D1756619

Victory at Gallipoli, 1915

Victory at Gallipoli, 1915

The German–Ottoman Alliance in the First World War

Klaus Wolf

Translated by Thomas P Iredale

Pen & Sword
MILITARY
AN IMPRINT OF PEN & SWORD BOOKS LTD.
YORKSHIRE – PHILADELPHIA

First published in Great Britain in 2020 by
PEN & SWORD MILITARY
An imprint of
Pen & Sword Books Ltd
Yorkshire – Philadelphia

ISBN 978 1 52676 816 2

Typeset by Aura Technology and Software Services, India.
Printed and bound in the UK by CPI Group (UK) Ltd, Croydon, CR0 4YY

Pen & Sword Books Limited incorporates the imprints of Atlas, Archaeology,
Aviation, Discovery, Family History, Fiction, History, Maritime, Military,
Military Classics, Politics, Select, Transport, True Crime, Air World,
Frontline Publishing, Leo Cooper, Remember When, Seaforth Publishing,
The Praetorian Press, Wharncliffe Local History, Wharncliffe Transport,
Wharncliffe True Crime and White Owl.

For a complete list of Pen & Sword titles please contact

PEN & SWORD BOOKS LTD
47 Church Street, Barnsley, South Yorkshire, S70 2AS, England
E-mail: enquiries@pen–and–sword.co.uk
Website: www.pen–and–sword.co.uk

Or

PEN & SWORD BOOKS
1950 Lawrence Rd, Havertown, PA 19083, USA
E-mail: Uspen-and-sword@casematepublishers.com
Website: www.penandswordbooks.com

Contents

List of Maps

Acknowledgements and Thanks

I would like to extend my heartfelt thanks to all those people without whom this English edition would never have appeared. First and foremost, my thanks goes to Thomas 'Tom' Iredale, who took the initiative for the translation, brought the case forward to the Gallipoli Association and did tremendous work, not only in the translation, but also in reviewing the original book, which has led to this new, revised edition.

My gratitude goes to the following people and organisations:

For the original German edition:

My wife Suzan for her everlasting patience and letting me spend so much time at my desk, in archives and at Gallipoli.

Count Jesko zu Dohna, Colonel (Ret'd) Klaus Hammel, Colonel Ullrich Kastilan, General (Ret'd) Klaus Reinhardt and Dr Norbert Schwake for their support and guidance; Lieutenant Colonel Thomas Eckel for the creation of the original cartographic material; Mr Turgay Erol, owner of the Deniz Kitabevi bookshop, for pictures from his collection and Eric Goosens and his wife, Özlem for their friendly support and hospitality in 'The Gallipoli Houses' during my trips to the Peninsula; Bernd Langensiepen for permission to quote from his book and to all the German families, who shared with me pictures and documents of their forebears active in Gallipoli; the staffs of the German Defence Attaché in Ankara and the German Consulate General in Istanbul, as well as the Orient Institute in Istanbul; the Bundesarchiv/Militärarchiv in Freiburg and Coblenz, as well as the Political Archive of the German Foreign Office in Berlin for their support in document and picture research; and the Volksbund Deutsche Kriegsgräberfürsorge (The German War Graves' Commission).

For the English edition:

The Gallipoli Association, for sponsoring the translation and publication of this edition; Stephen J Chambers for his steady encouragement and factual guidance; Michael D Robson, Tel Aviv, for help in proof reading, fact checking and editing; William 'Bill' Sellars, Eceabat, for his insightful observations and support; Bernard de Broglio, Australia, for help on the formation of the Turkish Air Arm; and Gunter Hartnagel, Germany, for his picture material.

Foreword

E ver since Klaus Wolf's book *Gallipoli, 1915: Das Deutsch-Türkische Militärbündnis im Ersten Weltkrieg* was published in German in 2008, I was one amongst many waiting for this book to be translated into English. Later I found out that this was also the author's hope, although that never reached fruition for one reason or the other. During the spring of 2017 the seeds of the idea were re-germinated during a drink with some friends in a bar overlooking the Dardanelles. This in turn led to meeting Klaus in 2018 during the Gallipoli Association conference when he delivered an excellent presentation, entitled 'Gallipoli Through German Eyes'. The conference audience was unaware that we were well underway with the translation, thanks to Thomas Iredale, and, supported by The Gallipoli Association, Pen & Sword Books Ltd were ready to publish this revised edition.

From a German point of view, with the end of the Great War Gallipoli rapidly became both a forgotten campaign and victory. Gallipoli has little national significance for Germany today, and nowhere near the scale that Turkey places on the campaign. This is not purely because the victory brought the Turks military prestige at a time when it was so badly needed, but because of the deeds of Mustafa Kemal Atatürk and the viewpoint that Gallipoli was the birthplace of modern Turkey. Amongst the allies a similar significance is placed on the campaign by Australia and New Zealand, where it has a similar, almost mystical, significance. For Germany there was none.

The integrity of Turkey and the Ottoman Empire was underpinned to a large degree by Germany. Military cooperation strengthened after the Ottoman army's defeat in the Balkan Wars when military assistance was needed to reorganise the Ottoman forces. Building on foundations already in place, thanks to General Colmar von der Goltz, Germany despatched a sizeable Military Mission under General Otto Liman von Sanders in 1913, which helped in the development of military training and the reorganisation of the Turkish armaments industry. At about the same time, the Turkish government invited British and French advisors to modernise the navy and shore-based Dardanelles defences. It is ironic that it would be the very same defences the allies would be pitched against in 1915.

With the outbreak of war and the welcoming of the SMS *Goeben* and SMS *Breslau*, any secrecy over the Turkish-German pact was no more. German Admiral Souchon was appointed commander in chief of the Ottoman navy and, with Enver Pasha's permission, made an unprovoked attack on the Russian seaports in the Black Sea in 1914. The Turks had been thrown into a powder keg that sparked the war between Russia and Turkey, and then Britain and France. A world war had begun, with Turkey becoming Germany's pawn.

How significant was Germany's help? Without German support I do not believe that Ottoman military forces would have performed as well in battle as they did during the campaign. Germany's contribution in leadership, equipment, munitions, medicine and training is notable and should not be underestimated. I would go so far as to say that without German involvement there would have been no Turkish victory, because there would have been no reason at all for the Allies to mount an offensive against the Dardanelles. By the very act of intervention, Imperial Germany had succeeded in bringing Turkey into the war and the campaign tied down the best part of half a million Allied troops. Indirectly, this aided the German efforts on the Western Front, if only to preserve the stalemate.

But what of the individuals? From the other side of the wire, this book tells stories of German command, bravery and sacrifice. Notable naval examples would include battery commander Lieutenant Hans Woermann, the first German officer to be killed in action in the region during the allied bombardment of Kumkale; naval engineer Lieutenant Arnholdt Reeder, who ensured that the minelayer *Nusret* steamed smoke-free to avoid detection by patrolling Allied vessels as she went to lay the fateful line of mines in March 1915; Lieutenant Commander Rudolph Firle, who jointly commanded the Turkish destroyer *Muavenet* that sank HMS *Goliath*; U21's submarine commander, Otto Hersing, who torpedoed HMS *Triumph* and HMS *Majestic*. Similar examples are to be found on land: such as Lieutenant Colonel Hans Kannengiesser, in command of 9th Division, instrumental in blocking the New Zealand attack on Chunuk Bair in August 1915; whilst Major Wilhelm Willmer, who commanded the Anafarta Group, defended Suvla Bay so effectively from the British landings. In the Gallipoli air war, the first Allied aircraft shot down was by Lieutenant Karl Kettembeil whilst flying in an Albatros C.III, piloted by Lieutenant Ludwig Preussner. Some of these stories are known to British readers, others may be new; but all helped Turkey secure victory at Gallipoli. At sea, on land and in the air the case for the significance of the German contribution to the Turkish victory is strong.

The hope is that this book will help to ensure that Imperial Germany's role in the Gallipoli campaign not being forgotten. Whilst there is no monument or cemetery in Gallipoli today for Turkey's brothers-in-arms, this work helps to fill that gap as a memorial to those that served Fatherland in the Great War.

Stephen Chambers
Gallipoli Association Historian

The Gallipoli Association:

Founded by Gallipoli veteran Major Edgar Banner in 1969, it is the foremost Association for the Gallipoli campaign. The Association's key focus is education; by raising public awareness of the campaign it encourages and facilitates study, with the aim to keep the memory of the campaign alive, ensuring that all who served in it and those who gave their lives, are not forgotten. The values of comradeship, endurance and determination to succeed against all the odds are just as important today as they were in those dark years.

Membership of the Association continues to grow worldwide, and is open to anyone today. Strong links have been established with official and other interest groups concerned with the campaign, notably in those countries, such as Australia, New Zealand, Canada, France, Turkey and now Germany, which participated significantly in the naval, land and air operations.

To find further details, the Gallipoli Association's website address is http://www.gallipoli-association.org

Introduction

Since my book was first published in German in 2008 I have dreamt of a translation into English. Benefitting from so many resources, documents and knowledgeable personal contacts from the English-speaking community, I wanted to be able to share my views of this almost neglected subject with a wider readership. Thomas Iredale has not only produced a translation but also a revised edition. His ability to understand older and often complicated German, catching the sense and combining it with his deep knowledge of the campaign, is a rare gift.

The Gallipoli campaign in 1915 was not only a struggle for control of the Dardanelles Straits between the Black and the Aegean Seas but also was one of the early phases in the First World War. The battles in this theatre of war near Troy were the culminating point in the struggle for deciding the decades old 'Eastern Question', in which the German Empire was able to secure as an ally the Ottoman Empire to the detriment of other major European powers. The Turkish victory at Gallipoli had far-reaching strategic implications on the course of the war. Moreover, it has an almost mystical significance not only for today's Turkey but also for Australia and New Zealand, which were on the losing side of this campaign.

For his part in the defence of the Gallipoli Peninsula, Mustafa Kemal, later called Atatürk, assumed his role as a folk hero and saviour of Turkey. As the first President of Turkey, he later steered the country in a Western orientation. In Australia and New Zealand, the defeat in Gallipoli is seen today as a major reason for the step to independence and severance from the British motherland.

From a military history perspective, Gallipoli was the first and only battle fought in the First World War where multinational armed forces and joint land, sea and air cooperation were exercised so extensively on both sides. This is of major significance.

Despite winning this campaign, the allied Central Powers lost the First World War and the victory in Gallipoli has faded from German consciousness. Nevertheless, German-Turkish friendship did not diminish and has endured for decades and up to the present day. Even now, the memory of this coalition has a high priority in Turkey and is still reflected in a benevolent attitude of the Turkish people towards Germany. Yet it seems the influence and role of Imperial Germany in Turkey has now lapsed into oblivion. Thus this book aims to serve as a comprehensive introduction to the German influence on the military development of the Turkish armed forces; to the role played by Germany in bringing Turkey into the war; and to the human and material resources provided by Germany in the defence of Gallipoli.

In this book I am primarily concerned with the German perspective. This has been largely neglected in historical reappraisals and accounts of the battles on Gallipoli.

The description of the life of German military personnel in Turkey and their participation and role in the battles for the Gallipoli Peninsula is viewed as it would have been then and – whenever possible – with contemporary reports and commentaries. The unavoidably one-sided and critical comments are there to show the contemporary *Zeitgeist* and problems of cooperation and are not written to open new wounds between two friendly nations. There is no intention to create a new German epic; my principal concern is to commemorate the many unknown and forgotten

German soldiers, who lost their lives in the course of these battles. Unfortunately, since there is no longer a German memorial on the battlefield itself and Gallipoli is not mentioned at all in the German military cemetery in Istanbul, a large part of this book is purposely devoted to this topic. Other operations in the Turkish theatres of war (Suez, Palestine, Mesopotamia and the Caucasus) are not pursued here – even if far more German soldiers and resources were used on active service in those theatres.

Klaus Wolf

Chapter 1

The History of German-Turkish military relations to 1913

The Ottoman Empire and Prussia looked back on a long tradition of military relationships that began in the middle of the 18th Century. During the Seven Years' War, King Friedrich II had proposed a defence alliance with Turkey and with it the intention of 'sending a capable and rational officer to Turkish headquarters',[4] who was to liaise between the Grand Vizier and Prussian headquarters. In 1756, the King first sent Captain von Varennes, his aide-de-camp, to be with the Prussian envoys Karl Adolf von Rexin and Major von Zegelin in Istanbul. However, the two soldiers were unable to influence the internal military issues of the Ottoman Empire because their mission was exclusively of a diplomatic nature.[5] The Prussian undertaking could only be made good with the arrival of the delegation of Colonel von Goetze, accompanied by Lieutenants von Schmidt and von Scholten, who were to assist the Grand Vizier in Istanbul from 1791 to 1792 in the reorganisation of the army. The first Prussian military advisory staff was soon to be faced with a special challenge, however, as the officers all marched with the Ottoman forces to take part in the Russo-Turkish War (1787-1792). Their participation apparently seemed to have been successful, as Lieutenant von Schmidt was decorated with the *Pour le Mérite* for his achievements there. When the two officers returned to Prussia in 1792, however, it would be another thirty-six years before Prussian officers were again deployed for duty in Istanbul.

In the years 1801 to 1804, Sultan Selim III made the attempt to form a Turkish army along European lines. At that time European officers who entered Turkish service, however, were mostly private individuals who had completed service in their own armies and were now adventurers, acting as advisers. Being non-Mohammedans, they had neither rights nor rank in the Turkish army and were not allowed to issue orders. The Prussian officers on the 'Moltke mission', who came to Turkey were, however, to be granted a different status. Sultan Mahmud II approached Friedrich Wilhelm III at the end of 1835 and asked for the despatch of Prussian instructors for his army. While this request was still being hesitantly considered in Berlin, two 'Prussian officers struck with *Wanderlust*', namely Captain Helmuth von Moltke of the Prussian General Staff and Second Lieutenant von Bergh of the 1st Guards Regiment, arrived in Istanbul,[6] where both of them had only envisaged staying a few weeks during their six months' leave. Von Moltke's qualities were quickly recognised and the Prussian captain was thus asked not to leave Istanbul. The King of Prussia then granted him an additional three months' leave, maintaining his Prussian army pay. Altogether von Moltke stayed in Turkey for more than four years. He spent twenty-eight months of this time in Istanbul, worked on the formation of a Turkish militia, made topographical drawings and travelled around Turkey. Together with Captain von Mühlbach of the Prussian Army, von Moltke served with the Taurus Army in the campaign against the Kurds and in the campaign against Ibrahim-Pasha of Egypt.

In 1836, the Sultan asked Friedrich Wilhelm III to send no less than eleven officers and four non-commissioned officers as additional Prussian support; a request which, however, he had to reduce after the intervention by other European states to three officers as staff advisers and an engineer to supervise the fortifications of the Dardanelles. In August 1837, three Army captains, Vincke, Fischer and von Mühlbach, arrived in Istanbul. Von Moltke himself described the task of

Captain Helmuth von Moltke in Istanbul. (*Self-portrait*)

Moltke monument in Tarabya.[9]

the Prussian officers as follows: 'As far as it is possible, our task is to sharpen up the old, somewhat rusty curved sabre *alla franca*, in the event that it should be needed.'[7] King Friedrich Wilhelm III was persuaded in 1838 by Prince August of Saxe-Coburg and Gotha to send additional officers to Turkey. The King, however, forbade seconding serving officers and only gave permission to delegate officers from the reserve. In 1838 the following officers on the retired list were thus sent to Istanbul: Lieutenant von Kuczkowski and, from the ordnance branch, Lieutenants Lüling, Wiesenthal, Schwenzfeuer and Wendt.

After the Taurus Army had been defeated at Nisib in June 1839 and Sultan Mahmud II had died in the July, further Prussian support from Berlin was no longer forthcoming and the three serving officers were recalled home. The five retired artillery officers were, nevertheless, allowed to remain in Istanbul and died there many years later as generals of the Turkish army. The Turkish commander, Mehmed Hafız-Paşa, gave von Moltke the following testimonial before his departure on 29 July 1839:

'He has performed his duties as a loyal and courageous man from the very beginning of his mission to this very moment, and has carried out his missions in an exemplary manner. I have been witness to the fact that this officer has shown evidence of courage and boldness and he has faithfully served the Ottoman government and even at the risk of his own life. Thus I have been entirely satisfied with him in all respects!'[8]

Because of its geopolitical position, the Ottoman Empire was a focal point of interest for the great European powers and therefore more or less affected by almost all conflicts of the late 19th Century. While the major European powers merely sought to secure influence in this region, the waterways between the Black and the Aegean Seas were Russia's lifeblood and she wanted to control these passages under all circumstances. Istanbul and the Ottoman ports were important for the exchange of goods as it was here that the trade routes between Europe and Asia met. The metropolis on the Golden Horn and the two narrows – the Bosphorus and the Dardanelles – gained political and military significance primarily because of their commercial importance. The waterways were easily controlled by the Ottomans, which the socialist theorist, Friedrich Engels,[10] on the occasion of the Crimean War[11] rated accordingly:

'The guns of Gibraltar and Elsinore cannot master the entire strait on which they are situated and need the support of a fleet to overcome this; the straits of the Dardanelles and the Bosphorus, however, are so narrow that a few well-armed fortifications erected in suitable places - as Russia would install without a moment's hesitation - would be able to defy the allied fleets of the whole world if they tried to invade them. Then the Black Sea would be nothing but a Russian lake [...] Trabzon would become a Russian port, the Danube a Russian river.'[12]

Therefore it is not surprising that Russia's strategic interest was to gain possession of Istanbul and the Narrows. Thus it was a constant element of Russian policy to work towards the disintegration of the Ottoman Empire and to prevent its revival or even reinforcement. As early as 1773, the French publicist Favier wrote: 'Russia's war with Turkey is primarily a trade war, for trade with the Black Sea is just as important for Russia as trade with America is for France, Spain and England [sic].'[13] Russia's dependence on the benevolence of the power controlling the passage through the Narrows was not only evident in the Russo-Turkish war of 1877/78, but also during the Italian-Turkish war (1912) and the Balkan Wars (1912/13), in which the Ottoman government, even though only temporarily, prevented the passage of ships. As on average over a third of all Russian exports went by sea through the Narrows, a loss of thirty million roubles per month was chalked up during these war years, thus reducing Russia's total trade balance by almost ten percent.[14] According to a memorandum from the Russian Ministry of Foreign Affairs of November 1914:

'The freedom of the maritime trade route from the Black Sea to the Mediterranean and back is therefore an essential condition of Russia's normal economic life and the continuous development of its prosperity [...] The strategic importance of the Straits is such that the state which controls them has the possibility of denying passage to warships into the Black Sea and back without the need for significant naval forces. In addition, the Straits provide excellent operational bases for fleet actions, both in the Mediterranean as well as in the Black Sea.'[15]

Therefore it was also in Britain's interest to have significant influence on the control of the Straits and thus to keep open its main trade routes and the sea route through the Suez Canal, opened in 1869, via the Mediterranean to its Indian possessions. The British were equally against strengthening the Ottomans, just as they also clearly understood the need to prevent control of the Straits by Russia.[16]

The geopolitical interests of France, Italy, Austria-Hungary and Germany in this area were primarily economic. Each nation wanted to pursue its own commercial ventures and needed a viable and solvent Turkey without, however, having the dominating influence of one of the other great powers in this region. Even as early as the Crimean War, European states had tried to maintain these interests and fought alongside the Ottoman Empire against Russia, in order to prevent Russia's supposedly strong growth in the Black Sea area. In the Peace Treaty of Paris in 1856, the territorial integrity of the Ottoman Empire was defined by the formulation 'every act and event that calls into question the integrity of the Ottoman Empire' would be regarded 'as a question of European interest'.[17] Karl Marx described this situation very succinctly in an article published by the New York Daily Tribune in 1853:

'Let us briefly [...] summarise the Eastern Question: the Czar, dissatisfied and annoyed that his whole monstrous empire is restricted to one single port for export, which is furthermore situated on a sea which cannot be navigated during one half of the year and can be attacked by the English [sic] during the other half, follows his ancestors' plan to gain access to the

Mediterranean. One after another, he cuts the remotest parts of the Ottoman Empire off from its body until finally Constantinople, its heart, must stop beating. [...] Counting on the cowardice and timidity of the Western powers, he [the Czar] intimidates Europe. [...] The Western powers, on the other hand, inconsistent, faint-hearted, always suspicious of each other, constantly encourage the Sultan to oppose the Czar, whose attacks they fear, to force him to finally give in, [and] for fear of a general war [...] their whole endeavour is directed only to maintaining the status quo.'[18]

Britain's elementary interest in a balance of forces on this geostrategic hub was demonstrated, among other things, by the British intervention in the course of the Russo–Turkish War of 1878. Russian troops had won an effective victory and were already at the gates of Istanbul. The prospect of an imminent conquest of the Straits by Russia alarmed the British, who sent their fleet to the Bosphorus and threatened a declaration of war should Russia continue its offensive. Russia had to avoid this conflict and was unwillingly forced to agree to the Peace Treaty of San Stefano, named after a suburb of Istanbul, on 3 March 1878. As the peace terms of this treaty were not acceptable to other European states, new conditions were negotiated at the Berlin Congress, organised by Bismarck. The biggest change was the division of Bulgaria, with the Ottoman Empire receiving back some of the losses suffered during this war. Russia regarded what came out of the Congress as a great disappointment and felt betrayed at the lost fruits of a costly victory.

The Ottoman Empire, which found its external borders shrinking and domestic politics degenerating into confusion, finally became the 'sick man on the Bosphorus'[19] through the loss of territories in the Balkans and as a result of the war against Russia. Serbia and Montenegro were granted full sovereignty by the Berlin Congress of July 1878; Austria–Hungary was granted the provisional right of occupation of the Ottoman Balkan provinces of Bosnia, Herzegovina and of Novi Pazar in the Sandžak region. What had constituted Bulgaria under the Ottomans was divided into an autonomous principality and the autonomous province of Eastern Rumelia. This situation brought Sultan Abdul Hamid to the conclusion that he once more had to seek outside help for the reorganisation of his forces. The reform of the army was urgently required for external defence against Russia and other powers; on the other hand, the Sultan saw himself threatened by the growing Young Turks movement and by national uprisings of ethnic minorities in the Kurdish and Arab parts of the Ottoman Empire. The German Reich seemed to the Sultan to be the most suitable partner for military aid. The Prussian army had demonstrated its military prowess by its discipline and success in the Franco–Prussian War (1870/71). Moreover, in contrast to the colonial powers Britain and France, the Sultan felt that Germany seemed the least likely to succumb to greediness.

After lengthy deliberation and consultation, Bismarck authorised the request to send officers for the army and administrative officials for the state apparatus. Previous discussions had taken place with the Great General Staff and, crucially for further development, with arms industrialists, in particular Krupp.[20] After Bismarck had clarified the question with Germany's alliance partner Austria–Hungary and established that relations between Vienna and Berlin would not be jeopardised, Bismarck explained his reasons for approving the mission to the Kaiser. He saw the new mission in the tradition of previous assistance and said that the other Powers would rather see German officers in place than to tolerate a rising influence of those great Powers already active in Turkey. However, political motives were decisive for Bismarck, as he explained to the Emperor:

'For the officers appointed to it, the Mission would provide the opportunity to advance their training and experience in unfamiliar conditions, and Your Government would gain more resources to influence Turkey.'[21]

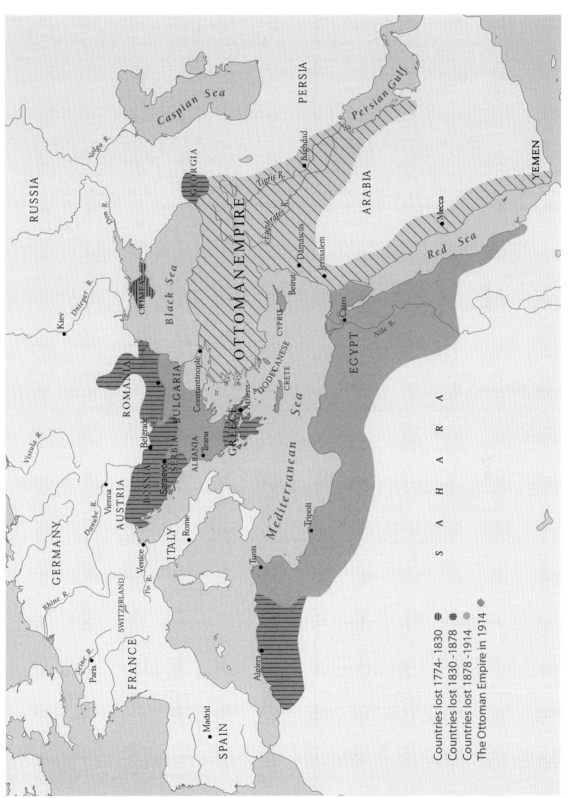

The Ottoman Empire, territorial losses and situation in 1914.

Countries lost 1774–1830
Countries lost 1830–1878
Countries lost 1878–1914
The Ottoman Empire in 1914

However, Bismarck tried to avoid anything that could make the mission appear political rather than military. The mission officers in Istanbul were officially banned from interfering in politics, and the German government avoided outwardly showing political support for the mission.[22] Clearly, Bismarck was less concerned with the influence that the officers could exert directly on Turkish politicians than with promoting a general positive mood in Turkey in Germany's favour. The goal was to have the Ottoman Empire as a friend and to prevent its joining up with anti-German alliances.

Meanwhile, a veritable 'Moltke legend' had been established in Turkey, since the fame of the now successful Prussian Field Marshal and victor of Sedan in 1870 also began to rub off on his former employer. In 1883, Sultan Abdul Hamid II said:

'In the time of his grandfather, Mahmut II, Field Marshal Moltke was here in Turkey. By failing to understand the great importance of this famous man, it was neglected at that time to benefit from his work, but his success was hindered by all kinds of intrigue and, finally, we made the great mistake of letting him go and thus depriving ourselves of his excellent services.'[23]

These and similar statements were exaggerated, and radically idealised Moltke's actual importance, since he had hardly ever been able to have any significant influence on the Ottoman forces at the time.

In the course of 1882 four officers, including Major General Otto Kähler, the Head of the Military Mission, entered the Turkish army after being granted permission by the German Emperor.[24] In 1883, General Colmar von der Goltz initiated training courses at the General Staff College in Istanbul. A year later, in 1884, Lieutenant Commander Starke began his service as naval adviser. After Kähler's death in 1886, General von der Goltz succeeded as head of the mission in the Turkish General Staff. The Goltz era should be regarded as an important phase in German-Turkish relations, for it tasked the Military Mission with intensive economic lobbying.

After arduous negotiations with the mistrustful Sultan, von der Goltz succeeded in enforcing his idea of a Territorial Force for Turkey and pushed through a law for the reorganisation of the army. He vigorously pursued this goal, which ultimately led to Turkey having a million men under arms in 1897, as well as establishing a militia 400,000 strong. By means of a new recruiting law, as well as the introduction of universal compulsory military service, he also masterminded the splitting of the whole Ottoman Empire into twenty-four divisional and 384 battalion areas. In addition, he wrote and published a manual for officers in the field, a tactical instructional manual, a two-volume treatise on the General Staff and training manuals on field duty and fortifications, all in Turkish. Von der Goltz and his work were judged thus:

Colmar von der Goltz ca. 1895. (*Sammlung Soytürk*)

'The excellent services rendered by Baron von der Goltz in the General Staff, his sound literary activity, the all-round nature of his education and his versatile, sophisticated personality, soon gained the special good-will of the Paşa circle and the keen interest of all military circles in Constantinople.'[25]

Von der Goltz and the other German officers, however, were confronted with the basic problem of a general unwillingness to cooperate amongst the Turks, as well as the Sultan's fear of sabotage against any suggestions for improvement. Sultan Abdul Hamid, who had himself come to power through a military coup, suffered the constant fear of being likewise overthrown. On the one hand, it appeared to be necessary to invite the German reformers to act as a deterrent to European powers as well as to be seen as a ruler willing to modernise by the Turkish people and Young Turk opposition. But, on the other hand, he did almost all he could to hinder any German success. Proposals for army reform were delayed or not taken up and, instead, German officers were occupied in senseless and time-consuming committees, which had little political influence or military relevance.

The fact that the military mission in Turkey was left in place despite the repeated complaints about the practical failures of Major General Kähler (1882–85) and later von der Goltz is an indication that, at that time in Germany, the value of having influence on the Turkish forces was clearly recognised. If German officers had been withdrawn from Turkey because of the military senselessness of their stay, there would have been a danger that their place would have been taken over by officers of other great powers. The German Ambassador, Hugo Prince von Radolin, told the Chancellor of the Reich:

'If, for political reasons, it does not seem appropriate to abandon an activity which does not meet expectations, there is nothing left but to submit to the immutable; to be satisfied with less success and lower expectations but, notwithstanding, to continue with tenacity and diligence the work that has been started, in order not to give up this position to foreign elements, instead of losing courage and throwing in the towel because everything is not as it is in Prussia.'[26]

However, the presence of German officers, with their opportunities for influence, led to a preference for purchasing weapons of German manufacture. Thus in July 1873, 500 cannons with ammunition were delivered, followed by another hundred guns from Krupp in 1877.[27] Krupp also received an order from the Ottoman government for 430 field guns at the end of July 1885 and in 1886 another 426 guns were ordered.[28] The Dardanelles forts were equipped with twenty-two medium and seven of the heaviest calibre coastal guns from Krupp.[29] Meanwhile, the Mauser and Loewe rifle factories supplied 500,000 rifles and 50,000 carbines to the Ottoman Army in 1887.[30]

After the departure of General von der Goltz in November 1895, the German Foreign Office decided to establish the post of military attaché in its Ottoman Embassy. The terms of reference, including those for Captain Curt von Morgen and Major Walter von Strempel, consisted of regularly reporting on Turkish military relations to the German High Command, procuring orders for arms and organising the placement of German officers in influential positions in the Turkish army.

In addition to significant Ottoman territorial losses over recent decades, the internal political crisis in July 1908 caused by the Young Turk revolution forced Sultan Abdul Hamid II in the summer to re-establish the Ottoman constitution of 1876. The insurgents were mainly young students and officers, among them Talat and Enver, who, whilst underground in Thessalonica and exiled in Paris, had conspired against the autocratic regime in Istanbul. Nevertheless, the German military mission remained in Turkey. Until 1908 three general staff officers, three artillery officers, two cavalry and two infantry officers, one engineer and one administrative officer, who were all on the active list of the German Army, were serving in posts in the Turkish army. A further seven officers were given leave of absence to carry out mapping assignments and a further two each of the cavalry, artillery and navy were seconded to act as instructors.[31]

On 5 October 1908, the Bulgarian Prince Ferdinand I, who was a member of the house of Saxe-Coburg, declared the independent kingdom of Bulgaria and himself Czar. On the same day, Emperor Franz Joseph placed the provinces of Bosnia and Herzegovina under Austrian military administration, thereby causing the Bosnian annexation crisis. When the Ottoman Empire, Serbia and Montenegro protested vigorously against the Austrian action, war threatened to break out. Russia, as the declared protector of all Slavs, and thus on the Serbian side, did not believe that it yet had enough military might to confront the Central Powers, especially so soon after the disastrous Russo-Japanese war of 1904-1905. Therefore Russia gave way to the German challenge and accepted the Austro-Hungarian annexation of Bosnia and Herzegovina. Serbia, which could no longer count on any military assistance, was also compelled formally to agree. Thus the crisis was superficially settled and the Ottoman Empire had to accept the loss of its two Balkan provinces in February 1909.

The renewed effort by Britain to gain influence in Istanbul and control of the Straits was observed with great suspicion by the Russians but could not be prevented. During the Crimean War and in 1878 Russia had had painfully to experience the Ottoman Empire's exercise of control over the transit route. In 1904 it was Britain that insisted in the Sultan's Palace on the closure of the Straits as a treaty obligation, to prevent the exit of Russian armoured cruisers and troop transports reinforcing the Czar's forces during the Russo-Japanese War and thus support Britain's Japanese ally.

There were critical reports in the middle of 1908 about the state of the Ottoman forces, especially the units stationed in Macedonia. There were revolts, refusals to obey orders and desertions. The reason for all this apparently lay in irregular disbursement of pay, but also in the cronyism of an ailing and opaque system of promotion with which Sultan Abdul Hamid II tried to control the army. Thus there were mutinies on a grand scale and the alienation of the army from the Sultan, providing the breeding ground on which the Young Turks' revolution could flourish. The position looked similar in the navy, which was in an even more desolate state.[32] During this period of unrest, von der Goltz travelled privately to Istanbul and paid a visit to the Sultan. Von der Goltz took advantage of this opportunity to point out the grievances in the armed forces and gave him a memorandum for the improvement of the Ottoman army.[33] As a result, Sultan Abdul Hamid asked the German Emperor, through von der Goltz, to despatch a specially qualified general staff officer who would be in a position to assist in the rectification of these deficiencies. This request was fulfilled by Wilhelm II in the middle of June 1908; the choice fell on Captain Aubert.

In November 1908 the Russian Ambassador in Istanbul reported on the negotiations between Turkey and Britain and the apparent conclusion of a secret agreement. The report concluded:

'Whatever result the negotiations between the Sultan's Palace and the British Government may have, the latter has already succeeded in securing a means of strengthening its influence in Turkey, by exploiting circumstances favourable to them.'[34]

This meant, first of all, transferring the reorganisation of the Turkish Navy to Rear Admiral DA Gamble RN, who also assumed command of the Turkish fleet. Apparently, the British also urged those responsible in Istanbul to push forward the upgrading of the Bosphorus defensive positions, since Russia, according to a British statement, would use the next favourable opportunity to force the opening of the Straits. These fortifications, of course, should only be directed to the north and did not concern the protection of the Dardanelles. Britain continued to play the role of a protective power over the coveted waterway; however, this did not enjoy the undivided enthusiasm of the Turks. When, in April 1909, the British fleet cruised off the Dardanelles, the Turks asked London for the reason. The answer was that the British fleet had received orders to assemble in Turkish waters 'to repulse any enemy action against Turkey by their neighbours'.[35] During this tense foreign policy situation, the Young Turks deposed Sultan Abdul Hamid II on 27 April 1909, sent him into exile and placed his brother Mohammed V on the throne. The 'Committee for Unity and Progress', the governing body of the Young Turks movement, now exercised *de facto* power in Istanbul.

Field Marshal (he had been given that rank in the Turkish Army on his departure in 1895) von der Goltz returned to Istanbul in July 1909 to explore the ground for a new and more comprehensive military mission, which he was to head. Von der Goltz, described in a book by George WF Hallgarten as 'an intriguing type, half scholar, half military, half German, half Turk, half aristocrat, half democrat, half general, half boy scout, too educated to be chauvinist, but too military not to be chauvinist'.[36] Von der Goltz remained until August and during this time produced a manual with advice for the German training staff instructors detached for duty in Turkish service. In this document he described not only the essential shortcomings of the Turkish army but also the Oriental mentality, which would have to be reckoned with.[37] A total of thirteen officers, under the command of Baron von der Goltz, were to be transferred for Turkish service.

Infantry training:	Major von Byern, Captain Schwarz, Captain Cretius and Captain Raven;
Cavalry support:	Major Veit, Major von Rogister and Captain von Frese;
Field Artillery:	Major von Anderten, Major Tupschoewski and Captain Binhold;
Construction Branch:	Hauptmann Muth;
Artillery and Engineer schools:	Lieutenant-Colonel Posselt and Captain Praetorius.[38]

All took up their posts on 15 October 1909 in Istanbul or in other locations at selected training establishments. At the same time, Colonel-General von der Goltz also returned to Istanbul, though he had only been temporarily given leave by the Emperor for this mission. Above all, von der Goltz tried to convince Turkish officers to acquire a certain satisfaction and seriousness in realistic training for war, 'to take them away from idleness, criticising, politicisation, clubs and coffee houses'.[39]

In the annual report on the Ottoman Army, Major von Strempel, the Military Attaché, noted that in 1909 significant progress could be ascertained in soldiers' training. The units around Istanbul and the European part of Turkey had been especially prioritised for modernisation. Nevertheless, in 1910 the reform of the Turkish army was still in its infancy, as the education and training of officers and non-commissioned officers took a long time. A further step was the reorganisation of the army groups on the recommendation of von der Goltz. Brigades should be abolished and thus a division would now consist of three regiments of three battalions each, plus a rifle battalion. In this way command level appointments could be reduced and duplication in staff work avoided. In January 1911 another seven German military advisors came to Turkey, including Major Eduard Weidtmann, Lieutenant Colonel Vollbrecht (Divisional Medical Doctor), Major Otto von Lossow and Captain Georg Gottschalk. Thus, at the beginning of 1911, the Military Mission had a complement of twenty-six officers.[40]

In the Yildiz Barracks on 28 March 1911 there was an incident during a parade taken by Lieutenant Colonel von Schlichting, in which he was shot by an Albanian recruit who felt that he had been wrongly treated.[41] This incident sparked discussion once again in Germany as to whether the Mission's officers were adequately briefed about the habits and cultural sensitivities in Turkey.

From the viewpoint of the German Military Attaché, Major von Strempel, the first successes of the so-called 'training regiments' were sound enough to try and arrange for Germans to occupy more important positions in the Ministry of War and the Army College. It was precisely these posts that were of particular importance since, up to now, the Ottomans did not want to have any foreign officers in these key locations. Von Strempel noted that the longer he was in the Ottoman Empire the more he believed that the number of German military advisers was far less important than their value as personalities. It was no longer easy to be a reformist because of the improved Ottoman level of attainment; moreover, in the Ottomans' memory, the accomplishments of men like Moltke or von der Goltz had 'to a certain extent spoiled the prices'. One Ottoman general had even proposed not extending any German contracts but to keep on engaging new military advisors until a von Moltke or a von der Goltz could be found again.[42]

Political developments at that time were dominated by the smouldering Balkan conflict. Italy opposed the expansionist Balkans policy of Austria-Hungary. Going behind the backs of the Triple Alliance Partners (the German Empire, Austria-Hungary and Italy), King Victor Emanuel of Italy met with the Russian Czar in October 1909 and assured him of support for Russian dominance in the Balkans. Encouraged by Russia, Serbia and Bulgaria formed the Balkan League against the Ottoman Empire and the Dual Monarchy on 13 March 1912. A few months later Greece and Montenegro also joined this alliance. Montenegro then declared war on the Ottoman Empire on 8 October 1912; Serbia, Bulgaria and Greece followed in mid-October and the First Balkan War began.

With the opening of the First Balkan War, the German government was faced with the question of whether German officers in Turkish service should actively participate in the hostilities. Although the reaction of the Chief of the German General Staff, von Moltke ('the Younger') was at first fundamentally opposed, it was, however, decided to permit six German officers to participate in the fighting in their respective functions. The Turkish army, however, was still in such a desolate state that even Cemil Paşa, the Governor of Istanbul, had to admit: 'We are not able to fight. I saw the soldiers during manoeuvres last year [...] with these soldiers, we cannot wage war.'[43] For the first time the war saw the command of a Turkish division given to a non–Muslim, when Major von Lossow led a Turkish infantry division during the battles at Çatalca.

The Ottoman Empire was, however, weakened by the Italo-Turkish War of 1911-12, which was only terminated by the peace treaty signed in Lausanne on the day the Balkan War was declared on 18 October. As expected, Turkey suffered a military defeat, which was partly blamed on the German instructors. In less than two months, the Ottoman Empire had lost almost all its possessions on the continent of Europe to the Balkan states. The Germans felt obliged to explain the debacle of the Turkish army. In spite of a detailed analysis of the circumstances, which had in fact little to do with the few German officers, this defeat was also viewed by the German military, both in Turkey and in Berlin, as a disgrace for the German Army. Reviewing his experiences in the Balkan War, Major Franz Endres wrote that it should be clear to every participant in the war, 'that the German reformist activity has been made a complete fiasco and consequently, German prestige has suffered regardless of the fact that the Germans were not to blame for it.'[44]

From the spring of 1912 the Ambassador of the German Reich in Istanbul, Baron Hans von Wangenheim, played an outstanding role in German-Turkish relations. He was a restless, clever and energetic man who, like no-one else in Turkey, represented and asserted the interests of Germany. A diplomat through and through, von Wangenheim was supposedly Wilhelm II's personal choice for this post. His abilities and charm were also highly regarded by his diplomatic colleagues. His Prussian striving for power, which he was able to assert to enormous success in Turkish government circles was, however, also deeply despised by the same group of people.

The American Ambassador, Henry Morgenthau, said of Wangenheim:

'Wangenheim linked the combination of a college student's jovial enthusiasm with the diligence of a Prussian official and the positive qualities of a man of the world. I remember this picture of a handsome man who sat down at the piano and improvised marvellous classical

Baron von Wangenheim. (*Deutsche Botschaft Ankara*)

Lieutenant Commander Hans Humann. (*Deutsche Botschaft Ankara*)

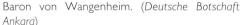

themes, then suddenly unceremoniously thundered out German drinking or popular songs. Wangenheim showed the same restless spirit when he flirted with the Greek ladies in Pera, or during the hours-long game at the table in the *Cercle d'Orient*, or bent Turkish officials to his will in favour of German interests; life was a game for him that was more or less played unscrupulously, and in which the man has the best chances who was stubborn enough and put success or defeat on only one card.'[45]

Von Wangenheim's report of 28 August 1912 shows the particular importance which he attributed to German reform activity in the Turkish military:

'Like Abdul Hamid, the *Union et Progrès* Committee has been overthrown by the army. The current government is also under its control. It was only a few days ago that the Minister of the Interior, Hussein Hilmi, was ordered by four generals, who had appeared before him on behalf of the Military League, to resign his post. It is not foreseeable who the army should oust from this position. In all likelihood, in the final analysis, it will still form the decisive factor in Turkey for a long time. Foreign governments, who want to exert influence in Turkey, will have to take this into account. As long as the army plays the leading role, Germany is in a privileged position against competing countries. For according to Turkish opinion, the armies of Turkey and Germany are brothers-in-arms. The majority of Turkish officers still believe in the absolute superiority of our military capabilities [...]. After all that I have seen and experienced here of our reform officers' activity, I can only but agree with Nazim's view that the Turkish army has less advantage with the employment of German officers appointed to command soldiers than those of instructors attached to the General Staff or the military education and training institutions. Although the first category of officers has been outstanding in the training of individual Turkish soldiers, there has often been friction between the German and Turkish mentality that did not make our officers more popular. Moreover, their achievements will always be more ephemeral and can only be felt within a restricted band. According to my insignificant opinion as a layman, it is less important to train Turkish officers and men according to German regulations than to train talented Turkish officers at home or here as instructors, so that they can translate German doctrine into the Turkish spirit and make it more clear to their subordinates. The main task of our officers will in future take on even more of a political nature and will be to cultivate and deepen the sympathies for Germany in the Turkish army by means of tactful, comradely behaviour.'[46]

Baron von Wangenheim, who was to later play a decisive role in strengthening German influence and nudging Turkey's entry into the Great War, was also not uncritically regarded in German military circles. In order to have direct influence on him, the future Naval Attaché, Commander Hans Humann, was despatched to Istanbul. Humann had been born and raised in Turkey. He was the son of the famous Pergamon archaeologist Carl Humann and had spent practically his whole life in Turkey; he not only spoke Turkish but he could also think like a Turk. This made him exceptional among the German officers in Turkey. Moreover, Humann and Enver had a friendly relationship, emanating from Enver's time in Berlin. Initially assigned the inconspicuous command of the 61 metre armed steam yacht *Loreley* on permanent station off Istanbul, his primary task was to establish a good relationship with von Wangenheim and set up a military intelligence office at the Embassy. Humann wrote about this:

'When I was appointed captain of the *Loreley* in 1913 I received only one order from Tirpitz, my boss at the time: to do everything to ensure a good relationship between the Mediterranean Division (which was actually an Orient Division) and Wangenheim, after Rear Admiral Trummler during his tenure had completely soured relations between the embassy and the navy, ending up with mutual accusations to the Emperor.'[47]

Humann tried to establish contact with the often moody and impetuous Ambassador through Wangenheim's wife, to whom he even explained his intentions quite openly. This strategy seemed to work, even if it often demanded of a lot of patience and empathy from Humann, who described this situation:

'I was fully dependant in my activities, accommodation etc., on the hospitality of the Wangenheims but also at the same time completely at the mercy of the whims and ideas of this quite impulsive person [...]. Because of our age difference, friendship with Wangenheim could only emerge by mainly obligating him and his wife to me, through constant friendliness and willingness to help in every conceivable matter. That worked and, through trustful cooperation, bore ripe fruit.'[48]

Admiral Souchon wrote in February 1915 about Ambassador Wangenheim:

'Wangenheim is absolutely gypsy-like in his nature, wholly subject to his moods. He often loses control, treats his wife and staff roughly, yawns, pulls faces etc.[...]. He often causes offence to both Turks and Westerners, which must be painstakingly made good again. [Rear Admiral] Trummler had a great deal of bad experience in his relationship with him and was therefore regarded in a poor light. From Humann and PW I learn all about W. As far as I am concerned, therefore, I avoid topics which would lead to annoyance or friction and thus get along with him, so I give Humann as much support as possible in his difficult dual role.'[49]

When the Russian government in the course of the Italo-Turkish war attempted to exploit the weakness of Turkey and obtain concessions for the exploitation of the Straits, there were defiant reactions in Istanbul. 'No Turkish government and no Turk can toy for a single moment with the idea that the Ottoman Empire may be placed in the position of becoming a Russian vassal.'[50] This adverse attitude of the Turks was supported by the other European governments and further isolated Russia on this issue. The British Foreign Minister even proposed sending an international fleet and, if necessary, wanted to place the Straits under international control. Germany, too, was to join this fleet with warships, and thus the heavy cruiser *Goeben* and the light cruiser *Breslau* were dispatched to the Mediterranean under the command of Rear-Admiral Trummler as the so-called Mediterranean Division (MMD). After the two ships parted in the Mediterranean, the *Goeben* went on to Istanbul, where she arrived on 15 November 1912 and remained for four months. During this time there was no participation in military operations but the German cruiser's shore detachment came ashore on 18 November to protect the European quarter in the city from any trouble. On his departure from the Bosphorus on 1 April 1913, Rear Admiral Trummler paid a courtesy visit to the commander of the British Mediterranean Fleet, Admiral Sir Archibald Berkeley Milne, on his flagship, the battle cruiser HMS *Inflexible*. During the visit, Milne pointed out the necessity of a German military presence on the Syrian coast; advice that he may have later bitterly regretted as, in the following years, the German Mediterranean Division became the decisive strategic power-factor in the Straits question.

Whilst Serbia, Montenegro and Bulgaria were able to agree on an armistice with the Ottoman Empire on 3 December 1912, Greece was still at war with the Turkish army. At the end of December 1912 the representatives of the warring factions met with the negotiators of the European powers at the London Ambassadorial Conference to discuss the future of the Balkans. The peace conditions of the Balkan countries were unacceptable to the Ottomans and the conference failed on 6 January 1913. After a *coup d'état* by the Young Turks, which finally disempowered the Sultan, the fighting with the Greeks flared up again. After the Turks were finally defeated on all fronts, an armistice with Bulgaria, Greece and Serbia (and a few days later with Montenegro as well), was able to be negotiated and came into force on 19 April 1913. On 30 May 1913 a preliminary peace treaty was concluded in London, again through the mediation of the European powers. As a result the Ottoman Empire had to surrender the island of Crete to Greece and renounce almost all European territories. On the European mainland there remained only a narrow stretch of land between the Dardanelles and the Bosphorus.

The London preliminary peace agreement, however, led to new conflicts between the former allies of the Balkan League, especially between Serbia and Bulgaria, who argued about the division of Macedonia. On 1 June 1913 Greece and Serbia joined forces to form an alliance against Bulgaria and, on 29 June 1913, the Second Balkan War broke out with an attack by Bulgaria against Serbia. A few weeks later, Montenegro, Romania and the Ottoman Empire joined the war against Bulgaria. At the request of Bulgaria, an armistice was concluded on 30 July 1913. In the ensuing peace agreement, Bulgaria lost most of its gains from the First Balkan War and the larger part of Macedonia fell to Serbia and Greece. In a later agreement, Bulgaria also had to give up territory to Turkey. Albania, which had been under Ottoman sovereignty until the London Ambassadorial Conference, became an independent state.

The Balkan Wars had a lasting impact, as the disintegration of the Ottoman Empire and Bulgaria led to ugly tensions between the successor states in the Balkans, finally culminating in the assassination in Sarajevo of the heir to the throne of Austria-Hungary, Franz Ferdinand, which thus sparked off the First World War.

Chapter 2

Paving the way for the 'Liman Military Mission', 1913

In order to secure the very existence of their fragile Ottoman Empire after the defeat in the Balkan Wars, the new rulers saw that the restoration of Turkish defence capabilities was urgently required. Once again, the Turkish leadership decided to use the proven help of German officers for this task. Shortly after the January 1913 revolution[51], Mahmud Şefket Paşa, who had previously figured as a broker for German-Ottoman arms deals and who also served as Minister of War, said to Cemal Paşa, one of the leading personalities of the Young Turks Committee and who was later appointed as the Minister of Marine:

'As far as our army is concerned, I believe that we can no longer remain closed to German methods. For more than thirty years we have had German instructors in our army; our officer corps has been thoroughly trained using German military procedures, our army is intimately familiar with the spirit of German training and German instruction. To change this now borders on the impossible. I therefore intend to have a German military mission on a grand scale and even, if necessary, entrust the command of a Turkish army corps to a German general and to place at the head of every unit the same German staff officers and subalterns and thus set up a model army corps.'[52]

Grand Vizier[53] Mahmud Şefket Paşa was personally concerned with both the reorganisation of foreign relations with the European powers, as well as conducting national affairs. He also worked extensively on the question of reorganising the army and the fleet. The British Naval Mission, now under Admiral Sir Arthur Henry Limpus, and a French Mission for the training and reorganisation of the *Jandarma* were already in situ and, on the instructions of Şefket Paşa, were to intensify their work. His intention was to reorganise the various departments of the Ministry of War, the General Staff, the military schools and armaments factories. He wanted to reduce the size of the army but improve its quality. This reduction in the number of men under arms was aimed to cover the costs of the reorganisation. On this basis, the Grand Vizier began negotiations with the German Ambassador, Baron von Wangenheim, and the Military Attaché, Major Strempel.

On 26 April 1913 Şefket Paşa gave von Wangenheim a detailed account of his domestic policy programme. It incorporated a division of responsibilities between European nations in the reorganisation of almost all aspects of the Ottoman State. The German Reich was to be allocated the reform of the army and its training methods, the importance of which Şefket underlined:

'For the reorganisation of the army I certainly count on Germany. This is the most important point of my programme. The army must be reformed from the ground up. To this end, the role of training officers, merely being placed here and there simply as advisers in our organisation, will not be nearly enough.'[54]

The special position of Germany in the reorganisation of the Ottoman State was again impressed upon von Wangenheim by Şefket Paşa in May 1913. Accordingly, the reform of the army was to be undertaken 'under the almost dictatorial direction of a German general'. This cosying-up between Turkey and Germany was observed suspiciously by the other European powers. The Turkish standpoint was defended against outside critical statements, and opportunistically glossed over. The Ambassador of the United States, Henry Morgenthau, reported on a conversation with Talat Paşa, the then Interior Minister and the most influential member of the Young Turks Movement:

> 'At this meeting Talaat frankly told me that Turkey had decided to side with the Germans and to sink or swim with them. He went again over the familiar grounds, and added that if Germany won – and Talaat said that he was convinced that Germany would win – the Kaiser would get his revenge on Turkey if Turkey had not helped him to obtain this victory. Talaat frankly admitted that fear – the motive, which, as I have said, is the one that chiefly inspires Turkish acts – was driving Turkey into a German alliance. He analysed the whole situation most dispassionately; he said that nations could not afford such emotions as gratitude, or hate, or affection; the only guide to action should be cold-blooded policy. "At this moment," said Talat, "it is in our interest to side with Germany; if, a month from now, it is our interest to embrace France and England [sic] we shall do that just as readily."
>
> "Russia is our greatest enemy," he continued; "and we are afraid of her. If now, while Germany is attacking Russia, we can give her a good strong kick, and so make her powerless to injure us for some time, it is Turkey's duty to administer that kick!" And then turning to me with a half -melancholy, half-defiant smile, he summed up the whole situation.
>
> "*Ich mit die Deutschen,*" he said, in his broken German.'[55]

The objectives of the Grand Vizier, as well as those of the Young Turks Committee, mirrored the interests of Berlin exactly. Economic investments, especially the construction of the Baghdad Railway, had to be safeguarded. Ambassador von Wangenheim said, 'Germany, which wants to keep Turkey, has, according to my insignificant opinion, an overwhelming interest in supporting the reform efforts of Mahmud Şefket.'[56]

An important strategic idea in the establishment of the Military Mission was the possibility of winning Turkey as a brother-in-arms in the event of a European war, since Berlin had already envisaged in 1913 the danger of a war on two fronts. In such a case, Turkey could be exploited as a flanking power of Russia in the Caucasus in order to weaken this potential opponent of Germany, to pin down her forces and, in turn, tie Russia down on two fronts.[57]

There was another reason for German interest in a reorganisation of the Turkish Army by means of German instructors. German military equipment used by Turkish forces, as well as the reforming and training of the army under the guidance of the then German Military Mission, were still being held responsible in the international press and by the Young Turks for the defeat of the Turkish Army in the Balkan Wars.[58] Behind this campaign were probably the interests pursued by Anglo-French armaments companies in competition against Krupp. Nevertheless, this press campaign also had its political consequences. If Germany's prestige could be lowered in the military field, other areas of German-Turkish relations could be damaged. In particular, German railway construction would have been at serious risk.[59] Ambassador Wangenheim saw in a renewed appeal for a German Military Mission the best opportunity to silence the critics of German training. In any case it was also necessary to counteract the readiness of other powers to step into Germany's shoes.[60]

The official Turkish request for the despatch of a German general for the reorganisation of her army was finally made on 22 May 1913. The Germans decided on the commander of the 22nd Division, based in Kassel, Lieutenant General Liman von Sanders, whose appointment was not uncontroversial. (Otto Liman was ennobled by the Kaiser in June 1913, taking 'Sanders' as his noble suffix, thus becoming Liman von Sanders.) In his credentials it was stated that he was

'… a superior divisional commander, who would be particularly suited to this position in every way. [...] [He] has an elegant military bearing, is adroit and versatile in the art of war. He had long been a member of the General Staff and had been most successful in a wide range of posts in the army.'[61]

Baron von Wangenheim, on the other hand, did not consider von Sanders to be suitable, observing that von Sanders, 'of all the generals considered as head of a military mission, he was undoubtedly the most politically unsuitable. [...] Liman has been excluded from a higher General Staff career because of his lack of tact.' From this von Wangenheim ironically deduced: 'This seems to have predestined him for the position here, which requires very special tact.'[62] Liman's subordinate, General Kress von Kressenstein, characterised him as incapable of adapting to foreign conditions and barely able even to grasp the oriental way of thinking. Liman was 'self-confident and vain, temperamental and irascible, suspicious and sensitive.'[63] And even Liman's adjutant,

Liman von Sanders. (*Bundesarchiv Koblenz*)

Enver Paşa. (*Author's Collection*)

Carl Mühlmann, who unreservedly emphasised the achievements of the German commander-in-chief in his publications on the fighting in Gallipoli, was himself desperately unhappy at having to work with him. During the fighting on the Gallipoli Peninsula, he wrote to his parents about his reasons for applying to get a general staff posting in a regiment and thus no longer having to act as von Sanders' adjutant:

> 'But all this is not the main thing; the main thing is that I would no longer be in the immediate vicinity of L. You know I always wanted to leave him; either I would have had to have given a false reason, as you know from our meeting last August, or there would have been a confrontation, whereby I would have been judged as ungrateful and he could have caused great damage to my military future [...] Oh, dear Dad & Mum, you do not know how hard these almost 1½ years with L. have been. If I did not have such an easy-going nature, I couldn't have stood it; these eternal rows with the Minister of War, Bronsart, the Ambassador, the continuous friction of the daughter [Liman's] with the families of the Mil. Mission, his nervousness in the car & on horseback, his colossal demands with regard to food and lodging in this relatively uncultivated country, in short, dear Dad & Mum, you can believe me, it was not easy.'[64]

General Hans von Seekt did not seem to have a good impression of General Liman von Sanders either:

> 'The selection of the Head of the Military Mission could hardly have been more unfortunate. In Germany, not suitable for the command of an army corps, he is to take over the new formation of the entire Turkish army. Even worse, the indifference to its development could not be fully stressed or admitted, that the basic principle has not been understood, that for the representation of a powerful nation in a foreign country, only the best would be barely good enough. General Liman von Sanders was known in the German army well enough to scare away the best from serving under him.'[65]

Liman von Sanders later wrote that the entire Army High Command was obviously not in full support of the decision to despatch the Military Mission and remarked:

> 'When I took my leave of Colonel General von Moltke at the beginning of December 1913, he told me, more or less, the following: "I do not understand why we are sending a Military Mission to Turkey. In view of their army's condition, which is beyond help anyway, this is quite senseless. I have at least inserted in the contract, that you can all be recalled in the event of a war." I then replied to the Colonel General that I had had no influence whatsoever on the appointment, nor did I volunteer for it.'[66]

The draft contract was approved by the Kaiser, the appropriate German military commands and Foreign Office, as well as by the Ottoman Council of Ministers during October 1913. Summoned to Berlin in November 1913, Liman von Sanders placed his signature under the contract, making the following note for himself:

> 'The task of the Military Mission is to be strictly military. The wording of the contract makes this fully clear. Statements made by many parties, as well as those in publications and newspapers, that the German Military Mission will also be politically engaged, are quite inappropriate. The fact that on the surface it has appeared as a political factor is a different

matter. The decision to despatch it has to be addressed as a political decision, because it was based on [our] Turkish policy, which had already been formulated.'

Liman von Sanders goes on to mention a talk with the Emperor, who told him during an audience at the end of November 1913:

'It must be quite irrelevant to you whether the Young Turks or the Old Turks are in power. Your only concern is with the army. Remove politics from the Turkish officer corps. Politicising is their biggest mistake.'[67]

Carl Mühlmann, however, saw the political consequences of the Military Mission as the pivotal point when he wrote:

'The target which is aimed for, namely the build-up of a powerful military force, has however, strayed from the framework of purely military business and received strong political weighting. For upgrading the [Turkish] army was tantamount to reinforcing Turkey; greater German influence on the army also highlights Germany's political influence in Constantinople. The question of army re-organisation by Germany thus elicited the problem with the Turks; it has compelled the great powers to take a stand on this question, both in regard to their Oriental and their German policies.'[68]

Whether the Kaiser's political intentions for an alleged 'Germanisation'[69] of the Ottoman Army were mentioned during the secret audience for the first contingent of the Military Mission on 9 December in the New Palace in Potsdam, is more than questionable. Von Sanders reported on what was said at this audience: 'The Emperor gave us a brief discourse in which he told us to uphold the honour of the German name abroad and to live only for our military duties'.[70]

After the bad experience of past missions, the success of which had been classified as very moderate, the Germans had now insisted on a more effective Military Mission, with greater powers to achieve a real strengthening and reorganisation of the Ottoman armed forces. The Turks also agreed to this[71] and, in particular, General von Sanders, as Head of the Military Mission, was assured that:

'He will be a voting member of the Supreme War Council and must be consulted on all questions on the army and defence. He is also the immediate commanding officer of all military schools, training regiments and foreign officers in the army. Thus the uniformity of training for the forces based on the German model is ensured. Whilst in post, the General may engage or dismiss additional foreign officers; those Imperial Ottoman officers under his command may only be assigned to other units with his consent. He may also select officers for training in Germany. General of Cavalry Liman von Sanders ranks immediately behind the Imperial Ottoman Minister of War, except when the Chief of the General Staff is senior to him. The German General is thus ranked as the second or third most senior officer in the Turkish Army. Furthermore, the General has full authority to inspect all military facilities and units. His task is the theoretical and advanced training of all Turkish General Staff officers.'[72]

Liman von Sanders arrived in Istanbul on 14 December 1913 with the first ten officers. On their departure from Germany, Prussian head-dress was worn but en route these were exchanged for the Turkish *fez*, evidently as a concession to their new masters. A total of forty-two officers was originally allocated for the Mission, all of whom arrived during the first months of 1914. By the outbreak of the war the Mission had increased to seventy-one members.[73] A personal budget of one million Marks (then worth about 240,000 US dollars) was made available to von Sanders to use at his own discretion.[74] He prepared himself for his task by studying the reports of former German reformers. It became clear to him that not only would it be difficult to effect radical influence on the Turkish Army but that too much theory and too little practice had so far been carried out in their training.

Moreover, he wanted to make rapid progress through personal influence on soldiers' training, based on German procedures. Von Sanders described his arrival in Istanbul:

'On the morning of the 14th of December, we arrived in Istanbul. At Sirkedji railway station we were received with resounding military music [...] present were a number of senior Turkish officers, among them the admirable Minister of War, Izzet Pasha, as well as the German officers who were already stationed in Istanbul. [...] To our great astonishment, the German Embassy was not represented at the reception of the Military Mission.'[75]

A few days after his arrival, Liman von Sanders was introduced to Sultan Mehmet Paşa,[76] with the Minister of War, Izzet Paşa, acting as interpreter. The delegation of the German Military Mission, equipped with such wide-ranging powers, was very controversial even in Turkish circles. It was regarded merely as a political and economic necessity, apparently viewing German–Turkish cooperation only with pragmatism and with little enthusiasm. After the assassination of Grand Vizier Mahmud Şevket Paşa on 11 June 1913, the power base had changed. Prince Said Halim Paşa was declared the new Grand Vizier and appointed Talat Paşa to the Cabinet as the new

The Liman Mission before leaving for Istanbul. Left to right: Major Perrinet von Thauvenay, Major von Feldmann, Captain von König, Colonel Bronsart von Schellendorf, Lieutenant General Liman von Sanders, Colonel Weber, Military Commissariat Councillor Buchardi, Major Nicolai, Chief Staff Surgeon (Major) Mayer, Lieutenant Mühlmann. (*Die Welt, 21 December 1913*)

Liman von Sanders being received by the Minister of War, Izzet Paşa, at the railway station. (*Ullstein Bilderdienst*)

Interior Minister. Talat Paşa had reservations about the German Military Mission since he was more of a Francophile. For example, apparently Talat Paşa said to Ambassador Morgenthau that Germany was going to be exploited - just as Germany intended to take advantage of the Ottoman Empire. A representative of the American Ambassador reported the following conversation with Talat Paşa in a memorandum:

> '"Why do you hand the management of the country over to the Germans?" asked this deputy, referring to the German military mission. "Don't you see that this is part of Germany's plan to make Turkey a German colony - that we shall become merely another Egypt?"
>
> "We understand perfectly," replied Talaat, "that that is Germany's programme. We also know that we cannot put this country on its feet with our own resources. We shall, therefore, take advantage of such technical and material assistance as the Germans can place at our disposal. We shall use Germany to help us reconstruct and defend the country until we are able to govern ourselves with our own strength. When that day comes, we can say good-bye to the Germans within twenty-four hours."'[77]

One of the greatest critics of the army reform under German leadership however, was Mustafa Kemal, who appealed to his comrades:

> 'It is madness to allow the Germans to control the army, which is the very foundation of our national existence and, in the event of a misfortune, the only guarantor of our survival. Are not the Turks able to reorganise their own army? Recourse to the Prussians is an insult to every one of us.'[78]

Kemal tried unsuccessfully to change the minds of the governing triumvirate of Talat, Cemal and Enver. Instead, he fell into disgrace, especially with Enver Paşa. After the death of Şefket Paşa, Izzet Paşa had been appointed Minister of War. He shared the view of his predecessor about German support and under his direction the relevant contract was drawn up and finalised in the War Office. Izzet knew von Sanders from his service as an officer with the Kassel Hussars and from the occasions when he had been instructed by him in the duties of a general staff officer. But Izzet's power was limited and in January 1914 his post as Minister of War was assumed by his keenest adversary, Enver Paşa, who was then only 32 years old. This change had obviously been enforced by Enver and Liman von Sanders expressly regretted this, writing later:

> 'One day in January 1914 Izzet Paşa did not appear in the Ministry of War, where the Military Mission also had its offices, and left someone to say that he was ill. I visited him the next morning in his *konak* [residence] and heard from him personally that he had had to resign.'[79]

Enver's reputation with the German military leadership was ambivalent. He was a well-known admirer of Prussian virtues and military achievements. He had spent many years in Germany, serving in 1909 as Military Attaché in Berlin, and he spoke fluent German. He seemed completely 'Prussianised' and was convinced of the effectiveness of German training, practices and weapons. He saw himself as a cross between Napoleon and Frederick the Great, with portraits of both hanging behind his desk. However, he was not considered by diplomats in Istanbul to be a special 'German friend',[80] but rather a pragmatist and Turkish patriot, who wanted to recoup the military strength of his country with German support. Enver's German-friendly orientation was valued and used, but his military skills were viewed critically. Von Hindenburg, who had experienced Enver more than once while Enver had been in Germany, wrote:

> 'In spite of all his great conception of wars in general, Enver Pasha, however, still lacked a thorough military, I may say, general staff training. This weakness was apparently not only to be found in all Turkish leaders but in their staffs as well. It seemed this deficiency was prevalent in the nature of Orientals.'[81]

The American Ambassador, Morgenthau, described Enver:

> 'He was quick in making decisions, always ready to stake his future and his very life upon the success of a single adventure; from the beginning, indeed, his career had been one lucky crisis after another. His nature had remorselessness, a lack of pity, a cold-blooded determination, of which his clean-cut handsome face, his small but

Visit of Kaiser Wilhelm II in Istanbul in 1917 on board the Goeben, with Enver Paşa saluting. (*Istanbul Archaeological Institute*)

sturdy figure, and his pleasing manners gave no indication. Nor would the casual spectator have suspected the passionate personal ambition that drove him on. His friends commonly referred to him as 'Napoleonlik' ···the little Napoleon··· and this nickname really represented Enver's abiding conviction.'[82]

Mustafa Kemal was never particularly impressed by Enver and was convinced that he

'[…] never got to the bottom of things. How his ideas and decisions were to be carried out were simply mere details for him. He was largely ignorant of military matters and he had not advanced upwards step-by-step with the command of a battalion and a regiment. [...] The result was that, whenever he gave orders to a division or an army corps, he never considered what was really essential and how the operation should be continued, acting almost like a non-commissioned officer, who gave forty or fifty soldiers the order to take a hill. The *Sarıkamış* disaster was a result of this attitude.'[83]

However, the most severe reaction to the appointment of the Liman Mission came from Russia. This led to a serious foreign policy crisis that lasted for several weeks, between 20 November 1913 and mid-January 1914. In St Petersburg the news of Liman's appointment was seen as a provocative denial of Russia's national prerogatives and interests. In addition to the far-reaching powers of both the General and the German Military Mission, the point which offered the greatest area of conflict was placing the 1st Turkish Army Corps as a future model corps under the command of Liman von Sanders. The assignment to the Corps was not part of the contract but was proclaimed by the Sultan's decree on 7 January 1914. This Corps was stationed in and around Istanbul and was thus responsible not only for the capital but also for the strategically important area of the Straits. Complications with Great Britain and France, who feared growing German influence on Turkey, were just as pre-programmed as the fierce Russian reaction was foreseeable. Liman von Sanders, however, emphasised in his memoirs the apolitical background of assuming this command. He saw it to have been pure expediency 'in the state capital, to create a practical example of training for war, in which Turkish officers could learn'.[84]

Liman von Sanders was only concerned with bringing about practical advances through direct influence on the troops, which had been hitherto denied to his predecessors by the lack of practical relevance. Subsequent events reveal this statement by the General to be quite plausible. Despite his personal military interpretation of his Mission, the fact was, however, that the Russians were deeply disturbed. The German Foreign Office was informed on 11 November 1913 by Baron Hellmuth Lucius von Stoedten, the German Chargé d'Affaires in St Petersburg, that:

'Russia would not be indifferent if, for example, the Dardanelles were to be strongly fortified and guns with a range of twenty kilometres into the Black Sea were installed at the [eastern] entrance [of the Bosphorus]. Such fortifications, carried out on the advice of German officers, could only be directed against Russia.'[85]

In fact, such plans did exist for the fortification of Istanbul and the Narrows under German supervision and, of course, equipped with guns of German manufacture.[86] But the French also suspected the strategic attempt by Germany 'to take possession of Turkish territory by the powers of the Triple-Alliance'[87] and saw the danger of being left behind in the continuing division of the Ottoman Empire. A telegram from the French Ambassador in Istanbul, dated 30 November 1913, stated that

'The disintegration of Turkey has already begun or is beginning and Germany, with help from the Ottoman government, occupies positions which secure it all the advantages in the division.'[88]

A diplomatic offensive by the Russians, with the aim of exerting joint pressure on all the Entente powers against the special position of General von Sanders, sparked British concerns. The Germans would have been able to argue on the basis of the fact that the British also had a military mission, equivalent in size and power to the German Military Mission.[89] Not only was Admiral Sir Arthur H Limpus the naval adviser, but he was also the Commander-in-Chief of the Turkish fleet. The defence of the Straits towards the sea was thus entirely in the hands of a British admiral and the British were afraid that their own influence would be reduced if the attacks on the position of General von Sanders became too virulent.[90] Indeed, Britain had even thought of recalling Admiral Limpus in order to invalidate Germany's argument in advance, but this idea was later rejected. The British Military Attaché also judged that the fact that von Sanders was in command of the 1st Army Corps was an obstacle in the German general's reorganisation of the army. Von Sanders would be tied up by too many organisational constraints, which would not be present if he only held a purely advisory position.[91] The Germans were certainly able to follow the sentiment of this argument. In a private letter, dated 17 December 1913, to Gottlieb von Jagow, the Secretary of State at the German Foreign Office, von Wangenheim frankly admitted that he was against this command from the outset, as it would hinder von Sanders' advisory activities too much. However, the Corps command was not the real reason for Russian protests. Russia feared much more the military strengthening of Turkey and the consolidation of the triumvirate of the Young Turks rule, which was emanating from the work of the Military Mission and Germany's uncontrolled influence. Von Wangenheim commented:

'The Russian opposition is therefore directed at the German mission in general. If Liman had not been appointed Commander-in-Chief of the Corps here the Russians would have found another part of our programme to protest against. It is a fortunate coincidence that effective assignment [of von Sanders] in Constantinople is precisely the point on which we can most easily give way. I was against the assignment from the outset.'[92]

The Germans were not aiming for the immediate seizure of the Straits, which would have been directed against Russia, but securing long-term German influence not only in the Turkish Army but also in the Ottoman Empire. This explains Germany's readiness to renounce von Sanders' Corps Command as the official bone of contention. The continued reluctant attitude of the German Government over the 'Corps question' was also interpreted by the Russians as 'the double-mindedness and indubitable insincerity of German statesmen in the question of the position of the German general, who has been appointed commander of the 1st Turkish Army Corps stationed in Constantinople'.[93] In St Petersburg, measures to impose sanctions were put in place to put pressure on the Turkish government. Russian ideas, however, of possibly occupying territory in Asia Minor would not have been feasible without the joint action and consent of both Britain and France. The Russians could not rely on this solidarity, as in such an event there was also the risk that Germany would send significant military aid to Istanbul in response. On the other hand, giving in to the 'Corps question' would have meant a weakening of Russia in the eyes of their British and French allies and thus a considerable loss of face.[94] What was necessary now was to find a way out of the problem that would humiliate neither the Germans nor the Turks, nor be interpreted as a sign of weakness and would not be understood by General von Sanders as a personal defeat. The simplest solution was to promote Liman von Sanders to be a Turkish Marshal. Von Wangenheim welcomed this compromise and on 23 December 1913 indicated his confidence in the solution to his Foreign Office: 'Liman's position will become stronger and more unassailable if, after some time, he relinquishes the command of the Corps and devotes himself exclusively to the task of reorganisation'.[95]

The command of a mere Corps was not appropriate to his new rank and had to be relinquished; but there was no loss of prestige for von Sanders because of his promotion. In his new rank of Marshal, he was appointed Inspector-General of the Turkish Army on 10 January 1914.[96] Whilst the German General, now a Turkish Marshal, saw nothing particularly remarkable in this (as Head of the Military Mission, he already had the right to inspect all branches of the Turkish Army and fortresses), the German diplomats involved were highly delighted.[97]

In Russia, though, the decision had now been finally taken to secure by all means their historic military-strategic goal – the mastery of the Straits. Czar Nicholas II commented in December 1913:

'As the most important condition for the steady development of South Russia, I continue to maintain that the Russian Black Sea Fleet must have absolute supremacy over the Turkish Fleet. For this reason, it is imperative to make extraordinary efforts for future supremacy in the Black Sea.'[98]

However, despite this grand design, Russian forces at that time were not yet powerful enough to achieve this goal. In any case, according to the Russian Minister of Marine, the two ships of the line that had been ordered by Turkey and were currently being built in Britain should be prevented from entering the Black Sea. These two modern warships would not only give the Turks 'a great moral uplift'[99], but would continue to prevent any Russian operations against the Straits. All in all, Russia felt that her own available military resources to throw down the gauntlet against Turkey would not be sufficient until 1916.

In the meantime the Germans still had to decide who was to become the Military Mission's Chief of Staff. The selection initially fell on Major Otto von Lossow, who was already in Ottoman service, but who was rejected by von Wangenheim:

While the Turks clearly recognise von Lossow's military achievements and tolerate his brusque attitude, everything depends on appointing a personality, especially during the first phase, in whom the Turks have every confidence and who can liaise between the Mission and the higher Turkish echelons.[100]

It was therefore decided that Major Walter von Strempel, the former Military Attaché, should take over this post. This appointment, however, was not seen uncritically, as von Strempel was obviously too well versed on the internal affairs of previous Missions.

Ambassador von Wangenheim noted on the appointment that, 'I have reason to suspect that some of the present reformers, who wish to continue their comfortable life, intrigue against von Strempel'.[101]

In Berlin it was also considered that the close relations developed by von Strempel to the Young Turks leadership could have a negative impact in any possible change of government and thus he could not be left as Military Attaché in Istanbul. Nevertheless, they wanted to involve him in the Military Mission and the Emperor himself agreed to assign the Military Attaché to it. When von Strempel was promoted lieutenant colonel in January 1914, Sanders proposed sending him back to Germany. Apparently, the good relationship between the former Military Attaché and leading

Ottoman personalities was too uncomfortable for von Sanders and he wanted to get rid of him. While the Embassy intervened to retain von Strempel, the Head of the Mission asked Kaiser Wilhelm II on 23 February 1914 finally to recall von Strempel, since he had apparently brought the Mission into too much contact with the Young Turks Party and thus may have caused it damage. According to von Sanders, von Strempel 'had distanced himself from the other members of the Military Mission, while on the other hand, with a certain high-handedness, went over the General's head'.[102]

The suspension of Major von Strempel caused considerable consternation amongst the German diplomats in Istanbul, who concluded that the Military Mission had lost its most capable personality. This example was only the beginning of a persistent rivalry between the Military Mission and the German diplomatic representation. It resulted of a great deal of friction, leading to inevitable poor consequences, during the war as a result of wrangling over competencies, influence and personal vanities. The Military Mission was also perceived as an annoying alien element by the Turkish military, which was not surprising, since in March 1914 all important positions in the Turkish General Staff and the Ministry of War were under German control. In order to ameliorate the impact of Germans being in key positions, Turkish officers were to be sent to Germany to be placed in command of appropriate German Army units, so that they would be able to 'form a better idea of the intentions and objectives of the Military Mission, of which they are now largely ignorant and therefore inwardly opposed'.[103]

It should be noted that General Liman von Sanders was obviously a very polarizing personality and always placed the needs of the service before diplomacy and finesse. He was an energetic, uncompromising and often unpopular superior. As was later shown, however, he nevertheless proved to be the correct and appropriate choice of commander, building up and leading the German Military Mission on the one hand and on the other pushing through operational requirements against Turkish resistance, therefore to plan and direct successfully the defence of the Gallipoli Peninsula. Any harsh judgment about von Sanders' less conciliatory nature should not ignore these facts.

Major Walter von Strempel. (*Deutsche Botschaft Ankara*)

Major Otto von Lossow. (*von Lossow Family*)

The Military Mission (MM) and the Mediterranean Division (MMD) until Turkey's entry into the war

At the beginning of 1914 the wrangling by the European Powers for favour and influence in Turkey was by no means over. Germany, however, took on special significance, given the ever-increasing size and influence of its Military Mission. The important task of the Military Mission was to create the conditions for a German-Turkish alliance, since German foreign policy made such a possibility dependent on the state of the Turkish army. To realise this, however, the Turkish army had first to be made fit to go to war. But even the Turkish Navy was not ready for action, despite British training assistance. This navy was of great importance to Turkey, especially as a strategic counterweight to Russia, and needed to be quickly bolstered. Therefore, in February 1914, Enver Paşa asked via Major von Strempel whether Turkey could buy two cruisers, already operational, from Germany, which would be superior to the Russian heavy cruiser *Averoff*.[104] This request was examined but no ships could be offered that matched this criterion. Nevertheless, the news of the intention to purchase such a warship trickled down to St Petersburg, where it was even said that the heavy cruiser *Goeben* was to be sold to Turkey, as reported by the Russian chargé d'affaires in Istanbul:

> 'Our military attaché told me as a result of the persistent rumours of the cruiser *Goeben* being handed over by Germany, that he had a confidential discussion with Major von Strempel, the former military attaché, now General Staff Officer, of General Liman. This gentleman stated categorically as follows: the German Emperor had already agreed to the sale of the cruiser *Moltke* to Turkey. The sale never went through, however, because of the high price, the protests by the Moltke family and the changed political situation. Should Russia, contrary to its promise allegedly given to Germany not to oppose the conclusion of a Turkish loan from France and prevent it [the loan], there is no assurance that the Emperor will not hand the *Goeben* over to Turkey. This hand-over is even very probable, according to Strempel, the more so since the case of Liman has still not been satisfactorily settled for Russia. Strempel asked our military attaché not to mention his name. The French military attaché, therefore, who called on Captain Schtcheglow, said that if the rumours of the sale of the *Goeben* were confirmed, this sale would be proof of general strategic preparation by Germany.'[105]

Although this statement was not at first taken seriously by the Russians and was regarded as deliberate disinformation by the Germans, this option of reinforcing the Turkish fleet was now known. Nevertheless, to emphasise the value of Turkey as a possible ally and as proof of German interest and a demonstration of military strength, the Mediterranean Division (MMD) was despatched to Istanbul. The MMD had been under the command of Admiral Souchon since 23 October 1913. The *Goeben* entered the Bosphorus on 15 May 1914 and anchored off the Golden Horn below the German Embassy in Pera. There followed a reciprocal series of sumptuous receptions on board as well as in the Embassy and also for the *Goeben*'s officers as guests of the Sultan. As the flagship's visit drew to a close and the coal stocks were topped up, a fire broke out in the Taşkışla Barracks in Pera and a third of the crew were despatched as firefighters. Three sailors lost their lives, a sad event, cynically commented upon by British Ambassador Sir Louis Mallet, for whom the political success of Admiral Souchon's visit stuck in his craw:

'When trying to extinguish a fire in the Tache Kéchla [Taşkışla] barracks, he [Souchon] was fatefully able to sacrifice the lives of three young sailors on the altar of Turkish-German friendship. If one remembers that Bismarck had said the whole Oriental question would not be worth the life of a single Prussian grenadier, then times do seem to have changed.'[106]

The visit of the MMD to Istanbul instigated a visit by the Commander-in-Chief of the British Mediterranean Fleet, Vice-Admiral John de Robeck, with the flagship HMS *Invincible*. The presence of the German warship had not been interpreted by the British as a courtesy visit but, more correctly, as a demonstration of German power and now had to be trumped. This did not achieve its aim, however, mainly because the Turks were still very mindful of the German sailors' help during the fire in the Taşkışla Barracks. In a letter dated 5 July 1914, Charles Lister commented wryly on *Invincible's* visit: 'The Admiral has now left us; his visit was a success, I think, and the Heir-Apparent went on board his ship. This was a score over the Germans, whom he did not visit.'[106a]

Slowly the efforts of German training support seemed to have been fruitful in some units at least, which were now to be harvested diplomatically. During a large parade for the Sultan and the Diplomatic Corps on 23 July 1914, von Wangenheim spoke with Cemal Paşa and tried to flatter him with the achievements of the newly-trained Turkish army:

'Now, Cemal Paşa, do you see what really extraordinary results have been achieved in a very short time by German officers? Here you have a Turkish army that does not differ from the best organised armies in the world! All the German officers unanimously praise the moral strength of Turkish soldiers, who have shown themselves exceedingly magnificent against all expectations. One can declare it a great success to be the ally of a government that has such an army.'[107]

This statement was, of course, a straightforward lie, since von Wangenheim very well knew about conditions in the Turkish army from persistent criticism by the Military Mission. He even wired Berlin in March 1914, noting that in three years only '200,000 tolerably trained men'[108] could be expected. The German influence of the Military Mission on Turkish troops had not gone unnoticed, especially by the international diplomatic corps. Once again, Ambassador Morgenthau wrote about these manifest successes of the German Military Mission:

'And now for several months we had before our eyes this spectacle of the Turkish army actually under the control of Germany. German officers drilled the troops daily – all, I am now convinced, in preparation for the approaching war. Just what results had been accomplished appeared when, in July, there was a great military review. [...] We now saw that in the preceding six months the Turkish army had been completely Prussianized. What in January had been an undisciplined, ragged rabble was now parading with the goose step; the men were clad in German field grey, and they even wore a casque-shaped head covering, which slightly suggested the German pickelhaube. The German officers were immensely proud of the exhibition, and the transformation of the wretched Turkish soldiers of January into these neatly dressed, smartly stepping, splendidly manoeuvring troops was really a creditable military achievement.'[109]

Proudly, von Wangenheim telegraphed to Berlin:

> 'During the jubilee celebrations of the Turkish Constitution a parade was held for His Majesty the Sultan, during which the German Military Mission's activity could celebrate an unexpectedly brilliant triumph, reflected in the impeccable bearing of the troops. General von Liman was congratulated all round. The ambassadors of the Triple Entente stayed away from this apparently undesirable drama.'[110]

The German–Turkish alliance was officially sealed at the beginning of August 1914. The emergence of the German–Turkish alliance might also be considered the result of the massive interference by the Entente Powers during the Liman crisis. It was the justified Turkish fear of encirclement by the 'hereditary enemy' Russia which, with the help of France and Britain, was obviously working towards ending the independent political existence of the Ottoman Empire. Cemal Paşa, the Minister of Marine wrote:

> 'We wanted to reorganise our army and therefore turned to Germany. The German Military Mission came to Constantinople, the result of which was a considerable increase in the fighting ability of the Turkish army and, at the same time, increasing the defence prospects of the Straits. It is perfectly understandable that the Russians were in opposition, since they had always regarded Constantinople as their legal heritage [...] but can it be assumed that this policy in the internal affairs of the neighbouring country would be carried out without the consent of England [sic] and France? Certainly not!'[111]

At the end of July 1914, Cemal Paşa was asked by Talat Paşa what he thought of a political alliance with Germany. Cemal had just returned from a visit to France, where he had tried to garner support but received no promises and he replied, according to his own records: 'I would accept without hesitation an alliance which freed Turkey from its isolated position'.[112]

On 1 August 1914 the German Ambassador was empowered by a telegram from Reich Chancellor Theobald von Bethmann Hollweg to conclude an alliance with Turkey 'if General Liman is convinced that Turkey is now prepared actively and effectively to intervene for us in the event of a war with Russia.'[113] This was not the only point. In a draft contract as early as 28 July, the Reich Chancellor had included the condition that, 'In case of Turkey going to war, Germany will retain the Military Mission. Turkey assures the effective execution of supreme command through the Military Mission.'[114]

The Ambassador saw the first condition fulfilled by the latest positive reports on the state of the Ottoman army. The Reich Chancellor's second condition was amended in the final text of the treaty: 'Turkey, on the other hand, guarantees the said Military Mission effective influence on the general army command, according to the agreements made directly between His Excellency the Minister of War and His Excellency the Head of the Military Mission.' The Ambassador added:

> 'The Turks want this wording with due regard for the fact that HM the Sultan is the Commander-in-Chief of the Turkish army. General Liman, however, officially told me beforehand that he had negotiated a detailed agreement with Enver, the Minister of War, which would ensure the reality of supreme command by the Military Mission [...].'[115]

The memoirs of Liman von Sanders do not confirm this phrase of the draft treaty as, in his opinion, the agreement between Enver and von Sanders did not take place and the comment had not been brought to the attention of the Head of the Military Mission. Accordingly, on 1 August 1914, von Sanders was called to the German Embassy in Tarabya for a meeting between Wangenheim and Enver. There he was told that a secret alliance treaty was being negotiated and they would like his advice on the role of the Military Mission in the event of Turkey's possible entry into the war. Von Sanders' reply was that the original contract for the Military Mission called for the recall of German officers in the event of a war. If, however, the Military Mission were to remain in Turkey and Turkey were to enter the war, then: 'German officers would have to be assigned to such positions, which would give them effective influence on the conduct of the war'. Sanders added to this text:

> 'The passage concerning the Military Mission was forthwith translated into French [the language of diplomacy], ensuring the Military Mission an *influence effective sur la conduite générale de l'armée*. I was not aware of the other content of the draft contract. When I requested this in writing at the beginning of September, this was refused in a letter from Baron v. Wangenheim dated 5 September.'[116]

The alliance treaty had been negotiated conspiratorially and without involving the Turkish Cabinet; it was signed by Said Halim for Turkey and by Baron von Wangenheim for Germany on 2 August 1914. It took place in the salon of the then summer residence of the German Ambassador in the Istanbul suburb of Tarabya. The conclusion of the contract was communicated to Cemal Paşa by the Grand Vizier, which he described in his memoirs:

> '[The Grand Vizier]: "and now I will tell you news which will certainly give you great pleasure. Can you imagine what it is?" "I guess," I replied after a moment, "that it is the decision you recently made with Enver Paşa, Talat and Halil Bey, at which I was not present. But I don't really wish to guess its content."
>
> "The German government has proposed an alliance with us," he said, "and since this proposal seems to us to benefit the country's interests, we signed the contract today with Ambassador von Wangenheim. Now! Are you satisfied with that?"
>
> The importance of the news, for which I was not prepared, shocked me very much. "If the provisions of the treaty really correspond with the interests of the country, this may well be regarded as an important political event," I replied. "It is an agreement which takes into account the interests of both parties and ensures the rights of the two parties equally, in a form which no government has yet accomplished", he said.'[117]

This treaty was a diplomatic masterpiece by Ambassador von Wangenheim, which thus sealed the previous unofficial military alliance between Germany and Turkey; but it caused a storm of international criticism.

In the same month, however, the MMD, with the presence in the Mediterranean of the heavy cruiser *Goeben* and the light cruiser *Breslau*, opened a completely new dimension in the course of German–Turkish relations and the German military presence operating in Turkey now took on a major strategic significance. From early 1914, the naval formation operating in the Mediterranean with Austrian and Italian naval units had already been preparing to wage war jointly at sea. To this end, during talks in Rome in January 1914, operational procedures and communication methods had been coordinated between the fleet commanders and the naval attachés.[118] The first task should be preventing the transfer of the XIX (Algerian) Army Corps from the French embarkation ports of Philippeville and Bône in Algeria. During the night of 1/2 August the mobilisation order had been received by the MMD. On 2 August it was also reported that hostilities against Russia had been opened and that war against France would be imminent.[119] Souchon, who was then with the MMD taking on supplies in Messina, received no support there from the Italian navy and, indeed, was required to leave port immediately. Souchon then requisitioned the steamer *General* of the German East Africa Line and conscripted all the men on this ship, as well as on the *Barcelona*, which was also in port. Since the Fleet Commander received no further orders from Germany, he took the decision on his own initiative to strike a blow against the fortified French embarkation ports, Philippeville and Bône, in Algeria. However, while the Mediterranean Division was still steaming towards the Algerian coast, there were already moves afoot for the deployment of this formation.

On 1 August, Ambassador von Wangenheim requested the despatch of the two warships as he cabled Berlin: 'According to reliable Austrian intelligence, Russian naval attack on the Bosphorus planned. Ambassador requests the *Goeben* to stiffen Turkish fleet, to keep Black Sea Fleet at bay, to secure cable connections to Romania and prevent a Russian landing on the Bulgarian coast.'[120] At the same time he also informed the Turkish leaders of this suspected Russian intention and offered German help. This offer neatly coincided with the news that the new warships, *Sultan Osman* and *Reshadiye*, nearing completion in England, had been confiscated on the orders of the First Lord of the Admiralty, Winston Churchill.

This British decision had a shocking effect in Turkey, which Cemal Paşa described:

'On 1 or 2 August, half an hour after Turkey had made the final payment for the *Sultan Osman*, the English Minister of Marine [sic] prevented the Turkish flag being hoisted on the ships and confiscated both the *Sultan Osman* and the *Reshadiye*. I will never in my life forget the pain and grief that I felt when I got this terrible news. This was the day when I clearly realized that the

Summer residence of the German Ambassador in Tarabya ca. 1890.[121] (*Deutsches Generalkonsulat*)

apparent friendly advice of Admiral de Robeck, Commander of the English [sic] Mediterranean Fleet, during his Constantinople visits, the thousand difficulties Armstrong had invented to delay the completion of the ship, had been nothing but pretexts for the long-cherished intention to take possession of the vessels.'[122]

Enver still tried to have one of the two warships sent to Germany, to be placed at the disposal of the German fleet, as on 1 August he no longer reckoned that they would be able to set sail for Istanbul. This suggestion was transmitted by von Wangenheim to Berlin, where it was approved by the Kaiser and answered on the same day by von Tirpitz: 'Turkish dreadnought *Sultan Osman* welcome in Germany. Set sail as soon as possible.'[123] However, neither of the warships could leave the British dockyards – they remained confiscated.

Wangenheim's proposal for the despatch of the MMD was welcomed by Prince Said Halim Paşa but it was preferred that a decision should be postponed until clarification of Bulgaria's reaction to the beginning of the war. Despite the wait-and-see attitude of Turkey, von Wangenheim asked the German Foreign Office to agree to despatch the MMD. This was initially rejected in Berlin: on the one hand the Emperor still did not have the exact content of the alliance treaty; on the other the German Admiralty staff saw little sense in an intervention by the MMD in the Black Sea. Only the personal intervention of Admiral von Tirpitz led to a change in this position.

Meanwhile Souchon continued preparing to attack the African coastal ports to destroy French shipping and port facilities there. In the late afternoon of 3 August the German Admiralty's signal arrived announcing the beginning of the war with France. Still on the voyage to Philippeville, at 3 am on 4 August, the MMD received the order: '51. 3. VIII. Alliance concluded with Turkey. *Goeben* & *Breslau* make course immediately to Constantinople - Admiralty Staff.'[124]

Souchon, however, stuck to his decision for an attack on Algeria and almost three hours later *Goeben* began bombarding port facilities, while *Breslau* opened fire on the port and ships at Bône. The result of this attack was less physical destruction but the resultant decision of the French Fleet Commander, Vice-Admiral Boué de Lapeyère, to bring his fleet into the area and from then on to form convoys - instead of engaging the MMD in battle - which he could easily have defeated with his superior force. His decision not only allowed the MMD to escape but also delayed the arrival of the XIX (Algerian) Army Corps in France by three days.

In the meantime the members of the Military Mission in Istanbul witnessed the mobilisation in Germany with bitter disappointment, as they obviously would not be involved in the fighting in their homeland and would have to remain in Istanbul. Lieutenant Colonel Heinrich Wehrle noted:

'On 3 August 1914 the officers of the German Military Mission in Turkey were assembled in one of the state rooms of the Ministry of War by the Head of the Mission, Cavalry General [and] Turkish Marshal Liman von Sanders. The Marshal gave a summary of the situation that had led to the mobilisation of the German armed forces, added that Turkey had also mobilised to protect her neutrality and concluded by reading a wire from the military cabinet that the role of the German Military Mission had not changed and that any request by individual members for home postings would not be granted. This dashed all hopes, for it was clear enough to us that we were now only confined to the forsaken role of observers.'[125]

The subsequent voyage of the MMD through the Mediterranean and the deliberations of the fleet commander to resupply and to disguise his intentions to the Allied naval leadership are not described here in detail. What is certain is that the Allied naval forces had clear superiority, as altogether their forces available to engage *Goeben* and *Breslau* in battle consisted of fifteen ships of the line: three battle cruisers; several armoured and small cruisers; eight destroyer flotillas; submarines and special ships.

Indeed, from 3.30 am on 4 August the British Mediterranean Fleet had been kept continuously informed about the exact position of the MMD, as a British cruiser of the *Weymouth* class kept the German formation in sight.[126] Italy's support for the MMD was also no longer certain and *Goeben* had considerable technical problems because of a defective engine system that prevented it from steaming at full speed. Even if the Allied forces apparently had very limited radio facilities, why the MMD was able to escape to the Dardanelles was the subject of a Westminster Parliamentary investigation later that month.

The possibility that the MMD was deliberately allowed to escape into Turkish waters, cannot be discounted – in my opinion, it is even probable. This assumption is supported by a note from the German Embassy of September 1914, in which it reported that the Grand Vizier had claimed that the British had 'let the Germans in'. Lieutenant Commander Hans Humann stated that:

'[...] according to reliable accounts, on request by the French government, the English [sic] naval commander, Admiral Milne who is accused of having allowed the German ships to enter the Dardanelles, be [should be] relieved. The Swedish ambassador here, who has close personal relations with our Ambassador, maintains that England [sic] had long ago sent an order to their Commander in the Mediterranean not to prevent the German warships entering the Dardanelles, since England [sic] is keenly concerned that the Straits do not fall into Russians hands. The source of this information believes [that he is] able to confirm that this order has not been modified in any way.'[127]

After an investigation of the incident, the British government made a statement in Parliament that:

'The conduct and dispositions of Admiral Sir Berkeley Milne in regard to the German vessels *Goeben* and *Breslau* have been the subject of the careful examination of the Board of Admiralty, with the result that their Lordships have approved the measures taken by him in all respects.'[128]

Nevertheless, on 20 September 1914 Rear-Admiral Troubridge was recalled from the Mediterranean to answer at his court martial for the breakthrough of the German ships. Although the court martial, which was held *in camera* from 5-9 September 1914, acquitted him, there were further enquiries. On 7 January 1915, the Earl of Selborne proposed a motion in the House of Lords that cast doubt on the veracity of the government's previous declaration. He suspected that the investigations against Admirals Milne and Troubridge would certainly not have been stopped had not something happened which, in the Admiralty's opinion, should not have occurred. The Earl of Curzon finally concluded the debate with the explanation that the two admirals had been acquitted, since they had done nothing but follow Admiralty orders. This may even be true, since the British Admiralty had repeatedly interfered in the powers of the Fleet Commander during the pursuit of the MMD. Orders were superseded by counter orders and sometimes even false reports were transmitted.

So much incompetence is neither credible nor probable, since the possibility of Germany bringing *Goeben* into Turkish waters had long been known. The motives for such a standpoint by Britain may well be sought in the historical roots of British imperial naval war politics in the 'Oriental Question'. Britain did not yet regard Turkey as finally lost to Germany and primarily saw her as a counterweight to Russia. In this role, the two German cruisers represented an expedient reinforcement of the Turkish fleet for balancing the forces in the Black Sea, especially since the

Admiralty had confiscated the two Turkish warships under construction. In addition, considerable German naval forces had been withdrawn from the Mediterranean or the North Sea and were now 'entrapped' behind the Dardanelles. The fact that these forces would be indirectly employed against their own fleet was, therefore, a tragic error on the part of the First Lord, Churchill, and which was not to be his last in connection with this theatre of war.[129] In writing of these events after the war, the Royal Navy's Official Historian, Sir Julian Corbett, came to the conclusion that one would have to speak of nothing else but 'of a grave disappointment, an unfortunate failure, with severe consequences …', which clearly referred to the political miscalculation that cost the lives of many thousands of British and Dominion soldiers.[130]

On 5 August 1914 the MMD received the radio message that the outbreak of war with Great Britain would be imminent, after she had already declared war at midnight the previous day. On 6 August, at 11 am, the MMD received a cable: '60. From the Admiral's Staff of the Navy: August 5, Entering Constantinople not yet possible for political reasons.'[131] On the same day the MMD was informed that it could not count on help from the Austrians and on 7 August it received another cable from Berlin: '64. 6 August, from the Admiral's Staff of the Navy: His Majesty the Emperor is convinced that *Goeben* and *Breslau* will get through successfully. Admiral.'[132] Souchon's intention was now clear and he had no other choice but to make for Istanbul, not only because of boiler leaks but also as his inferior force would not have been able to do battle successfully against the Allied units in the Mediterranean. Nevertheless, Souchon turned on the British formation that was shadowing the MMD in order to shake them off. During the engagement that followed the *Breslau* received a hit.

At about 10.00 pm, Souchon sent a radio message to the Embassy in Istanbul:

'Bowalor Constantinople. Militarily essential [to] attack enemy in Black Sea. Do utmost that I can pass through Straits without delay with permission of Turkish Government even without formal consent. Position at noon 7 August Cape Matapan. Establish immediate FT [radio/telegraph] connection. *Goeben*.'[133]

This telegram was supposed to go via a Greek telegraph station but the transmission was rejected because it was a violation of neutrality and therefore had to be sent to Izmir via the steamer *General*, which served as a relay station, and was forwarded on from there.

On 10 August, at 1 am, Souchon received a radio message from the Naval Attaché, Lieutenant Commander Humann, in Istanbul, who had already asked Cemal Paşa on 8 August to provide coal for the Mediterranean Squadron: 'Enter – demand fortress to surrender – take Dardanelles barrier pilots. Turkey fleet command of English officers rescinded.'[134] On the same day this order was amplified by a radio message from Germany: '70. From Admiralty Staff of the Navy. 9. VIII. It is of the utmost importance that *Goeben* enters Dardanelles soonest. Confirm.'[135]

At 5 pm hrs on the 10 August 1914, Admiral Souchon and his ships were granted passage through the Dardanelles. A pilot was ordered and a Turkish torpedo boat was promptly sent, thus entering the Dardanelles in its wake could be made unhindered. Colonel Hans Kannengiesser described this historical moment:

'On the 10 August 1914, I was at the usual lecture by the Minister of War Enver Pasha, when, contrary to custom, in the middle of the lecture the servant announced Lieutenant Colonel von Kress – the renowned and later proven leader of the Suez Canal expeditions. It therefore had to be a very urgent matter. Kress: 'The Çanakkale fortress reports that the German warships *Goeben* and *Breslau* are hove to at the mouth of the Dardanelles and request safe passage. Fortress asks for immediate instructions as to which measures the commanders of the forts at Kum Kale and Siddul Bahr should take.' Enver: 'I cannot decide now. I must speak with the Grand Vizier.' Kress: 'But we have to telegraph immediately.'

It was a difficult decision for the otherwise decisive Enver Pasha. He battled with a heavy, inner struggle without outwardly showing anything. At last he said briefly, 'They should let them in'. We two Germans felt a great weight fall off our shoulders. But Kress was not yet satisfied. 'If the English warships follow the Germans, should they open fire on them, if they want to enter at the same time?' Enver considers anew. 'The matter has to be decided by the Council of Ministers and this question could still be left open for the time being.' Kress: 'Excellency, we cannot leave our subordinates in such a situation without immediate, clear orders. Should they open fire or not?' Enver: (after another pause for consideration) 'Yes.'

A rattling sound could be heard as the bolts of the Dardanelles gates flew open.'[136]

Enver Paşa said to Cemal Paşa and others gathered around the table of Prince Yali on 11 August 1914: 'A son is born unto us'[137], alluding to the two ships that his decision allowed to pass through the Dardanelles.

The Goeben enters the Dardanelles. (*Bundesarchiv Koblenz*)

Hoisting the Turkish flag on the Goeben during her passage to Istanbul. (*Bundesarchiv Koblenz*)

The British pursuers were indeed denied passage – an act that *de facto* now meant the surrender of Turkish neutrality. The British then responded with the warning that if the German ships were to proceed to the Black Sea, the Dardanelles would be forced.[138]

Ambassador Morgenthau describes this moment with bitter admiration for Ambassador von Wangenheim:

'"The *Goeben* and *Breslau* have passed through the Dardanelles!" He (Wangenheim) was waving the wireless message with the enthusiasm of a school boy whose football team has won a victory. Then, momentarily checking his enthusiasm, he came up to me solemnly, humorously shook his forefinger, lifted his eyebrows, and said, 'Of course, you understand that we have sold these ships to Turkey!' 'And Admiral Souchon,' he added with another wink, 'will enter the Sultan's service!' Wangenheim had more than patriotic reasons for this exultation; the arrival of these ships was the greatest day in his diplomatic career. It was really the first diplomatic victory which Germany had won. For years the chancellorship of the empire had been Wangenheim's laudable ambition, and he behaved now like a man who saw his prize within his grasp. The voyage of the *Goeben* and *Breslau* was his personal triumph; he had arranged with the Turkish Cabinet for their passage through the Dardanelles, and he had directed their movements by wireless in the Mediterranean. By safely getting the *Goeben* and the *Breslau* into Constantinople, Wangenheim had definitely clinched Turkey as Germany's ally. All his intrigues and plottings for three years had now finally succeeded.'[139]

The Goeben: renamed Yavus Sultan Selim. (*Bundesarchiv Koblenz*)

The Breslau: renamed Midilli, at anchor in the Bosphorus. (*Bundesarchiv Koblenz*)

The fact that this decision quickly led to the first consequences is demonstrated by a radio message that the MMD received at about 10 pm from Istanbul the same day:

'Pass through Straits, ignore if Turkey raises protest. […] Dardanelles blocked with mines; take pilot. Headquarters informed and agreed. Inside Straits 2 steamers with 4000 French reserves held back by Turkey, hopeful of removal by Germany. Ambassador agreed with opening hostilities in Black Sea.'[140]

On 11 August two German steamers, *General* and *Rodosto*, also reached the Dardanelles and passed through without problems, although a number of French and British ships lay at anchor outside the Straits. Why the Allied fleet allowed the two German steamers to pass without incident cannot be established. On the same day, Souchon was brought by *Corcovado* to Istanbul, to meet with the Embassy, the Ministries of War and Marine and the Head of the Military Mission for a conference on 12 August. On 12 August, the Head of the MMD, Admiral Souchon, sent a telegram to Berlin:

'The Turkish Government has received *Goeben* and *Breslau* with enthusiasm. Cooperation with the Turkish Navy has been initiated. I intend to proceed as soon as possible against the Black Sea. Require as many German naval officers and good crews as possible to complement Turkish warships. Please send ammunition as soon as possible. There is enough coal in Istanbul.'[141]

In order to disguise the handover of both German cruisers, Admiral Souchon was to hoist the Turkish flag. Von Wangenheim signalled Berlin: 'Admiral Souchon carrying out the authorised *ruse de guerre* to hoist a foreign flag, is shortly due to arrive tomorrow or the day after under Turkish colours in Constantinople.'[142] Thus Turkish flags were hoisted by both cruisers during passage through the Dardanelles and in this way concealed the MMD's transfer to Turkish ownership.

A few days later the two German warships appeared off Istanbul flying Turkish flags. After the ships had anchored in the Bosphorus, on 16 August Cemal Paşa, the Minister of Marine, accompanied by a number of Turkish naval officers and men, came on board, thus demonstrating the transfer of the two Imperial German Navy ships into Ottoman service. From now on *Goeben* would be known as *Yavus Sultan Selim* and *Breslau* as *Midilli*. Admiral Souchon was simultaneously made commander of Turkish naval forces. The fact was, however, that these ships had neither been given nor sold to Turkey, it was but a political feint, even if rumours were circulating that both ships had been bought for eighty million Marks.

Although some Turkish sailors and officers had been taken on board, the ships always remained under German command, even if the crew now wore a Turkish fez. Ambassador Morgenthau described an incident that clearly underlines this situation:

'The German officers and crews greatly enjoyed this farcical pretence that the *Goeben* and the *Breslau* were Turkish ships. They took delight in putting on Turkish fezes, thereby presenting to the world conclusive evidence that these loyal sailors of the Kaiser were now part of the Sultan's navy. One day the Goeben sailed up the Bosphorus, halted in front of the Russian Embassy, and dropped anchor. Then the officers and men lined the deck in full view of the enemy embassy. All solemnly removed their Turkish fezes and put on German caps. The band played *Deutschland über Alles*, the *Watch on the Rhine* and other German songs, the German sailors singing loudly to the accompaniment. When they had spent an hour or more serenading the Russian Ambassador, the officers and crews removed their German caps

Breslau officers with their new headgear. From left to right: Back Row: Hildebrand, Dr. Wunderlich, Surgeon Essig, Mackensen, Baden, Ritschel, Boltz, Schevket, Lt Cdr Carls, Lt Cdr von Mohl, Linnenkamp; Middle Row: Wachs, Lt Cdr Grabau, Cdr Kettner (Commandant), Engineer Gronemann, Mahmut; Front Row: Dönitz, Wodrig.

and again put on their Turkish fezes. The *Goeben* then picked up her anchor and started southward for her station, leaving in the ears of the Russian diplomat the gradually dying strains of German war songs as the cruiser disappeared down stream.'[143]

On 14 August 1914 Tirpitz wrote to Souchon, describing how he wished the German fleet to act quickly in the Black Sea and confirming the despatch of the requested personnel reinforcements.

'You cannot imagine how important it is for the Navy and otherwise that you succeed in the Black Sea [...]. The Russians in the Black Sea can be poorly estimated. Do not be swayed by the size of their boilers. The top speed of the big Russians is not over 18 [knots]. In reality, lower. Marksmanship is bad as well. God willing, the Turks and Bulgarians start first so you have a free hand. It is of utmost importance that the Balkan states go along with us. We will ship out everything you need – men and materials. Breathe life into the Turkish fleet! If all hopes of Turkey etc. end up being in vain, you will be let out from the Bosphorus, using a mock battle with coal steamers. Then you can at least get a round trip and at least honestly use up ammunition. One more thing, for both our Navy and our position in the world – for which we are fighting – it will be of utmost importance that a Turkish army threatens the Suez Canal. If all goes well against the Russians even without the Turks, all our interest would then be centred on the Suez Canal. Generally, there is little regard for this unique influence of sea power by either the army or our diplomats. You could discuss this matter again with Humann and then with the Ambassador and Liman. God be with you, and us.'[144]

His interesting assessment of the limited strategic capabilities and political foresight of General Liman von Sanders was valid to a degree, though the pessimism about Baron von Wangenheim was not.

Obviously inspired by the grandiose promises of the commander of the German Navy, just one day later, on 15 August, the Fleet Commander requested the transfer of additional personnel. On 19 August, Souchon received news that his request for the assignment of officers and men for service in the Dardanelles and the Bosphorus, had been granted:

'The intention is to despatch the following personnel to Turkey:

1. For coastal defence: two admirals, 10 naval officers, 100 artillery gunners, 50 naval gunners, 30 rangefinders, 20 mine-layer NCOs, 30 mine artificers.
2. For ships: 10 naval officers, 10 engineers, 1 shipbuilding engineer, 17 gunners, 12 gun barrel artificers, 12 signallers, 50 torpedo technicians.
3. 200 mines with a torpedo officer, several warrant officers and depot officials.'[145]

These additional personnel were ordered to depart on 18 August 1914, which meant an astonishingly short warning time for the men concerned. Hardly anyone would have guessed how long it would take for this deployment to arrive in Turkey. Lieutenant Commander Firle reported on the journey of these naval personnel, who were disguised as civilians:

'The next morning – it was 18 August 1914 – a special train was ready for transport, filled with naval detachments, primarily Marine Artillery, from Cuxhaven, Lehe and Wilhelmshaven. Setting off on time, we travelled at 50 km/h and at noon arrived at Lehrter railway station in Berlin. We were received by representatives from the Navy Office, then the whole detachment was led to a Guard Regiment's barracks. Here there were civilian clothes spread out on long tables and representatives of several department stores fitted us out hurriedly with civilian suits. So that there would at least be a small difference, I had trilby hats given to the officers and warrant officers. Then the order was given: assembly point this evening 7 o'clock at Görlitzer railway station. I went to the Imperial Navy Office for more detailed instructions, where I expected and received further orders and information about the real objective. I learned that the destination was Istanbul and that all personnel were to serve on board Turkish warships under Admiral Souchon who, with *Goeben* and *Breslau*, had now been given command of the Turkish fleet. The Foreign Office issued everyone with a false passport, listing them as engineers, shipbuilders, technicians, fitters etc. [...]. Romania was extremely hostile and we had to surrender our passports and get off the train. Only when we handed over a corresponding sum of gold, of which we had a whole sackful, to pay for several broken light bulbs and other damage to the train, did things run more smoothly. The only snag was when the passports were going to be returned and the detachment commander, instead of collecting them all together, came up with the idea of calling them out individually, causing a mild panic, since none of us could remember the name on his passport. But gold smoothed things out here as well.'[146]

On 17 August 1914, Souchon sent a report to the Navy Office in Berlin:

'The Ambassador is of the opinion that operations in the Black Sea are still premature. He attaches utmost importance to the presence of *Goeben* and *Breslau* within the Narrows for the time being, until Turkish mobilization has advanced further. Eight torpedo boats have been

The Goeben in the dockyard at Istinye Bay. (*Bundesarchiv Koblenz*)

placed under my command. German and Turkish ships are consolidating in joint exercises in the Marmara Sea. I am advancing the war readiness of Turkish ships with all possible means. Am cooperating on improving the fortifications of the Dardanelles and Bosphorus, have organised a mine clearance division, coastal signalling facilities. Am supporting preparation for the planned army transports. Have fitted out steamers *Corovado* and *General* as auxiliary cruisers.'[147]

In anticipation of the arrival of the new personnel, Admiral Souchon had already issued training instructions on the same day:

'To increase the battle readiness of Turkish ships and boats, *Goeben* (Captain Ackermann) takes over – *Torgud Reis*, *Goeben* (Lieutenant Commander Madlung) – the torpedo boats, *Breslau* (Commander Kettner) – *Messudje*. Mission: appropriate preparation of ships for war, safe operation of weapons, ship clearing with substitute crews, fire control exercises, *Abkommschießen* [exercise of heavy and medium armaments by firing smaller calibre ammunition through a specially-fitted barrel lining], torpedo launching, black out, torpedo boat defence, leak control, simple signal procedure etc. Try to instil through example, advice and convincing persuasion. Treat officers and men individually, rough handling in our experience easily alienates the Turks and makes them indolent. First and foremost, concentrate on weapons of attack and general awareness. Training of defensive capabilities must be deferred. *Goeben* and *Breslau* have to help each other out with training staff.

Unnecessary items and people should be removed as much as possible from Turkish ships. This should, however, be requested with great consideration so that the Turks do not lose their good spirits. *Goeben* and *Breslau* must at all times be regarded by the Turks as masters in the art of warfare and military presence. German crews must be clear on this point. Under all circumstances the wearing of shabby clothing must be avoided.'[148]

In a report to the MMD in August, Lieutenant Commander Pfeiffer assessed the state of Turkish destroyers and torpedo boats as catastrophically bad:

'Until the arrival of the German crews, the Turkish torpedo boats had enjoyed an easy-going life in the Golden Horn. They were safely moored to buoys, were outwardly flawless with paint, all brass parts gleam in the sunshine. [...]. For the maintenance of the boats and their entire fittings, almost nothing had happened since delivery to Turkey. [...] After only two-day practice runs, the boats had to have a long break to carry out the most urgent repairs. [...] The general practical abilities of Turkish engineers were, or are still, very low. [...] The guns on all boats were consistently well-maintained on the outside. [...] On the other hand, the telescope sights were quite neglected. Misfires often occurred with ammunition during firing practice and also later in an emergency, which is partly due to improper handling. [...] The officers were unfamiliar with artillery firing of any kind. No-one had been trained in range-finding. [...] not even a single torpedo had ever been launched from one of the boats since delivery from the manufacturer. [...] The torpedo tubes were coated thick with paint. Moreover, on many boats the spring balance did not work.'[149]

On 27 August Souchon assessed the situation of the Turkish navy in an internal paper:

'Almost nothing has been done for battle training [...] Exercises at night have never taken place. Signalling ability is at an unspeakably low level because there was never any instruction until now. [...] Almost all radio/telegraph devices in Turkish ships are unusable. The importance of torpedoes has also been so superficially taught that this important weapon in the hands of Turkish officers currently constitutes more of a danger to our own ships. The use of artillery is also carried out with un-warlike methods.'[150]

This low standard of training was naturally attributed to the British Navy Mission, which had been previously responsible for it; naturally, it was suspected that the capability of the Turkish Navy was intentionally allowed to fall into neglect.

After the two admirals, Guido von Usedom and Johannes Merten, together with fifteen naval officers and 281 naval gunners, arrived on 25 August 1914 in Istanbul, the Special Command of the Imperial Navy in Turkey (*Sonderkommando Kaiserliche Marine Türkei*, abbreviated '*SoKo*') was formed, and was placed under the command of Admiral von Usedom. He was tasked with improving the fortifications of the Narrows whilst Admiral Mertens functioned as the liaising element to the Turkish General Staff for the Dardanelles. This left Admiral Souchon to concentrate on serving as Fleet Commander, with the primary responsibility of improving the operational readiness of the Turkish Navy. According to entries in the MMD's war diary, German personnel were now on board all ships of the Turkish navy; the German fleet crews now totalled about 1,600 men. The British Embassy watched this development with unease. Charles Lister wrote in a letter on 20 August 1914:

'Things here have naturally gone from bad to worse; German sailors arrive by scores, and German merchantmen are being fitted out from the German Embassy as auxiliary cruisers to have a go the Russians in the Black Sea, it is thought. We are simply powerless and expect to have to pack up any day. The Turks are quite *tête montée*. The Ministers say that they know nothing of these batches of German sailors arriving, and are in any case wholly impotent.'[150a]

Just *Breslau* and *Goeben* on their own now provided the Turkish Navy with adequate fighting power compared to the Russian navy. There were fourteen German officers and fifty-five seamen on *Turgut Reis* and *Barbaros*, with two officers and ten seamen on *Berk*. On each torpedo boat of German origin there were six engineer officers and eight seamen.

The German naval officers and men were variously assigned to the installations and batteries on the Dardanelles and immediately began training and site reinforcement. As an independent and separate formation, the *SoKo* did not report to either the Military Mission or the MMD. Apparently the Kaiser, who was close to Admiral von Usedom, wanted to give him a post to help him gain a certain modicum of war glory. Although the Admiral was judged to be rather slow and lethargic, he had found favour as the long-term commander of the Imperial Yacht *Hohenzollern*. Thus the energetic Admiral Souchon was lumbered with a more senior admiral, which did not please him at all, and this led to a great deal of interpersonal friction. Since accommodation in Istanbul was not available for Admiral von Usedom and his staff, all were quartered with Souchon on board the *General*, the MMD's supply ship, also used as an accommodation ship. The General Inspectorate of Coastal Fortifications under Admiral Merten was established in the Ministry of War. Thus there were three admirals on the Bosphorus, of whom Souchon and von Usedom could report directly to the Emperor in their immediate assignments. The nature of the collaboration between the admirals had not been definitively settled, with von Usedom only receiving the instruction that 'His Majesty the Emperor expects you to be subordinate to the political opinions of the Ambassador and to maintain close liaison with Admiral Souchon.'[151] Souchon wrote:

'However, living aboard the *General* also has its disadvantages. I'm always there with von Usedom, who blathers a lot and corresponds with the Cabinet Chief, is indisputably indiscreet and,

Admiral Merten (Second right) and Admiral von Usedom (r) with German officers; The naval officer in the background is Lieutenant Prince Reuss. (*Bundesarchiv Koblenz*)

since he has very little to do, concerns himself with things that are none of his business. Recently, he even came out with "I'm the senior admiral here". This, of course, makes me keep my distance from him.'[152]

In the following months, the SoKo Turkey, the MMD and also the Military Mission formed three at times rival German military agencies in Turkey, since everyone was careful not to give the other too much of a say. Even for the Navy Staff in Berlin the relationship between the different agencies in Turkey was no longer clear, so that von Usedom wrote to Berlin on 23 April 1915:

'Repeated queries in the recent past make it seem desirable to summarise the clarification of the position and the task of the Special Command of the Imperial Navy on the one hand and the Turkish General Inspectorate of coastal questions and mine systems on the other, by the Central Authority at home. If this has not happened so far, this is primarily due to the gradual development which things have so far taken here.'[153]

He explained how the various services should be properly regulated for the future, underling 'that the Turkish Government had not asked for the Special Command, but was presented with a *fait accompli*, as this not insignificant force arrived, while the country was still at peace.' He also asked for him to be given the 'higher jurisdiction for the commander of a German force in war and abroad', since at that time he was still subject to the military jurisdiction of the Mediterranean Division.

Lieutenant Commander Humann later wrote in a memorandum to Dr. Jäckh about these various German commands:

'The multiplicity of the German command [...]. Through the impossibility of holding sharply defined areas of responsibility on a narrowly defined joint battlefield; through the differentiation of the characters and views; through the all too human traits, such as ambition, envy etc, [...]. This situation has quite fatal consequences [...]. The result of our work is deteriorating [...] strong dampers for mood and work satisfaction [...] Among the Turks, this greatly reduces our standing (city gossip).'[154]

In his assessment, he concluded that the entire German naval contingent would have been better off if it were to have been led by only one admiral.

Meanwhile, the expectations of all the warring factions on the Western Front had been disappointed by not being able to gain a quick and glorious victory. After initial gains on the ground and strategic chess moves, it had degenerated into static trench warfare, so in the middle of September 1914 the Central Powers felt themselves compelled to press for Turkey's early entry into the war. This, however, was delayed by the Turks and was even wholly rejected in some government quarters. Although Turkey had concluded the assistance agreement with Germany, nothing had happened in Turkish quarters since then. Germany urged Turkey to enter the war, expressed, amongst other things, on 7 September 1914: 'It is desired that Turkey should soon join the fight, at the latest after the speedy completion of the Dardanelles defences'; or 'Everything possible should be undertaken to get Turkey to cut loose against Russia'.[155] Turkish mobilisation was sluggish, mainly due to the tense economic situation in the country. In September all Germany's hopes rested on Enver Paşa, whose position as Minister of War was not yet strong enough for him to act alone.

An Imperial Ottoman *Iradé* [decree] was issued on 11 September, appointing Rear-Admiral Souchon as Commander-in-Chief of the fleet and Commander Madlung to the command of the Destroyer Flotilla.[156] Two days later, the British Ambassador, Sir Louis du Pan Mallet, informed

The *General*, the station ship used for accommodation and staff, at anchor in the Golden Horn.

the Grand Vizier at the palace that the British Navy Mission under Admiral Limpus would now be withdrawn. The Grand Vizier expressed his regrets, to which the Ambassador replied that the Ottomans had inflicted this upon themselves by their poor treatment of British officers.[157]

Enver's first attempt, on 14 September, to obtain permission for Souchon to allow patrols in the Black Sea with the intention of provoking incidents with Russia, were quickly stopped by the Turkish Cabinet. Souchon received the following message from Cemal Paşa, the Turkish Minister of Marine:

'Putting the fleet out to the Black Sea on 15 September is not permitted. This is a political undertaking for the Turkish government; only the Cabinet can make this decision. Your Excellency is not empowered to decide about it, neither is the Minister of Marine, nor the Deputy Commander-in-Chief. I request preparation of a review for 17 September.'[158]

Admiral Souchon was very dissatisfied with this order and noted in the MMD's war diary: 'This telegram is an affront by the Minister of Marine. I have nothing to do with him in questions that concern the operational use of the fleet.'[159]

After Admiral Limpus and his staff had made a farewell visit to the Minister of Marine on 15 September 1914, the delegation left Istanbul a day later. Firle noted in his diary: 'The British Navy Mission with Admiral Limpus at its head has finally left today. I hope they all go to Odessa, to try to practise their talents for reorganisation on the Russians, perhaps with the same good results as here, i.e. negative [emphasis by Firle].'[160] Surprisingly, however,

Admiral Souchon as Commander-in-Chief of the Turkish Fleet with his staff on board the *General*, from left to right: Turkish Chief of Staff Enver Bey, Admiral's staff officer Commander Busse, Admiral Souchon, Lieutenant Wichelhausen, Admiral's staff officer Büchsel, Turkish Flag Officer Lieutenant Hakki. (*Bundesarchiv Freiburg*)

British officers were popping up weeks later in Turkish arsenals and the Navy School, still able to continue working against German efforts.

On 17 September the Turkish fleet, under the command of Admiral Souchon, was drawn up in Pendik, an area south-east of Istanbul, for review before the Sultan. After this the fleet practised battle formations with cruisers and torpedo boats. Souchon used the opportunity to urge Enver Paşa and the German Ambassador again to decide on an attack on Russia, but this was rejected by the two on this occasion because of the unfavourable situation in the Cabinet, as well as the lack of good news from other theatres of war. Thereupon Admiral Souchon sent a telegram to the head of the German Staff Office in Berlin:

'As often as possible, the fleet is lying off the capital, to bolster the confidence of the weak, discordant and unreliable Cabinet against the tempting offers from the Ambassadors of England [sic], France and Russia and to revive the popular mood in our favour.'[161]

As still no change of opinion by the Turkish Minister of War had come about, Souchon tried his luck on 18 September with the Grand Vizier. He complained to him of the 'indecisive, perfidious attitude of Turkey'. Souchon felt himself held back by promises and fleet reviews and, by the evening of 19 September, there had to be authorization to go on practice runs in the Black Sea, 'otherwise he would act as his military conscience dictates'.[162] Of course, the impatient German admiral, who was obviously also being put under pressure for success by Germany, did not receive an answer and noted his frustration in the MMD's war diary: 'Because I have received no reply from the Grand Vizier regarding putting out to the Black Sea, I am not going to approach the Turkish government any more'.[163]

After Enver Paşa had at last given his approval for short forays by destroyers in the Black Sea, Lieutenant Commander Kettner was ordered to set sail on 20 September 1914 with three ships. Kettner wrote:

'Before leaving, the Admiral had given me verbal instructions, that if I encountered Russian warships and, if at all feasible on the pretext of an attack by them, to engage them myself, thereby initiating war. As a result, both in this and all subsequent trips in the Black Sea, I had a huge responsibility on my shoulders, because I had the immediate consequence of war in my hands. But I knew that the political negotiations with the Turks were not yet so far advanced ... For such an important decision, however, I thought a concise written order from the entire government should be issued. During the forays we did not see any Russian warships.'[164]

Admiral Souchon then visited Enver Paşa once more, to get him to at least agree to another 'exercise' and thus he could deliberately provoke an incident with Russia.[165] This exercise was, however, again cancelled. Admiral Souchon was beside himself and wrote to Ambassador von Wangenheim on 21 September that the Turks should now be threatened in order to force them to come to their senses and become brothers-in-arms:

'Head of Division asks Ambassador to consider, in the case of Turkish betrayal, he would be obliged above all else to destroy the Turkish fleet and at the same time to occasionally instil this train of thought to leading Turkish personalities in order to bring them to make a stand against England [sic].'[166]

The German Ambassador signalled to Berlin on the same day that the Turkish Government had decided that it would not be against any German fleet actions in the Black Sea but it would not allow Turkish ships to take part.[167] That the German cruisers in question were flying the Turkish flag seemed to have been overlooked in Enver's tactics.

From a Turkish point of view, the overall strategic situation could not be ignored - a victory by Germany or the Central Powers was no longer self-evident during September 1914. Thus Enver lost an important point of argument because he had always wagered on Germany being victorious. A decision needed to be taken quickly before further unfavourable reports reached Istanbul, which would weaken the German position.

This decision could be accomplished in two ways: through a considerable payment of money (two million pounds sterling) to buy a moral obligation from Turkey; or a direct order to Admiral Souchon to attack Russian ships, which would create a reason for going to war. But despite this direct payment by Germany and all the other benefits already granted to Turkey, it was still not possible to get a rapid entry into the war. In addition, the death of King Carol of Romania created doubts about Romania's political future and direction, which could possibly lead to a further weakening of the Central Powers. It was therefore decided in the Turkish Cabinet to negotiate with Berlin a further six-month postponement of Turkey's entry into the war.

Crew of Goeben undergoing drill on the pier at Istinye. (*Bundesarchiv Koblenz*)

On 26 September 1914, Enver Paşa gave the Fleet Commander a verbal order that the fleet should be cleared ready to make for the Black Sea. Subsequent negotiations within the government now released the fleet for a foray in the Black Sea, but it would not take the responsibility for any engagements that resulted. Admiral Souchon had to continue to wait until the final consent of the Ottoman Government was assured. Many ministers, among them the Grand Vizier, who had signed the treaty with Germany, as well as Cemal Paşa, the influential Minister of Marine, were still in favour of remaining neutral.

For the first time, on 3 October 1914, firing practice by *Goeben*, *Turgut* and *Barbaros* was carried out against a towed target. The Fleet Commander was not satisfied with the result; according to his assessment, the gunnery of the Turkish ships was still completely inadequate. He described the political situation:

'Since the Council of Ministers had expressly stated that the departure of the fleet depended on its approval, I decided to present them with *faits accomplis* by gradually despatching more and more units into the Black Sea at the same time. After the firing exercises, the ships of the First Division were anchored near the exit to the Black Sea to give the population as much of a show of the great ships as possible... The Inspector-General of the Coastal Artillery is asked to get ready for offensive operations against enemy forces off the Dardanelles. He will release three small torpedo boats to the fleet, which are to be serviced and trained by the flotilla.'[168]

Enver Paşa, Admiral Souchon, Admiral von Usedom and General Bronsart von Schellenberg met on 6 October aboard the *Goeben* to go to the Dardanelles to observe gunnery demonstrations there. During the voyage, Enver Paşa proposed to Admiral Souchon, in his role as both Turkish Admiral and Fleet Commander, a closer relationship with the Turkish government. This arrangement, according to Enver, would in no way affect the current German position and also make it possible to enable the Council of Ministers to allow the fleet to undertake sorties in the Black Sea. The reform of the fleet could be better promoted by the greater influence which could be exerted on officers and men.

The German Ambassador held a meeting on 11 October with Ministers Enver Paşa, Cemal Paşa and Talat Paşa. It was affirmed by the Turks that the war would have to be begun, since these men had an overwhelming majority among the leading politicians as well as the army and navy being both firmly in their hands. They simply demanded that the two million pounds promised should be paid beforehand. Furthermore, the result of this discussion was to be kept secret from the Grand Vizier, the Turkish Ambassador in Berlin, Mahmud Mukar, and Cavit Bey.[169] Lieutenant Commander Humann wrote a letter, dated 13 October, to Dr Jäckh, showing that his optimism was, however, still very much dampened:

'There is no question of this at present, and it is all about if and when Turkey will participate in the war. [...] Whether it will be possible for them to achieve significant military successes with the means at their disposal seems doubtful to me. Only our ships, *Goeben* and *Breslau*, have military value. [...] At the moment, it looks as if he [Enver] really has a decisive majority in the Cabinet and in *comité*, to get going as soon as the money is available.'[170]

Lieutenant Commander Humann finally received an order from the Ambassador to speak with Enver personally and to have the order to attack issued. The written order of 18 October stated:

'Lieutenant Commander Humann is tasked by the Deputy of the Supreme Commander to carry out the following order which is written in both German and Turkish. The order is to be issued to the senior German naval officer on all Turkish ships and only opened on the signal of the Fleet Commander and then passed to the Turkish commander. "War against Russia has broken out. The senior German naval officer on board has precise instructions from the Deputy of the Commander-in-Chief as to how the ship is to fight. Act exactly according to the orders given to you by the senior German naval officer on board."'[171]

In his telegram of 21 October, Enver Paşa clearly stated the intentions for entering the war to the Chief of the German General Staff, General von Moltke:

'The Turkish armed forces are instructed to carry out or prepare the following actions: 1.) The fleet is to gain naval superiority in the Black Sea by attacking the Russian fleet without declaration of war. Timing at the discretion of Admiral Souchon.'

These intentions were followed by a further six orders to the Turkish ground forces.[172]

While Turkish units continued firing exercises and repairs, Admiral Souchon was still waiting for permission from the Minister of War to launch the fleet in the Black Sea for an attack on Russia. The ships were, however, already prepared for such operations and the German commanders got relevant plans of attack ready. In the war diary of the MMD, Souchon wrote on 22 October:

'The Admiral should soon receive a secret order from Enver Pasha, as well as a letter from the Minister of Marine, to the individual Turkish commanders to obey the Admiral in war and peace. The intention of appointing me as a Turkish Admiral has been dropped by the Turkish Government, as I suspected. It was handled all very quickly. Now I hear nothing more of it. The letter of the Minister of Marine to the individual commanders would suffice for my purposes of having the Turkish commanders unconditionally in my hand.'[173]

At a meeting between Enver and Humann on 22 October in Tarabya, the Minister of War presented a telegram that he wanted to give to the German 'war leadership'. In addition, he showed Humann the order already signed by him to the Fleet Commander, with the request to attack Russia without a declaration of war. On the same day he wanted to talk with Cemal Paşa and Talat Paşa, and then send the order to the Admiral that day or the next. In a note which he addressed to the Ambassador, Humann wrote:

'At the same time, Enver Pasha issues a command to all the Turkish commanders with this content: That they obey Admiral Souchon, whom His Majesty the Sultan had designated as Fleet Commander, faithfully and on all occasions, both in war and peace. [...] The fact of this telegram is, in my opinion, of unusual significance and I respectfully recommend the Ambassador briefly reply to the Minister of War, who will not be unresponsive to this.'[174]

All the German commanders were assembled on 23 October and briefed about the planned 'warlike operations in the Black Sea' and received sealed orders that should only be opened after receiving a special signal.[175]

A day later, on 24 October, Enver wrote Humann a note saying the decision had now been made and that the Grand Vizier would be asked for his consent the next day. He said, 'Now tell the Ambassador that I [here it is not clearly legible] either *will give* or *have given* Souchon the enclosed order, so that he may nevertheless attack with the fleet on my responsibility.'[176] In this order, also dated 24 October 1914, addressed to the Commander of the Ottoman Fleet and the Ottoman General Souchon and signed by Enver, it stated:

'The whole fleet is to carry out exercises in the Black Sea. If you find a favourable opportunity, attack the Russian fleet and in this case – before commencing hostilities – open my order given to you personally this morning. In order to prevent transportation of material to Serbia, act as agreed. The Deputy Commander-in-Chief. Signed Enver.'[177]

Apparently the delivery of this order was further delayed, as Admiral Souchon wrote in the War Diary on 25 October:

'Together with the Minister of Marine and the Minister of the Interior, the Minister of War announced that he continues to advocate going into action. Promised orders are due today. If they arrive, the prospect of getting to open the order is slight. Halil, the President of the Chamber, is to go to Berlin to reach agreement on the most politically favourable time for Turkey to open hostilities. The attack of the Turkish fleet alone would not find resonance in the Islamic world. The army is not yet ready to begin operations, either in the Caucasus or the Suez Canal.'[178]

On 26 October the German Army Command agreed by telegraph to all points of the operational planning, but put emphasis on an immediate naval operation in the Black Sea. On the same day the order from the Minister of Marine was issued to Turkish commanders.

'You and others are called upon to render literal obedience to the orders of Admiral Souchon, who has been appointed Admiralissimo of the Turkish Fleet whilst in the Black Sea for training purposes and I require that you unhesitatingly carry out all that is necessary to comply with these orders as the situation requires. Cemal Paşa.'[179]

Souchon commented on this part of the order: 'Although this version does not correspond to the agreed text *"in peace and war"*, it will provide sufficient assurance that my orders will be executed'.

Thus on 27 October 1914 all battle-ready ships of the Turkish fleet steamed into the Black Sea at 2.54 am for 'fleet and reconnaissance exercises'. At 3.45 am the Turkish and German commanders of the *Breslau, Hamidiyi, Berk* and *Peyk* held a joint conference on the *Goeben*. Admiral Souchon said 'that he intends to attack Russian ports with the tacit agreement of Enver Paşa',[180] who was said to have issued the following secret order: 'The Turkish fleet is to gain naval superiority in the Black Sea. Seek out the Russian fleet and attack them without a declaration of war, wherever you may find them.'[181]

The fleet operational planning was as follows:

'1. *Midilli (Breslau)* and *Berk* are to make for the eastern part of the Black Sea, where *Midilli* is to lay mines off the Kerch Strait; meanwhile *Berk* is to make for Novorossiysk and to broadcast the impending destruction of the oil base, grain storage and ships, so that people can be brought out of danger. After laying mines in the Kerch Strait, *Midilli* is also to make for Novorossiysk and destroy facilities and ships there.
2. *Hamdiye* is to make for Theodosia to destroy the grain silos.

Bombardment of Novorossiysk, picture taken from the Breslau. (*Goeben Voyages, p 140*)

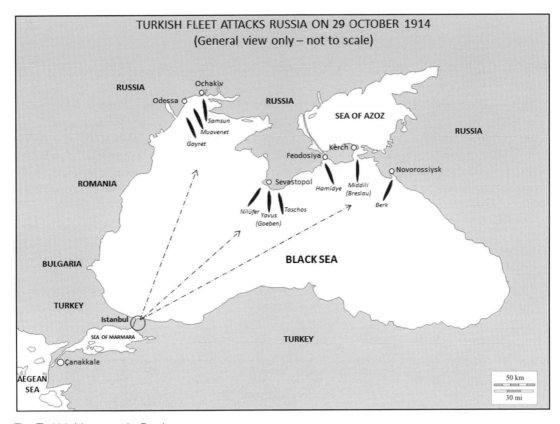

The Turkish Navy attacks Russia.

3. *Gayret*, with the Flotilla Commander, and *Muavenet* are to make for Odessa to destroy one or possibly more Russian warships and steamers as well as the harbour facilities.
4. The minelayer *Nilüfer* is to lay mines off Sevastopol.
5. The minelayer *Samsun* is to lay mines off the Ochakiv channel.
6. *Yavus (Goeben)* is to bombard warships lying in Sevastopol. *Taschos* and *Samsun* are to sail together with *Yavus* in mine sweeping formation.'[182]

After pointing out the strict secrecy of these orders, even after their execution, the ships received the following flag signal at 5.45 am: 'Do your utmost, it is all about the future of Turkey'.[183] On 28 and 29 October the Turkish fleet attacked the Russian Black Sea Fleet, as well as the port facilities in Sevastopol, Odessa and Novorossiysk.

The condition of the Ottoman Navy was still inadequate at this time and, above all, the level of training of naval personnel meant that they were anything but combat ready. Souchon accepted this risk, relying on German support within the crews of the Turkish ships. Lieutenant von Mellenthin, who commanded the torpedo cruiser *Berk*, described the lead up to his ship's attack:

'I used one part of the evening (27 October) to translate into Turkish the war orders received together with the First Officer and to make him aware of the importance of this mission. As such, they would be passed on to the Turkish commandant, who does not speak English. With the best will in the world, however, I was not able to discern any enthusiasm for the war. [...]

Lieutenant Hans-Joachim von Mellenthin
(*Sammlung Soytürk*)

The Turkish commandant is being slowly eased out of the picture, but with all due consideration. As the weather gradually deteriorated, the state of the crew became increasingly miserable. The movements of the ship could still be regarded as very pleasant, and yet the Turks lay perched like corpses in every corner, quite motionless. [...] Such was the situation, when the ship was detached at 18.00 hrs (October 28) to make for Novorossiysk. As I had thought it would be, it now happened. I could no longer manage to get a speed of 13 nautical miles. What I had always been able to achieve on the *Breslau* by jollying up the people, especially the engineers, no longer worked. [...] So only the German engineer and I were left there. Then a hefty discussion took place with the commandant. I personally fetched the navigation officer, who lay seasick in the mess, as he had to act as interpreter. Then we went to the chief engineer and then together to the commandant, where a discussion in a not too friendly tone lasting ten minutes was sufficient to make my point of view clear to them. Most crestfallen and upset, the chief engineer then disappeared into the engine and boiler room. My engineer and I divided the control of Turkish personnel between us [...] The closer we got to the mouth (Novorossiysk), the less the Turks took part in navigation [...] but even more was the fear of the enemy and the mines.'[184]

On 29 October, the Fleet's attack was reported to Turkish Headquarters and on the same evening the Cabinet met and was informed about it. Cavit Bey published a description of this meeting, in which mostly ignorance and surprise about the Turkish attack on Russia were feigned:

'Enver showed himself highly delighted, but was alone in this; he had indeed left us in uncertainty about the action. A little later Talat appeared, who was very boastful. He knew about everything, but pretended not to have been informed. The last to arrive was Cemal Paşa. The Grand Vizier gave him Souchon's telegram, which he read with puzzled amazement. He then demanded Enver's explanation of the events. The whole thing was a complete farce.'[185]

Admiral Souchon commented on the attack in a letter to his wife dated 31 October 1915:

'Even though it should not be overlooked that the whole enterprise was greatly favoured by luck and weather, the overall success is due to the excellent conduct and professional training of German personnel. With great efforts, surpassing the limits, with whatever the training officers and men may have accomplished with professional joy, austerity, iron will and toughness, the Germans attached to Turkish ships have reaped the rewards of subsequent success for their hard work in recent months.'[186]

Souchon was apparently disparaging about the Turkish crews, when he mentioned to Cemal Paşa on 1 November 1914: 'I informed him about the desolate worthlessness of the Turkish fleet, of the non–performance of personnel'.[187]

This judgment was not only hard, but it was also unjust, as the Turkish Fleet, like the Army, was indeed not yet fully trained and battle-ready. He could have launched the attack on Russia without Turkish ships, but obviously he also wanted to demonstrate unequivocally a Turkish attack to the outside world without making German dominance too obvious.

After the successful attack the Turks then wanted to push for more naval action in the Black Sea, which prompted Admiral Souchon to draft a memorandum restricting the tasks of the fleet to a realistic level:

'The task of the Turkish Fleet is primarily to protect the Narrows. This can be done by their presence in the Narrows, by shadowing guard vessels, by supporting and advancing the installations and by torpedo boat attacks on enemy ships stationed at the mouth. Secondly, the Turkish fleet is to seek to keep the waters of the Bosphorus free from the enemy, so that coal from Heraclea and goods from Romanian ports can come by sea to the Bosphorus. Bigger tasks will not be allocated to the Turkish Fleet, which is not only numerically but also materially and manpower-wise inferior to the enemy. In particular, a battle with the Russian fleet would mean the sure destruction of the Turkish Fleet without any significant damage to the enemy, because the Turkish ships can neither sail nor shoot.'[188]

He made this statement in the context of the continuing demands on the Navy to send convoys in the Black Sea and to protect them. These troop transports were destined for the Caucasus front, but they could not be adequately protected and there were repeated losses to troopships as well as their escorts. In this regard, it is interesting that Liman von Sanders had apparently not been privy to the plans for the attack on Russia, as he says in his memoirs:

'The news of the battle came as a surprise to me, because I had not been informed by the German Ambassador or Admiral Souchon, with whom I had not spoken since our differences on the prospects of a Turkish attack on Egypt, that in the current tense situation the Turkish fleet was to put into the Black Sea. A few weeks ago, on 20 September, after I had been informed by a reliable source that Baron von Wangenheim intended to send *Goeben* and *Breslau* to the Black Sea under the German flag, I went to Therapia and urgently warned the Ambassador against this.'[189]

This demonstrates how very isolated von Sanders was from the circle of German decision-makers in Istanbul and his memoirs reveal that he even believed the rumours of a Russian provocation in the Bosphorus, and it was only as a response that the Turkish fleet attacked Russia in retaliation.

The attack on the Russian naval forces and the bombardment of Russian ports on 29 October 1914 were presented to the Turkish Cabinet as accomplished facts, even though several members had been assumed to have been privy at least to the intention of an attack on Russia. Nevertheless, retrospectively, there was more condemnation than approval from the Cabinet. On 30 October, Souchon's entry in the MMD's war diary stated:

'The Prime Minister rejects responsibility for belligerent action, thus crisis in the Ministry. A decision is demanded from the Minister of War. In consideration of today's *bayram* [holiday] festivities, put off till this evening. Minister of War tasked by Prime Minister to recall [the MMD from the Black Sea]. He will telegraph with a condition: if breaking off hostilities possible without loss and Turkish coastal defence assured. The Minister of War expects the Admiral to ignore telegram. That corresponds to what I expected. The Minister War and the

Minister of Marine are expressing their congratulations on my success. They will assert their will, which corresponds to our political needs, since they have the majority in the committee.'[190]

The Grand Vizier, Said Halim, especially seemed deeply concerned and thus demanded that Talat take action to avoid a war with Russia. When Talat, apparently not from his own conviction but simply to comply with the Grand Vizier's request, asked the Russian Ambassador, M. Giers, what could be done to sway the Czar, he replied that Russia would expect all German officers to be immediately removed from the Turkish Army and Navy. This demand naturally could not be complied; as a reason, Talat later told Ambassador Morgenthau, '... because Wangenheim, Enver and I have decided that the war shall now come'.[191]

On 2 November 1914, Russia declared war on Turkey. The beginning of the hostilities and the collapse of Russian-Turkish relations were followed in early November by Great Britain and France declaring war on Turkey. On 15 November 1914, an 'Islamic Holy War' was declared in Istanbul against both the enemies of Turkey and those of Germany.[192] In hindsight, Turkey's joining forces with the Central Powers was only possible as the result of a constellation of various factors: The negative attitude of the Ottoman leadership towards the other European great powers, who wanted to solve the 'Oriental Question' to the detriment of Turkey; the decision to deploy an extensive German Military Mission; the availability of the Mediterranean Division in the Black Sea, exacerbated by Churchill's confiscation of the two Turkish warships; a few influential and assertive figures, such as Enver Paşa, Cemal Paşa, von Wangenheim and Admiral Souchon; and the weak leadership of the rest of the Turkish Cabinet.

While Germany vigorously and stringently pursued its goal, the other European powers did not fully realise the consequences of their passivity. The Turkish Parliament submitted to the actions of a few politicians and soldiers and later tried to dissociate itself from them. The attack against Russia should be seen in this context as a chain of circumstances which, however, would surely not have come about without the constant lobbying and pressure, as well as being finally executed by Admiral Souchon. The attack took place merely with the silent agreement of the Minister of War. Souchon congratulated himself in his notes when he wrote, 'I have thrown the Turks into a powder keg and sparked the war between Russia and Turkey'.[193]

Only after the Mediterranean Division arrived in Turkey did the German military presence come to possess a strong political dimension and the wherewithal for strategic action. Up to the summer of 1914 the Military Mission had only made modest progress to improve Turkish military capabilities and had no influence on Turkey's readiness to enter into the war on the side of the Central Powers. The political significance of the Mediterranean Division was first recognised by the German Ambassador and later firmly exploited by Admiral Souchon. After Turkey's entry into the war, the *Goeben* and *Breslau* lost their political impact quickly and could only now be employed in their original tactical and purely military roles.

Admiral Souchon. (*Sammlung Soytürk*)

Chapter 4

Everyday life and work in the Military Mission (MM), the Mediterranean Division (MMD) and the Special Command (SoKo) in Istanbul

This chapter looks at the everyday life of German military and naval personnel in Istanbul as well as inter-service cooperation with their counterparts in the Turkish forces. To begin with, however, the state of the Turkish army, with which German officers were confronted on their arrival in 1913, should be examined.

The state of the Turkish armed forces after the heavy losses during the Balkan Wars of 1911/1913 was, unsurprisingly, deplorable. Amongst all ranks and at every level there was an ominous lack of solid military training. Even those officers who had been through higher training institutions often lacked the insight and understanding of separating theory and practice from one another and adapting to an actual situation. The officers recruited from the ranks were good front line soldiers but, as illiterates, they often did not have the necessary qualifications for leading troops. Particularly difficult were the conditions in the Arabian units, in which, for political reasons, most of the officer appointments were reserved for Turks. Most of these officers did not have a good command of Arabic and required an interpreter to communicate with their men. The welfare of subordinates in the spirit of 'comrades together' was not widely adopted by Turkish officers and the troops did not have a trusting relationship with their leaders. Lieutenant Colonel Hans Kannengiesser reported that obvious attention to rank and file soldiers was looked down upon by Turkish senior officers. Kannengiesser's habit of handing out cigarettes to soldiers as a small mark of attention was commented upon as undesirable:

To Sami Bey and perhaps other Turkish superiors, this way of taking care of people was very disagreeable. [...]Sami Bey asked me not to ask the men how they were. There would also be shameless types, who might say the opposite. That would then be a fatal thing. My answer, that this was precisely the purpose of my question, so that grievances could be stopped, was incomprehensible to him.'[194]

The simple rank and file soldiers did not seem to need very much and showed stubborn equanimity in suffering and deprivation. In his memoirs Kannengiesser described the simple, Turkish soldiers:

'His requirements for accommodation and food are quite ridiculously low, if one wants to speak of requirements at all. He is accustomed to sleep on hard ground from an early age. The Turks don't know beds at all, at the most carpets or mattresses that are taken out at night from a closet and placed anywhere on the floor. Rice and meat is a feast for them. Iron rations, if available, consist of a piece of bread and a few olives [...] soup in the morning and more soup in the course of the afternoon towards evening.'[195]

Military training suffered from a lack of good instructors and adequate equipment. Like the officer corps, the feeble, weak, non-commissioned officers were not equal to their training responsibilities;

thus the training of soldiers remained far behind requirements. To this was added a comparatively low physical performance, which was a consequence of general malnutrition.

Equipment had been largely lost in the Balkan Wars and it had not yet been possible to replace it. Turkish armament production was limited to infantry and field artillery ammunition; heavy guns, machine guns and even rifles had to be procured from abroad. Heavy artillery and the requisite munitions were a significant deficiency. The weapons that were available were of different origins and made uniform supply and distribution to unit level almost impossible. Modern communication facilities were almost completely absent.

It is not surprising, therefore, that German estimates about the state of the Turkish armed forces were dire. In the middle of March 1914, only a few months after Liman von Sanders had begun his work, the Chief of the German General Staff, Colonel General von Moltke, wrote to his Austrian colleague, General Conrad von Hötzendorff:

'Militarily speaking, Turkey is at rock-bottom! The reports from our Military Mission are simply miserable. The army is in a state that belies all description. If we used to speak of Turkey as 'the sick man', we have to now speak of a dying one. It no longer has any life force and is irrevocably on its last legs. Our Military Mission is like a group of doctors, huddling around the death bed of an incurable patient.'[196]

Two months later, Moltke still had no better opinion of the Turkish military and said to Conrad von Hötzendorff during a meeting in Carlsbad, the spa resort in West Bohemia: 'The Turkish army is absolutely worthless. It has no weapons, no ammunition, no uniforms. Officers' wives go begging on the street.'[197]

In a private letter of 3 April 1914, the Kaiser wrote from Corfu:

'News of the Turkish army, which I received in strict confidence, portray the situation as completely desolate and realistically, so to speak, irremediable and almost hopeless, especially the great number of cases of plague and deaths; more than 2,000 sick in Adrianople [now Edirne] alone. Among these, there were 60 cases of cholera.'[198]

These negative assessments reflected the judgements expressed in the first reports of the Chief of the Military Mission, but also led back to the bitter disappointment of German officers due to the obvious failure of their efforts in Turkey. As late as 18 May 1914, Moltke wrote in a memorandum: 'To want to count on Turkey in the foreseeable future in favour of the Triple Alliance or Germany must be described as completely off the mark.'[199] However, by the end of July 1914, von Sanders' opinion seemed to have changed and Ambassador von Wangenheim reported on his behalf that

'… the reorganisation of the Turkish army was now so far advanced that in case of war Turkey would be able to field four to five well-equipped and fully battle-ready army corps without risking a catastrophe such as at the outbreak of the Balkan War. Even a very short time ago the Military Mission regarded it as quite definite that Turkey could not wage war for several years.'[200]

These first positive results, of course, could by no means only be accomplished with the original complement of the Military Mission. Even before the outbreak of war, General Liman von Sanders had decided to enlarge the Mission, which had at first been fixed at forty-two officers. In order to expand the Mission's influence into the provinces, he asked in the middle of March 1914 for the dispatch of three German officers as regimental commanders for Erzincan in Eastern Anatolia. In the middle of June the Mission Chief informed the military cabinet that his annual allowance for officers' pay had been increased by 8,000 Turkish pounds and asked for the assignment of ten officers, two sergeants and six senior NCOs who could be used as sergeants and staff-sergeants. On this occasion he could also report that he had succeeded in placing German officers in important positions in the Turkish Ministry of War. However, an appointment in the Ministry did not mean being able to work there successfully or even to be accepted, as foreign officers were not familiar with rudimentary procedures characteristic of the country; or else they were not amenable to them. Rear Admiral Albert Hopmann, for example, reported on a conversation he had conducted with the Minister of War and noted:

> 'Particularly resented is the present practice that the personnel files of the Turkish officers' corps should be handled by a German officer, as is currently the case, overseen by Lieutenant Commander Büchsel, the Head of Section II. A foreign officer knew far too little about the Turkish officer and his character in order to be able to decide on such delicate questions. When I said that the impartiality of such an officer was the best remedy against favouritism in the Turkish Navy, he replied: "Favouritism," adding a gentle smile, "without any favouritism, nothing moves in Turkey".'[201]

In the summer of 1914, Enver Paşa approached the German Head of Mission to ask for the dispatch of six German general staff officers, who were to be assigned as general staff officers to army corps. Because even German non-commissioned officers now entered Turkish service, the Military Mission compiled a special contract form for them. The contract, as was also customary for officers, was concluded between the candidates and General Liman von Sanders, who alone was responsible for their promotion. The duration of the contract for non-commissioned officers was set at one year and could be terminated by the Head of the Mission in cases of 'obvious complete unsuitability' with three months' notice. At the outbreak of war, increasing numbers of German personnel, including other ranks of the Army and Navy, as well as civilian staff from war industries, were interested in having an assignment to Turkey. With the opening of hostilities, Liman von Sanders proposed that German military personnel who were on leave in Turkey and could no longer return to Germany should be recruited into the Military Mission and assigned to mobile units. The Prussian Ministry of War agreed with this proposal.

An assignment in Turkey, therefore, was obviously not unpopular. Requests by officers to be stationed in Turkey seemed to be on the increase. Good connections with relevant authorities often made it possible to grant such requests, though it did not always correspond to the requirements of the Military Mission. This often resulted in officers filling unimportant posts, underemployment or even complete inactivity. At the end of 1914 Liman von Sanders approached the German authorities with the request that the assignment 'of elements not on morally solid ground and who believe they can lead a life of adventure here, as was the case in the Balkan Wars, should be avoided in the interest of Germany's reputation'.[202] Proven considerations did not always play a decisive role for a transfer to the Military Mission. For example, a memorandum explained why an applicant had been rejected: 'H. would not prove to have any usefulness to either Germany or Turkey but only for himself. It is purely his private matter. H. wants a transfer to further his professional career.'[203] The request had come from a philology student who hoped to improve his Turkish language skills. Similarly, a request was made to the Special Command (*SoKo*) to examine whether a medical student, 'could work as a voluntary assistant in the German hospital from 1 December to 15 January'. The applicant 'only asks for free board and lodging'.[204] In another case, an air corps staff sergeant, who had personal difficulties in his unit in Germany (the report spoke of an 'unstable character'), submitted an application. At the end of 1915, a Mr J Feller, the owner of the Ludwigsau Textile Mill in the Bavarian town of Lauingen, on the Danube, wanted his son, Roman Feller, to be transferred to Istanbul, because he intended to establish a military textile factory in Turkey after the war. The Bavarian military authorities concluded that 'it was essentially a question of the initiation of economic relations, which would certainly be in the interests of the Bavarian textile industry'.[205]

All the requests, sponsored by friends and acquaintances in the Fatherland, meant an additional burden each time for duty stations in Istanbul, as they had to examine all such requests, find suitable postings and units, as well as providing accommodation. In mid-April 1915 the Ministry of War in Berlin issued a decree that 'requests for the transfer of German army personnel to Turkey' would be met only when 'they served to satisfy the exigencies of the service expressed by the Turkish Government and if these exigencies are acknowledged here'. On 23 December 1915, Lieutenant Commander Hans Humann, the Naval Attaché at the Embassy in Istanbul, issued a general directive on who was the competent authority for personnel matters after the number of direct recruits in Istanbul had steadily increased. This directive also confirmed the inconsistent leadership and different competencies of the various branches of the forces in Istanbul.

Personnel who were required to be 'boots on the ground' and who would take an active part in operations had to be requisitioned directly from Prussian military headquarters in Berlin by the Head of the German Military Mission. The personnel requirements of the 'German-Ottoman naval forces' were to be submitted by the Head of the German Mediterranean Division to the Navy Cabinet, which also dealt with requests for 'coastal defence' submitted by 'Naval Special Command Admiral von Usedom'. In principle, therefore, all official requests for assignments in Turkey had to be directed either to the Military or Navy Cabinet and not to 'German or Ottoman authorities in Constantinople'. The order concluded:

'The number of officers and officials who wish to come to the Orient theatre of war is apparently extraordinarily great. Bearing in mind the difficulty of filling the constant need for officers etc. for the German Army and the Navy itself, all parties involved are urged not to assign more German officers and officials to Turkey than is absolutely necessary for the given tasks. It has already happened on several occasions that officers etc. who have come here did not find the field of work they expected and did not see the hopes with which they had pursued such a command fulfilled.'[206]

However, about a year later, the Bavarian authorising officer at Supreme Headquarters had to explain to his superiors in Munich that 'as in the Prussian army, apart from official channels, there is still a private channel of personal recommendation'. This would usually be more effective. Liman von Sanders still requisitioned officers by name, who were usually assigned to him. Therefore Bavarian officers had no choice but in some way or another to draw his attention to them. Mühlmann thought that the despatch of so many German officers was 'too much of a good thing'. He said quite bluntly that, 'in the case of what was at stake', namely, the 'expansion of German power in all areas' in the Near East, the 'selection process of German officers' could not be thorough enough. If respect for the personality of German officers was lost, according to Mühlmann, then success in fulfilling his task would also be denied. A growing resentment within the Turkish officer corps was making itself felt at the apparent 'flood' of German officers: competent Turkish officers felt disadvantaged in their prospects for advancement. Indeed, the Germans did not always prove that they could do things better than the Turks could.[207] As a further reason for the burgeoning tensions between Germans and Turks during the war, Mühlmann recognized the 'wrong basis of working together', which meant that the Military Mission's contract, prepared in peace time, would not be adaptable for the conditions of war. The more Turkish self and national awareness grew during the course of the war, 'the more oppressive the contract shackles felt' but von Sanders energetically opposed adapting them. Turkish officers reacted to the fact that a large number of Germans who were staff officers in 1915 subsequently became Turkish divisional and corps commanders.

Another reason for friction was that the officers who were assigned to Turkey had not been adequately prepared for their new duties. In Germany there was scarcely an officer with experience in Turkey who could have been able to train them or, at least, to brief them suitably. They were usually only offered platitudes or the obvious, for example that one should only negotiate with Turks in the presence of a German witness; there were more such nonsensical sentiments. In his memoirs, Kannengiesser criticised this state of affairs:

> The Germans, who arrived in such numbers during the course of the war, should have been appropriately instructed. They very often hurt the cause and themselves in the mistaken belief that, having a dashing figure and zeal, they could treat Turkish officers and men in the German manner. It was a great mistake to assume that German standards and German regulations can be applied willy-nilly to Turkish conditions.'[208]

The question of the dual loyalty of German officers in Turkish service was certainly a significant issue. Were they primarily German officers, or should they follow Turkish rules? This dilemma understandably nourished Turkish mistrust.

It is therefore no wonder that as early as December 1914 the British Ambassador in Greece passed on rumours to London, emanating from his Greek colleague in Istanbul, that there was allegedly a great dislike of German officers in Turkey. A few days later it was said that there had been a fight between German and Turkish officers in Istanbul, in which two Germans had been injured. At the beginning of 1915 reports from Greece spread about anti-German feeling in Istanbul. On 26 January 1915 the Greek newspaper *Hestia* published a report on growing resentment against German officers in Turkey. When, at the beginning of May 1916, Major Guhr came to Turkey to take over a Turkish division, an experienced member of the Military Mission told him that the German officers' relationship with their Turkish counterparts was far from expectations. In July Naval Attaché Humann expressed criticism of those assigned German officers, who, in his view, 'did an enormous amount of damage'.[209]

The Turkish authorities raised concerns when it emerged that German officers expressed displeasure about their Turkish allies in their letters and during their home leaves. The Turks launched a protest after such remarks, through indiscretion, had even appeared in the French press and demanded an official enquiry. The Military Mission attempted to shift the responsibility to officers attached to 'special expeditions' and who did not belong to the Mission.[210] It appears as though the main source of the Turkish complaints could be traced to Major Franz Carl Endres, who served on the Turkish General Staff and who had been with the Military Mission since the Balkan Wars.

As was to be expected, the assignment of Turkish personnel in German units or ships, such as crew members of *Goeben* and *Breslau*, created heightened potential for conflict. Kress reported that German officers did not understand how to handle their Turkish subordinates correctly nor did they have the capacity to ensure that the Germans under their command used the right tone in dealing with their Turkish counterparts. There were even cases of physical mishandling of

Turkish soldiers by Germans. German officers' inadequacy in Turkish (incidentally one of the most difficult languages for a foreigner to master) has already been mentioned. German officers and, above all, officers of the General Staff, had quickly to accept that, being in charge of an official Turkish assignment, it was indispensable to be both orally and literally fluent in Turkish. As very few German officers possessed this ability, many matters were decided without their knowledge and so they often (correctly) felt ignored and useless.

The reinvigoration of Turkish officers' self-confidence, especially after the end of the Gallipoli campaign, was accompanied by further discord and resentment between the officers of both nations. At the same time, clashes between German and Turkish officers over the ski command for the Caucasus Army caused a great deal of raised eyebrows. After a few minor incidents, a Turkish captain demanded to be saluted by a German lieutenant, at which the German unit commander (a major) told him in the presence of other Turkish officers: 'In my presence, you do not give orders to any German officer'. Another incident that typically reflects these sentiments happened during an artillery training exercise, which was being carried out by Lieutenant Martin Nitzsche at a gun emplacement in the Dardanelles. He not only had the gun crew fire, but also summoned the battalion commander, Captain Hakki, to do the fire-controlling. At this, Hakki complained that his honour had been deeply offended, being called upon in the presence of his subordinates to carry out duties which were not commensurate with his rank. Turkish senior officers agreed that this was a slight and demanded a suitable apology from Lieutenant Nitzsche. In his defence, Nitzsche said that he required that all commanders must be familiar and in full control of subordinates' duties, whilst it had not been pointed out to him by other Turkish officers in attendance that such training procedures were demeaning; thus he would not render an apology. Already the incident files were mounting up and the reactions of both parties reveal the degree of mutual misunderstanding and differing views on training and leadership.[211]

A very graphic description of the state of German–Turkish relationship comes from the pen of Lieutenant Colonel Kannengiesser who, as a commander of troops, had intensive contact with his Turkish comrades and subordinates. He described the Turkish character as being defined by:

'... a need for good form, respect for dignity and a great objection to vehement scenes and irascible behaviour. Vehemence is a violation of good manners. It is rude to say 'no'. They say 'yes', but it may not necessarily get done. They do not report any unpleasant things to their superiors, because he would be annoyed. [...] This equanimity, this immobility, is basic to the Oriental character and finds its typical expression in 'keff' [keyif], the delight of nothingness; this may be a result of religious fatalism or the debilitating influence of the climate [...] In any case, on this basis, a trait is formed, of which the Turk is a true master - passive resistance. This generally negative character of the Oriental is now facing off against the positive up-front character of the Germans in all the various military departments.

Coming from the cold North, we German officers were trained in a tough, sometimes gruff, manner and saw respite in clear, forward-thinking organisation and in preventive measures. We were focussed on the enemy by our field service regulations, that an unsuccessful action weighed more than sitting around waiting if you had to make a choice. 'Haste is from the devil', says the Turk, while the Germans have a strong tendency to feverish haste. Well, we Germans are here at the culmination point of our military activity and under enemy fire, instead of being kindred souls as already described with the calmly waiting-and-seeing Turks, who like to remain with something up their sleeves, avoid unnecessary effort and are fully convinced that, when it comes down to it, they will always find some small way to get out of a situation. They hope for 'last minute luck' and have often been successful in this.'[212]

In spite of these observations, Kannengiesser concluded that 'the German–Turkish brotherhood proved itself brilliantly and at Gallipoli it had borne fruit'; but this can only be his personal perception or perhaps subsequent idealisation of this relationship. He did report an incident which, however, was allegedly caused by an interpreter's mistake:

'A severely wounded German captain, unfit for service in the field but still fit for the tropics, was assigned to train a Turkish depot regiment. On the first day he visited the soldiers' living quarters, kitchens and other facilities in Asia Minor and, being used to German conditions was, of course, appalled. In conference with his company commanders, he promised that everything would be different and in his eagerness, the rather vulgar but not uncommonly used German expression *Schweinerei* [pigs' mess] slipped his tongue. There is nothing more disgusting to Turks than *domuz* (pig). The Turkish interpreter, whether it was malicious or unconscious, I don't know, translated the ominous word as if the captain meant it for the members of his regiment. Thus, this German was doomed from day one, all his subsequent efforts were in vain and without him even suspecting why. Even the civilian population of the small town avoided him because he had called the Turks "pigs".'[213]

Cases of misconduct by German officers in Turkey occurred repeatedly. Captain Erich Serno reported in his diary at least two cases in which German officer pilots had engaged in the black market by 'renting out' railway wagons to merchants for large sums of money when the wagons were officially designated solely for use as military transport. Obviously, the fact that these cases were commonly known did not enhance German prestige.

Cultural differences and conflicts repeatedly dogged German–Turkish relations and sometimes German soldiers were regarded as behaving improperly, since moral standards were different. Opportunities were also sought to discredit recalcitrant German officers. For example, Captain Reclam was accused by Colonel Şefki Bey, commander of the Bosphorus Narrows, of 'drunkenness, a bad life style and insulting behaviour'. Colonel Şefki apparently had great problems working with German officers and his accusations were examined but could be disproved. Colonel Şefki was removed from his post by Enver Paşa but promoted to GOC, the commander, of the 19th Division; the Turks also demanded the reassignment of Captain Reclam. The incident that had sparked the uproar of Turkish sensibility appeared in a report of 19 August 1915:

'The matter in question about the ladies is briefly this: Reclam and a married reserve lieutenant called Koch, with his wife, held an afternoon function to repay hospitality at a viewpoint far beyond Kawak. There the house of the rescue station had been made available for use by German officials and officers. During the afternoon, the group went down to the beach in a remote bay there and the young men and women, using separate bathing huts, went bathing. The fact that ladies in Turkish dress also took part created the tension.'[214]

On the other hand, the report by Colonel Şefki was certainly not unfounded, as he felt annoyed about the occasional evening drunkenness of German soldiers in public, especially during the fasting month of Ramadan, and demanded:

'It is necessary to prohibit this conduct as otherwise great offence will be aroused in the officer corps, other ranks and local inhabitants. I would therefore ask you to present this to the

Minister of War or to submit this letter to him. I do not wish to write such things officially. I ask the following:

1. Prohibit the Germans from drinking openly;
2. No drunken approaches to Turkish ladies;
3. An absolute prohibition of relations with Turkish women, especially in or near the fortress.'[215]

Şefki's demands do not seem to be excessive and the behaviour of the German soldiers being criticized is borne out by various judgments of courts martial held in Istanbul. In most cases the offenders were merely posted back to Germany, such as Reserve Lieutenant 'D', because of 'public offence through drunkenness in uniform and constant relations with little boys'.[216]

Disciplinary, as well as criminal offences by German soldiers, were punished under the German Military Criminal Code and prosecuted under military jurisdiction. Serious offenders were often reduced in rank or imprisoned, for which some cabins were set up as prison cells on the accommodation ship *Urla*, which was moored in Istinye. Offenders sentenced to detention were thus able to serve them out in Istanbul, but apparently the number of cells was sometimes not sufficient, so that prisoners were occasionally transferred to the prison fortress of Cologne; this had to be requested separately for each individual case.[217]

Admiral Souchon, who had applied for higher jurisdiction in October 1915 for himself as Head of the Military Mission,[218] was against such prison transfers. But he also showed an understanding of his men:

'I am in a difficult position to confirm such harsh judgments, in wartime, of 10 years' imprisonment. I can mitigate them, but lack a guiding rule for them. The whole gravity of the law must, in my opinion, weigh against incorrigible rascals, who cannot even pull themselves together in wartime; but, on the other hand, understand the case of a family man in the Territorials or perhaps Militia, who rebels against the pure disenchantment of military order. It will be a relief to me in this connection when I have court martial counsellors again, especially senior and experienced people.'[219]

Lieutenant Rudolph Firle commented rather sardonically on one occasion, when Admiral Souchon, accompanied by his Second Admiral's Staff Officer, Lieutenant Commander Erich Schlubach, visited the arrest cells of the MMD:

'Admiral with A 2 on board to inspect his hobby horse, the arrest cells, also a pleasure. He said he wanted to bring in the pastor to at least pester the fellows. I was more for them facing firing squads or doing hard labour building roads and strongholds.'[220]

The concern in the cases of indiscretion and improper behaviour, especially concerning contact between local ladies and German soldiers and civilians, finally led to an order issued by Admiral Souchon at the end of 1916:

'The constantly and rapidly growing number of judicially punishable offences gives me cause to remind all superior officers with disciplinary responsibilities to pay particularly careful attention to their subordinates. The influence of long times at anchor and the seduction emanating from local conditions are becoming more and more noticeable. They harbour great dangers for discipline and the morals of our people. Of course the main danger stems from

The crew of the *Breslau* on shore in Bursa. (*Bundesarchiv Koblenz*)

relations with females. Even the relatively harmless, fixed relationships with local Levantine and other girls are undesirable, especially when the idea of the possibility of marriage is considered. Such relationships, if they are recognised as serious, should be broken up by timely re-assignment. Much more serious are relations with lower classes of women. It can be safely assumed here that espionage is being carried out on a grand scale. The suspicion is particularly justified against the prostitutes in the Galata quarter. The men must take care that they watch each other's backs. Women who try to acquire military information must be reported immediately. It must be brought to the men's attention that they have to consider that this segment of the local population is largely hostile to us [...] a further danger looms on the part of the local merchants and traders.

A number of cases have been discovered, leading to investigations of customs fraud and misappropriation due to bribery by local merchants. The usual way is to try to get items through the field post office free of customs duties; another, taking over of part of a war delivery by the supplier himself, after the goods concerned have been imported free of customs duties as war goods. For all deliveries, greatest caution and strict control must be applied when placing and receiving orders for goods [...] Observation of these activities must still be conducted for the time being in secret, but any clues which may serve to expose this activity should be made known. It is up to commanders to find ways and means to counter these harmful influences. Where it is prevalent, weak characters or unruly elements have to be removed. Timely removal should also take place wherever NCOs and men mismanage supply stocks. Regular clean sweeps by newly-arrived replacements from home must be continued. The new arrivals – and particularly the younger ones – should not be left to themselves until they have been warned of the specific local dangers.'[221]

Not only was too little adaptability to local conditions criticised, but also the other extreme of 'becoming a Turk', which symbolised a man giving up his national identity. Thus Liman von Sanders observed the following behaviour, which he judged as an unnecessary annexation of Turkish custom:

'The founding of the German-Turkish Friendship House in Constantinople, for which Professor Jäckh had collected great sums, had to be regarded by the Turks as currying their favour. This was the last thing we should do. Better a certain restraint which the Turks appreciate and respect and seemed to me to be more worthy of the German name. Many inaccurate judgments, most of which culminated in the exaggerated praise of cultural progress, have been spread throughout the Fatherland by fleeting visitors and so-called country experts. To our dismay, there were Germans in Constantinople who believed that after a few weeks of taking up their official duties that they had to assume Turkish customs. In the room of the Grand Vizier I once met three civilian gentlemen wearing the Turkish fez, who silently greeted me with the Turkish greeting of the right hand to heart, mouth and forehead. When I inquired about the names of these improbable looking Turks, who looked quite familiar to me, I heard that they were actually Germans - one was called Schmidt - who had been assigned to an official post a short time ago.'[222]

The behaviour and presence of German soldiers on the streets of Istanbul was also sceptically viewed by international observers and diplomats. Thus, Ambassador Morgenthau described the situation bitingly and, probably, with exaggeration:

'German officers were almost as active as the Turks themselves in this mobilization. They enjoyed it all immensely; indeed they gave every sign that they were having the time of their lives. Bronssart, Humann, and Lafferts were constantly at Enver's elbow, advising and directing the operations. German officers were rushing through the streets every day in huge automobiles, all requisitioned from the civilian population; they filled all the restaurants and amusement places at night, and celebrated their joy in the situation by consuming large quantities of champagne – also requisitioned. A particularly spectacular and noisy figure was that of von der Goltz Pasha. He was constantly making a kind of vice-regal progress through the streets in a huge and madly dashing automobile, on both sides of which flaring German eagles were painted. A trumpeter on the front seat would blow loud, defiant blasts as the conveyance rushed along, and woe to any one, Turk or non-Turk, who happened to get in the way! The Germans made no attempt to conceal their conviction that they owned this town. Just as Wangenheim had established a little Wilhelmstrasse [shorthand for the German Foreign Office] in his Embassy, so had the German military men established a sub-station of the Berlin General Staff. They even brought their wives and families from Germany; I heard Baroness Wangenheim remark that she was holding a little court at the German Embassy.'[223]

He went on to note:

> 'I really think that the most influential seat of authority at that time was a German merchant ship, the *General*. It was moored in the Golden Horn, at the Galata Bridge, and a permanent stairway had been built, leading to its deck. I knew well one of the most frequent visitors to this ship, an American who used to come to the embassy and entertain me with stories of what was going on. The *General*, this American now informed me, was practically a German club or hotel. The officers of the *Goeben* and the *Breslau* and other German officers who had been sent to command the Turkish ships ate and slept on board. Admiral Souchon, who had brought the German cruisers to Constantinople, presided over these gatherings.'[224]

Morgenthau was not completely wrong in his observations. Thus typical German behaviour, like pursuing 'Teutonic traditions' - such as skittles or beer evenings, as well as summer rambles with loud singing - found little popularity among the population. Nevertheless, the theme of German-Turkish brothers-in-arms was repeatedly published, especially in the Fatherland. Ernst Jäckh, in particular, often gave lectures about his idealised view of a Germanic-Islamic global domination in various social and diplomatic circles, but this did not echo how the German community in Istanbul felt.

There were, however, German officers, who had a different view of their Turkish brothers-in-arms and who were capable of self-criticism, such as Commander Hans Humann, who on 17 March 1916 wrote to Captain Ackermann, who commanded the *Goeben*:

> The German is not a very fortunate coloniser, even in peace-time, and certainly not in colonising through his own *persona*. He always appears in two extremes: either as an unswerving, pure confessor of the virtues of his homeland, against which nothing can match up; or as a spineless ideologist, who always sees the good in the alien being and soon becomes absorbed by him. The one has too much, the other too little of what is necessary for living and working abroad, of learning and understanding the essence of a foreign nation. German military personnel who come down here, unfortunately, tend to veer exclusively and particularly strongly in the first direction. Unfortunately, officers too often appear only as victorious soldiery, whose foolish and inconsiderate actions and conduct are a great affront to the local civilian and military people.'[225]

The differences in the food rations between the Turkish and German troops aroused the displeasure of many Turkish soldiers. It must have fuelled their envy that, while they had to live under the most primitive conditions and often even on the breadline, the units of their German allies were better and more abundantly fed. However, German soldiers did work hard to ensure the supply of their customary fare. For example, on the hills above Istinye harbour market gardening was carried out by members of the MMD and, to ensure the supply of fresh meat, they also had their own small pig breeding facilities.

Medical services in Istanbul had been brought to an improved standard because of German aid and thus could cope with the many health problems of German military personnel. In addition to the German hospital in Istanbul, which was mainly staffed by German doctors and nurses, there was also a German field hospital near Bighali on the Gallipoli peninsula. So-called 'convalescent homes' were set up for recuperation from chronic diseases and injuries. In addition, several German doctors were distributed among various hospitals in Istanbul and other cities.

Agricultural work by members of the Mediterranean Division in Istinye. (*Bundesarchiv Koblenz*)

For many Germans, health problems were often attributed to the unfamiliar diet and sometimes inadequate hygienic conditions. A particular illness for stokers on board ships was pneumonia, which, as a result of the coal dust, smoke and cooling-off under draughty ventilation shafts during breaks, often became chronic and had fatal consequences. Typhoid and dysentery were often prevalent and there were some cases of cholera. Some of the senior officers were no longer young and thus particularly prone to such illnesses; Admiral von Usedom in one of his reports to the Kaiser, noted Admiral Merten: 'Vice Admiral Merten reported sick on 28 June and is in the German Hospital in Constantinople. Whether he can recover well enough to be fit for re-assuming his post here seems doubtful to me.'[226] Usedom did not like Admiral Merten; in another report on him Admiral Usedom wrote with malicious irony: 'In spite of his low resistance to climatic influences and frequent dysentery, he was of the opinion that with his boundless energy and untiring zeal in two years of work, he had rallied Turkish officers and crews to co-operation and increased efficiency.'[227]

At times, the optimistic self-assessment of German medical proficiency could be shattered, as the wording of a telegram on 6 November 1915 showed: 'Sub-Lieutenant Kraft seriously ill with typhus – condition critical due to imminent intestinal perforation. Best care available. Chief Physician Schleip, German Hospital.'[228] Lieutenant Kraft died the same day. The story of the failed efforts by his father, Rear Admiral Kraft from Wilhelmshaven, to bring his son's body home to Germany, illustrates clearly that even the best miltary connections did not always guarantee success. It also shows how painful it must have been for families to know their loved ones were buried far from home, in this case in Istanbul. Probably knowing Rear Admiral Kraft well, Admiral Souchon had personally wired his condolences to the Kraft family, also on 6 November. The Krafts desperately tried to have the body repatriated to Germany, as the following exchange of telegrams shows.

'Telegram No. 550 for Mediterranean Division, 7 November 1915: Admiral Kraft wired: Request immediate repatriation my son's body from Constantinople to Hamburg – all costs will be paid. / Telegram to Admiralty Staff Berlin, 7 November 1915: Sub-Lieutenant Kraft died of typhus 6 November. / Telegram No. 559 for Mediterranean Division, 8 November 1915. Rear Admiral Kraft requests despatch of coffin with his son's body through Schenker and Son Forwarding Agents addressed to Reich Navy Office address. Wire reply if repatriation possible. Admiralty Staff. / Telegram to Admiralty Staff Berlin, 10 November 1915: Repatriation of body provisionally impossible – will be embalmed for later transfer. Divisional Chief, signed Humann.'[229]

Obviously the wishes of the parents could not be followed, as Sub-Lieutenant Kraft was interred in the military cemetery in Tarabya and lies buried there to this day.

There were several cases of typhoid fever during that period and a doctor, who was 'urgently required for typhoid epidemics in Aleppo and lines of communication', had been summoned back from his own medical recuperation by telegram on 14 November 1915. In one case, the inquiries of an anxious mother were even transmitted via official channels. Thus, Constantinople was cabled on 12 November 1915: 'Mother of Sub-Lieutenant Prince Reuss requests news of her son's condition'[230] as it was suspected that he was probably suffering from typhus. On 8 December 1915, Prince Reuss, who had in the meantime been promoted to lieutenant, was on forty-five days leave 'for recuperation of his health', which was regularly granted to wounded or sick personnel.

In addition to providing for German soldiers and civilians, the MMD also established polyclinics to improve medical care for the Turkish population in the immediate vicinity of one of its unit's location and for the dependants of Turkish soldiers. The most famous clinic was located in Emirgan, a small village near Istinye, where the MMD had its berth and was run by naval doctor Willrich.

Naval convalescent home in Yeniköy, on the Bosphorus.

ERICH SELLIN   BERLIN w
Hof Photograph   Unter den Linden 19.

Chaplain to the German Embassy, Count von Lüttichau. (*Ev. Pfarramt Istanbul*)

Navy Chaplain Ludwig Müller. (*Author's Collection*)

From its opening in the summer of 1915 until the end of the war, this clinic treated 147,434 patients. Since treatment was free of charge and the good reputation of the German doctors spread beyond the immediate vicinity, their capacity was soon reached. Drugs that initially came from MMD stocks were not enough. Standards could only be maintained through donations from Germany, such as by the initiative of Ambassador von Wangenheim's wife, who was able to raise additional funds through the Red Cross in Berlin.[231] In addition, a naval convalescent home was established in Yeniköy for personnel of the Mediterranean Division and the Coastal Inspectorate who were wounded or temporarily unfit for duty.[232]

The first man of the cloth to care for the spiritual well-being of German personnel was the Embassy Chaplain, Count von Lüttichau, who had officially assumed the function of a navy chaplain on 31 October 1915. He not only held religious services for soldiers in Istanbul, but later was also alongside the fighting troops in Gallipoli. He was accompanied during these visits by senior officers, but insisted that all his conversations with sailors and NCOs should take place without their 'supervision'. Count von Lüttichau came under enemy fire several times during such visits to the front lines and received the Iron Cross Second Class. His duties were so numerous that additional clerical support was repeatedly drafted from Germany to assist him. However, it was difficult to obtain suitable chaplains, since ordained ministers, Roman Catholic or Protestant, were relatively few in number, especially those who had the necessary physical fitness and robust health for the conditions. On 23 January1916, the *SoKo* wired Berlin that 'Pastor Weiker cannot take up post Turkey. Please send replacement immediately. Navy Chaplain Count von Lüttichau alone cannot cope with work.'[233] His ministry was highly esteemed, especially by the fighting troops; and he was popular with senior officers as well. Lieutenant Colonel Kannengiesser wrote on 24 July 1915: 'Count L. for lunch here, good conversation. When he left, feeling as if a piece of home went away.'[234] In due course assistance was despatched: Navy Chaplain Ludwig Müller was assigned to Istanbul when Count von Lüttichau was transferred to the German Asia Corps in Palestine.

In mid October 1915 von Lüttichau travelled to Berlin to recruit additional pastoral assistants and to organise the founding of a German Soldiers' Club in Istanbul. Support for the latter came in the form of a telegram from the German authorities in Istanbul: '… because Count von Lüttichau has exercised pastoral care for the Mediterranean Division in a self-sacrificing manner since the beginning of the war, his proposals are quite justified.'[235] The new Soldiers' Club was located at 51 Pera Street [now *Istiklal Caddesi*], diagonally opposite the *Tokatlyan* Hotel, and was opened on 19 December 1915 with an afternoon programme and talk. On the invitation for the event it stated: 'A visit to the club, which provides all German military and naval personnel who are in Constantinople with a place of recreation and informal companionship, is highly recommended.'[236] Later this Soldiers' Club made the headlines in an article on 11 March 1916, when Ludwig Ganghofer, a Bavarian journalist (and a poet who wrote in dialect) submitted a report about his visit to Istanbul. He remarked that the presence of German troops was obviously being intentionally minimised:

'The only indication that it was German was to be found in a tiny, barely hand-sized sign with the inscription 'German Soldiers' Club'. I was told that the German words had earlier been in half-metre-high letters, mounted on a large signboard, with a black, white and red border. This signboard had to be removed, because it disturbed the newly-flourishing Turks. Indeed, it was done – perhaps on a day when we had sent a few hundred million Marks, German guns, German shells and a thousand young men in field-grey with German hearts and German blood to Constantinople.'[237]

These and other statements from Ganghofer did not resonate well everywhere in Istanbul. Commander Humann wrote a counter article, in which he tried to explain that the removal of the sign was because it had to be in accordance with Turkish regulations and that these must be adhered to. Furthermore, 'These signs are not just hand-sized, but in an 80:40 cm format. The above-mentioned regulations are an expression of the new nationalism, which is not only supported by the Turkish government, but also by us.' Humann pressed his attack on Ganghofer, continuing: "Through his article, the author shows that he is an expert writer; but neither is he a politician nor a true journalist because he clearly does not understand the need to examine the situation and events as to their causality, their inner purpose and context.'[238] Irrespective of the contretemps, the Soldiers' Club was a very well-received social facility, especially since access to many local restaurants and pubs had been put out of bounds for soldiers.

Further support and information for German soldiers was to be found in their newspaper *Am Bosporus* [*On the Bosphorus*], which was published from 1917 onwards. A small editorial staff collated monthly information from other theatres of war, tips and advice on life in Istanbul, as well as instructional articles from military authorities for the enlightenment of all troops stationed on the Bosphorus. The editorial staff reported directly to the Chief of the Military Mission, General Liman von Sanders. As early as 1915, the *Wissenschaftliche und technische Osmanische Militaer-Zeitschrift* [*Scientific and Technical Ottoman Military Journal*] had been published under the name

Die Verteidigung [*The Defence*] in Istanbul. The editor-in-chief was Mehmed Zeki. The journal was printed in both German and Turkish and its goal was to throw the best light on the German-Turkish military brotherhood.

Of particular importance for almost all the military personnel was the award of decorations, which were very numerous, especially after the battles on Gallipoli; therefore the medals themselves were sometimes in very short supply. On 25 November 1915 the Mediterranean Division telegraphed to Berlin: 'Request Iron Crosses: 10 First Class, 100 Second Class to replenish stocks'.[239] German decorations were not only given to those serving in their own forces, but also frequently awarded to Turkish officers and occasionally even to private soldiers. An order of 11 March 1915 permitted the 'Head of the Special Mission in Constantinople and the Head of the Mediterranean Division' to authorise the award of the Iron Cross Second Class 'due to the theatre of war being so far away'.[240] Awards of the Iron Cross First Class continued to be subject to 'Application through His Majesty'. From the documents available on the MMD and Coastal Inspectorate, it can be seen that applications for the award of decorations, along with citations and subsequent award confirmations, created a considerable amount of administrative work, for some requests were submitted as individual applications for up to eighty personnel at a time. Again and again award applications were rejected and yet the MMD still tried to push through awards for the Iron Cross First Class with further arguments - often couched with slight irony - as illustrated by the application for Lieutenant Commander Erich Schlubach.

> His Majesty, the Emperor and King, has rejected the application with file reference G 8215 of 7 November 1915 requesting Iron Cross First Class to Lieutenant Commander Schlubach, the Mediterranean Division Admiral's A 2, because the officer had not been directly involved in active naval operations of the U-boat. Whilst I will notify this most important decision to the Imperial Command, I have the honour to humbly inform you that recently a similar application for a U-boat Half Flotilla Chief of the High-Seas Fleet has also just been rejected. Signed v. Müller, for the Imperial Command of the Mediterranean Division.'[243]

Decorations were ceremoniously exchanged to consolidate German-Turkish relations. With this in mind, Admiral Usedom telegrammed: 'Urgently request award of the Iron Cross First Class to Enver and Cevad for their great meritorious service in Dardanelles'.[244] This request came after several Turkish lower ranks had already been awarded the Iron Cross Second Class and Admiral Usedom wanted to avoid stirring bad feelings with these two very senior members of the Alliance.

For German soldiers of all ranks, the Turkish War Medal, also known as the 'Iron Crescent Moon' by the Germans and the 'Gallipoli Star' by the Allies, was a coveted award. This decoration was only available in one class and it was, as the lowest available distinction of valour, on a par with the Iron Cross Second Class. Thus there was no automatic award for having taken part in a battle; the medal could be awarded for exceptional valour and war services to soldiers of all ranks and branches of military forces. The decoration was created on 1 March 1915 by Sultan Mehmed V Reşâd. The centre of the crescent featured the Sultan's official seal (*tughra*) and 1333 - the awarding year 1915 - engraved on it as the Islamic synonym. Although the award was worn directly pinned to the uniform and without a neck ribbon, there were also bars for participation in special battles. The award of this decoration could be made not only by the Sultan himself but also by Enver, the Minister of War, Marshal Liman von Sanders, as well as Admiral Souchon as commander of the fleet. The versions manufactured by the Turks were simple metal stampings and coloured with red paint, but finer versions were produced in Germany using silver and red enamel for private clients. The Turkish War Medal was awarded to almost all personnel in the Mediterranean Division, the Special

Command (SoKo), and to everybody in the Military Mission. Admiral Souchon, however, was obviously not very enthusiastic about this award when he wrote to his wife on 30 July 1915:

'Today I have been awarded the Turkish War Medal, which is given to everyone who has already received another war decoration and from now on will be awarded instead of other war medals. It is a brick-red filled nickel-plated star, worn without a ribbon on the right breast, which unfortunately, as you can imagine, looks horrible, but quite Turkish. This includes a red-white button-hole ribbon, similar to the design of our black-and-white ribbon.'[245]

On 21 October, he once again contemptuously remarked to his wife about von Usedom and the importance attached to the Ottoman decorations: 'He (von Usedom) has become so Turkish that he wears the buttonhole ribbon of the Iron Crescent Moon over that of the Iron Cross and asks me for permission to keep his fur hat on when in my room.'

A remark of Souchon's, in a letter dated 29 October 1916, illustrates his low opinion of Turkish decorations when he indirectly judged their value as not being particularly high: 'A year ago war broke out between Russia and Turkey. I awarded a great number of Iron Crescent Moons and other Turkish war medals as souvenirs.'[246]

Admiral Souchon himself, however, was only reluctantly considered for appropriate military awards. While General Liman von Sanders, Admiral von Usedom and even Enver Paşa were decorated with the *Pour le Mérite*, Admiral Souchon had only received the Iron Cross First Class. Count von Metternich, the Ambassador of the German Embassy, as successor to the recently

Above: Turkish War Medal [241]

Right: Able Seaman Wolfgang Schrader [242] with his Turkish War Medal

deceased Baron von Wangenheim, sent an unusual request to the Chief of the Admiralty Staff in Berlin on 21 February 1916:

> 'May Your Excellency allow me to touch upon a matter which is outside my competence, but is of importance to the overall interests of our German position here. Your Excellency is more aware of Admiral Souchon's merits than I, and therefore I only need to mention how his dashing breakthrough in the Dardanelles made a major contribution to bringing Turkey on to our side in this war. [...] I should now like to beg Your Excellency for generous reflection of whether you consider it right and proper to entreat His Majesty the Kaiser to award the high distinction, *Pour le Mérite*, to Admiral Souchon.'[247]

The answer came fairly swiftly from Berlin on 8 March, stating that the request 'Would have little prospect of success' since 'an award of the *Pour le Mérite* was only possible after a very recent deed and that the cases specially cited from 1–3 lay too far back in time, in order to be able to use them as justification.'[248] Perhaps ironically, Souchon, who evidently knew nothing of the Ambassador's efforts, viewed and critically judged Metternich as a diplomat through whom no serious representation of German interests in Turkey could be achieved. He reported von Metternich's departure on 3 October 1916:

> 'Metternich is leaving today; unfortunately I cannot wave him bon voyage behind the train because good old Wichelhausen will be sitting in it, but I will ask the Lord God to spare Prussia and Germany from using such officials, who have forgotten where their duty lies.'[249]

However, he was not left unrecognised and, perhaps as compensation, Souchon received a communication, dated 7 April 1916, which informed him that he was awarded 'the Swords to the Red Eagle Order Second Class with Oak Leaves and the Star to the Red Eagle Order 2nd Class with Oak Leaves and Swords'.[250] Eventually he was awarded the coveted *Pour le Mérite,* in October 1916 – despite the fact that the request in early 1916 was turned down and Admiral Souchon had not performed any 'recent' outstanding deeds.

In addition to the Turkish War Medal, other Turkish orders were awarded to German officers, such as the Imtiaz Medal,[251] the Liakat Medal,[252] the Order of Osmania [253] and the Order of the Medjidie.[254]

The relationships between German servicemen and civilian women in Istanbul was a sensitive subject. The less salubrious kind of relationships resulted in frequent cases of sexually transmitted diseases, but the more pleasant kind, though rarer, even led to marriage. An early military directive was promulgated to prohibit German servicemen stationed in Turkey from getting married; of course there were exceptions to that ruling, which required special permission from the Navy Cabinet or the Army General Staff. One example was the intended marriage of Sub-Lieutenant Karl Dönitz, who had come to Turkey as an officer of the crew of the *Breslau* and had started paying court to General Weber's daughter, who was living in Istanbul with her father. On 6 November 1915, Admiral Souchon wrote to his wife: 'This morning the news arrived of the engagement here of that upstanding Sub Lieutenant Karl Dönitz, *Breslau*, with the nice daughter of General Weber – the 4th such engagement under my flag in the MMD'.[255] However, simple approval by the Fleet Commander was not deemed sufficient and was why official permission had to be obtained from the Admiralty Staff in Berlin. The request came in a telegram from the Mediterranean Division to Berlin dated 8 March 1916:

> 'Sub-Lieutenant Dönitz humbly requests official permission for a wartime marriage with *Fräulein* Ingeborg Weber, daughter of Major General Weber, Prussian Army, Commander 100th

Infantry Brigade [sic]. Both Protestant, assured that [his] income corresponds to requirements, submission documentary verification very difficult now due distance from here.'[256]

Dönitz and his fiancée Ingeborg must have been very happy on that Sunday, 7 May 1916, finally to receive the news from Berlin that they had both eagerly awaited: 'Permission granted for Sub-Lieutenant Dönitz to marry Ingeborg Weber'.[257]

An equally delicate issue, one which led to dissatisfaction and envy within the German contingent, were the visits of wives and family members to an active service area. While it was possible for personnel of the Military Attaché's Staff and the Military Mission to bring their families to Istanbul, the crews of the MMD and the Special Command (SoKo) could only see their families and wives during their annual leave in Germany. This soon resulted in some ladies beginning to travel on their own account from Germany to the Bosphorus. In September 1914 the American wife of Lieutenant Commander von Müller arrived in Istanbul and very quickly got on Admiral Souchon's nerves:

'She is simply a burden to everyone here with her American friendliness, since she cannot remain sitting in her shabby hotel. Her favourite hang-out is our shore-based cipher office, as I almost regularly find her there smoking and drinking tea and apparently feels quite at home.'

The wife of *Goeben's* gunnery officer, Lieutenant Commander Arnold Knispel, had also made the journey to join her husband and was also mentioned in Souchon's journal, when he wrote: 'Frau v. Mueller isn't even thinking of leaving and Frau Knispel doesn't seem to want to budge either'.[258] These visits also encouraged other officers and men who wanted to claim the same right for themselves, insofar as they could personally afford to cover the costs of the journey. The flood of travel applications was so great that the Admiralty Staff in Berlin responded to one such application in a telegram on 28 February 1915:

'Since requests from wives for a pass to be issued to travel to Constantinople are received almost every day, it is urgently necessary to point out that passes may only be issued when special reasons apply. These reasons are, for example, serious illness or being wounded, cases of death. Details of the specific reasons for Mrs Neuschmann and her son are hereby requested.'[259]

Little attention, however, was paid to this directive, because in the following months there were also frequent questions asking to know the 'specific reasons' for travel applications. Finally, in February 1916, the Admiralty Staff decreed that 'passes for the dependants of officers, officials and men of the Imperial Navy [...] for travel to Turkey may only be issued by the Imperial Naval Office'. The abating of the fighting on the Gallipoli front and the opening up of surface traffic through Serbia seemed to have increased the flow of visitors by military dependants still further. Finally, the Military Attaché in Istanbul demanded, in April 1916, a ban on visiting the city:

'Since the introduction of the Balkan railway [connection], the number of officers' wives wishing to pay a visit to their husbands in Constantinople has been constantly increasing. This is by no means conducive to the execution of military duties, for it is natural that the ladies, who are here for a longer or shorter time, want to see as much as possible of Constantinople and the surrounding areas and that therefore there is much gossip about excursions, pleasure trips etc. There seems to be a danger that the awareness of being at war will be lost. I believe, therefore, that it would be a good thing, also in the case of the areas behind our German fronts, if there were to be a fundamental ban on German officers based in Turkey bringing their wives and families to Constantinople.'[260]

This proposal was obviously not enforceable, as it would have meant unequal treatment when contrasted with those officers already living with their families in Istanbul. In June 1917, a final decision was made by letter from the Supreme Command:

'Ludendorff, in a letter to the Secretary of State, insists that, besides no Army wives, no Navy wives should be permitted to come to C'ple. Perhaps this is against Mrs Pieper [wife of Navy Captain Waldemar Pieper], who has already become very unpleasantly noticeable? It is unjust, however, that civil servants can have their wives here.'[261]

The wrangling over this problem finally resolved itself when the poor supply situation in Istanbul ceased to make a sojourn there a pleasure, thus putting a stop to the flow of dependants from Germany.

Chapter 5

The Fortification of the Dardanelles

T he Dardanelles had ancient, centuries-old fortifications, yet upgrading the installations had not kept pace with the progress of technology. The main focus of the improvements lay in the defence of the Straits against a naval attack from the west.

The key fortifications were on both shores of the Dardanelles, where there were coastal batteries and forts directed towards the Aegean Sea. A fleet that broke through this barrier could fire on them from the rear and theywere practically defenceless against an attack from the landward side. As early as 1836 Helmuth von Moltke had written about the early use of the Dardanelles fortifications after his visit to Çanakkale:

'Some daring and fortunate naval actions of the English [sic] have spread the general view that shore batteries cannot defend against fleets, which are of course superior in the number of

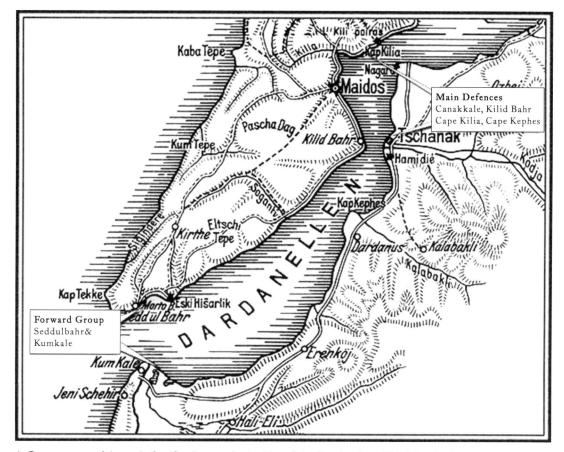

A German map of the main fortifications on both sides of the Dardanelles. (*Eckel Graphics*)

the guns. Such an enterprise was that of Lord Duckworth in 1807. At that time the defensive positions of the Dardanelles were in the most pitiful state the English [sic] squadron sailed by, almost without finding opposition. [...] If the artillery is organised in the Dardanelles, I do not think that any hostile fleet of the world might dare to sail through the straits; one would always be obliged to disembark troops and attack the batteries at the Narrows.'[262]

The fortification of the narrows comprised two groups. A forward group was formed by two batteries: on the Asian side at Kumkale (Fort Orhanié); and on the European shore at Seddulbahr. These batteries consisted of a total of twenty guns of various calibres from 15 to 28 cm, old models without rapid-fire devices and with short range, apart from four guns with a range of just fifteen kilometres. The main fortifications were formed around a group in the vicinity of Canakkale – Kilid Bahr – Cape Kilia – Nagara.[263] Only near Cape Kephes, on the Asian shore, was there a medium forward battery. Altogether there were about eighty guns of the most disparate kinds available, which hardly corresponded to the demands of an effective coastal defence against modern warships. Moreover, the construction of the fortifications was not up to date. The facilities dated mostly from the Russian-Turkish war of 1877/78 and were either made up of brick walls or simple earthworks. The batteries were open and there was neither armoured protection nor concrete. The guns were almost exclusively of German manufacture (Krupp) and their delivery from Germany by sea was still possible until mid-1914. The installation of the heavy cannons under the direction of German experts required great enterprise; some forts were even constructed around the weapons.

The foundation and bearing of a heavy gun in Fort Hamidie before the insertion of the gun carriage under the supervision of German officers. (*Goosen*)

Admiral Souchon wrote a considered note about rumours of an Allied naval attack grew at the end of 1914:

'I do not think that the English [sic] and French will force the Dardanelles, because they are not able to decide between themselves who should pay the price with Dreadnoughts. So many good mines lie in the long, sinuous passage and so many cannons and soldiers are positioned on both shores that the attacker must count on a major operation in all circumstances. Even if, after appropriate losses, he then gets some ships through into the Marmara Sea, he can undertake nothing significant further unless he can establish himself on the shore with the help of substantial landing forces.'[264]

Souchon was, therefore, in agreement with an evaluation made by General Liman von Sanders, who asserted:

'Hence, a crucial success could only be achieved by the enemy if a large troop landing against the Dardanelles is synchronised with the breakthrough of the fleet or takes place ahead of this. A troop landing only following the breakthrough would not have artillery support from the fleet that had already broken through.'[265]

Until the assumption of responsibility of the Dardanelles fortifications by German officers in 1914, they had been completely neglected by the Turks, at least according to the judgment of German experts. This deficit had been recognised early on by General von Sanders and he wanted to take

Turkish crew around a 21 cm heavy gun in the Dardanelles. (*Bundesarchiv Koblenz*)

over responsibility for these defensive arrangements, although they were still subordinate to the British Naval Mission's area of responsibility. Nevertheless, even the Turks considered the 'Limpus Mission' as incapable of fulfilling this task; it was pejoratively called 'ridiculous' and Admiral Limpus was judged a 'weak and soft character'. Compared with the British, the German Military Mission was considered to be of 'towering' superiority.[266] Enver welcomed the intention to put the fortifications under German responsibility. For that reason, a German naval officer would first be transferred to the army as a matter of camouflage and later posted to the Military Mission in Istanbul. This expert for coastal fortifications was to be assigned to General Weber, the Inspector General of the Turkish Engineer and Pioneer Corps. By this means the Germans not only wanted to acquire control over the extension of the fortifications but also to ensure they would be supplied by German industry.

Nevertheless, this intention was not effected immediately; in the War Diary of the MMD, Admiral Souchon noted on 27 August 1914:

'The forts have still mostly never fired a shot. Absolutely unclear ideas about fire control. The mines deployed lie for the most part 70 or 80 metres apart and can apparently lie no longer than four weeks with certainty in the same place.'[267]

Ambassador von Wangenheim had informed the German Foreign Office a day earlier that he could only support an attack in the Black Sea if the Dardanelles had been secured.[268]

Command and control of the Dardanelles was not clearly regulated and was split into different areas of responsibility. Admiral von Usedom had taken over command of the fortifications of the Dardanelles and the Bosphorus in September 1914. As a delegate of the Turkish headquarters and with direct responsibility to Enver Paşa, there was, in addition, Admiral Merten in Canakkale. However, Cevad Bey, a Turkish colonel, was the commander of the Canakkale Fortress Command. All troops assigned to coastal defence in the southern part of the Gallipoli Peninsula, as well as those for the defence of the Straits on the Asiatic coast, were subordinate to him. Admiral von Usedom reported on 5 June 1915 about the command and control structures there and his intentions as to how to optimise them:

'The command structure of the Straits fortifications is not able to be so clearly organised as it should be in a military sense, because of the somehow strange developments in the local circumstances. Now I judged that the time had come to centralise the organisation more and first achieved a situation that both straits fortresses – as far as it also concerns warfare and defensive measures – were subordinated directly to me as 'Governor-General of the Straits', while I remained affiliated to the Main Headquarters. This new position corresponds to that of an Army Command. On 24 April, when the signs increasingly pointed to renewed hostile action against the Dardanelles, the Minister of War on 25 April transferred to me the direct command over land and sea forces in the Dardanelles fortress area; while I agreed at the same time with the head of Your Majesty's Mediterranean Division, in his position as Turkish Naval Commander, that elements of the fleet should also be subordinate to me, as long as they stayed in the fortress area but, however, authority for allocation and withdrawal of these elements remains with the Naval Commander.'[269]

Most of the German officers, NCOs and other ranks who came from the Mediterranean Division (MMD) or the Special Unit (SoKo) were distributed among the fortifications and of whom Admiral von Usedom proudly commented: 'Despite the recognition of the purely German character of the troops subordinated to me, I succeeded in them taking over the most important batteries in both straits; Turkish soldiers are used in these batteries only as 'auxiliaries' and reserves'.[270]

As an example, Lieutenant Commander Wossidlo took command of the Hamidiè fort to the south of Canakkale with its 35.5 cm guns. Approximately 170 of the remaining Germans worked together with the Turkish crews of the fortifications and, essentially, provided their training. The mobile artillery, which was under the command of Lieutenant Colonel Wehrle, undertook an important role in the Straits' defence. Wehrle commanded the 8th Heavy Field Artillery Regiment and with his troops, including a training battalion, he had moved to the Dardanelles in September 1914. The heavy field artillery batteries, which had been distributed to both shores, were to conduct the defence against ships penetrating into the Dardanelles from constantly changing positions, as well as monitor the minefields against sweeping. Firing and alert exercises, as well as the intelligence and supply services, had only previously been rehearsed very insufficiently.

Lieutenant Colonel Wehrle wrote about the state of the gun crews and the weapons:

'Soon after its institution, the training battalion fired, in the presence of the Marshal (Liman von Sanders), from a concealed position against a drifting target. Because of the lack of practice and suitable aiming procedures, the result was exceedingly pitiful. I explained the reasons to the very disappointed and angry Commander-in-Chief and assured him that firing procedures would be practised that would exclude such failures. I was firmly determined to have all batteries fire against moving targets; but everything was lacking to be able to carry out even a simple procedure based on precise range finding, as is required for coastal firing.'[271]

Wehrle set up provisional range finding devices made of oak and practised firing at moving targets, as well as rapid repositioning of the light guns. He wrote:

'I can touch quite briefly on the following period, which was equally strenuous for the regiment and me. Every day brought new disappointments and bit by bit I recognised that we had to start completely from the ground up. All German concepts of the independence of the junior commanders melted away; from the simple gunner up to the battalion commander there was no duty which did not have to be demonstrated or done by oneself. The constant fight against unpunctuality, sluggishness, deceit and abuse of official power could only be dealt with by means of the most austere punishment.'[272]

Lieutenant Colonel Wehrle.

Turkish 7.5 cm quick firing cannon on Gallipoli. (*Bundesarchiv Koblenz*)

However, in a report by Admiral von Usedom dated 18 December 1914, the first results were sent to Berlin:

'The training of the Turkish artillery crews in the coastal facilities has continued and produced very good results. The last firing exercises in both straits proved not only considerable progress in accuracy but also in the management of the batteries by the Turkish officers, of whom a larger number has turned out to be trainable than was previously assumed.'[273]

He further explained appreciatively:

'Lieutenant Commander Gehl, who has been posted to the Special Unit [SoKo] and operates here as a major of Army Engineers, has done very well in refurbishing old mines and has been masterful in finding and using existing material that was unknown to the Turkish officers.'

Numerous dummy positions were built to draw enemy fire. The US Ambassador, Morgenthau, who had visited the Dardanelles at the invitation of the Germans, described the implementation of this idea:

'South of Erenkeui, on the hills bordering the road, the Germans had introduced an innovation. They had found several Krupp howitzers left over from the Bulgarian war and had installed them on concrete foundations. Each battery had four or five of these emplacements so that, as I approached them, I found several substantial bases that apparently had no guns. I was mystified further at the sight of a herd of buffaloes––-I think I counted sixteen, engaged in the operation – hauling one of these howitzers from one emplacement to another. This, it seems, was part of the plan of defence. As soon as the dropping shells indicated that the fleet had obtained the range, the howitzer would be moved, with the aid of buffalo-teams, to another concrete emplacement.

"We have an even better trick than that," remarked one of the officers. They called out a sergeant, and explained his achievement. This soldier was the custodian of a contraption which, at a distance, looked like a real gun, but which, when I examined it near at hand, was apparently an elongated section of sewer pipe. [At the] back of a hill, entirely hidden from the fleet, was placed the gun with which this sergeant had cooperated. The two were connected by telephone. When the command came to fire, the gunner in charge of the howitzer would discharge his shell, while the man in charge of the sewer pipe would burn several pounds of black powder and send forth a conspicuous cloud of inky smoke. Not unnaturally, the Englishmen and Frenchmen on the ships would assume that the shells speeding in their direction came from the visible smoke cloud and would proceed to centre all their attention upon that spot.[274]

The American Ambassador wrote about his meeting with Lieutenant Colonel Wehrle:

'The first fortification I visited was that of Anadolu Hamidié (that is, Asiatic Hamidié), located on the water's edge just outside of Çanak. My first impression was that I was in Germany. The officers were practically all Germans and everywhere Germans were building buttresses with sacks of sand and in other ways strengthening the emplacements. Here German, not Turkish, was the language heard on every side. Colonel Wehrle, who conducted me over these batteries, took the greatest delight in showing them. He had the simple pride of the artist in his work, and told me of the happiness that had come into his days when Germany had at last found herself at war. All his life, he said, he had spent in military exercises and, like most Germans, he had become tired of manoeuvres, sham battles, and other forms of mock hostilities. Yet he was approaching fifty, he had become a colonel, and he was fearful that his career would end without actual military experience.'[275]

A clearly limiting factor in the defence of the Dardanelles lay in the meagre ammunition stocks. This was caused by an inadequate logistics organisation and the limited possibilities of manufacturing large-calibre ammunition in Turkey. As at that time there was no secure land connection through the borders of friendly nations, support could only be given with difficulty from German war industry. New aiming and signal technologies were procured from Germany and smuggled through Bulgaria and Romania into Turkey. Walter von Schoen wrote about the transport of munitions and munition parts:

'The most ingenious means had to be taken to bring ammunition and technical equipment 'from the rear' through Romania. Machine guns were hidden in cement blocks for the 'construction of the Baghdad road', breech blocks and spare parts rested on the bottom of barrels filled with oil, many freight wagons had double walls in which many useful things could be stowed away.'[276]

All available supplies of artillery ammunition as well as naval weapons already in Turkey were sent to the Dardanelles. Among them were also twenty-six *Carbonit* sea mines, which had come via devious ways from Germany. These mines were to play a critical role in the coming battle – they were used by the mine-layer *Nusret* for the devastating line of mines in Erenkeui Bay.

The Mediterranean Division provided not only staff but also ships' heavy guns, which were dismantled for this purpose in the Istinye Shipyard, transported in smaller boats to the Dardanelles and then incorporated into the gun emplacements. On 2 March 1915 Admiral Souchon sent to the Dardanelles: two 8.8cm guns with ammunition; on 9 March 200 15cm shells; on 16 and 20 March respectively, twelve mines and later two 15cm guns from the *Goeben*.[277] In addition, the mine fields and the torpedo battery at Kilid Bahr, under the professional management of Lieutenant Commander Gehl, had been clearly improved.[278]

In this situation it was a piece of luck that Captain Pieper, the former captain of the Imperial German Navy cruiser *Yorck*, was posted to the MMD. Pieper had been accused of being responsible for the loss of the *Yorck* on 4 November 1914 in a German minefield close to Wilhelmshaven in the North Sea, and thus for the death of 336 sailors. He had been sentenced by a court martial to a form of imprisonment, known as *custodia honesta*, whereby he could move freely around the citadel where he was confined and receive visitors but could not leave it. Pieper was given probation for military war service and released from his confinement. He was, therefore, not unhappy to come to Turkey and put this incident behind him. Souchon wrote:

'I have put a great deal of effort into ensuring that the unfortunate *Yorck* commander, Captain Pieper, comes here for coastal defence. The start of his sentence will be suspended until the end of the war. He is an experienced gunnery specialist and will be able to rehabilitate himself in the Dardanelles fortifications.'[279]

Captain Pieper. (*Sammlung Soytürk*)

When, for personal reasons, Admiral von Usedom did not want to have Captain Pieper in the Dardanelles, Souchon was able to convince Enver Paşa to use Captain Pieper as Head of the Turkish Ordnance Department. In this capacity he performed both astonishingly well and decisively and very quickly improved the quality and output of production from the different armaments factories in Istanbul. Now even von Usedom, who had initially turned him down as a staff officer on his own staff, found words of praise in recognising his achievements. He reported: 'Captain Pieper applies himself to his duties with great devotion, even when new supplies have not yet reached the front line. By regulating available supplies, he has ensured the continuation of the battle.'[280]

After the successful battles on the Gallipoli Peninsula, von Usedom was even more lavish in his praise: 'I am not going too far if I suggest that without the achievements made by Captain Pieper and his organisation the enemy attacks on the Gallipoli peninsula could not have been beaten off in the long run.'[281]

In a detailed report of 25 January 1916, Captain Pieper, who now held the rank of a Turkish major general, summarised the work of the Ordnance Inspectorate, which was subordinated to him:

'In this respect an excellent cooperation with German spirit has developed, which is felt here with particular joy and which has not been affected by the slightest differences. Elsewhere in this report it was explained how the quality of the munitions was made the object of special care and control. In this respect the contribution of the ordnance officers was particularly valuable, who have proved themselves very able in controlling, mixing and also to a large extent in manufacturing [the munitions].'[282]

In his report Pieper described the difficulties in the supply of raw materials and the expansion of the munition production plants. For those reasons, not only were facilities brought in that had been requisitioned from occupied territory but German-speaking metal working specialists were employed. They had already been active in Turkey and could now train the growing number of Turkish workers. His report contained a detailed list of the personnel in his department, showing that all divisions were headed by German officers, whilst many experts, such as ordnance specialists, in the rank of sergeant, were involved in production. Altogether there were: seventy-four service officers, officials, engineers and chemists; forty-seven master craftsmen; and 659 workers brought in from Germany, who trained and supported more than 14,000 workers in all the Turkish armament factories.

Shells of calibres from 7.5cm to 21cm were produced and fuse production was undertaken for twenty-one different kinds of shells. Some of the raw materials for the shell factories came from the railway workshops; however, shell fragments were also collected from the battlefield and re-smelted. Gunpowder had to be produced and a firing range was established close to Istanbul for testing weapons and ammunition. New weapons and equipment, i.e. guns, fire control devices, rifles and close combat weapons, such as rockets, stick grenades, mines and bomb throwers, were produced, all of which were used, mainly from the summer of 1915, in the battles on Gallipoli.[283]

Notwithstanding this progress, owing to the high expenditure of ammunition by the continuous employment of Turkish artillery, there were still bottlenecks in the supply of shells for the Gallipoli front. This situation caused Ambassador von Wangenheim to telegraph Berlin on 1 July 1915:

'General Pieper, organiser of the Turkish armaments production, told me that if 400-450 wagonloads of ammunition could be sent here immediately it would help him to sustain supplies for the critical period of about one month, which time is needed to bring production up to the necessary level for the effective defence of the Dardanelles.'[284]

All this hard work by Captain Pieper brought a much-desired reward; it was now so highly appreciated that the Kaiser decreed, on 8 December 1915:

'… in recognition of his excellent merits in connection with the ordnance and particularly for munitions production in Turkey, which has substantially contributed to the previous success of the allied Turkish armed forces, the remaining part of the court martial sentence of 28 December 1914 of imprisonment (*custodia honesta*) is remitted.'[285]

Chapter 6

The Sea Battles for the Dardanelles

Turkey's entry into the war on the side of the Central Powers did not bring about the strategic advantage for which Germany had hoped. Bulgaria and Romania did not join the alliance with the Central Powers and remained neutral. Thus a direct overland transportation link between these allied states was still missing and this was of decisive importance for delivering essential weapons and ammunition to Turkey. Even Romania insisted on its neutrality and no longer permitted freight from Germany to pass through its territory, which had previously been possible by paying bribes.

In mid-November 1914, based on reports from Istanbul, the Foreign Ministry emphasised in a memorandum to the German High Command that the number of mines in the Dardanelles and the army's ammunition would hardly suffice for two battles, so that ensuring a transit route to Istanbul through Serbia became one of the most important tasks of German war planning.[286] The document pointed out that should Turkish requirements not be fulfilled due to shortage of ammunition, then the possible negative consequence could be the mobilisation of the entire Balkans against the Central Powers. On the other hand, as a positive effect of a campaign against Serbia, and thus by keeping the Turkish army as an ally, then 700,000 Turks as well as a further 400,000 men of the Bulgarian army could be made 'usable' for German purposes. Towards the end of November 1914 Austro-Hungarian troops tried to defeat Serbia but during the first half of December this offensive ended in a severe rout and the Central Powers' withdrawal from Serbia. The overland route to Turkey remained blocked.

Field Marshal von der Goltz was again posted to Istanbul in November 1914, transferred from a controversial period as military governor of Belgium. This assignment had been engineered on the initiative of Ambassador von Wangenheim, who evidently wanted to be rid of the recalcitrant General Liman von Sanders and hoped that he would be better able to exercise influence on the conciliatory old Field Marshal.[287] When von Sanders learned of Wangenheim's efforts to bring back von der Goltz, he tried to dissuade the head of the Military Cabinet in Berlin and stated that, in his view, his relationship with the Ambassador was not as bad as was apparently mistakenly assumed. Von Sanders received support through a letter that Lieutenant Colonel Thauvenay, a member of the Military Mission and now quartermaster at Turkish Headquarters, wrote to the Under-Secretary at the Foreign Office. In the letter, Thauvenay tried to excuse the conflicts between the Head of the Military Mission and the Ambassador, indicating that it was due to the General's military integrity and straightforwardness. He considered von der Goltz was unfit to have an active role in the Turkish military, since he had already 'sinned enough in the Turkish army' and what was needed was 'not a smiling advisor but a firm hand'.[288] This entreaty was unsuccessful however, and von der Goltz arrived in Istanbul on 12 December 1914. But not even von der Goltz himself knew for what purpose he had been assigned to Turkey. He had received no clear instructions or support from either Germany or the Turks. Von der Goltz was not made subordinate to the Military Mission, had no other powers and was therefore not suitable for the German Ambassador's intention, which was namely that he should act as a replacement for Liman von Sanders. On the contrary – in a telegram on the departure of the Field Marshal from Berlin, it was said that the posting was 'merely an act of courtesy and has nothing to do with warfare or military operations'.[289] This was understandably unsatisfactory for von der Goltz, who still regarded himself as the figurehead of German–Turkish cooperation and was now bitterly disappointed with his dubious status and lack of recognition:

> 'Here I am only to hold a purely honorary position. Not even an adjutant was to be allocated to me. […] Any rights, powers or courses of action to gain influence have not been granted to me. I was not authorized to recruit other officers. All these rights, especially a significant monetary fund, however, were placed at General v. Liman's disposal, were contractually guaranteed to him, and the Military Cabinet nervously ensured that I was not interfering with these rights.'[290]

Nevertheless, at the beginning of February 1915 the Sultan gave von der Goltz the function of an advisor at the Turkish headquarters and let him take part at General Staff meetings. Although he felt like a 'spare wheel' in this position he nonetheless gave expert advice to the Turkish leadership and wrote assessments and reports to Berlin. Thus during these weeks von der Goltz principally viewed his task as explaining to Istanbul the war question against Serbia and in supporting the new Chief of the General Staff, Erich von Falkenhayn, with his assessments. He saw the advantage of a military operation against Serbia as of grand strategic effect, both in Turkey and in the Balkans, and wrote to Falkenhayn:

> 'If, on the other hand, we succeed in bringing the Balkan states over to our side through early success in Serbia, our prevalence over Russia would be finally settled. We have Bulgaria and as soon as we or our allies are with strong forces in Niš the rest will follow on. Then the well-equipped Turkish army of six corps, now inactive in Thrace and Constantinople, can be used.'[291]

Von Falkenhayn was not against this line of reasoning, but had to keep his eye on all the theatres of war and thus saw no possibility of carrying out a major offensive against Serbia. Even the Austrian Chief of the General Staff, Franz Conrad von Hötzendorf, saw no chance of even a limited operation against Serbia in order to open just a single corridor as a transport route.

Meanwhile, on 3 November 1914, the Allies had launched a first attack on the entrance to the Dardanelles – apparently, however, more with the intention of probing the defence capability or damaging installations than trying to make a breakthrough. Lieutenant Colonel Wehrle reported:

> On the morning of the 3rd at 7 o'clock, 10 English[sic] and French ships of the line were lying in two semicircles at the entrance of the strait, and fired at the two forts at Kumkale and Seddulbahr from a position 16,000 metres away, where no Turkish guns could reach. Out of the slight morning mist, muzzle flashes constantly light up, the forts are shrouded in smoke and dust from which continuous tongues of flame rise up. Half an hour later a tremendous white cloud of smoke appears over Seddulbahr, and stayed in the air for minutes. A [sound like] heavy thunder is heard. The ships peel off and disappear in the haze. That was the start, but a bad start. Through an incomprehensible act of carelessness by a coastal battery, many hundreds of hundredweights of old gunpowder had remained piled up in an underground storage area. This storage area was hit by a shell and the whole battery, along with 5 officers and 60 men, were blown to pieces.'[292]

After this attack and during the following weeks it remained quiet in the Dardanelles. This afforded the Turks more time to continue their preparations for defence. An additional Turkish artillery battalion had been assigned in mid-December for the defence of Beşika Bay (just slightly north of Nagara); Lieutenant Colonel Wehrle first of all had to put this unit through some basic training:

'Simply looking at them, my head was shaking in disbelief and even my Turkish battery commanders, who were used to many things, remained speechless at this pile of military destitution. The battalion was taken in hand and two days were needed to restore order and bearing. First, everything went to the delousing facility, which was set up in a bakery. Meanwhile officers and NCOs of the Howitzer Regiment were tasked to inspect materiel and equipment, any items deficient were noted and indents placed with the quartermaster. Fourteen days later Marshal Liman v. Sanders visited the battalion in its firing position. Chance would have it that just at the time, when we were standing in one of the batteries, a destroyer was approaching the shore. The Marshal gave the order to fire. This battery had never before fired a single live shot. I prompted the battery commander, checked the sighting and the first shot near the target caused the boat to turn off. The battery was praised and was very proud. The following day, a French cruiser appeared and gave us thanks with 60 heavy shells, which it fired – not at the battery but against a dune 200 metres away, which I had set up at night, using tree trunks as a decoy.'[293]

Meanwhile, new calls for help went out from Istanbul to Berlin. On 30 December, Ambassador von Wangenheim announced that, with the continuing geographical isolation of Turkey, 'the moment could be foreseen where Turkish thirst for action and will to fight may cease'. On 4 January 1915 Falkenhayn was notified about a meeting of the generals and admirals stationed in Istanbul regarding the ammunition situation in Turkey, where they concluded that even with the most economical consumption, 'the ammunition for the army and navy would only last until mid-March'. Admiral von Usedom, who was responsible for the defence of the Dardanelles, had also stated that 'he could vouch for the defence capability of the Dardanelles against a first attack, but that he could not give the same guarantee for a repeated attack'.[294]

Churchill had discussed the question of opening the Dardanelles in November 1914 in the context of a new strategic offensive in southern Europe to win over the Romanians, Bulgarians and perhaps the Greeks as allies; however, this plan was not pursued due to a lack of available forces. Only at the beginning of January 1915, in response to a request from Russia, who wished to take the pressure off their Caucasus front, was further planning resumed in London. However, since the British Secretary of State for War, Lord Kitchener, did not want to make troops available for the Orient Front, the commander of the British Mediterranean Fleet, Vice Admiral Sackville Carden, was asked how this task could be achieved. He replied on 5 January that although he could not take the Dardanelles by a surprise rush attack, he could take them with the fleet in a large and extended operation. This statement formed the basis for the decision of the British Military Council on 28 January 1915, which recommended an attack on the Dardanelles solely as a fleet action.[295] Preparations for this attack took several weeks. In mid-February it was believed that the plans for attack were ready. On 19 January, Russia had been informed of the intended operation; in London it was expected that with the operation to force the Dardanelles, Russia would at the same time carry out a naval attack on the Bosphorus and a landing on the Turkish Black Sea coast. This, however, was rejected by Moscow due to insufficient forces being available.

Meanwhile the Allied fleet, lying off the Dardanelles, had been considerably strengthened. In addition to the sixteen large British battleships and cruisers, four French battleships and the Russian protected cruiser *Askold* arrived in January, so that at least twenty-one large warships were now off the Dardanelles. At first the Allied fleet limited itself to continuous monitoring of the entrance to the Dardanelles. From mid-January 1915, there were signs that the Western powers intended an attack on the Straits. On 15 January a French submarine broke through the defensive anti-submarine net stretched across the Dardanelles. Through the courageous intervention of Navy Lieutenant Prince Reuss, who set course in a small ship towards the submarine and dropped depth charges, the submarine was forced to surface at Nagara and fired on by coastal batteries. The Austro-Hungarian Military Representative in Turkey, Field Marshal Lieutenant (*Feldmarschalleutnant*) Josef Pomiankowski, reported:

'As an enemy submarine appeared shortly thereafter, it was immediately fired upon and severely damaged, leaving the commander with no choice but to surrender. The crew was captured, but the boat - it was the French submarine *Saphir* – was towed to Constantinople, where I had the opportunity to inspect it. *Saphir* belonged to a very outdated type, and was also much neglected. German naval officers told me that in the German fleet boats of this type no longer existed.'[296]

Beginning on 2 February, individual ships began to shell the outer fortifications. On 19 February the Anglo-French fleet again shelled the outer fortifications of the Dardanelles with twelve warships. Admiral von Usedom described this in detail and thus gave an example of the leadership qualities of the German forces taking part:

'The French used their heavy artillery, the Englishmen [sic] followed soon thereafter with their medium artillery, so that now broadside salvoes were being fired at three minute intervals against all four forts. The batteries were heavily hit; and clear hits could be made out in the fort at Seddulbahr and in the Kumkale battery. At Fort Orhanié the clouds of smoke from the explosions were right in front of the traverses. The ships came closer and closer to the forts. Apparently they believed the batteries to have been fully destroyed. This now gave Orhanié and Ertugrul the opportunity to counter-fire at 16.45 hrs. At the same time all hell broke loose, in which all the ships now seemed to take part. At intervals of 40 seconds, salvo followed salvo. At times, the forts were completely obscured by the black clouds of the explosions. Nevertheless, Orhanié and Ertugrul continued firing. Towards 18.00 hrs, the enemy broke off the bombardment. The battery commander of Orhanié, Lieutenant Hans Woermann, as well as the Turkish interpreter and telephonist, who had been in the second observation station of the battery, were killed at 16.10 hrs by 2 shells of 15 cm calibre, after being forced to abandon the first observation post as a result of it being hit. Deputy Ordnance Technician Joerss, sheltering with others outside the battery, assumed the post of the dead battery commander. Since the phone line was out, he no longer had communications with the other batteries. On his own initiative, when the second enemy ship came into bearing from the left, he opened fire at a distance of 44 hm [4400 metres]. Then the Englishman immediately turned to starboard to increase the range.'[297]

The losses caused by this attack totalled four dead, including two Germans, and nine wounded on the Turkish side. Lieutenant Colonel Kannengiesser wrote about this attack:

'The first attack on 19 February 1915 was aimed at the outer forts of Seddulbahr and Kumkale at the entrance [of the Dardanelles], which were fired at from long range, and vanished under a dense hail of shells, smoke, dust and splinters. Aircraft directed the fire. How can 30-year old

Fort Seddulbahr before the bombardment on 19 February 1915.

guns with quite outdated traverse and firing methods counter this? As Carden withdrew his ships when darkness falls, the loss of people and materiel is insignificant.'[298]

The destruction was judged to be low in relation to the estimated 800 to 1000 shots fired by the Allied naval guns. At Kumkale, only a 28-cm gun had been permanently knocked out, but Fort Seddulbahr had suffered greater damage. In preparation for the breakthrough and also for landing operations, the forts at Kumkale and Seddulbahr were systematically bombarded almost every day. With field artillery support, the forward Turkish infantry managed to beat off the smaller Allied daylight landings, which were aimed at demolishing gun barrels and ammunition bunkers in the forts. On 25 February 1915 the Allied fleet made another attack on the outer forts, which were almost completely destroyed after a seven-hour bombardment.

These initial experiences of the Allied fleet and their limited visible successes led to new British operational planning. The experience during the British fleet's 1807 Dardanelles breakthrough was also remembered, in which, after entering the Marmara Sea, fleet re-supply was disrupted by Turkish troops on either side of the Dardanelles. Therefore land forces had to be included in the planning to secure the coastal areas after the breakthrough. The basic decision was made on 16 February 1915, but it was only on 10 March that the total strength of the Expeditionary Force was finalised: four English divisions and one French division. However, the exact operational role for this force had not yet been defined. It should follow the outcome of the fleet operations, which were maintained. Thus there was still no joint or coordinated operational planning for the deployment of Allied naval and land forces.[299]

Despite the Entente's limited success so far, the attacks on the Dardanelles had caused great concern in Istanbul. Although Turkey had already been a Central Powers' alliance partner for several months, deliveries of much needed supplies from Germany still could not be transported there and unrest began to grow against the background of the imminently anticipated attack on the Dardanelles. On 1 March Enver wrote to von Falkenhayn that the situation was serious, as the Allied fleet was gradually destroying fortifications and could thus force a passage through the Straits. In a second telegram of 8 March, Enver recalled the precarious situation and described the opening-up of an overland transportation route through Serbia as the 'vital question for Turkey'.[300] On 10 March, Admiral von Usedom wrote to von Falkenhayn: 'Despite the relatively meagre success of the enemy, destruction of all the Dardanelles fortifications cannot be prevented in the long run, if the munitions and mines which have been on order for months do not arrive as soon as possible.'

The Foreign Office warned:

'Should the Dardanelles and Constantinople fall, this would not only signify a great moral boost for the Entente, with immense repercussions for all of Islam and for Turkey's existential endangerment, but also a revitalisation of the war effort in Russia and France, thus not only prolonging the war but also driving all the Balkan states (Bulgaria and Romania) into the arms of the Entente.'[301]

Meanwhile, a major Allied landing operation at Kumkale on 3 March underlined the urgent nature of the munitions question. The almost 400 man strong landing detachment of the Royal Marine Light Infantry was, however, beaten back. The attackers suffered casualties totalling seventy dead and wounded. From the equipment left behind, the Turks concluded that this was not just a temporary landing but was apparently intended to occupy permanently the extreme tip of the Asian side of the Dardanelles.

However, the attacks now beginning to be made against the inner defensive positions only made little progress. To carry these out the fleet had to enter into the waters of the Dardanelles and thus loose its freedom of movement and 'passive' protection. In addition to the danger from the guns of the defence emplacements and the minefields in the waterway, the attackers also faced the threat of the mobile 15 cm howitzer batteries on both sides of the coast. The ships were therefore forced to manoeuvre quickly, which consequently reduced their firing accuracy. Thus they succeeded in neither destroying the Turkish batteries nor in clearing the numerous minefields.

On 5 March the batteries at Kilid Bahr, on the opposite side of Canakkale, were shelled by indirect fire. This attack was reciprocated by indirect fire from the Turkish ships of the line, *Barbarossa* and *Torgut*. In anticipation of these battles, the German captain of the *Barbarossa*, Lieutenant Commander Joachim von Arnim, had already been ashore to set up a fire control observation post on the heights of the southern peninsula. Although this post came under fire later, as it had revealed its position by the use of signal ammunition, by a rapid relocation the post could continue support the Turkish ships for effective fire. In the days which followed these observation posts were expanded, surveyed and connected to telephone exchanges. Lieutenant Rolf Carls, the gunnery officer of the *Breslau,* was commended for his actions in this work.[302]

On the morning of 7 March, two large British warships, the *Agamemnon* and the *Lord Nelson,* accompanied by several French vessels, entered Karanlik Bay and began shelling Dardanos and the inside forts. Firing at the same time from Kaba Tepe, the *Queen Elizabeth* bombarded the forts, while HMS *Dublin* shelled the Bulair fortifications from the Gulf of Saros. The British warships moved inside the straits to push closer to the forts, but then they came within range of the Turkish coastal artillery. The naval guns fired in quick succession, but the warships withdrew after a short

A naval artillery observation post on land: standing left, Lieutenant Franz Wodrig, right Lieutenant Rolf Carls. (*Sammlung Soytürk*)

time because of the hefty resistance and without having inflicted (or incurred) any significant damage. During the bombardment it was observed that the Allied ships remained mostly in the Bay of Erenkeui, where they were largely outside the range of the fortress guns. Again and again, the 15-cm howitzers commanded by Lieutenant Colonel Wehrle, expending the then huge tally of 800 shells, had fired on the enemy warships in the Dardanelles, which forced them to keep moving and thus ensured that the ships simply 'wasted ammunition'.[303]

Even though by night there were entire flotillas of ships, protected by smaller vessels and destroyers, trying to clear the minefields, the Turks were constantly laying new mines. A special line of mines, which had been laid in the turning circle of retiring Allied warships, was to acquire decisive significance. The planning was carried out by Major Nazim Emin, the Chief of the Dardanelles Mine Service, who had a comprehensive knowledge of the currents and depth conditions. The Coastal Inspectorate assigned the minelayer *Nusret* for this task, while Naval Engineer Lieutenant Commander Arnholdt Reeder, of the German Imperial Navy, represented the SoKo (Special Command) on board. A torpedo specialist, Lieutenant Commander Paul Gehl, was assigned by the Straits Command to be on board *Nusret* as well.

Lieutenant Commander Reeder submitted his report to the MMD on this operation, which made a major contribution to thwarting the Allied naval attack of 18 March 1915:

'On 7 March, at 11.30 in the afternoon [sic], I went on board the minelayer *Nusret* with Hafis Nasimi, the Turkish Mine Captain and Petty Officer Rudolf Bettaque, the German torpedo-man, to make the necessary preparations for minelaying. While I was personally double-checking the engine room and then got the boilers ready for smokeless sailing,

The Nusret in the Dardanelles. (*Deniz Kitabevli*)

the torpedo-man, Bettaque,[304] and the Turkish mine-laying crew cleared the mines ready for launch. Two German NCOs and stokers were at my disposal for the operation of the engines and boiler. This was to guarantee that my commands were executed quickly and correctly. At 5 o'clock in the morning I had the anchor raised. The weather was good for this operation. A light mist lay on the water, which gradually turned into a steady rain. With an average of 140 revolutions, the minelayer made its way from Nagara along the Asian coast.

Since it was still dark and several minefields had to be negotiated, great caution was needed. However, the Turkish Mine Captain knew the critical points exactly, and so *Nusret* arrived safely at its destination. Throughout the voyage, [engine] revolutions were maintained according to my orders. This enabled me to sail completely smokeless, although the Turkish *Eregi* coal is very unsuitable for this purpose. At 07.10 hrs I had us turnabout and bound for home; simultaneously, I had the mines laid at 15 second intervals by Hafis Nasimi, the Turkish Mine Captain. Overall, 26 mines were laid in the general direction of SW-NE. Meanwhile the morning was already beginning to turn grey. The enemy guard piquet had apparently already withdrawn; within the Dardanelles no enemy ship could be seen. The visibility towards Canakkale was too low due to the rain and the dark background. With reasonable certainty I can therefore assume that the laying of the mines was not noticed by the enemy. At 8 o'clock in the morning, I was able to anchor again at Canakkale.'[305]

This line, which had been laid with twenty-six Carbonit mines supplied from Germany, remained undetected until the attack on 18 March 1915. Churchill later wrote that 'the *Nusret* may have changed the world', as these mines shattered the dream of reaching Istanbul.

This example of effective cooperation between Turkish and German military personnel has unfortunately been wholly ignored since by the Turks and this successful minelaying operation attributed exclusively to the Turkish crew.

The Allied fleet attacks on the Dardanelles, as well as mine clearance, were therefore far less successful than was assumed by the British and French. Nevertheless, rumours were heard in Istanbul that a successful attack by the Entente was imminent, causing unrest and sometimes panic in the city. When an official visit to the fortifications by the Diplomatic Corps was organised, the Austro-Hungarian Military Attaché, Josef Pomiankowski, reported:

'We left Constantinople on the morning of 14 March. As far as I could tell, Enver Pasha had organised this excursion mainly for the American Ambassador, Mr. Morgenthau, who spread the most alarming rumours among the diplomatic corps, about the hopeless situation of Turkey and the forthcoming appearance of the Anglo–French fleet off Istanbul. [...] The greatest interest was aroused by the battery at Dardanos, so named after the still visible ruins of the eponymous city of antiquity. This battery was located at the top of the heights and visible from afar, consisting of a one-metre high earthen breastwork of the ordinary type, behind which cannons were placed so that the barrels could shoot just above the ridge line. To protect the gun crew, they were provided with small steel shields., The enemy ships (especially on 7 March) had already bombarded this battery with a thousand shells, without somehow damaging it. By contrast, the entire area in front, as well as the forward part of the earthworks, were literally ploughed up and turned over by shells. On the protective shields one noticed only two dents, which apparently originated from exploding fragments. The crew serving the guns had suffered no losses; however, on 7 March, a shell had hit the observation post of the battery commander, which was about 15 steps away, and had killed him, along with

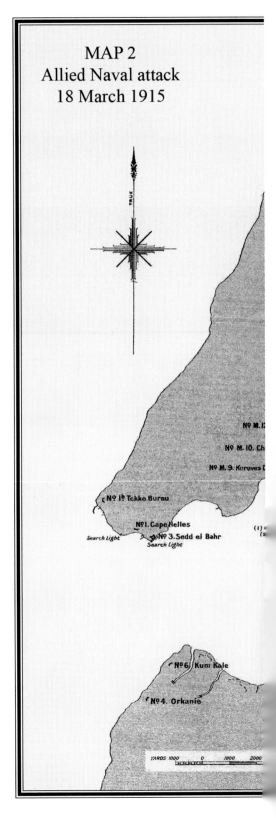

MAP 2
Allied Naval attack
18 March 1915

The Naval Battle of 18 March 1915.

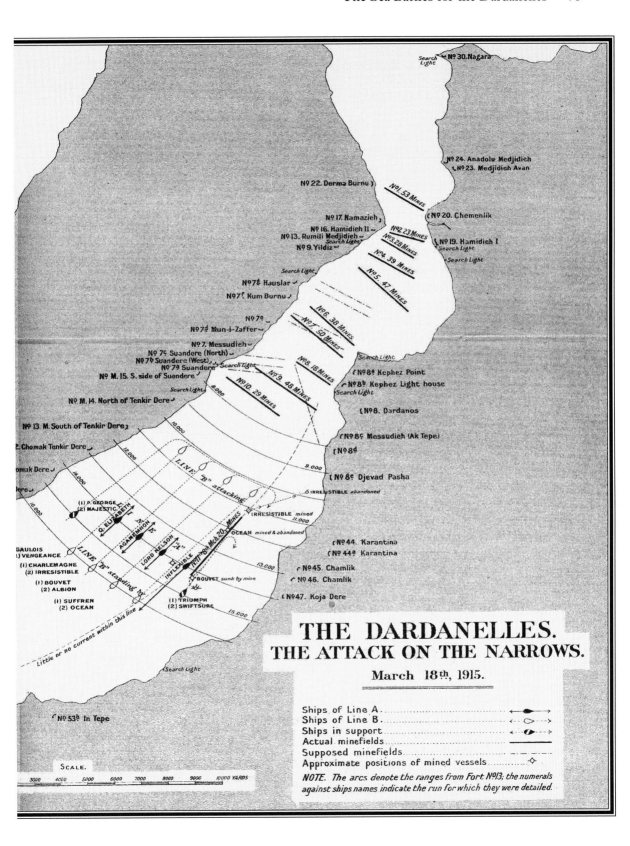

No 30. Nagara

No 24. Anadolu Medjidieh
No 23. Medjidieh Avan

No 22. Derma Burnu

No I. 53 MINES

No 20. Chemenlik

No 17. Namazieh
No 16. Hamidieh II
No 13. Rumili Medjidieh
Search Light
No 9. Yildiz

No 2. 23 MINES
No 3. 28 MINES

No 19. Hamidieh I
Search Light

No 4. 39 MINES
Search Light

No 7c Hauslar
No 7b Kum Burnu

No 5. 47 MINES

No 7e

No 7d Mun-i-Zaffer

No 6. 38 MINES
No 7. 50 MINES

No 7. Messudieh
No 7c Suandere (North)
No 7b Suandere (West)
Search Light
No 7a Suandere
No M. 15. S. side of Suandere

No 8. 18 MINES
Search Light

No 8a Kephez Point
No 8b Kephez Light house
Search Light

No M. 14. North of Tenkir Dere
Search Light

No 9. 48 MINES
8.000

No 10. 29 MINES

No 8. Dardanos

No 13. M. South of Tenkir Dere

10.000

No 8c Messudieh (Ak Tepe)
No 8d

Chomak Tenkir Dere

12.000

LINE "B" attacking

9.000

No 8e Djevad Pasha

omak Dere

14.000

IRRESISTIBLE abandoned

ere

16.000

(1) P. GEORGE
(2) MAJESTIC

Q. ELIZABETH

IRRESISTIBLE mined
11.000

OCEAN mined & abandoned

GAULOIS
(1) VENGEANCE
(1) CHARLEMAGNE
(2) IRRESISTIBLE

AGAMEMNON

LORD NELSON

LINE "A"
INFLEXIBLE

No 17. 78th Mch 20 MINES

No 44. Karantina
No 44a Karantina

(1) BOUVET
(2) ALBION

13.000

BOUVET sunk by mine

No 45. Chamlik
No 46. Chamlik

(1) SUFFREN
(2) OCEAN

LINE "B" standing by

(1) TRIUMPH
(2) SWIFTSURE

No 47. Koja Dere

15.000

Little or no current within this line

Search Light

No 53b In Tepe

THE DARDANELLES.
THE ATTACK ON THE NARROWS.
March 18th, 1915.

Ships of Line A	⟶
Ships of Line B	⟵•⟶
Ships in support	⟵•⟶
Actual minefields	▬▬
Supposed minefields	▬ ▬ ▬
Approximate positions of mined vessels	◇

NOTE. The arcs denote the ranges from Fort No 13; the numerals against ships names indicate the run for which they were detailed.

SCALE.

3000 4000 5000 6000 7000 8000 9000 10000 YARDS

other soldiers near him. In the afternoon we visited the forts of the European side, then returned aboard the *Jürük*, which started the journey back in the evening and arrived in Istanbul on the morning of the 16th.'[306]

On 18 March the major Allied naval attack began, aiming to force a passage through the Dardanelles. Sixteen large warships, accompanied by many destroyers and minesweepers, approached the entrance of the Dardanelles. However, their approach had already been discovered in the early morning of that same day during the first flight of the new squadron at Canakkale. Captain Erich Serno, together with Lieutenant Commander Karl Schneider, the 2nd General Staff Officer at von Usedom's headquarters, had made a reconnaissance flight. They spotted the enemy fleet and immediately afterwards warned of the apparently imminent attack. Schneider reported:

'Early in the morning, we climbed up [...]. We were flying at an altitude of 1,600 metres. The aircraft was at its ceiling. We realised that we had just flown over old Troy. At Tenedos we easily counted forty ships at anchor. All types were represented [...]. Six battleships now headed in line towards the mouth of the Dardanelles. The battleship *Inflexible* led with the admiral's flag flying.'[307]

Both knew what this gathering of ships meant and flew back immediately to report the impending attack. As far as was possible in the short time available, coastal batteries and artillery units could

Coastal artillery in a firefight against an observation post on Rabbit Island. (*Bundesarchiv Koblenz*)

be forewarned, Six large British battleships, including the *Queen Elizabeth*, with her 38-cm guns, started to attack the defences at Canakkale and Cape Kephes at around 11.30 am - initially staying out of range of the forts.

The Turkish coastal batteries and the mobile artillery units returned fire at the incoming French squadron, which consisted of four battleships and passed the line of British warships at about noon. All the battleships now came closer to their targets – but also within the range of the defending artillery. At around 2 pm the French squadron, which was under great pressure, was relieved by a squadron of six older British battleships. The battle then took an unexpected turn for the Allies, as the French battleship *Bouvet* hit a mine at about 2 pm, capsized in just two minutes and dragged almost the entire crew of 600 men down into the depths with it. Some of the other French ships were badly damaged and retired; the *Gaulois* was heavily damaged by artillery and a mine explosion and had to be beached at Tenedos. At 4 pm the *Inflexible* hit a mine and was barely able to escape out of coastal artillery range into safe waters. Shortly after, the *Irresistible* was hit so badly that she was abandoned and sank in the evening. These heavy losses caused the Allied Fleet Commander to break off the attack at 5 pm. When trying to take the *Irresistible* in tow, the *Ocean* also hit a mine and later had to be abandoned as well. The remaining nine English warships departed the Dardanelles westwards at full speed.[308]

That date, 18 March 1915, marked an unforgettable day of victory for the defenders of the Dardanelles and is still celebrated every year in Turkey – especially in the Armed Forces – as 'Canakkale Day'. The attackers had suffered heavy losses and forfeited the initiative, while the defenders had suffered relatively little damage. Admiral Souchon wrote home about the day's events:

'Yesterday's heavy attack by the English [sic] and French on the Dardanelles ended as a great success for us. Here there is a great joy of victory. The French battleship *Bouvet* ran on to one of the mines laid on 6 March, and sank immediately. The English [sic] battleship *Irresistible* remained shot up, lay immobilised, the English [sic] battleship *Ocean* managed to steam away slowly with a heavy list. A destroyer sunk. Minimal loss on the Turkish side. In total, 2 heavy guns are damaged, of us Germans 2 dead, 7 badly, 7 slightly wounded. Hopefully the Englishmen [sic] will come again today and suffer such losses again. If they really want to succeed, they will have to do it before all the damage to the earthworks, telephones, etc. is completely repaired. Patching up will naturally be the case again this morning.'[309]

As recognised later, the losses suffered by the Allies had been achieved to a large extent by the mines laid on 8 March by the *Nusret*. The Allied fleet had thought this area was already swept clear. In addition, in the days prior to 18 March, there had been no incidents in the area of this particular line of mines. However, it is not clear whether all the ships that sank were all as a result of mines. Von Usedom wrote about this in his report:

'When *Bouvet* came into sight of the headquarters observation post at around 14.00 hrs, a strong smoke emission and listing could be observed, which got bigger and bigger. Three minutes later, *Bouvet* sank. From the speed of its sinking it was concluded that it had run into one of the mines set in the Erenköy Bay on 8 March, especially as it was also in the longitudinal location of this barrier. From later reports by the forward observers and Lieutenant Colonel Wehrle, commanding the howitzer batteries on the European shore, it became clear that the ship had suffered its heavy damage, whilst east of the mines, through artillery fire from Fort Anatoli Hamidié, causing the rapid sinking. It can also be concluded from the behaviour of the other ships that the enemy itself had not reckoned with the presence of mines, for *Triumph*, *Majestic*, *Suffren*, *Gaulois* and *Charlemagne* were heading for the scene of the accident. *Suffren* launched a boat. Motor boats, destroyers and later some mine-sweepers were trying to fish out survivors. In the process, a destroyer sank when hit by shells from the howitzer batteries, and sometime later a mine-sweeper. [...] During this time, Dardanos had been able to clear its guns and at 6 o'clock in the evening, opened a lively and effective fire against *Irresistible*, which was sunk at quarter-past seven in the evening.'[310]

This report puts into better perspective the sometimes over-exaggerated performance and impact of the mines laid down by the *Nusret*. It also shows the viciousness of this merciless battle, as even vessels that were clearly engaged in saving the lives of shipwrecked sailors and which had already put themselves into the minefield danger zone were nevertheless fired upon. Today this would be a clear violation of international military law, which prevailed at that time. This indictment must be made against the German and Turkish forces that took part in this battle and, in retrospect, casts a shadow on their victory over the Allied fleet.

The losses of the Allied fleet were high. Of eighteen ships, six had sunk or been put out of action for a long time. On the side of the defenders, however, only 114 men, including twenty-two German soldiers, were killed or wounded. Of a total of 176 guns, including those of the mobile howitzer batteries, only nine were destroyed. The forts had not been substantially damaged – even though massive numbers of shells had been fired at the fortifications. Of the ten lines of mines in the Dardanelles, nine were still intact. However, the ammunition situation on the Turkish side was critical after this battle. The medium howitzers and minefield batteries had fired half of their ammunition. The five 35.5-cm guns of the fortress artillery had only 271 rounds left; for the eleven 23-cm guns there were only between thirty and fifty-eight rounds available per gun; while the reserve of high-explosive shells, the only effective munition against the battleships, was almost completely used up. A second, similarly heavy, attack would therefore have been difficult to fend off due to a lack of ammunition; a third attack would probably not have been opposed.[311]

In the course of the battle, Major Binhold, a German commander of a field artillery battery, experienced an example of the Turkish custom whereby it was not common practice to pass on bad news. Binhold despatched his Turkish aide-de-camp to find out what had happened to a 15-cm howitzer that was being brought forward. The adjutant found the gun; it had fallen down a slope and the crew were in the process of recapturing the oxen. Returning to his CO, the ADC reported that the howitzer was not far off. Hours later, the aide was sent again to look for the long overdue howitzer. He found that the recovery work was still in progress, but reported back that the howitzer would arrive soon. Not a word of the accident was mentioned as such, as it would surely just lead to trouble. As more time passed by, Binhold set off on horseback himself during a lull in the fighting and saw that the ox-team was finally approaching the position. The circumstances of the delay were eventually explained; because he was familiar with the Turkish mentality, Major Binhold took a lenient view and closed the matter with a simple admonition.[312]

After the 18th, the Commander-in-Chief of the Straits sector, Admiral von Usedom, immediately transferred the remaining ammunition available in the Bosphorus batteries to the Dardanelles. He also had ammunition from the fleet reworked for the calibres in use at the Straits. Mines were brought from Trebizond and Smyrna, even though they were indispensable there too. Although some stocks could be replaced from the modified munition factories in Istanbul, the Turkish government continued to urge Germany finally to provide adequate supplies.

Three days after the Allied naval attack, von Falkenhayn again tried to persuade his Austrian ally to campaign actively against Serbia. Enver Paşa also urged support for the opening of the land route to Germany and said optimistically in a letter to von Falkenhayn on 23 March:

'I do not want our alliance with Germany and Austria to be a burden for these powers, but I am only anxious to help the allies with all we have at our disposal. This would be done to a much greater degree if Serbia is subjugated, thereby ensuring a reliable Bulgaria, as well as making Romania docile, and establishing an open route between us and Germany–Austria. I hope to be able to make other significant forces available for common purposes. Turkey still has half a million trained soldiers in reserve, who can be deployed immediately if armaments are available.'[313]

This letter underlined the strategic importance of Turkey and strengthened von Falkenhayn in his planning. The resulting demand by the German government to the Austro-Hungarian Chief of Staff, Conrad von Hötzendorff, to carry out the Serbian campaign was answered with requests for troops from Turkey. Austria thought such an advance would be possible if Bulgaria took part, Germany provided four divisions, and Turkey '[protects] Bulgaria against Greece and Romania if they intervene and [...] as far as possible, with about two corps [participate] under the Bulgarian Supreme Command directly.'[314] At the beginning of April 1915, von der Goltz was able to deliver a letter from the Kaiser to the Sultan, which announced the start of a Serbian campaign in the 'near future'. This came after von der Goltz himself had been appointed as mediator to Conrad von Hötzendorff to explain the necessity of the war option against Serbia.

Enver responded to the demand from Vienna for troop dispositions on 12 April. In a letter to von Falkenhayn, Enver agreed to 'provide two Army Corps to the Bulgarian Army for a joint operation against Serbia'.[315] But once again the campaign against Serbia did not materialise, which is why Berlin had to think of different ways of solving the transportation problem for ammunition. It even considered using Zeppelins and large aircraft but, unsurprisingly, these methods were rejected because they were impractical.

The defence against an Allied landing operation at the Dardanelles, which was growing more likely with each day that passed, now had to be planned quickly, taking into account the lack of material support from Germany.

Chapter 7

Preparing to Repulse the Allied Landings

Following the naval attack of 18 March, the Anglo–French fleet held back from further attempts to force the Dardanelles. The failed breakthrough brought the British government to the conclusion that the defensive installations of the Dardanelles should now be overcome by a land attack, which would then enable the fleet to sail through the Straits. Under the command of General Sir Ian Hamilton and General Albert d'Amade, an Anglo–French expeditionary force of five divisions, with a total of 75,000 men, was formed. A significant portion of this force consisted of the Australian and New Zealand Army Corps, the initials of which formed the name ANZAC.[316] The collection and concentration of troops in Egypt and the islands in the eastern Mediterranean, however, took time and they were only ready to launch an attack on the Dardanelles at the end of April 1915, almost five weeks after the naval attack.[317]

Until this time the defence of the coastal zones on both sides of the Dardanelles had only been half-heartedly planned by the Turkish High Command. The order of battle stipulated that the northern (European) side was to be defended by the First Army and the southern (Asian) side by the Second Army. Thus, the dividing line between the armies ran along the Straits of the Dardanelles, which would have rendered any uniform command for defence very difficult. Liman von Sanders considered this situation as threatening:

'The 1st Army would then have its front to the south, the 2nd Army its front to the north. Defence of the outer coast of the Gallipoli peninsula, with its dominant heights and defence of the Asian coast at the mouth of the Dardanelles, was dispensed with! It was the weakest defensive measure you could think of.'[318]

On 23 February, therefore, von Sanders wrote to the Turkish Minister of War, pointing out the dangers in this planning. He argued that a Turkish army would have to be stationed in Gallipoli to defend against any enemy landings and another in the vicinity of Istanbul. Enver initially rejected this proposal without an explanation.

Not satisfied with this, von Sanders took up the matter on 1 March with von Wangenheim and the Head of the Military Cabinet in Berlin; whether this German pressure moved Enver Paşa to change his mind cannot be proved. On 24 March the German Fleet Commander, Admiral Souchon, approached War Minister Enver and asked that General von Sanders take command of the Gallipoli defence. Souchon was said to have emphasized that although the current commander, Essad Paşa, is an 'excellent soldier', he did not have great experience and the requisite 'heavy-weight as a field commander'. The efforts of defence planning in the area of Istanbul were clearly to be seen; but on Gallipoli everything was lacking. Souchon went on that only by using all resources and with the greatest possible speed could the conditions there be so improved that 'the prospect of success in repulsing the expected landing of enemy armies could be met'. An hour after the interview, General von Sanders was appointed Commander-in-Chief of the Fifth Army.[319] Sanders wrote:

'Now at last, on 25 March, Enver decided to form a separate army, the Fifth, for the defence of the Dardanelles. My constantly renewed efforts to bring about such a decision from Turkish headquarters had of late received effective support from the German Embassy and Admiral Souchon; Admiral von Usedom, however, after his experiences in China, would not yet believe in the probability of large landing operations.

Late on the afternoon of March 24 Enver asked me to wait for him in my office. He came soon afterwards and asked if I were willing to take command of the Fifth Army, to be organized for the defence of the Dardanelles. I assented at once and informed him that the troops now there would have to be reinforced at once as we had no time to spare.'[320]

Field Marshal Baron Colmar von der Goltz, now aged 72, had entertained high hopes of taking command of the army at the Dardanelles. He had been firmly counting on it and when it never came he was accordingly disappointed. He wrote to Germany:

'One sign of Enver's confidence [in me] was that when I undertook my usual rounds of the headquarters at the end of March on the Sultan's behalf, to push the Serbian campaign forward – now finally starting – he offered me Supreme Command in the Dardanelles. It was agreed that I should assume it on my return. As soon as I left Constantinople I learned through the newspapers that Liman had been appointed in my place. How that came about I have never been able to determine very clearly. On 15 April I was appointed to the Supreme Command of the 1st Army.'[321]

But even this new appointment for von der Goltz was not without some controversy, since Enver had made no previous consultation with Liman von Sanders about it, although Liman's

Field Marshal Colmar von der Goltz in 1915. (*Author's Collection*)

Admiral Guido von Usedom in 1915. (*Gunter Hartnagel Collection*)

competence as Inspector of Turkish forces had provided for this. Thus von der Goltz had to endure further humiliation:

> 'When my appointment as Commander-in-Chief of the First Army had not yet been publicly announced, Liman objected to my appointment on the basis of his contract as well as on the basis of a clause in the Treaty of Alliance, which grant him 'decisive operational influence'. This protest officially went to the German Embassy here. Had I first asked at our Supreme Headquarters, as the Ambassador had suggested to me, the matter would have been brought to the attention of the Military Cabinet, and it would then have been undoubtedly decided to my detriment just the same.'[322]

While General von Sanders and Admiral von Usedom were obviously not happy with the arrival and appointment of Field Marshal von der Goltz, Admiral Souchon was, on the other hand, rather pleased:

> 'Usedom is annoyed that von der Goltz is coming here, because then he can no longer put on airs. By the way, he should be as happy about it as I am, because Goltz is a very sensible man and carries a lot of weight with the Turks, so that hopefully more uniformity comes down the line.'[323]

Although the continued internal friction between the German officers and diplomats assigned to Turkey had so far had no direct impact on the fighting, the clashes were inexcusable stupidity and disloyalty. A poor effect of these disagreements was described at the time by Lieutenant Commander Hans Humann:

> '… through awkwardness, personal [resentment], and the all too human foibles of senior German officers, our position vis-à-vis Enver is more weakened than necessary: Liman shows Souchon's letter to Enver, Usedom tells Enver that Goltz is constantly writing reports home and thus putting the actions of the other German commanders in the wrong light, Liman points out to Enver Usedom's ignorance of warfare and his particularistic attitude towards cooperation. Liman tries to push Bronsart out, Bronsart tries to justify his position by discrediting Liman, and so on.'[324]

Liman von Sanders left Istanbul one day after his appointment and arrived in Gallipoli early on 26 March to set up his headquarters in the village of Galata. He had communicated his arrival by telegram to Admiral Usedom, to whom he wrote on 25 March: 'Your Excellency informed [I have] arrived [in] Gallipoli to take over command of divisions against enemy landings. Going first to 5th and 7th Division then request consultation [with you] for cooperation.'[325]

His staff was made up almost exclusively of Turkish officers – the Germans were his two adjutants, Captains Carl Mühlmann and Erich Prigge, as well as Captain Frese, the headquarters commandant. His chief of staff was Lieutenant Colonel Kiazim Bey, a sensible, educated and tactful officer, who had already been serving under Sanders for several months and possessed the rare gift of being able to get along well with him.

It was noticeable that von Sanders did not have a German General Staff officer on his team. However, this may have possibly been due to the fact that he wanted to have more willingly obedient staff around him who would carry out his orders and believed that he could find them more easily among Turkish officers. Von Sanders was known for not being appreciative of the often

Staff of the Fifth Army, sitting from left to right: Cevat Paşa, Dr Süleman Numann Paşa (Chief of the Medical Service), Essad Paşa (Commander III Army Corps) (2), General Liman von Sanders (3), Vehib Paşa (4) and Lieutenant Commander Rauf Bey (5). Standing behind Sanders: Kazim Bey (Chief of the General Staff) and (with aiguillette) his adjutant, Captain Erich Prigge. (Bundesarchiv Koblenz)

critical opinions voiced by his German officers, which he regarded more as unjustified opposition. In addition, he considered that his orders, edited and transmitted by Turkish General Staff officers, better reflected the way of doing things in the Turkish forces and thus would be more readily accepted and executed than if they had been handled by German General Staff officers. While a Turkish General Staff formed a link between the German Commander and the Turkish troops, a German General Staff could possibly have led to the separation and isolation of the German commander from his Turkish troops.

After a thorough reconnaissance of the ground, von Sanders arrived at an assessment of the terrain and the resulting possibilities for an Allied attack:

'The most important works and batteries dominating the straits of the Dardanelles lay on the southern, Asiatic coast. The island of Tenedos, occupied by the enemy, lay right in front of this shore and the large and small Bays of Besica (Bashika) were particularly suitable places for landings. It was possible here to place large forces on the Turkish shore. As the works and heavy batteries of the fortress were arranged only for a struggle for the possession of the waterway, an advance and attack against our rear after his landing on the Asiatic shore, offered excellent chances to the enemy. Road communications here were tolerably good. Hence this was the place of greatest danger.

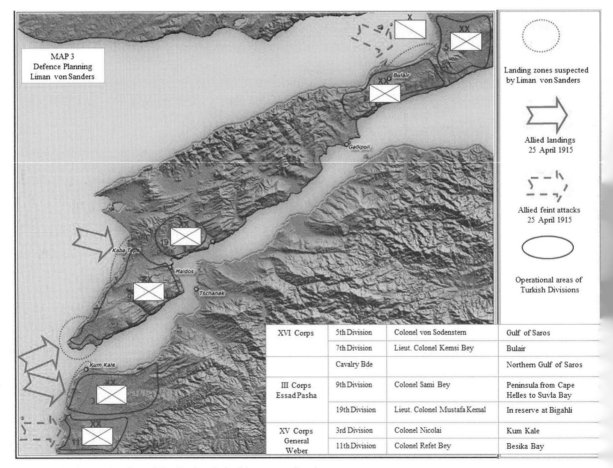

The Defence planning of the Peninsula by Liman von Sanders.

On the Gallipoli Peninsula there were three places that had to be considered as specially important and in danger. The first was the southern point of the peninsula at Seddulbar (Sedd el Bahr) and Tekke Burnu, because this terrain could be covered by the guns of the enemy's ships. After a successful landing at the southern point there rose before the enemy the most conspicuous, bald height of Eltschitepe (Altchy Tepe) [Achi Baba] as the next decisive objective, up to which the gently rising ground offered no great obstacles of ground. From the top of the Eltschitepe (Achi Baba) Ridge a part of the Turkish works and batteries along the coast could be taken under direct artillery fire.

The second place suitable for a quick decision was the coastline on both sides of Kabatepe [Gaba Tepe]. From here a broad plain, broken only by a flat elevation, led directly to the town of Maidos, on the straits. From the heights on both sides of Maidos the batteries of the fortress could be silenced with certainty. North of Kabatepe the steep heights of Ari Burnu lay close to the coast with a well-protected landing place. If the enemy directed his main attack on Maidos by way of Kabatepe it was necessary for him to hold the heights of Ari Burnu because they flanked the plain mentioned.

The third especially important place for a landing on the European side was the vicinity of Bulair on the upper Gulf of Saros [Xeros], where the peninsula is not more than five to seven kilometres wide. It afforded no direct artillery effect against the fortress and the grounds for deciding the question of a landing here became strategic. There the peninsula could be cut in two and shut off from communication with Constantinople and Thrace. If the enemy occupied the narrow ridges between the Gulf of Saros and the Sea of Marmara,

General Liman von Sanders' staff quarters in Galata, near Gallipoli. (*Bundesarchiv Koblenz*)

General Weber. (*Sammlung Soytürk*)   Colonel Nicolai. (*Sammlung Soytürk*)   Colonel von Sodenstern. (*Sammlung Soytürk*)

the Fifth Army would be cut off from every land communication and the communications by water would become endangered as soon as British long range guns, assisted at night by search lights, commanded this narrow part of the Sea of Marmara. Hostile submarines had devoted their attention to the mine field since the beginning of December and attempted to enter the Sea of Marmara; they would be instrumental in completing this separation.'[326]

In accordance with his assessment of the terrain and suspected enemy intentions, von Sanders divided the Fifth Army in mid-April into three groups of two divisions near the possible landing sites. He decided the distribution and deployment of his forces, which would counter as many as possible of the enemy's potential attack points and which would provide him with the greatest possible flexibility. The XV Army Corps - commanded by General Weber – were concentrated on the Asiatic side: around Besika Bay, the 11th Division; and, further north, at Kumkale, the 3rd Division (under Lieutenant Colonel Nicolai). The 5th Division (Lieutenant Colonel von Sodenstern) and the 7th Division were positioned as XVI Army Corps on the upper Gulf of Saros in the area of Gelibolu-Kavak for the defence of Bulair. The 9th and 19th divisions, which were to defend the entire southern tip and west coast, formed III Army Corps under Essad Paşa, the former commander of all troops on Gallipoli. The 19th Division, under Lieutenant Colonel Mustafa Kemal, was initially intended as a mobile reserve in the Bighali area. The northern shore of the Gulf of Saros was the sector of 1 Cavalry Brigade.[327] Von Sanders suspected the main focus of the enemy attack would be on the isthmus at Bulair - probably because this narrow strip of land was the most vulnerable area of his entire command. Here he decided to place the main focus of the defence. Although von Sanders - as mentioned - did not want to have German General Staff Officers on his own staff, several positions in Fifth Army's formations were filled by Germans - starting with the General Officer Commanding XV Corps, General Weber, and the two divisional commanders already mentioned. Thus not only the overall command of the operation but a third of the senior troop commands were in German hands. Additionally there were German officers in command of artillery units as well as advisory staff officers at corps and divisional levels.

The composition and strength of the Turkish divisions was different from their German counterparts. In general, an infantry division comprised three infantry regiments, each with three battalions (each having about 1,000 soldiers), a machine gun company, a field artillery regiment of two sections, a reconnaissance squadron, a pioneer company and a medical company – a total of approximately 10-12,000 men. Apart from its six divisions, with a total strength of about 60,000 men, the Fifth Army still had the Light Reconnaissance Brigade at its disposal - but no other support forces such as artillery at army or corps level. Means of transport were scarce and, in the early phases, there was no air support. These forces, inadequate for a full coastline defence, had to be more effectively exploited through a more flexible operational plan, since: 'whatever might be in store, in view of our weak forces, our success depended not on sticking tight, but on the mobility of our three battle groups'.[328]

It was von Sanders' intention to leave only relatively weak forces for reconnaissance and delaying tactics directly on the coast and to maintain strong and mobile reserves in depth. The order to his divisional commanders was therefore:

> 'First: strengthening the places on the coast that are suitable for enemy landings and reinforcing and making obstacles from wire etc. Second: these positions are to be held by companies of the main forces, connected by patrols and sentries, and the battalions of the advanced posts are to be kept centrally in the sectors. Third: in the case of enemy landings, those outposts that are too weak to prevent a landing are to delay the enemy advance. This should give the main forces time to reach the endangered points and throw the enemy back into the sea.'[329]

This concept corresponded to the operational idea that the force commander would have the ability to regain the initiative after the attack – thus echoing the traditional and proven school of German general staff training. However, this idea was hardly compatible with the Turkish mentality, which planned for a defence geographically as far forward as possible with almost all available forces and without large reserves. It also did not take into account the immense firepower of the Allied warships that could support the landings. Such an operational plan had already been drafted by Essad Paşa and his divisional commanders, including Lieutenant Colonel Mustafa Kemal, before the arrival of the German general. Understandably, they reacted very disapprovingly to the plans of Liman von Sanders.

Since the new defence concept required special skills from both commanders and troops, von Sanders ordered an intensive training programme. Special emphasis was placed on night marches and attacks, as well as field exercises, for which extra training areas on the peninsula were created. All of these were designed to inject fresh thinking and new mobility to the units, which until then had operated statically. The track and road network was, as far as possible, repaired and expanded by additional labour battalions. These units consisted mainly of non–Muslim Turks, i.e. Greek, Armenian and Jewish soldiers. There were no through roads on the peninsula at the time. While there were footpaths that could be used by pack animals in single file, they did not allow for towing field artillery or supply wagons.

The rearward connections to Istanbul were a particular problem since, despite the nets strung across the Dardanelles, Allied submarines had broken through and made supply by ship unsafe in the Sea of Marmara. Provision had therefore to be made for the case that the sea route would be completely unusable for a long period of time. The nearest railway station on the line from Istanbul

A Turkish ox-drawn ammunition column on Gallipoli.

to Uzunköprü was seven days' march from Gallipoli, the road connection to it was poor and there was a lack of adequate means of transport.

To alleviate this problem, small food and ammunition depots were set up near the coastline positions. In order to carry out the possible requirement to ferry troops between the European and Asiatic shores, transport ships and ferries were berthed in the various ports along the Dardanelles. Field fortifications on the most vulnerable shores were reinforced, with all operations required to be done at night to avoid enemy reconnaissance and artillery fire. Von Sanders noted:

'The available Turkish means of obstruction were in as short supply as were the tools, but we did the best we could. Torpedo heads were used alongside regular land mines and the fences of gardens and fields were stripped of their wood and wire. At places particularly suitable for landings, barbed wire was stretched under water.'[330]

In addition, flanking support was to be provided by the heavy German machine guns and artillery. The Commander of all Fifth Army engineer units, Major Alexander Effnert, was a driving and resourceful force in all these preparations, which were to pay off, especially at the southern tip of the peninsula. Von Sanders did not know how much time he had to prepare for the defence. He had already said to Lieutenant Colonel Kannengiesser on 27 March: 'If the English would only allow me 8 days!,[331] unaware that he would have four weeks before the Allies landed.

The Turkish preparations for defence had been closely observed by the Allies. Admiral de Robeck reported to General Sir Ian Hamilton, who had just arrived at the Dardanelles front:

'The Gallipoli peninsula is being fortified with great haste. Thousands of Turks are working like beavers all night, making trenches, redoubts and laying barbed wire. Although one has not yet seen any of them, every morning brings fresh evidence of their nocturnal activity. All landing places are now dominated by lines of trenches and effectively camouflaged. [...] The Germans apparently have taken the Turks firmly in their hands, and all that labour quite splendidly carried out by the Turks.'[332]

The Turkish officers themselves, however, viewed the German engagement at Gallipoli rather critically. For example, Major Izzetin, Mustafa Kemal's chief of staff at the 19th Division, wrote in his diary:

'Today Liman von Sanders, accompanied by the Corps Commander, Esat Paşa, came to Maidos and visited the coastal fortifications. Liman Paşa is commander of the 5th Army, Cevat Paşa commands the fortifications, Usedom Paşa has the Coastal Inspectorate and Weber Paşa is the commander of the mixed forces on the Asiatic coast. It seems the Germans want the defence of the Dardanelles to be in their own hands.'[333]

That the assessment of the enemy's situation by the German commander of the Fifth Army was correct and that he had ordered adequate and flexible operational planning against the background of information available to him was demonstrated by the attack plan and its implementation by the Allies. In contemporary Turkish assessments, General von Sanders is nevertheless still accused of having unnecessarily taken forces from the front lines with his idea of deeply-staggered reserves. Thus, the landings could not have been immediately stopped and the enemy would therefore have the possibility to form bridgeheads, which would have led to high casualties later. Pomiankowski wrote:

'Confidentially I heard at the time that both Enver and other military figures disagreed with the defensive measures taken by the Marshal and ascribed to them the success of enemy forces landing on the peninsula. Liman had not judged the general situation properly, having given too much importance to the Bulair area and the Asian sector, and hence his forces were not properly distributed. The main force - four divisions - should have been directed not to the designated external sectors but to the centre, i.e. Seddulbahr-Ari Burnu-Canakkale, while only one division each would have sufficed for the Gulf of Saros and the Asian shore. Furthermore, it had been a mistake to schematically arrange matters so that only weak observation and security forces were to be placed everywhere on the shores, whereas the main forces, on the other hand, were to have been held together in the rear. On the contrary, it would have been advisable to occupy adequately those places where landings were to be expected, i.e. the southern tip of the peninsula, then the area around Ariburnu, for defence; and the defence plan at these points to prevent the landing directly instead of being based on counter-attacks. In view, however, of the enormous artillery superiority of the enemy, the latter had to be very costly and had little chance of succeeding.'[334]

The Turkish view of the von Sanders' planning was often already critical during the war itself; but it became much stronger after it ended. In September 1925, Legation Councillor Braun von

Stumm, of the re-established post-war German Embassy in Istanbul, took part in a tour of the Gallipoli battlefields with Turkish officers and politicians. In his travel report, he noted:

'[The General Staff lieutenant colonels, Galib Bey and Nihad Bey] gave lectures during the trip on the meaning of the fighting and on the tactics of the Army Command, which did not lack somewhat bitter criticism of the German High Command under Marshal Liman von Sanders. [...] It had also been emphasised on several occasions that the units and formations involved in the battles were purely Turkish, with only sixteen Germans participating in the fighting as staff, an assertion which is hardly true. Moreover, the talks were moving in the direction of attributing the *Ghazi* [Mustafa Kemal Atatürk] solely with the credit for the successful defence and the retreat of the English [sic].'[335]

Even today, Turkish opinion is still largely characterised by works that lay the blame for the high casualties exclusively on the German leadership. One can read, for example:

'The reason for these casualties lay in the few senior German commanders of the Turkish army in the Gallipoli battle and in particular the German commander who led the battle. The German commanders increased the price of our victory. They caused the higher losses of the Turkish army. Using the defensive concept of the commander of the Fifth Army, Liman Pasha, he turned the Gallipoli peninsula into a honeycomb on which bees could gather. As a result, he kept half a million English [sic] and French soldiers on this honeycomb but Turkish soldiers paid the price with their blood. The main reason for these losses was that Liman Pasha gave the enemy the chance to land on the shores, as he changed the tactics originally planned by the Turkish commanders. Then the German divisional commanders and the Army commander often launched counter-attacks more by chance, and by day and night, that were not commensurate with war tactics.'[336]

It is always easy to evaluate a plan of action measured by the course of the battle from a retrospective point of view, since the opponent's dispositions and the result are all known. However, in the light of the information available at that time, the assessment of the terrain and the forces available, the operational plan worked out by General von Sanders was, in my view, not only appropriate but also extremely clever, particularly with his concept of mobile battle engagements with strong reserves at the rear for rapid deployment for fast force concentration. The original division of forces, which had provided for an even distribution of all the forces along the coast and with no significant operational reserves, might have enabled a rapid breakthrough from individual Allied landing sectors. Concentrating on Bulair was justified, as a landing there could have bypassed and undermined the entire defence of the southern tip of the Peninsula.

Despite significant reinforcement of the Fifth Army, von Sanders had still not been provided with sufficient forces to defend all the stretches of forward coastline strongly – although at that time, for example around Istanbul, six further divisions were uncommitted and were not released by Enver. If these troops had been used according to Sanders' early request instead of only being moved to Gallipoli during operations, the defence could have been planned and carried out differently. Whether the high losses were actually attributable exclusively to the German leadership will be examined - and refuted - in the following chapters. It was certainly never the intention of General von Sanders to allow the enemy to make a landing in order that they commit large numbers of troops and so keep that strength from fighting in the Western theatre of the war. This view contradicted his apolitical nature and his military straightforwardness, with which he also faithfully planned and led the defence of the Peninsula.

Chapter 8

The Landings on 25 April 1915

The strategic goal of the Allied landing[337] was the elimination of the artillery threats on the shores of the Dardanelles, thus allowing the clearance of the minefields and thereby freeing the passage for the Allied fleet through to Istanbul. To accomplish this, General Hamilton had to land his forces as quickly as possible, smash the Turkish defenders and take possession of the Peninsula. He would thus dominate the shores of the Dardanelles and then be able to seize the fortifications on the waterway from the rear. His landing plan envisaged simultaneous landings at two points on the Peninsula, together with a diversionary attack on the Asiatic shore. At the same time, a feint landing was to be made in the Gulf of Saros, near Bulair.

The Australian and New Zealand Army Corps (ANZAC) was to land near Gaba Tepe, south of the Ari Burnu bluff, on the west shore of the Peninsula. Then it was to seize Koja Chemen Tepe to protect its left flank, advance on Maidos and thereby disrupt the Turkish communications lines. The British 29th Division was to land in the southern area of the Peninsula on five stretches of beach, named S, V, W, X and Y, in the area of Cape Helles, Seddulbahr and Achi Baba[338] and from there to attack the inner coastal fortifications and ultimately to capture them. The French were to land on the Asian side of Kum Kale and Yeni Shehr in order to tie up the Turkish forces deployed there and to appear to threaten the coastal fortifications at Canakkale. In the Gulf of Saros – contrary to the assumption of Liman von Sanders – a landing was only to be a feint to tie down Turkish forces for as long as possible. The landings were set for the morning of 25 April 1915.[339]

On 24 April an extensive exercise was carried out by the 11th (Turkish) Division on the Asian shore which, like all the manoeuvres at that time, also included an operation against a landing attempt, including the necessary relocation of forces and mutual reinforcement. Only in the late afternoon did Liman von Sanders return with his staff to the town of Gallipoli. In the early morning of 25 April heavy gunfire preceded the Allied landing. General Liman von Sanders' adjutant, Captain Carl Mühlmann, described the moment:

'On April 25 the seriousness of the war began for us; until then, it had simply been an interesting and harmless experience for us. [...] I woke up at 05.00 hrs on Sunday morning; the sun and the blue waters of the Dardanelles reflected into my room, but the continuous, sometimes distant, sometimes nearer, thunder of cannons did not fit in with the peaceful picture. Prigge and I decided to get up and investigate at the same time. As we arrived at Liman's quarters, he stood half-dressed on his doorstep. At the same time a General Staff Officer came rushing in, [saying] the enemy had landed at Seddulbahr and Ari Burnu (north of Gaba Tepe) and that a huge transport fleet in the Gulf of Saros lay off Izidze under the protection of numerous warships. Since from the latter message a landing in the Gulf of Saros seemed to be imminent, the 7th Division, based at the town of Gallipoli, was immediately alerted and ordered to march in the direction of Bulair. Liman was unfortunately a bit nervous and instead of staying at the central point, the AOK [Army High Command], where all the telephone lines converged, he swung himself onto a horse and rode with both of us to the heights near Bulair. Of course all the messages arrived one to two hours later and the

Captain Mühlmann. (*Deutsche Botschaft, Ankara*)

whole interaction between him and the AOK remaining in Gallipoli was made very difficult; it only just about worked. As soon as we reached the top we saw a heavy bombardment crashing down on the main fort of Bulair. At times the whole fort was shrouded in smoke, it could be believed that nothing remained intact after these heavy naval shells exploded; but looking at the damage afterwards, if the target had not had a direct hit, then it is not that bad. The shell holes are huge. Especially gigantic are those from the 38cm shells of the *Queen Elizabeth*. But while the damage is localised, one has to admit, however, that the effect on morale is enormous. From the heights, we only had a limited view and we were able to take cover behind a small hedge, hardly moving. Here we also received the news of the enemy landing at Kum Kale and asked Essad Pasha for permission to transfer the G.Kdo (Army Headquarters) to Maidos, which was willingly approved, as two of his divisions were fighting there.'[340]

Liman von Sanders did not seem surprised by these reports, as in essence they confirmed his own appreciation. He wrote:

'From the many pale faces among the officers reporting in the early morning it became apparent that, although a hostile landing had been expected with certainty, a landing at so many places surprised many and filled them with apprehension. My first feeling was that our arrangements needed no change. That was a great satisfaction! The hostile landing expedition had selected those points which we ourselves considered the most likely landing places and had specially prepared for defense.'[341]

Von Sanders was so firmly fixated on the idea that the enemy's main thrust would be at Bulair, that he judged the landings elsewhere were just a distraction: in fact it was the other way round. He remained on site with his adjutant, Mühlmann, who described the situation in the Gulf of Saros:

'The picture was really impressive; twelve mostly large transport vessels, a large battleship, two cruisers, some destroyers. During my two hours of observation the transport ships, which rode very high on the water, were motionless and no long boats [for landing troops] could be seen; the warships sailed here, sometimes there and ventured close to the coast of the Peninsula, firing at everything that showed itself. When I returned to S we had a meagre breakfast. Gradually, it was evening and we hoped he would soon give the sign to return to Gallipoli. But, to our astonishment, he decided to stay the night on the heights; the purpose was not revealed to us, because there was no telephone line from the Army Command Headquarters to us.'[342]

While the Army commander waited spellbound for the landing that was not to take place at Bulair, the situation in the south of the Peninsula was critical. That area, and along the entire west coast to Gaba Tepe, was only defended by the Turkish 26th Infantry Regiment, with its command post

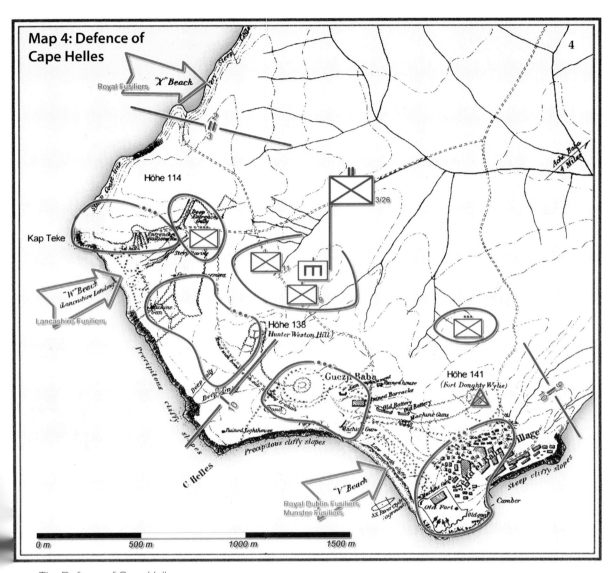

The Defence of Cape Helles.

in Krithia. While the 4th and 2nd Battalions (4/26 Regt. & 2/26 Regt.) west of Krithia had been used to protect the west coast, the 3rd Battalion (3/26 Regt.), led by Major Mahmut, with around 1,000 men, had to protect the entire southern tip at Seddulbahr.

Mahmut's battalion had only taken over the area on 23 April and immediately continued to build up the existing defences. Above all they were busy installing wire obstacles, digging trenches and siting, for flanking use, the four 37mm pom-poms which had been handed over by the previous battalion. The battalion had no artillery of its own in support of its companies deployed forward and the regimental artillery could not fire directly on these stretches of beach.

On the morning of 25 April, after heavy naval bombardment, the 29th Division, under Major General Hunter-Weston, began the attack in daylight on Tekke Tepe and Seddulbahr. At Y Beach, on the left flank of the 29th Division, approximately 2,000 soldiers of the King's Own Scottish Borderers, a company of the 2nd Battalion, South Wales Borderers, and the Plymouth Battalion of the Royal Marine Light Infantry had to land at this northern area on a very small stretch of beach. The commander of the 26th Infantry Regiment had not suspected an attack here and therefore had only positioned very weak forces of his 2nd and 4th Battalions (2/26 Regt. & 4/26 Regt) in defence.[343] The British were able to land almost unopposed at 5.45 am and already, at about 6.00 am, two company-strong reconnaissance detachments had been sent inland which, according to British records, allegedly even made it through to Krithia. However, why they did not encounter Turkish troops of the 26th Infantry Regiment's staff or the 2nd Battalion (2/26 Regt.), who were there as regimental reserve, cannot be explained. However, the British soldiers in this sector had no further orders and withdrew back to the beach and awaited further instructions. It was 3 pm before they began to set up defensive positions and they were barely prepared for the counter-attack by the 3rd Battalion of the 25th Infantry Regiment at 5.30 pm. At the landing zone, where there had been the least casualties and from which the furthest advance into the interior during the entire operation was made, heavy fighting now erupted and the British suffered severe casualties. Close combat ensued and the invaders were pushed back further and further towards the beach. The war diary of the King's Own Scottish Borderers described the situation:

'...several times the enemy approached within ten yards of our position... so close did the enemy reach to our lines that in one place a German officer walked up to our trench and said, "You English surrender, we are ten to one". He was thereupon hit on the head with a spade.'[344]

At X Beach, which was also only defended by a weak force of the 2nd Battalion, 26th Infantry Regiment, two companies of the Royal Fusiliers landed almost unhindered at 6.30 am, against whom a section of only twelve Turkish soldiers could hardly offer meaningful resistance. However, after landing, the troops had no further orders to advance inland or to seek contact independently with flanking troops. They thought that they were merely intended as a divisional reserve to protect the left flank of W Beach. The two companies were almost thrown back on 26 April by the counter-attack of the Turkish 25th Infantry Regiment. However, on the same day, the 1st Battalion, Border Regiment and the 1st Battalion, Royal Inniskilling Fusiliers were landed as reinforcements, so this landing could be held - albeit with heavy losses.

On the south-west side of Cape Helles, W Beach was about 350 metres long and forty metres wide at the lowest point. The beach was mined and defended with extensive wire obstacles. The only passage was up through a stream bed that was easy to defend. In this area, the 12th Company of the 3rd Battalion, 26th Infantry Regiment was deployed. The Turkish positions and defences had not been destroyed, as had been hoped, by the preceding naval bombardment. The disciplined Turkish soldiers held their fire. Only when the leading boat of the Lancashire Fusiliers reached the beach, did the attackers come under heavy flanking fire from both slopes. Most of the Fusiliers did not even reach a small rise in the ground at the end of the beach that would have given them cover. Many of them had already been killed or wounded in the boats. Eventually the Lancashire Fusiliers were able to gain a foothold here, but the Turkish company had inflicted 533 casualties on the 950 attackers and almost detroyed an entire battalion. For valour in the fighting on this stretch of beach, six Victoria Crosses (VC) were awarded to men from this battalion of the Lancashire Fusiliers.[345]

About 300 metres long, V Beach was bounded on the left by Cape Helles and on the right by the old 17th century fortress of Seddulbahr. Immediately ahead was Hill 141 and on the left Hill 138, the dominant heights and intermediate points to be taken. This stretch of beach was

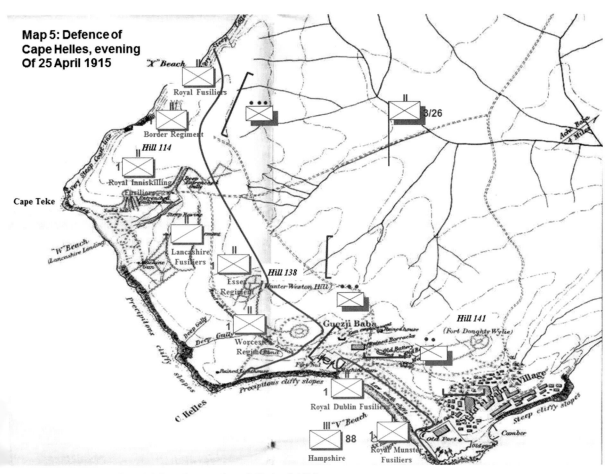

The Defence at Cape Helles, the evening of 25 April 1915.

defended by the 10th Company, 3rd Battalion, 26th Infantry Regiment, with flanking support provided by four 37mm pom-poms. The 1st Battalion, Royal Dublin Fusiliers landed from a line of rowing boats, tethered together by ropes, and pulled by motor pinnaces. A large number of infantry were aboard a converted 4,000 ton collier, the *River Clyde*: 1st Royal Munster Fusiliers, together with a company of 1st Royal Dublin Fusiliers and a company of 2nd Hampshire Regiment. The ship had exits from its hull cut out above the waterline. Through these holes approximately 2,000 soldiers were to leave the ship after it had been run aground, and then make their way to the shore, over catwalks and barges which had been connected together.

The towed boats of the Dubliners left HMS *Clacton* at 06.00 am. After the prior bombardment, everything was quiet on the shore and the Dublin Fusiliers at first believed that they would meet with no appreciable resistance. But as the boats approached the beach the defenders opened a withering fire on the landing troops. Of 700 men, only 300 reached the beach, many of them badly wounded. They sought shelter behind the sand banks and under overhanging shore sections. The *River Clyde* followed closely behind this first wave and ran on to the beach at full speed. Two

View from the RIVER CLYDE to V Beach (taken after the evacuation of the Allied troops). (*Deutsche Botschaft, Ankara*)

companies of the Munster Fusiliers now left the transport and tried to reach the beach but were mowed down by the fire of the Turkish defenders. British losses were over 70 percent.

At 09.00 am another company made a new attempt; but this failed as well. However, the commander of the 29th Division, Hunter-Weston, aboard the *Euryalus*, remained unaware of this dramatic development on V Beach and at 8.30 am he ordered the main contingent to begin the landing. At 9.30 am, he had the advance party link up with W Beach. For this purpose a third attempt to leave the *River Clyde* was made by a company of the Hampshire Regiment which was also all but wiped out. In charge of the main contingent, Brigadier General Henry Edward Napier, GOC 88 Brigade, was killed in an attempt to land his force. Finally, at 10.21 am, General Sir Ian Hamilton, who was following events from his command post aboard the flagship *Queen Elizabeth*, ordered Hunter-Weston to break off the operation. The question of whether the Worcestershire Regiment, as the Divisional Reserve for V Beach, could possibly be landed on a stretch of Y Beach, was postponed for several hours. Eventually, these troops were landed on the still bitterly contested W Beach, which led to further confusion there. The 1,000 men remaining aboard the *River Clyde* waited until nightfall before attempting to reach the beach again. Two of the battalions which had landed on V Beach - the Royal Dublin Fusiliers and the Royal Munster Fusiliers - were so damaged that they were later temporarily merged into a mixed battalion known as the 'Dubsters'. Of the 1,100 original men of the Royal Dublin Fusiliers, only eleven survived the campaign at Gallipoli unharmed.

On S Beach, at Morto Bay, to the east of the defensive section of the 26th Infantry Regiment, three companies of the South Wales Borderers landed without great losses and had this area quickly under control. They even took the top of Eski Hissarlik Point and held it against Turkish counter-attacks.

Only the men of the 3rd Battalion (3/26th Regt), commanded by Major Mahmut, were present for all of these landings in the early phases. The main concentration of defence was with the 12th Company at W Beach and the 10th Company at V Beach. Despite his successful defence, Mahmut had to withdraw the 12th Company, which threatened to break under pressure from the troops that had landed. He had already set up his battalion reserve north of Tekke Tepe in the X Beach sector and Seddulbahr at V.

In the V Beach sector the company commander of the 10th Company was killed in the morning. Sergeant Yahya took command of the remaining sixty-two men and fought and held against six enemy battalions. Today a memorial stone commemorates the deed: 'Sergeant Yahya and a heroic platoon fought with all their hearts against three regiments [sic]. The enemy thought these wonderful men were a division. They served God and were with Him in the evening.'[345a]

The fight was now mainly about the possession of Hill 138, which was finally taken by British troops towards 3 pm. Mahmut had called for reinforcements from the 9th Division soon after the attack in the morning; however, the first two battalions of the 25th Infantry Regiment, Lieutenant Colonel Nail Bey, and parts of the 9th Field Artillery Regiment, only reached the southern tip of the Peninsula at about 9 pm. Major Mahmut's battalion had been almost completely wiped out by that time; but until then he had successfully fought back a vastly superior enemy. At the southern tip of Gallipoli, of a total of about 9,000 British soldiers who landed, 3,000 were killed or wounded on 25 April.

On the Asiatic coast, Major General Weber was the commander with responsibility for its defence. In this sector, following intensive shelling, around 3,000 soldiers of the 6th French Colonial Regiment landed at Kum Kale at around 10.45 am. This was much later than planned - probably the strong current in the Dardanelles had delayed the operation. The attack was obviously intended only as a feint that should tie down Turkish forces on the Asian side for as long as possible. The town of Kum Kale itself was only defended by an infantry platoon of the 3rd Division. No obstacles had been made on the shores, as a defence in depth was to be conducted at the bridge over the River Menderes and along the river's course. The French troops who landed were mostly Senegalese and French Foreign Legionnaires and, supported by the preceding naval bombardment, they were quickly able to overwhelm the infantry platoon, led by Lieutenant Ali Effendi, in Kum Kale and capture the place with two companies and only minor casualties by around 11.15 am.

Meanwhile the battleship *Henri IV*, designated for immediate fire support, entered the Dardanelles and was able to intensify the bombardment of the defending 3rd Division. Since the shore was only slightly higher than the waterline, the ship's gunners could see and range far inland. They destroyed the bridge over the River Menderes, which meant that the French troops now advancing from Kum Kale could not march further east but only to the south. There they took Yeni Shehr, which was in flames after being razed by the bombardment. The last battalion, together with the artillery, had landed by 5.30 pm. Kum Kale and Yeni Shehr were now prepared for a defence of this apparent bridgehead.

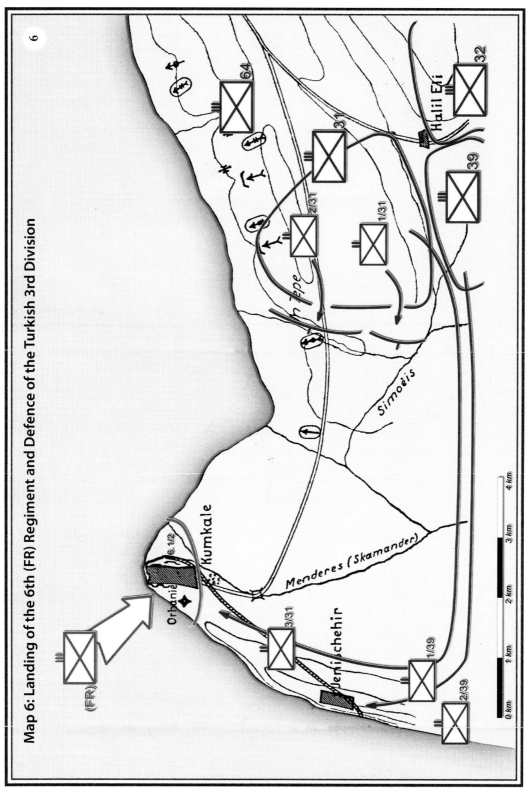

Map 6: Landing of the 6th (FR) Regiment and Defence of the Turkish 3rd Division

The Landing of the 6th (Fr) Regiment and the Defence of the 3rd Division.

Meanwhile Lieutenant Colonel Wehrle had ordered forward his best howitzer battery under Captain Ali Tewik Effendi and provided it with 200 shells. The battery took up position east of the River Menderes and was very effective against the French troops still at Kum Kale. During the night, Colonel Nicolai, the commander of the 3rd Division, had had parts of the Turkish 31st Infantry Regiment advance against Kum Kale from the south across the then still intact Menderes Bridge and it then prepared the defence to the east of the Menderes. The 39th Infantry Regiment attacked the French at Yeni Shehr. The attacks against Kum Kale were beaten off by French troops on the eastern edge of the town, while Yeni Shehr reverted to the Turks.

To effect a surprise, the ANZAC landings at Ari Burnu began without any preparatory bombardment early in the morning, at 4.15 am on 25 April. This sector was secured by the 2nd Battalion of the 27th Infantry Regiment under the command of Major Izmet Bey. In command of the 27th Regiment was Lieutenant Colonel Şefik Aker. This latter regiment, except for its 2nd Battalion, which was committed to the Ari Burnu section, was to act as reserve and, together with its two other battalions, was held in readiness near Maidos.[346] The defence planning for the entire Ari Burnu section was described by the commander of the 3rd Battalion, Major Halil Bey:

'2nd Battalion: defends Arı Burnu and the Gaba Tepe area. 7th Company of the 3rd Battalion, 9th Mountain Artillery Regiment, with half a machine-gun company in position on the heights behind Arı Burnu and 3rd Battalion and the Arı Burnu Company and Gaba Tepe field guns are under the command of the 2nd Battalion's commander. Half the machine-gun company select their positions so that the northern beach of the Arı Burnu-Gaba Tepe area can be covered by their arc of fire.'[347]

Captain Faik, OC 4th Company, watched the approaching enemy fleet, silhouetted in the gloom of the early hours of 25 April. He informed his battalion commander and moved to an even better observation point.

'This time around, I saw an even larger number, which in my opinion were heading straight for us. As ordered, I informed the Division Headquarters by telephone. It was around 2.30 am. I was connected to Lieutenant Nuri Effendi [...] and made my report. "Hold the position," he replied, "I'll inform the Chief of Staff." After a while, he came back on the phone and asked, "How many are warships and how many are transports?" "It's impossible to tell in the dark," I answered, "but there are many." That ended the conversation. A short time later the moon sank on the horizon and the ships were now completely invisible. We alerted the reserve platoon and ordered it ready. I watched and waited.'[348]

The 1st Australian Division should have landed in three waves in the southernmost part, about one and half kilometres north of Gaba Tepe. Today it is no longer possible to establish why the landing took place further north on the beach section at Arı Burnu, known today as ANZAC Cove, and not - as originally planned – at Gaba Tepe. Whether it was a sudden change of plan or a navigational error, the troops only realised when they got ashore that they had obviously not landed at the intended location. They were now on a beach where they had to overcome the steepest slopes and gullies of the entire Peninsula. However, they were on a section of beach that was much better protected against direct artillery fire and was less prepared for defence. From here the route to the first objective of the attack, Koja Chemen Tepe, lay over a kilometre closer and needed hardly any lateral movement towards the defending Turks. All these factors could lead to the conclusion that the landing site had been changed at short notice but this had not been passed on at brigade level.

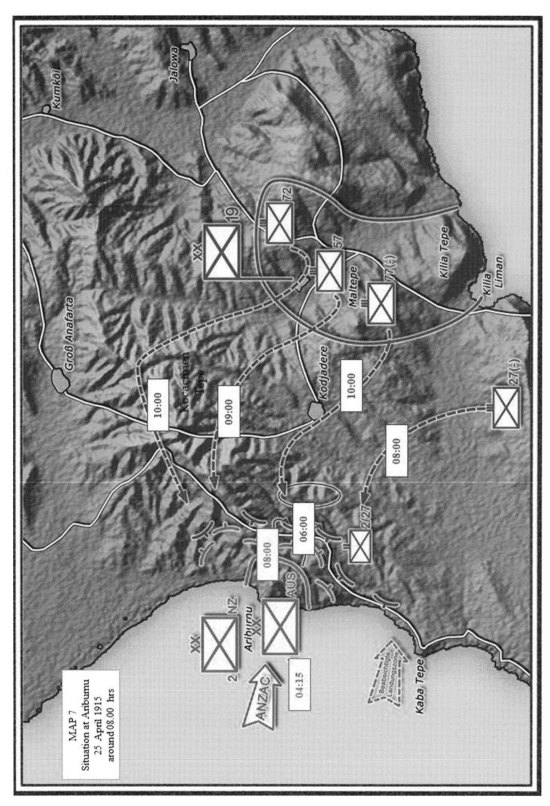

The situation at Ari Burnu, 25 April, at about 8.00 am.

The unexpected landing point – except for the fact that it was initially confusing to the troops – tactically had more advantages for the attacking Anzacs. If it had really been an error, it follows that subsequent landings could have taken place at the originally intended place; but this did not happen and this even though the alleged oversight had long been realised.

At 4.20 am, Lieutenant Asim, 3rd Company, 2nd Battalion, which had conducted a night exercise with the rest of the 27th Infantry Regiment the night before, sent the decisive message to the Divisional Headquarters: 'The enemy has begun his attack at Ari Burnu'.

Due to reports which had already been received, a serious attack was assumed and under the plan that required calling for immediate reinforcements. For this purpose the units of the 27th Infantry Regiment, which had returned to the Maidos area after the exercise, were alerted and immediately ordered to march forward. Captain Faik, meanwhile, took up the fight with his 4th Company:

'I saw a machine gun shooting from a boat off Ari Burnu. Some shots passed over us. I ordered the platoon back to the trenches on the ridge that towered over Ari Burnu and sent two groups under Sergeant Ahmet to the trenches on the middle ridge, from which one could see the beach. I ordered the redeployment by telephone and went to the flank with the reserve platoon.'[349]

Major Halil Bey, commanding officer of the 3rd Battalion, 27th Regiment (front left) and Lieutenant Colonel Mehmet Şefik Bey, commanding officer of the 27th Regiment (front centre).

Numbering approximately 1,500 men, the 9th, 10th, 11th and 12th Battalions of 3 (Australian) Brigade attacked the heights in small groups, which, immediately after the landing, were disorderly and uncoordinated due to the confusion arising from the unexpected landing site. Because the units were all mixed up, no uniform leadership was in place. They only slowly gained ground but took the first heights against resistance from units of the 27th Regiment, which withdrew further up the heights under enemy pressure. In the northern area, the heights were still in the possession of the 2nd Battalion of the 27th, which was able to continue to rain flanking fire from there on the troops landing at Arı Burnu. In the same way, the Turkish troops to the south were able to make use of their position in Gaba Tepe, which flanked the Australian Brigade. After the 3rd Battalion, 27th Infantry Regiment, arrived and the first field howitzer battery had been placed in position on the heights behind Gaba Tepe, the Arı Burnu landing area could now be shelled by shrapnel. The 1 and 2 (Australian) Brigades, which had landed with about 2,500 soldiers as the main body of the 1st (Australian) Division on this narrow strip, now came under fire from the defenders.

The Anzac losses were high; using boats that had ferried in new troops, the wounded were taken back to the warships whenever possible. By around 6.00 am almost 4,000 soldiers had landed at Arı Burnu and faced the few hundred Turkish soldiers of the 2nd and 3rd Battalions of the 27th Regiment. The outnumbered defenders now had to hold on, according to Liman von Sanders' operational concept, until reinforcements from the rear could be brought up.

The commander of 3 Brigade, Colonel Ewen Sinclair–MacLagan, who only landed with the second wave, now began to organise his troops. However, this was almost impossible, as more and more small groups, independently and with little coordination, tried to eliminate the Turkish positions in the north and to silence the artillery position at Gaba Tepe or continue to attack east against the heights. The units of the 27th Regiment had moved back to the second ridge line and took up positions again. While Colonel Sinclair–MacLagan now wanted to concentrate the attack, initially coordinated in the south and against the second ridge, he did not know that individual units of forward troops were already on the third ridge, the so-called Kemalyeri[350], and had advanced further eastwards than any Allied soldiers would ever achieve in later months. There they were discovered, at about 9.30 am, by approaching Turkish troops and immediately attacked. The Australian troops moved to Plateau 400 and there defended themselves against the advancing Turks. The Australians in this phase of the battle were concentrated against the threat on their right flank, i.e. from Gaba Tepe, where other Turkish forces were suspected to be; and that changed the focus of the attack, which was actually planned against the Koja Chemen Tepe.

The deployment of 2 (Australian Brigade), which was supposed to continue attacking Koja Chemen Tepe on the left as its main objective, was now used to protect its own right flank, which further reduced the attack's momentum and strength. Intended as a divisional reserve, 1 Brigade remained on the beach. At 8.39 am, Lieutenant General Birdwood, GOC, Australian and New Zealand Army Corps, reported that Plateau 400 had been taken, three Krupp cannons captured and 8,000 men landed. Meanwhile, Major Halil, whose men of the 3rd Battalion (3/27th Regt) were completely overwhelmed by the magnitude of their defensive task, reported to the commander of the 9th Division: 'The enemy is currently attacking the heights behind Gaba Tepe. We have no reserves left. It seems that our reserve forces are distributed along the entire front line of Koja Dere in all directions to Koja Chemen Dagh and Gaba Tepe.'[351]

Major Halil's communications to the commander of the 27th Regiment, Lieutenant Colonel Şefik Bey, were disrupted. Nevertheless, he received further support from his own artillery, which fired more and more shrapnel against the Australians attacking through the valleys. Australian artillery support was sparse, since the few guns landed could not be brought into favourable firing positions quickly enough from the beach. The naval guns of the Allied warships could not intervene effectively, because the troops of both sides were too close to each other and there were no artillery observation reports to allow for accurate Allied firing on the Turkish reserves to the rear.

The first Turkish reserves arrived at around 8.00 am, from the camps south of Gaba Tepe and from the 27th Regiment, which had already been alerted and deployed at 4.30 am. General von Sanders' operational plan, though risky and costly, seemed to have worked. The 27th Regiment continued to defend its position from its second and third line positions, with three machine guns in support, and repeatedly launched local counter-attacks. Although these troops were completely exhausted by the previous night's exercise and the hours spent in defence, they were able to hold on until reinforcements arrived. At 8.30 am, parts of the 2nd (Australian) Brigade watched the approach of more Turkish forces from the south and below Koja Chemen Tepe. This missed the opportunity for a surprise attack against inferior forces and marked the turning point for the fight at Ari Burnu. The units now arriving came from the 19th Division, commanded by Lieutenant Colonel Mustafa Kemal. He was awoken early in the morning by the noise of the guns and wrote of that moment:

'I spoke on the telephone to ...Essad Paşa, at Gallipoli. He said that no clear information about what was going on had yet been obtained. It was at 6.30 am that I learned from a report that arrived from Halil Sami Bey that a force of enemy had climbed the heights of Ari Burnu and

Colonel Mustafa Kemal.
(*Sammlung Soytürk*)

that I was required to send a battalion against them. Both from this report and as a result of my personal observations that I had carried out at Mal Tepe, my firm opinion was, just as I had previously judged, that an enemy attempt to land in strength in the neighbourhood of Gaba Tepe was now taking place. Therefore I appreciated that it was impossible to carry [out] my task with a battalion but that, as I had reckoned before, my whole division would be required to deal with the enemy.'[352]

With two-thirds of his division, the 57th and 77th Infantry Regiments and a mountain battery, Kemal marched towards Koja Chemen Tepe and a hill later named Kemalyeri after him. He initially held back his 72nd Infantry Regiment, which consisted mainly of Arabs, as a reserve because he did not have full confidence in this formation. After his troops arrived, at about 9.00 am, east of Hill 700 (Baby 700), he reconnoitred further west with some officers. When he met some malingering soldiers of the 27th Regiment there, he ordered them to go back into position and if necessary to fight with fixed bayonets against the advancing enemy. He immediately ordered his 57th Regiment to follow suit; and they attacked the Australian troops at 10.00 am. The contested Hill 700 remained the key area for the following hours and then the following days. It was the British intermediate goal on the way to Koja Chemen Tepe; but it was also the north-eastern pivot of the defence. Hill 700 changed hands five times on this first day. Kemal threw all his reserves into battle and, presumably, gave his famous command here: 'I don't order you to attack, I order you to die'.

The 57th Regiment was almost completely destroyed in these counter-attacks. Major Zeki Bey of the regimental staff reported that the 2nd Battalion (2/57th Regt.) almost ceased to exist after an attack on the slopes at Fisherman's Hut, west of The Nek.

The 57th Regiment was brought up to strength again by taking soldiers from the 72nd Regiment. At 10.15 am the Turkish counter-attacks became so fierce that ANZAC Headquarters reported that Russell's Top could not be held, and the entire Australian reserve, 1 Brigade, was sent to reinforce the northern front. A battery of the Indian Mountain Artillery, laboriously brought up to 400 Plateau, was withdrawn in the afternoon as it had come under heavy Turkish fire.

The Turks dominated the heights, had artillery superiority and made counter-attacks on the Australian lines, using reinforcements that kept coming in. However, there were also problems of coordination on the Turkish side. The 77th Regiment, also comprising mostly of Arabs who barely spoke Turkish and were therefore not easily controlled in battle, was deployed between the 57th Regiment, which fought in the north, and the 27th Infantry Regiment to the south. The two flanking regiments were not aware of this insertion of troops. As the 77th Regiment came under heavy Australian machine-gun fire, it took evasive action and fell back and at the same time dragged along units of the 27th Regiment, leaving the Lone Pine area undefended for some time. The exhausted Anzacs, however, did not push on and could not benefit from this situation.

The battles here that day also led to large losses on both sides. Despite the considerable numerical superiority of around 13,000 Anzacs, landed by the afternoon, pitched against a total of only 8,000 defending Turks, the attackers were not able to achieve any significant territorial gains.

The Turkish fleet and the *Sonderkommando* (SoKo) also acted promptly on 25 April. Admiral von Usedom, who was in Istanbul at that time, immediately returned to the Dardanelles. The *Turgut Reis*, under the command of Lieutenant Commander Fedor Rosentreter, had been able to open indirect fire against two small Allied cruisers on 24 April. The *Turgut's* 28 cm guns could also fire on

Turkish and Arab soldiers of the 77th and 27th Infantry Regiments in defence at Ari Burnu (*Bundesarchiv Koblenz*)

the attacking Allied ships, this fire being directed from the observation posts previously established on land. Lieutenant Commander Rolf Carls reported:

'The next salvo is well-placed, I fire as fast as the *Turgut's* old guns can manage, and then I saw four hits on transports and battleships. In the meantime, a salvo bursts on land a hundred metres in front of us. Apparently it was meant for us, but still it was not dangerous; right after it, the second one bursts fifty metres ahead of us. I instruct my people that if the enemy fires on our post to go behind the rear slope. Then the third one hits ten metres in front of us. Everyone gets down, waiting for the exploding fragments to go over us and then run down the slope. A salvo from the *Turgut* is still underway. We still have to carry out the observation. I run forward with my ordnance Petty Officer. A salvo hits us again, barely five metres away. We can still observe the *Turgut's* salvo. It was a hit. From the camouflaged gully, fire control can still carry on.'[353]

Admiral Souchon, the Fleet Commander, sent the *Barbarossa* on the 25th to provide additional artillery support. The MMD's war diary contains the following entry for that day:

'*Barbarossa* ordered at 7 o'clock in the evening to make way to the Dardanelles. Lieutenant Commander Rohde vice Lieutenant Commander von Arnim (sick) as commander. Admiral v. Usedom goes to Dardanelles so that the defence rests in one hand and especially [to ensure] that the Turkish commander does not arbitrarily do anything stupid. As agreed, order issued by Enver Pasha, who places all land and naval forces of the Dardanelles under Admiral von Usedom.'[354]

To be clear, this order of Enver's meant that Admiral von Usedom commanded all the troops in the fortifications and the naval units in the Dardanelles. The Turkish Fifth Army was not affected by this order.

General Liman von Sanders remained on the heights of Bulair all day but increasingly came to believe that Bulair was only a feint attack. As the enemy had not landed there by evening and Essad Paşa was pleading for reinforcements for his hard pressed troops fighting in the southern part of the Peninsula, von Sanders was finally convinced and felt able to hand over elements of the divisions held in readiness at Bulair. Nevertheless, he remained up on the heights after dark.

The overall situation on the evening of 25 April as it presented itself to von Sanders was as follows: in the south, on the Asian side, the 11th Division reported a large concentration of the enemy's naval and transport ships in and around the Big and Small Beşika Bays and thus threatening a landing. Farther north, near Kum Kale, parts of the 3rd Division were fighting French troops, which had been landed there under massive support from naval artillery. At the southern tip of the Gallipoli Peninsula, namely at Seddulbahr, at Tekke Burnu, at the mouth of the Sigin Dere and at Morto Bay, strong British forces continued to fight weak units of the 9th Division's 26th Infantry Regiment around the landing bridgeheads. The whole area was under heavy fire from British naval gunnery, but the Turkish defence still seemed to be holding. At Gaba Tepe and at Ari Burnu, Allied troops had been disembarked from their transports and warships and were advancing towards high ground. Again, the defence seemed to be holding. In the upper Gulf of Saros, several warships were on station and had fired on the coast and fortified heights. Several large ships, possibly with troops on board, lay farther back. Signs of them leaving the ships had not been observed. In several places landings or preparations for them had been reported, so that the main Allied thrust was still not clearly defined so far as von Sanders was concerned. The goal of throwing the enemy back into the sea before it had established itself on land had not been achieved at any place.

The initial successful defence of the Gallipoli Peninsula on 25 April can, in my assessment – and despite some inadequacy on the part of the attacking Allied troops or their leadership, be attributed almost exclusively to the Turkish troops who fought outstandingly and valiantly at all three landing sectors. Although the operational plan of General von Sanders was successfully carried out, he was fixated for too long on the possible landing at Bulair. By noon on 25 April he should have realised that Sir Ian Hamilton had placed his emphasis in the south. Thus time was unnecessarily wasted in determining the focus of the defence and in concentrating the Turkish forces.

The successful defence of the first day cannot be attributed to a single commander. If anything, the major part of this success lies in the superior performance in the south of the Peninsula, at Cape Helles, by the 3rd Battalion, 26th Infantry Regiment under Major Mahmut Bey, and the men of the 27th Infantry Regiment under Lieutenant Colonel Şefik Bey, defending the Ari Burnu area against a far superior attacking force until reinforcements could be brought up.

Mustafa Kemal, who deployed his entire division against the express orders of his superiors and caused enormous casualties amongst his 57th Infantry Regiment in counter-attacks, wanted, however, to claim credit for the day's success. He was not shy in belittling the contribution of his Turkish comrades. Since he was obsessed with expelling the attackers from their positions before they became entrenched there, he repeatedly ordered desperate attacks by his devoted but completely exhausted infantry:

'There is no going back a single step. It is our duty to save our country, and we must acquit ourselves honourably and nobly.'[355]
'He reported to Essad Paşa that the tactical situation was good, but that the most important factor "was that everybody hurled himself on the enemy to kill and to die. This is no ordinary attack".'[356]

Mustafa Kemal continued to send his troops into action in small groups and at various points, without having a coherent plan and instead of concentrating his forces in one place and therefore being able to break through the ANZAC line. He wrote: 'I persisted in the idea of attacking with the utmost vigour and fierceness, and I was sure that with the throwing in of the reserves and support forces such an attack would achieve a decisive result.'

Robert Rhodes James commented on this approach: 'If it had been left to Kemal, there would hardly have been a Turkish soldier alive in the ANZAC area by the beginning of May'.[357]

On 3 May Mustafa Kemal wrote directly to Enver Paşa about the fighting on 25 April, going over the heads of both his Corps commander, Essad, and the Fifth Army commander, von Sanders:

'I had earlier explained to you the special importance of this sector as compared with all other sectors. The measures which I had taken as Maydos Area commander might have stopped the enemy coming ashore. But Liman von Sanders Paşa does not know either our army or our country, and did not have time to study the situation thoroughly. As a result, his dispositions left the landing sites totally unguarded and facilitated the enemy landings. When the enemy landed four brigades at Ariburnu, I was informed [of this] by sector commander Colonel [Halil] Sami. I attacked the enemy's left flank and threw them all back into the sea. But the enemy landed the same number of troops in the same place and counter-attacked. I repelled them, having no choice but to attack superior enemy forces with the reinforcements at my disposal. [...] But the terrain and the lack of skills of the commanders round me made it impossible to achieve a definite result. [...] I urge you strongly not to rely on the mental ability of the Germans, headed by von Sanders, whose hearts and souls are not engaged, as ours are, in the defence of our country. I believe that you should come here in person and take over the command as the situation requires.'[358]

These statements are essentially inconsistent with the evidence, as Mustafa Kemal's 19th Division on 25 April probably did not engage units of 2 and 3 (Australian) Brigades until around 10.00 am. While he certainly drove them again and again off Hill 700, he could never have thrown these troops back into the sea. Obviously Mustafa Kemal avoided mentioning the achievements of the 26th and 27th Infantry Regiments as he, too, would clearly have had to have given these troops full recognition for their success in the forward defence.

Despite these facts, in Turkey the energetic immediate defence of the Gallipoli Peninsula is almost exclusively associated with Mustafa Kemal; however, the high casualties are solely attributed to the decisions of General Liman von Sanders. This is a falsification of the evidence, has unfortunately found national acceptance and continues to be perpetuated in current Turkish publications and at memorial sites.

Chapter 9

The Fighting from 26 to 28 April 1915

The Allied command had little clarity about the state of the battle at Kum Kale on 26 April. The commander of the French troops, General d'Amade, had throughout the day asked permission from Hamilton to re-embark the troops at Kum Kale. This landing, apparently intended only as a diversionary attack, was under strong pressure from the Turkish 3rd Division. In the morning hours of 26 April, however, ships' heavy guns were able to intervene effectively and inflicted severe losses on the Turks. Several units gave themselves up. It was reported that a group of Turks, showing the white flag indicating that they wanted to surrender, then overwhelmed the French troops who came to take them in and so were able to force their way into Kum Kale. There they fought for some time, until finally they were overwhelmed by the French. The Turkish officer responsible for the white flag deception and eight of his soldiers were then summarily executed.[359]

The fighting continued until the early hours of 27 April, ending with the French withdrawal that General d'Amade had already ordered on 26 April. This took place without appreciable Turkish

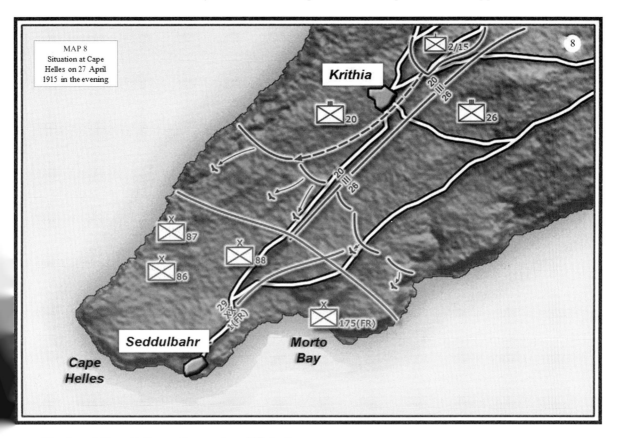

Situation at Cape Helles on the evening of 27 April.

intervention and the troops thus released were now able to reinforce the right flank of the British attack at Morto Bay. The French casualties in the fighting around Kum Kale came to 758 men, substantially less than those of their opponents; over 2,300 Turkish soldiers were killed, wounded or captured. With the French withdrawal, the Asiatic shore was again completely in Turkish hands and played no further role in the battles that followed. Although the landings at Kum Kale had at first tied down the 3rd and 11th Divisions, they were not sustainable. Nor could they keep these Turkish forces from the fighting on the peninsula in the long-term. Hamilton was obviously too focused on reinforcing the southern front on the Gallipoli peninsula and did not see the risk that the same Turkish forces that he might have successfully overcome at Kum Kale would sooner or later be facing him again at Krithia.

On the southern part of the Peninsula, in the Y Beach sector, the British losses amounted to 697 men - including the Commanding Officer of the 1st Battalion, King's Own Scottish Borderers, Lieutenant Colonel Archibald Stephen Koe. Reinforcements had not been sent, despite desperate requests. Hunter-Weston was fixated on the fighting at the tip of Cape Helles and assigned no importance to the appeals for help from this particular sector. Although Hamilton had recognized the crisis around Lieutenant Colonel Matthews, he did not want to intervene in the operational control exercised by the divisional commander. Matthews himself had not received any reports from divisional command for twenty-nine hours. Finally, Hamilton did order a French brigade to reinforce Y Sector, but it was impossible for him to get a clear picture of the situation from aboard the *Queen Elizabeth*. On the morning of 26 April, partly in confusion and obviously without clear leadership, groups of soldiers began independently to re-embark from Y Beach. By 7.00 am several hundred men had already returned to the warships. The evacuation continued under its own momentum and even Matthews, though aware that the Turkish troops had retreated, could not prevent the exodus. Thus, large quantities of equipment and ammunition remained ashore but without the Turks making use of it later. Units of the Turkish 25th Infantry Regiment had moved farther south to reinforce their defences.

Y Beach was now lost to the Allies and the great opportunity that had resulted from the unopposed landing of approximately 2,000 soldiers of the King's Own Scottish Borderers, a company of the South Wales Borderers and the Plymouth Battalion of the RMLI was squandered through unnecessary hesitation and weak leadership. These troops could have advanced to Krithia and tied up the Turkish reserves there. More troops landed in this sector could have attacked the southern landing areas from the north-west and the Turkish defence in the south might even have collapsed on the second day.

The W and V Beach sectors were now defended by about 1,000 men of the Turkish 25th Infantry Regiment, who arrived there on the evening of the previous day and had reinforced the remainder of the 26th Infantry Regiment. With daylight beginning, the shells of the ships' guns began to rain down again. At V Beach the exhausted British troops attacked the old Fort Seddulbahr, occupied it quickly and began to take the village, fighting street by street. The struggle against the spirited defence by remnants of the 26th Infantry Regiment lasted until about 3 pm, at which time the Turks withdrew further north and dug in again. The defenders were totally exhausted and their many wounded could not be treated locally. Mühlmann, who had relinquished the post of Adjutant to von Sanders, and was now assigned as a General Staff Officer to Sodenstern, in the Turkish 5th Division, described the state of the wounded whom he encountered:

'Soon we came across the wounded from Seddulbahr, mostly injured on their hands or feet; no medical facilities available. So the poor wounded had to make it to the dressing station about 20km away, where they were treated until reaching the military hospital in Maidos.'[360]

A Turkish field hospital in the dune positions of Gallipoli. (*Bundesarchiv Koblenz*)

Although the British were now able to take the dominant Hill 141, the Royal Fusiliers did not consolidate further and for the time being were content with this local victory. On the evening of 26 April Hunter-Weston and his 29th Division controlled the now extended landing area at Cape Helles with about 20,000 men. Only weak units of the 9th Division had made contact with the Allied invaders, whilst the remaining troops of the 26th Infantry Regiment and the 20th Infantry Regiment of the 7th Division continued to prepare for defence further to the north-east, just south of Krithia. Liman von Sanders had ordered the staggered withdrawal of the 7th Division from Bulair to the southern part of the Peninsula and now went himself to General Essad Paşa's command post, which was less than five kilometres behind the lines of Ari Burnu.

By 27 April, Hunter-Weston, on board the *Euryalus*, was able to establish a line from the former landing area at X Beach in the west, to Eski Hissarlik, as a jumping off point for a further attack against Krithia. He had parts of the French division, which had meanwhile landed in Morto Bay, on the right flank, and two British brigades, the 88th in the middle and the 87th on the left, as well as the 86th in reserve, So far he had not encountered any significant resistance from the Turkish defenders.

Meanwhile, on 26 April, von Sanders had considered it necessary to identify the two geographically separate combat zones on Gallipoli, placing each under its own command. In Ari Burnu, Mustafa Kemal was given command of what later became known as the Northern Group.

The troops fighting at the southern tip, the subsequent Southern Group, were subordinated to the GOC of the 5th Division, Colonel von Sodenstern. Both groups were commanded by Essad Paşa. Mühlmann described this reorganisation:

'About 9 pm, after we had ridden all over, we saw a few lights & came across the Staff of the 9th Div hidden in a few gullies, together with Essad. The command structures were quickly regulated. The troops present at Seddulbahr were subordinate to Sodenstern, 9th Div & the parts of 7th Div now coming forward as Southern Group. The troops at Arı Burnu, 19th Div & later 5th Div as well, which replaced another Div from Const[antinople] at Bulair, form the Northern Group under the Div Cdr of the 19th Div, Kemal Bey. Essad was in command of both groups.'[361]

On the second day of the attack Liman von Sanders was finally prepared to release more reserves from Bulair. Nevertheless, this decision was not easy for him at this time, as ships of the British fleet were still in the Gulf of Saros. He handed over the command of the remaining troops at Bulair to his Chief of Staff, Lieutenant Colonel Kiazim Bey. Von Sanders later explained his reasoning:

'As the responsible leader, the withdrawal of all troops from the shores of the upper Saros Gulf was a serious and far reaching decision for me. But it had to be risked on account of the great

Headquarters of III Army Corps. Seated at the table, Essad Paşa, left of the table, Sedat Doğruer Bey, right of the table, Fahrettin Altay Bey.

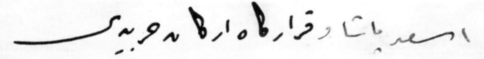

superiority of the enemy in the southern part of the peninsula. Had the British noticed this weakness, they probably would not have hesitated to take decisive advantage of it!'[362]

The ADC to von Sanders, Mühlmann, described the subsequent measures:

At 06.00 hrs on the 28th, I was hastily summoned to S [von Sanders], who, in contrast to the previous day's intelligence, had just received a new communication that the enemy had been greatly reinforced at Arı Burnu & Seddulbahr, [and] reinforcements were therefore necessary. As a result, not only the 7th but also the 5th Div were to be brought up via Maidos. I should immediately go to Sodenstern & provide practical assistance to the troops to be shipped via Gelibolu, as well as the appropriate occupation of the Bulair position.'[363]

The units of the Turkish 5th and 7th Divisions, which had arrived by boat in Maidos, had been ordered by Essad Paşa, on the morning of 26 April, to join the Southern Group near Seddulbahr, where they were incorporated as reinforcements. Of the remaining units of the 5th Division, some smaller elements had to be transferred to Ari Burnu to reinforce the 19th Division there. Of course, given the fragmentation of forces, operations such as counter-attacks or relieving larger formations were difficult to carry out. Within only a few days four divisions had been merged, as was the 11th Division later, which had been brought over from the Asiatic side: this was a situation that was also heavily criticised by Mühlmann:

'Unfortunately, the operation against Seddulbahr came out of the fear that the enemy would daily reinforce himself at Seddulbahr and increasingly gain a firm foothold. All possible troop units hastily rushed from different divisions arrived here, usually without kit, to be led into battle, despite several days of transportation & tiring marches, and lacking knowledge of the terrain.'[364]

Von Sanders now saw the need to reinforce the forces of the Fifth Army as a whole and reported this to Istanbul. Along with his request for reinforcements, he also asked Enver to send him German officers; among others, he urgently asked for the assignment of Colonel Kannengiesser: 'To Enver Pasha. Please send Colonel Kannengiesser immediately to take over command of the southern portion of the Gallipoli Peninsula. Signed, Liman von Sanders, 26.4.15.'[365]

At first Kannengiesser was to take command of the newly formed Southern Group; but then von Sanders obviously decided differently. Kannengiesser described the moment when he reported to von Sanders on 29 April and his disappointment is more than clear:

'Events always happen, however, quite differently to what one has anticipated. I was almost immediately to experience this again. Directly after we had made fast before the town of Gallipoli I reported to the Marshal, who explained that I had to take over the 5th Division in place of Col. von Sodenstern, who had already taken the position allotted to me as commander of the South Front. It had taken me longer than G.H.Q. had expected to come from Constantinople, although I had lost no time.'[366]

The surprises continued for Kannengiesser. When he wanted to take over his intended 5th Division, units of which had meanwhile been relocated from Bulair to the Ari Burnu area, there were no troops left that could be handed over to him: Mustafa Kemal had already merged this division into his own.

'Nobody knew anything of the 5th Division. I finally found, west of Koja Dere, a small clump of tents. This was the staff of the 5th Division, from now onwards my own Division. The Chief Staff Officer was with Mustapha Kemal Bey. Where the troops were they did not know.

   'We climbed a steep cliff to Kemalyeri, as this place was called, after Kemal Bey. He was extremely astonished when I presented myself to him as commander of the 5th Division and told him I intended to take over my own troops. "That's quite impossible," he told me, "as the 5th and 19th Divisions are completely mixed. I have arranged a big attack for tomorrow." I recognised that it was impossible to make any alterations at the moment and agreed to his conducting the action over the whole front provided that, at the first possible opportunity, I took over command of my own Division.'[367]

A Turkish attack on 28 April on the front of the Northern Group at Ari Burnu, launched against the Anzacs, again failed. Because of the difficult terrain and poor communications, what had been planned by Kemal as a simultaneous attack along the entire line evolved into a fragmented series of bold but suicidal attacks that could be repulsed everywhere. General Birdwood wrote in his diary, 'Had Turks attacked in unity in one place, they must have got through'.[368]

   The only result of these attacks was that the Turks would in future desist from daylight attacks in order to avoid the fire from the Allied ships. The losses in the ANZAC section were again enormously high. In just six days, the attacking British, Australian, and New Zealand troops had lost 6,554 soldiers, of whom 1,252 had been killed. The Turkish losses were significantly higher, especially as a result of the counter-attacks. The Turkish General Staff estimated the losses at about 14,000 men, many of them killed or who later died of wounds. Despite significant German support, the Turkish Army's medical services were not as well organised as that of the Allies and the mortality rate of their wounded was much higher.

Chapter 10

The Three Battles for Krithia

In his telegram from Istanbul very soon after the landings, Enver Paşa urged pushing the attack against the Allied troops that had landed at Seddulbahr, Teke Burnu and Morto Bay, throwing them off the Peninsula. On the other hand, Major General Hunter-Weston intended, by all means at his disposal, to push the decision his way in the Helles sector. The following battles were subsequently named by Allied historians as the Three Battles of Krithia; this nomenclature referred to their attacks and did not necessarily encompass the Turkish counter-attacks.

The British 29th Division was ordered to dig in on 27 April and prepare a defence against Turkish attacks. Although reconnoitring parties had discovered that the Turks had set up their defences more than three kilometres to the north, the British apparently lacked the strength or the will to follow up any success at that stage. Their supply situation was still critical and so far only twenty-eight artillery pieces had been landed. Hunter-Weston nevertheless ordered an attack for the morning of 28 April. His plan of battle was an attack on the forces positioned to the far left of Krithia, while holding back a little in the centre and then slowly shifting the attack further to the north-west. On the left and in the middle were units of the 29th Division and on the right the French Division. The plan therefore constituted a flanking movement, difficult to coordinate,

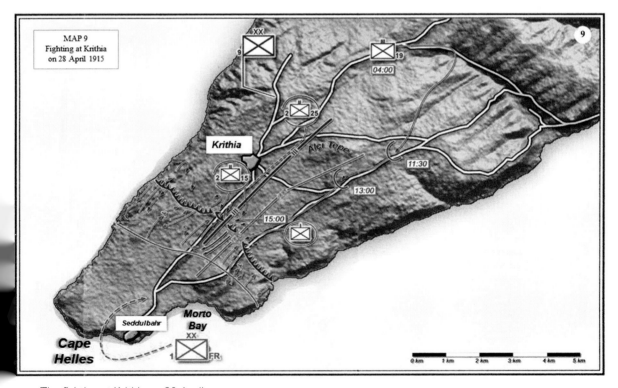

The fighting at Krithia on 28 April.

against unknown enemy positions, without sufficient artillery support and with troops who were still exhausted. To make matters even worse, there was again a timing issue, as some units did not get their orders until the planned attack had started. However, Hunter-Weston believed that he could take this risk, as he assessed the resistance capability of the Turkish troops as weak and, in his opinion, they were still retreating to the north.

The First Battle of Krithia began on 28 April at 8.00 am with a bombardment by the battleships, which were hove to off the coast. At first the attack on the left flank went according to plan and Krithia seemed theirs for the taking. In the middle, however, the attack lost its coherence, as orders were forgotten or misunderstood, and each unit attacked where it deemed fit. By noon the entire attack had lost its momentum and the situation was unclear. On the right flank the French had tried to cross the Kereves Dere but had been beaten back there by entrenched Turkish units, who knew how to take advantage of the rugged terrain. In the centre, forces of the 19th Regiment, which had been brought to the front by forced march during that very day, launched a counter-attack at around 3 pm against the flanks of the two attacking Allied divisions. Hunter-Weston now lost control of the battle. Even though individual British units had come up close to Krithia, they were not supported there. The British troops withdrew and the fighting was over by 6 pm on the same day. The First Battle of Krithia was one of the most intensive battles of the entire Gallipoli campaign, with the Allies suffering 3,000 casualties out of the approximately 14,000 soldiers who took part.

The troops on both sides were exhausted, but the Allies also had supply problems, since bad weather prevented stores being landed by sea. The devastating result of the first fighting for Krithia put paid to Hamilton's strategy of a lightning strike to take the Peninsula. The Allied forces had been badly damaged and were severely demoralised, while the Turks were now able to prepare additional defensive positions on the slopes of Alçi Tepe (Achi Baba) and bring over additional forces from the Asian shore. In the meantime, von Sanders prepared the Southern Group's counter-attack for the night of 1/ 2 May, while simultaneously launching further counter-attacks in Ari Burnu against the Anzacs. On 1 May Mustafa Kemal again ordered his troops forward against the ANZAC lines. In his order of 30 April, he wrote: 'Our front in comparison with the enemy is not weak … the enemy's morale has been completely broken down. In continually digging trenches, he is seeking a refuge for himself.'[369]

However, this Turkish mass attack wavered in the rifle and machine gun fire of the Royal Naval Division fighting alongside the ANZAC forces. Colonel Kannengiesser observed this attack, led by Mustafa Kemal, which was composed of forces drawn from four different Turkish divisions. Kannengiesser was very critical, describing his impression of the Turkish soldiers:

'I must say that the first general impression which I received of the conduct of the Turkish troops in battle was not particularly complimentary to them. Quite a number of battalions had failed during the attack.

It was particularly difficult for me to obtain a clear appreciation of the situation, because I only heard Turkish spoken, which I did not understand. My interpreter, Zia Bey, appeared to have little or no appreciation of the real tactical position … […] The best will and the best ability in the world could not be used in action so long as it was impossible to converse directly with the non-commissioned officers and men, and reports and orders were received through the interpreter either incorrectly or were badly translated.'[370]

It should be borne in mind, however, that the troops Kannengiesser criticised had already been in action for six days, had suffered heavy casualties and had hardly any officers and NCOs left. Nevertheless, Mustafa Kemal also took this lesson to heart and commented later: 'the battle, which lasted for 24 hours, had caused great fatigue to our troops, and so I gave an order for the attack to stop.'[371]

The hard lessons learned caused Essad Paşa strictly to forbid any further frontal assaults. The decision in favour of the resultant positional warfare was justified by Kemal: 'There was no other means of protecting our homeland but to dig in on the line which had been won and to hold on there.'[372]

Mustafa Kemal's order for defence ended:

'All soldiers fighting here with us must realise that to carry out completely the honourable duty entrusted to us there must not be one step towards the rear. Let me remind you all that your desire to rest does not merely mean that you are being deprived of your rest but may lead to our whole nation being so deprived until eternity. I have no doubt that all of our comrades agree on this, and that they will show no signs of fatigue until the enemy are finally hurled into the sea.'[373]

On 30 April, Colonel von Sodenstern, commanding the Southern Group, was ordered to attack the Allied positions with all his available forces, which amounted to a total of twenty-one battalions. Apart from the 9th Division, which had hardly any troops of its own, and the 7th Division, which was just as severely weakened, Sodenstern would be receiving fresh troops from the 11th Division, which was en route after their fast march without kit from the Asian shore, as well as units of the 5th and 3rd Divisions. Captain Mühlmann, who had been assigned to the staff of the Southern Group as General Staff Officer, wrote to his parents about his new post:

'At last he [von Sanders] consented; I was assigned to accompany Colonel von Sodenstern as General Staff Officer. I was happy & I am sure you will approve of my decision. I have thereby assumed a completely different independent post & have – I can modestly say – conducted

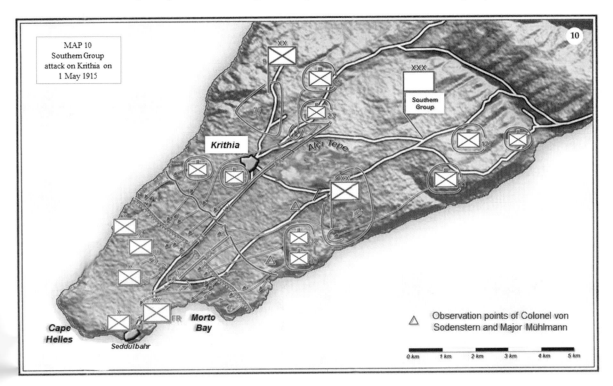

The attack of the Southern Group near Krithia on May 1, 1915.

operations with mixed troops with a strength of almost an Army Corps & although under the most difficult external & internal conditions over 6 days & under General Weber, now have an interesting & comfortable life. These weeks have seen me get a General Staff Officer's uniform, the Iron Cross 1st Class & Imtiaz Medal in Silver.'[374]

Mühlmann went on to describe the preparations for the attack set for 30 April:

'In the afternoon I took a short nap to keep myself fresh. Then, on a hill close to us, [...] worked out an inspiring order of the day, stating, in a few words, that the soldiers were defending their religious and political liberty. I will send you a transcript. In the evening, at 9, the two divisional commanders had been summoned to discuss everything in detail and & to clear any doubts.'[375]

Drafted by his adjutant, the same order of the day was given by von Sodenstern to his soldiers before the forthcoming attack:

'Soldiers! You must drive the enemy, who are at Seddulbahr, into the sea. The enemy is afraid of you; he dare not come out of his trenches and attack you. He can do nothing more than wait for you with his guns and machine guns. You are not afraid of his fire. You must believe that the greatest happiness awaits him who gives up his life in this Holy War. Attack the enemy with the bayonet and utterly destroy him! We shall not retire one step; for if we do our religion, our country and our nation will perish! Soldiers! The world is looking at you! Your only hope of salvation is to bring this battle to a successful issue or to give up your life gloriously in the attempt.'[376]

Another order from Sodenstern to his regimental commanders was more than clear, since it was apparent that he felt that the quality of leadership by Turkish officers in battle left much to be desired:

'Let it be clearly understood that those who remain stationary at the moment of attack, or who try to escape, will be shot. For this purpose machine-guns will be placed behind the troops to oblige such people to advance and at the same time to fire on the enemy's reserves.'[377]

The terrain over which the attack was to be fought was described by Mühlmann:

Near Salem Bey Tschiflik [çiftlik = farm], which is now our home – in a rugged, partially pine-covered valley – is a coastal battery observation post, which offers an excellent view of the foothills to the coast, which will be transformed in a few hours into a fierce battleground. Like a bastion, the Hissarlik Plateau, which is occupied by the French, rises up. L. [Liman von Sanders] is worried that they will place heavy artillery batteries there, making our shore batteries quite uncomfortable; then there is a treeless hill, where two hollows rise up from our side from the elongated Kereves Dere Gorge, then there are lower lying meadows & arable land; finally, on the right flank, at last, heathland again, traversed by a deeply winding ravine. In general, although flat at a first impression, the area looks like it has a lot of cover & hollows, which, luckily, lead around our rear positions & reserves to the front line.'[378]

On the evening of 1 May at Krithia all available forces of the Southern Group were ready to launch their counter-attack. As night fell, the units of the 9th and 7th Divisions, with white sleeve markings for mutual recognition, were taken to their jumping off positions. The attack began at 10 pm as planned, but no reports came in to the Southern Group staff. Mühlmann wrote:

'Shortly after 10 [pm] weak infantry fire began in some places, which soon stopped. Messages unfortunately very sparse, as the division staffs were too far behind & therefore only received sparse & late messages from their front lines. Shortly after midnight the news came from the 7th Division on the left wing, that the enemy's forward positions had been taken, and now the main positions were being advanced upon. A great burden dropped off my shoulders, as I will never forget these hours; but I was – I may say it – the driving force before the attack & I felt a huge responsibility.'[379]

As still no reliable reports arrived for the staff of the Southern Group, in the early hours of the morning Sodenstern and Mühlmann set off personally to observe the attack.

'In the meantime, at 3.00 am, heavy infantry and artillery fire again and we suspected the storming of the main position; at 03.30 am it was very quiet, even the ships did not fire, so that my hopes were steadily rising, the enemy had been thrown into the sea or captured. How else to explain the silence? So we rode back to Salem Bey Tschiflik at dawn to await further news at this central point. I thought it would have been better to have ridden further forward, but accepted the validity of the reasons given by Sodenstern. Shortly before we went down, in a sombre but confident mood, to Salim Bey Tsch., lively infantry and artillery fire began again. We quickly rode back up to the heights of the observation post & saw – it really hurt me – our lines of troops going back up the slope. In thin lines, the troops withdrew to the high ground north of Hissarlik. They particularly came under fire from the warships lying off the Dardanelles, which were firing on their left flank & rear. Unfortunately, the Canakkale Fortress Command artillery did not support us enough, although the day before I had personally asked Devad [Cevad] Pasha, the governor of the Dardanelles. [...] So, of course, the troops have suffered great losses, not only when going back under the naval bombardment from three sides, but also during the day, by the flanking fire of the *Agamemnon*, which is now my sworn enemy & I wish it is speedily sunk by a German U-boat.'[380]

By 1 May the Allies' morale and supply situation was much better than it had been two days earlier. As the weather had improved, supplies and reinforcements could now be landed and brought in unhindered. The troops were rested and well looked after in their positions when the Turkish artillery opened fire at around 10 pm. Turkish troops attacked over several hundred metres of open terrain and could only break through in two places in the opposing lines. These breakthroughs were made on the positions of the Munster and Dublin Fusiliers, who had suffered heavy losses on landing. However, the attacking Turks were halted by the Royal Fusiliers and the Royal Scots, and the lost positions were retaken. This action was recorded in the diary of Sergeant Dennis Moriarty, 1/Royal Munster Fusiliers:

'About 5 p.m. enemy started a heavy shrapnel fire on our trenches. [...] 9 p.m. they started an attack, I am sure I will never forget that night as long as I live. They crept right up to our trenches (they were in thousands) and they made the night hideous with yells and shouting Allah, Allah. We could not help mowing them down. [...] My God, what a sight met us when day broke this morning. The whole ground in front was littered with dead Turks.'[381]

On the flank of the 7th Division, attacking from the left, a breakthrough on the defending French division was initially successful, assisted by artillery support, and here also the old positions would be taken again in the course of the battle. After a successful Turkish defence, the Allied troops immediately launched a counter-attack. The 87 Brigade, on the left of the 9th Turkish Division, gained almost 500 metres of ground and thus reached the forward Turkish positions, which, however, were regained by the Turks during the course of the day. In his letters Mühlmann gave an account of both this initial defeat and the counter-attack that was ordered by Liman von Sanders:

'Blow upon blow followed & every new situation gave me physical pain. Under these circumstances we did not want to repeat the attack, but a message from L. [Liman von Sanders] forced us to do so. I was dead tired and you can reckon up just how many hours I have slept the last few nights & also the food was neither abundant nor nutritious. Nevertheless, the necessary orders were issued; for the new attack two new battalions were now available, who had arrived in the evening after a long march. At 07.00 hrs we rode off to the observation post of the 7th Division, who had placed their artillery forward on a height with a commanding view. Fortunately we did not attack – because it would have certainly failed, since only two new battalions were available – the enemy now went over to the attack. [...] About 03.00 hrs on 2 May we received reports that the enemy attacks had been repulsed all along the line. The question next arose as to whether one should not launch an attack on the weakened & exhausted enemy; but the two new battalions had not yet arrived. It was not until 03.30 hrs that they turned up; so we could be quite certain, that with a daylight attack we would be annihilated by the ships' guns. This consideration was the decisive factor; the two battalions, also totally exhausted by their long march, were withdrawn to cover and the two divisions ordered to hold their positions at all costs & to dig in there.'[382]

Even though the Turkish attack had failed, the Allied troops had nevertheless suffered heavy losses. The French contingent had more than 2,000 wounded and killed; in the 29th Division, a disproportionate number of officers and senior commanders had been killed, including five battalion commanders and the commander of the artillery brigade.

Von Sanders had already ordered the next attack with fresh forces for the following night of 2/3 May – a great challenge in view of the heavy fighting which had already taken place, the supply situation and the difficult integration of forces. On 2 May Colonel Kannengiesser, who had started off as commander of the 19th Division at the Northern Group, was ordered back by Liman von Sanders to be deployed in the Southern Group at the main point of defence. Kannengiesser reported there on the same day at around 11 pm to Colonel von Sodenstern at his command post. On his way to the south of the peninsula, Kannengiesser impressively described the intensity of the fighting:

'By 10 o'clock in the evening I rode out from Serafin Tschiflik, and my guide was the sky, reddened as from an enormous conflagration. [...]

The closer I approached the battlefield the more powerful was the impression on the eye and ear. I recognised the continuous flashes from the fleet that lay in a half circle round the Peninsula and bombarded the land with ceaseless fire, giving an impression of power and might which I can scarcely describe.[...]

Even later, in August 1917, in the battles in Flanders, I did not have the same overwhelming impression of concentrated shelling as during this period.'[383]

The Turkish fleet provided personnel and material support for the Fifth Army. Admiral von Usedom had reported to the Fleet Commander that there was a shortage of machine guns on the front lines. Admiral Souchon reacted to this and noted in the war diary of the MMD on 30 April:

> 'Enemy troops landing at Kaba Tepe launched attacks on Turkish positions during the day. *Barbaros* supporting the army with indirect fire. Incredibly, the Fifth Army, as Usedom reports, lacks machine guns. I will provide all that can be spared from the ships of the fleet.'[384]

The *Goeben* and *Breslau* now provided officers and men. Under the command of Lieutenant Wilhelm Boltz, forty-four men and eight machine guns made their way from Istanbul to the Dardanelles.[385] This group later merged with the naval gunnery observers who were already present there, and were then formed into the so-called 'German Naval Shore Detachment', with Boltz in command. Almost all of the officers and men had had infantry training, having been assembled as a Marine Infantry Company from the 1st and 2nd Sailors' Division in Kiel and Wilhelmshaven. They had taken part in the international blockade of Montenegro in 1913 and consequently had already been on board the *Breslau* in Pola during the same year. The task of the marine infantry was to fight on land as well as carrying out watch and gun duties on ship. This is the reason that the MMD had at its disposal a number of heavy machine guns, on which the sailors were well trained.

The Naval Shore Detachment of the Breslau. (*Bundesarchiv Koblenz*)

When the detachment arrived at Gallipoli on the afternoon of 3 May, it was immediately ordered to report to the Southern Group. Lieutenant Boltz wrote about an incident which occurred on the way:

'On 3 May, at 15.00 hrs, my detachment arrived in Kilia, and here I received orders to march to the Southern Group to report to Colonel von Sodenstern. In the rush, they had not found time for my sailors, who still wore German uniforms, to change into Turkish ones, so we were often halted when night began to fall. It was not until 23.00 hrs that I was able to report to the commander of the Southern Group in Ali-Bey Tschiflik, Colonel von Sodenstern, who gave me the order to send four machine guns via Krithia to Seddulbahr. The four other guns were be used at Kereves Dere. I assumed command of the latter, delegating command of the guns for Seddulbahr to Petty Officer Schubert. On our way up we had already heard the thunder of the ships' guns as well as lively infantry fire. But the route to Kereves was still under the heaviest artillery fire from the enemy fleet, and the valley itself was full of troops, ammunition wagons, and pack animals carrying boxes of infantry ammunition. Everywhere, shot-up carts and dead animals presented an obstacle that was difficult to clear where the path cuts deeply into the rock. Nevertheless, the unit marched forward silently, in exemplary order. Shortly before arriving on the battlefield, the section sent to Seddulbahr came back to me, as it had not been possible for them to get through there. [...] On the point of setting up my machine-guns in position, an unexpected event suddenly occurred. A company of an Arab regiment, coming up from the side of the valley and only led by a Tschausch [çavuş = sergeant], had noticed my people and surrounded them, thinking that they had Englishmen [sic] in front of them. The uniform of the German Navy was unknown to these people and trying to make myself understood with my poor knowledge of Turkish was difficult, especially to an Arab. When I threatened to free myself by force of arms, the Tschausch approached me at gunpoint. I raised my Browning - a critical moment, only resolved through the intervention of the General Staff Officer of the Southern Group, Major Mühlmann, who quickly made the people understand that we were Germans.'[386]

Mühlmann described this incident:

'Having arrived on top of the hill, a little farther, from where we had been sitting two hours ago with Sodenstern, I was stopped by Turkish infantrymen who excitedly told me that they had captured English machine-guns. My astonishment cannot be described as other than anger when I recognised that our six German machine-guns from the *Breslau* were in the midst of the so-called Englishmen. During the night they had already been stopped through non-recognition of their uniforms, roughed up and not really allowed to proceed forward. And now, at this crucial moment, when the Turks had so few machine-guns, our six good machine-guns, well-served, would have been able to achieve extraordinary results, but I found them to have been 'captured'. Of course, I immediately cleared things up & ordered them to continue to go forward into position.'[387]

The accounts written by Kannengiesser also make it possible to have more insight into the difficult situation regarding the organisation and supply of this Army Corps:

'In the morning, at 5 o'clock, von Sodenstern and I met in the 'Staff quarters' – a little clay house in the middle of a small bare spot called Salem Bey Tschiflik. The three canvas beds occupied the room. Instead of windows, holes had been punched in the thatch of the sides. It was very cold. [...]

The 7th and 9th Divisions had their normal supplies. For the attached units that had been put in piecemeal difficulties arose that Sodenstern settled out of hand by requisitioning herds of sheep that he discovered during his ride through the Peninsula a few days previously, although such action was strictly forbidden. The troops received in this way at least meat and a little bread. I gratefully remember here a battery which lay close to Salim Bey Tschiflik that admirably looked after the rationing of the staff of von Sodenstern.

As a matter of fact this staff was not particularly well off. There was actually nobody of any real account there in spite of the fact that Sodenstern had more than an Army Corps under his command. The few men that he had, even including the able Major Mühlmann, could not possibly replace a properly constituted General Staff. There was not a single telephone line to any of the divisions and, added to this, there was the language complication, the extremely difficult tactical position where we were and the complete confusion existing among the troops.'[388]

At this phase of the defensive battle the first plans started to emerge in Istanbul as to how the Turkish Fleet could also provide support for the defenders. The War Diary of the MMD for 2 May stated:

'Meeting with Enver Pasha regarding the situation. I explain to him about the cooperation of the fleet in defence of the Dardanelles, and that tomorrow I sail with the flagship to try and shell the Kaba Tepe position of the enemy landing. Major von König, before going back to Gallipoli, gave me a very hopeful report of the situation on the Gallipoli peninsula on behalf of General von Liman. The Turkish troops are doing very well.'[389]

But the use of the *Goeben* was short-lived, as it was too big and unwieldy in the Straits and could easily have fallen victim to Allied naval guns or air raids. But, with the unique appearance of his largest ship, Admiral Souchon at least managed to boost the morale of the troops, even though the *Goeben* simply steamed back to Istanbul the following day. Nevertheless, Souchon appreciated the need for support for the land forces and summarised the position on 3 May:

'Situation on Gallipoli not particularly good. Above all, there is an absence of collaboration between General Liman, Essad Pasha and the Fleet. Essad Pasha has no German officer on his staff and refuses all help from Lieutenant Commander Rohde. The preparations at Gaba Tepe for shore defences against landings were inadequate.'[390]

In the shipyard at the Golden Horn in Istanbul, the *Torgut* had been specially modified for indirect fire support in the Dardanelles and now she made her way to Gallipoli on 8 May. From Mühlmann's accounts of the preparations by the Southern Group staff, his criticism of von Sodenstern is clear; the Colonel obviously was not equal to the task before him:

'Three infantry regiments of the 15th Division arrived; six battalions, plus a battalion of the 11th Division, and a new heavy battery. All wanted to have orders; ammunition, food and medical service had to be organised, but I was alone; good old Sodenstern, by the way, is a great man, but would be better off as a battalion commander in Arolsen [a quiet town in Germany], as the situation was way over his head. There was no support for me except a totally incompetent Turkish adjutant & two officer cadets who translated the orders from German into Turkish; that comprised the whole staff for a body of troops or, better said, motley collection of troops, numbering around 30,000 men! So that night of 2/3 May the attack was to be repeated, hopefully with more success. The necessary orders were all issued in good time, which means to say I issued them early, then had the unfortunate job of transmitting them, passing them on by phone, which didn't work properly, so that unfortunately they arrived late at the most forward front line.'[391]

The front was divided into two halves by the Krithia-Seddulbahr road: on the right, the 9th Division under Colonel Sami Bey; on the left, the 7th Division under Kemsi Bey. A total of twenty-four battalions were used, that is the 7th and 9th Divisions in their entirety, as well as units of the 3rd, 5th and 11th Divisions. The commander of the Southern Group still had no heavy guns at his disposal, but did have just enough field artillery with sufficient ammunition supplies on hand. In the course of 3 May Colonel Remsi Bey, commander of the 15th Division, arrived on the battlefield with five battalions, on which Kannengiesser commented: 'He spoke very good German and impressed one as fresh and efficient. New hopes arose that during this night we should finally be successful.'[392]

The attack started again in the night hours. Mühlmann wrote:

'At 22.30 hrs the attack was launched. All imaginable instructions had been given; at any rate we all had the feeling that we could not have done more. Soon we left our position at the rear & went on the road leading to Seddulbahr, as far forward as telephone cables had been laid: we were at the position of the 7th Division. An overview of the battlefield was of course not possible despite the moonlight, which shone from about midnight. Again heavy infantry and artillery fire started up; the 9th Division was to go up against the line Tekke Burnu-Helles Burnu; the 7th Division against the line Helles Burnu-Seddulbahr, and the 15th Division attacked against Hissarlik. Around 02.00 hrs the 15th Division called for reinforcements; we gave it our last battalion & I moved further forward with Colonel Kannengiesser, who had come to us the day before. We rode to a spot close behind a forward battalion, dismounted there and, with rifle fire whizzing round our heads, went behind the slope of the hill often mentioned, northeast of Hissarlik. Now I have to agree with Sodenstern, we were now well forward, close behind the firing line, but there was not much to see & leadership in the fighting was also not apparent. It is curious what skill the senior Turkish leaders have to disappear. Also, the pictures we saw were not very pleasing. Instead of proceeding silently in fixed directions, the infantrymen, screaming like nursery schoolkids, dodged here and there; the officers also failed here. Divisional and regimental commanders were not to be seen, so that Sodenstern himself had to order the last battalion to attack & give it its final instructions. We stayed there about half an hour, without being able to clearly see in which direction the battle was going. The stray bullets of the infantry that were constantly buzzing around our ears could easily have hit us as well, as they fell into the grass beside us. We could see that up ahead, surrounded by the action of battle, and without any telephone connection, battle leadership was even less possible & so we went back to our old position, the little gorse hill on the road to Seddulbahr. Since there were neither clear nor unclear reports from the divisions & as the daylight approached, I decided to ride forward to ascertain the state of the struggle. I went forward at a gallop on my trusty Kerim [his horse] with an interpreter. Slowly the day, 4 May, began to break.'[393]

The report of the intelligence officer of the Fifth Army confirmed the sad outcome of the battles. On 4 May, at 7.00 am, he noted:

'At 04.55 hrs, the 15th Division commander reported that he had taken Seddulbahr. On the right flank, the attack went just as well, until this flank came to the enemy wire obstacles & was halted there. I saw our own infantry at Seddulbahr and to the west of it. The enemy was completely defeated and thrown back behind Seddulbahr and up to Ertrogul. But we still did not have Ertrogul as yet. Unfortunately, it was getting light. The poor soldiers, who had carried out this attack excellently, were without leadership, as there were rarely any officers to be seen at the front. They had all been killed or wounded on the field of honour. The men did not know what they should do, and ran back and forth like sheep as shells from the enemy ships came from all sides and unfortunately the whole attack had to come to a sad end. Our losses were indescribably high. Whilst withdrawing we lost as many as we did in the attack. The infantry which had gone forward occupied its old positions again. Major Lange on the right reported that he can hold his position. The dashing, energetic 15th Division commander, Remsi Bey, who was with the whole attack on the first front, also reported that he can also hold his position. The 7th Division reports the same thing. I have no confidence in these. I've just come from the front and am now with Rifaat, riding towards Kara Tepe. I'm in Chanak at midday.'[394]

Ready for action – a Turkish machine-gun position with German officers. (*Bundesarchiv Koblenz*)

Lieutenant Boltz described the attack:

'The news spread like wildfire of the intervention of German machine guns in the Turkish line, and soon the general attack began again. The guns were brought forward bit by bit, and from the Kereves Dere we managed to drive the enemy from their positions back to the beach; the English [sic] trenches were occupied. Finally I found myself in the English positions with three machine-guns and brought the withdrawing enemy under heavy fire. Two of my guns had become unserviceable by being hit, the other three had not been brought along due to no gun crews being available. At daybreak the Turks had to withdraw as a result of the devastating fire of the enemy fleet, which bombarded from a distance of about 15 kms. The trenches we had taken were cleared again. The enemy infantry in no way disturbed the slow withdrawal of the Turkish lines of troops. Over on the enemy's side, there seemed to be no leadership this morning.'[395]

By the morning the attack had failed and had to be broken off. The Shore Detachment's first mission was successful, even though it was not able to save the attack completely. But it suffered casualties; three soldiers were killed, seven wounded and a machine gun was no longer usable.

Mühlmann judged why the counter-attacks of the Turks had failed, again not sparing his criticism of the leadership:

'Before I continue, I want to tell you the reasons for the failure of the attacks. First of all the contribution made by the participation of the [Allied] fleet, which could fire on the Turks' attack from all sides with about twenty batteries of their heaviest calibre. Then the attack had been rushed. The concern that the enemy would reinforce and entrench more each day in Seddulbahr led to bringing in troops from wherever they were available, and these without their kit – yes, and sometimes without their big packs. After being several days on transport & after a long march, the troops then arrived at the battlefield & barely had time to orientate themselves properly on the terrain. Of course, food and water supplies were not working as under regular circumstances.

Another aspect was the lack of training of the officers and men. Of course night attacks are one of the hardest kinds of attack & the troops have to be specially trained. Unfortunately, this was not the case with the men who came here. Instructions at the last moment do not help. The officers, too, failed completely; the senior leaders all remained at the rear, where they lost all influence on the course of the battle, and the junior officers, like their troops, were ignorant of night attacks and their technique. And yet, in spite of all these things, the attacks carried out by this untrained, leaderless infantry, but inspired by the best spirit of martial aggression, would have succeeded if the 9th Division, on the right, had not let us down.

On both nights regiments of the 7th Division, according to a number of reports, penetrated as far as the landing areas of Seddulbahr and threw bombs at the landing barges; but since the 9th Division, in spite of all their orders to attack, only made feeble attempts to move forward, the enemy, since they were not held down there, could use his forces opposing the 9th Division to turn against the right flank of the advancing 7th Division & force its withdrawal. Is that not a pity? So much blood flowed in vain as a result. For the 7th Division, which had to go back in daylight under hell fire from three sides, the losses were of course very, very heavy. You have to give the soldiers the highest recognition that they did not fall apart; I am once again totally convinced that everything can be achieved with these kinds of men. As I was up on the heights on the morning of the 4th, it would have been possible with the help of some energetic officers to restore order to the confusion, yes, indeed, even to go on the attack again, if daylight had not threatened. I could hear cries from all around: "Where shall we go? Nobody tells us. We have no officers." And they all went around confused. It was really shocking. And, despite the enormous losses & failure of the planned goal to actually throw the enemy into the sea or capture them, these continued attacks had had considerable success; according to later newspaper reports, the enemy had suffered high casualties and his morale was greatly shaken, as the later attacks have shown.'[396]

Kannengiesser had been watching this battle and concluded:

'I personally was forced to the conclusion that we dare not attempt further fighting of this description, and that it was my personal duty to report my conclusions to the Marshal. Following my return from the battlefield at dawn on the 4th May, I asked by telephone for permission to report to the Marshal about the position of affairs.'[397]

He stated his case before von Sanders and not only pleaded to give up trying to drive the enemy entirely from the southern peninsula but also suggested that General Weber be entrusted with the Command of the Southern Group. Sanders replied that, 'He is already on his way and should arrive here in a few hours' time'.[398]

Captain Mühlmann gave his opinion on the Southern Group's change of leadership:

'General Weber arrived late in the evening; since the attack methods had failed, positional warfare will now be started & for this, being a logistics & fortifications officer, Weber was the right man. I was very happy that he had come, for Sodenstern was not up to the task in the long run and I also felt too much a layman with the construction of defensive positions for positional warfare, with obstacles, mines, etc.'[399]

The official replacement of Colonel von Sodenstern was justified with the alleged claim that he had suffered a serious knee injury, even though it was obvious that the unsuccessful counter-attacks had been the real reason for his dismissal. Nevertheless, he received the Turkish Imtiaz Medal from the hand of General Weber when he arrived at 10 pm on 4 May at the command post of the Southern Group.

General Liman von Sanders now refrained from further major counter-attacks. As the Allied forces were also exhausted by the continuous day and night battles, the defending Turks gained time to reorganise their troops and bring in reinforcements. Lieutenant Boltz, who on 4 May had been ordered to occupy the Turkish trench furthest forward with the remnants of his Shore Detachment, reported that conditions there beggared 'all description'. The foremost trench was barely a metre deep and filled with excrement. Saps were non-existent, so any detected approach instantly brought down enemy fire for approximately twenty minutes.

Mühlmann wrote during a brief respite in the fighting:

'On 5 May at 04.30 hrs we rode to the observation post of the 7th Turkish Division & from there to a hill at the 9th Division; Weber wanted to get an impression of the terrain & the troops. But there was not much to see; the troops were hidden in the folds of the countryside &, through the confusion, the Division Commanders did not even know where & which units of the four different divisions lay in their sectors. So the order was given to hold the forward positions at all costs & to restore order wherever possible.'[400]

The Second Battle of Krithia, as the Allies named it, began on 6 May and lasted until 8 May. In the previous days, all available reinforcements had already been ordered to Helles by General Hamilton as he wanted to push for a decisive action there. Two infantry brigades and twenty Australian field guns, which were actually intended for the ANZAC front, were diverted south. On 1 May the 29th (Indian) Brigade, with its four battalions, had also landed at Cape Helles.

Lord Kitchener wrote to Hamilton on 3 May: 'I hope the 5th will see you strong enough to press on to Achi Baba. Any delay will allow the Turks to bring up more reinforcements and to make unpleasant preparations for your reception.'[401]

Hamilton envisaged planning an attack at night, while Hunter-Weston, still coping with the impact of heavy casualties among his officers, wanted to avoid a counter-attack at night. The reason for this was that in the darkness he would have to do without the support of the naval guns. Hunter-Weston's plan did not envisage a new operational variation for this attack, which was to begin at 11.00 am after the usual artillery preparation. The French on the left flank were to take Kereves Valley and British troops, positioned on the right and centre, had Krithia and Achi Baba as their targets. The intelligence on the location of Turkish troops was very inaccurate, but the greatest shortcoming of the Allied planning and execution again proved to be that insufficient information was provided to the troops about the aims and the exact plan of attack. The divisional orders could not be distributed until seven hours before the start of the attack and some units did not receive them at all. This meant that, at company commander level especially, there was not enough time to prepare themselves and their troops for attack. A battalion of the Lancashire Fusiliers had to march from the beach to the starting positions on 5 May and find their way in the darkness, which for them was likened to 'jumping off a balloon any old where'.

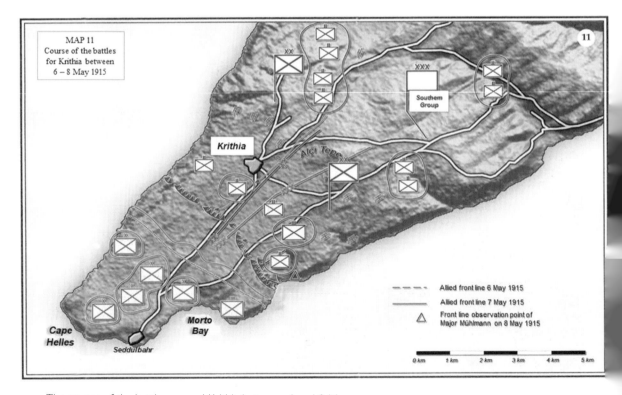

The course of the battles around Krithia between 6 and 8 May.

On 7 May Colonel Kannengiesser was ordered to report to the staff of the 9th Division to act as 'adviser' to its commander, Colonel Sami Bey. The reason behind this was probably the obviously hesitant attacks of the days before, which General von Sanders mainly attributed to Sami Bey's lack of leadership ability. Kannengiesser's first impressions in his new assignment confirmed this assumption:

> 'Sami Bey was a man of a comfortable, passive nature, mostly to be found in his tent, which lay much too far back in the neighbourhood of the field hospital; who spoke a little German and showed himself at first to be not unapproachable, although somewhat suspicious. [...] Sami Bey was of the same opinion, as many Turkish officers in the field felt that "the Germans, having forced us into the war, can now show us what they themselves do".' [402]

This was how Kannengiesser experienced the following days of this battle in the 9th Division.

On all three days the battles began in the morning practically at the same time each day - on 6 May at 11.00 am, on 7 May at 10.00 am and on 8 May at 10.15 am – naturally after the usual artillery barrage to soften up defensive positions but which, however, did not have the desired effect. Each day the Allied forces were able to make slight local gains, but the Turks, in defence, were able to forestall any decisive breakthrough.

French trenches at Kereves Valley.

Lieutenant Boltz, still deployed with his machine gun sections of the German Naval Shore Detachment in the front line with the 7th Division, which was west of the Kereves Valley, described this Allied attack in all its tragedy and brutality:

'In thick columns, always 50 to 60 men all bunched-up, they were death-defying in their advance, offering the Turkish artillery and our machine guns an easy target. In rows they were mowed down, but more and more columns were detailed to storm forward. When our machine guns had completely expended all ammunition, the crews took rifles from the dead Turkish soldiers and continued to fire at them. It was not until 17.00 hrs that the attack was halted. The enemy must have had tremendous losses on this day. The red trousers and red caps of the French offered excellent targets.'[403]

Boltz was wounded in the foot during the fighting on 7 May and he had to hand over command to Chief Petty Officer Schubert. When Schubert was twice wounded in the head the next day, Petty Officer Seckendorf assumed command of the Shore Detachment. Prior to all this, however, Boltz had requested, because of his recent loss of twenty-two men, via Fifth Army Headquarters, that the fleet assign as reinforcements a younger officer, a doctor, two mechanics and thirty men.[404]

The commander of the Southern Group, General Weber, was optimistic in his description of the situation on 7 May:

At 12.45 hrs on 6 May, after the foreshore had been heavily bombarded by the ships' guns, a thin line of [Allied] soldiers advanced from the area around Hissarlik. The soldiers came under effective fire from Turkish light artillery. In the centre, the enemy advanced in strong numbers. The Turks deployed individual battalions, and after a short time the enemy's forward movement collapsed under our fire. The 21st Infantry Regiment, which did especially well here, gained ground up to the landing stage of Seddulbahr, our losses low. A forward battery lost only two men and an ammunition wagon. I am convinced that any further enemy advance can be stopped. Our troops have more or less returned to their old positions. Through better use of the terrain, the effects of bombardments from the ships will not be felt as much. The night passed quietly. We control Hissarlik from the heights northeast of it, so that it will be difficult to move forward there. I intend to give the enemy no peace every night. Signed Weber.'[405]

The Allies, however, did not realise how much the Turkish troops had suffered from the uninterrupted fire, especially from the ships, and that repeated requests had come from Turkish commanders to be allowed to withdraw to a line further north, on the slopes of Eltschi Tepe (Achi Baba). However, General Weber refused, as he had received clear orders from General von Sanders to hold these positions at all costs. The terrain was most favourable for the defenders, who had fortified and connected with trenches the natural obstacles, such as riverbeds and recesses.

Up to 7 May scarcely any ground was gained by the Allies; and Hamilton had now come ashore to direct personally the final phase of the battle. The orders for 8 May were again simple, but were again only delivered to the troops a few hours before the attack was due to begin. Four battalions of New Zealanders were to attack Krithia, which was defended by nine Turkish battalions. The 29th Division was to attack on the left again, while the French, on the right, would again try to take Kereves Valley. After fighting began on the morning of 8 May, reports came to Allied headquarters, at about 1 pm, that the artillery had still not been able to silence the Turkish machine-gun positions. Furthermore, the artillery had suffered a supply breakdown and therefore could no longer provide adequate fire support. By 3.30 pm it was clear that the New Zealand and British troops were back in their starting positions of the morning, at which time the French troops had not even started to move out of theirs. Hamilton saw a last chance to achieve a breakthrough by a unified attack along the entire front. But even this desperate final attack failed, the troops suffered considerable casualties and were now finally exhausted.

The German Naval Shore Detachment, now under the temporary command of Petty Officer Seckendorf, had moved into position at Kereves Dere on the evening of 7 May, where they were able to repulse the attacks of 8 May. But the situation was critical and Boltz, despite his wounds, again took over command. Towards 5 pm the Allied attack was renewed once more and the left flank of the 7th Division was able to halt it, supported by the German machine guns deployed there. However, when the Turkish counter-attack should have begun, the front at the 9th Division collapsed anew. Boltz reported that at that moment the main task of his Detachment was to provide cover for the Turkish withdrawal and hold on as long as possible. When the German Naval Shore Detachment finally had to withdraw, three machine guns were made unusable and left behind, since there had already been too many casualties among the German operating crews. The following night the area could have been retaken by a Turkish counter-attack, but the machine guns had either been destroyed or buried. The Turks were at the end of their tether. Mühlmann described his impressions of the last phase of this battle from his position on the left flank:

'But now back to 8 May. Just as I did a few evenings ago with Halil, the commander of the right subsection of the Division on the left, I now wanted to see [about things on] the extreme left flank for myself [sic!]. Staying along the coast, in the sights of a battleship, which, despite the close distance, did not waste its shells on me, I walked down the Kereves Dere, where I saw sights just like in my first recce. Arriving in the reserves of the left flank sector, I did not immediately visit the commander, the very capable Colonel Salvi, but went alone to the forward trench lines. What I witnessed along this way was deeply upsetting and an eloquent testimony to the fierce fighting that has been raging uninterruptedly since 1 May.

A terrible smell of corpses polluted the air; the artillery fire remained silent, but there was lively rifle fire, the bullets whizzing left and right around my ears, the floor was covered with bodies, some of which had already decayed. The work of reinforcing the trenches was lamentable, showing no signs of any system and was completely inadequate. The sap trenches were filled with corpses, so that everyone, myself included, and all reinforcements, would have to cross open ground to reach the front line, instead of being able to use the imperfect cover of sap trenches. Cartridge boxes as well as other items of equipment were scattered everywhere. Latrines were non-existent; piles of human waste everywhere added to the pollution of the air. The foremost trench, the firing line, hardly provided cover for kneeling riflemen; I hunkered down there, bullets flying around & talked with the people, who naturally made an overstrained, nervous impression. They only fired sporadically, but instead of taking up their spades to improve the position, sat there idly. As they had received their soup the previous night, they expected to receive something that night as well. In the morning, news had just arrived that 80,000 Russians had been captured in Galicia; I told them this in my broken Turkish to give them some encouragement & I also had the impression that they would hold their ground. As I left they immediately began to dig; really such undemanding, willing soldier material.

They were so concerned that I should be under proper cover. I then went slowly back the same way & this walk was the most unpleasant of all the moments I have experienced under enemy fire; a rushing hail of bullets behind me & always the feeling that the next bullet will hit you in the back. When you are facing into a storm of bullets, the feeling is not nearly as unpleasant. I was very happy when I was back and seated hale and hearty in Colonel Sahir's tent & now heard his opinion. Sahir himself had been in Seddulbahr with his regiment in the attacks on 1 May, and had lobbed bombs onto the jetties. He also attributed the failure of the attacks to the failings of the 9th Division, which was to have advanced to the right of the 7th Division. He also expressed quite pessimistic views about the current situation & spoke of the high casualties; I expressed my astonishment that the trenches etc had been so poorly made and it turned out – one could hardly believe it possible – that no sappers were forward! The Division had four or six sapper companies!

I promised him both to remedy this immediately, and also to move out the dead, as far as they could not be buried in situ, using the pack animal trains returning empty, and bring ammunition, food & other pieces of equipment & gave him encouragement, so that I parted with the understanding that the left flank would also hold its position. On my way back, as night had fallen, the sky was lit up by searchlights & flares which the English [sic] had and which could hover freely in the air for several minutes, illuminating all the surroundings as bright as day, and more than was necessary.'[406]

On the evening of 8 May, Hamilton wrote to Lord Kitchener: 'The result of the operation has been failure, as my object remained unachieved. The fortifications and their machine-guns were too scientific and too strongly held to be rushed, although I had every available man in today.'[407]

This battle had cost the Allies nearly 6,000 casualties; the 29th Division had lost 10,000 men since landing on 25 April and of the 22,450 French soldiers, 12,610 had been killed or wounded between 25 April and 12 May.

Among the forty-four Germans who had started out with the German Naval Shore Detachment, only seven were fit for action after the battles; the rest had been either killed, wounded or had died of illness. The wounded were taken to Istanbul, mostly by ship, and treated there in the infirmary on board the *General* or in the German hospital. The actions of the Shore Detachment were extensively praised in the War Diary of the MMD, as illustrated by this entry on 8 May:

'Of the machine-gun companies sent to the Dardanelles, 20 men are already dead or wounded. I immediately sent replacement machine gunners. According to General v. Liman, the machine gun company has rendered him invaluable support. Their arrival in the Turkish lines without an interpreter or Turkish escort could easily have been fatal to them. The Turks took them for Englishmen, removed their weapons and field-glasses and wanted to shoot them until it was possible to clarify the situation and get a German speaking sergeant assigned [to them].'[408]

The high rate of casualties during the battles not only met with criticism from the Turkish upper echelons, but also from Field Marshal von der Goltz, commander of the First Army. On one occasion, he stated that the 'Ypres kind of slaughter of our boys should not be repeated here', and issued a letter counselling that infantry attacks needed to be well prepared by artillery beforehand. This letter was delivered to General Liman von Sanders, who replied to General Headquarters in Istanbul and derisively rejected 'the drivel of an old man'. Shortly afterwards von Sanders ordered the 2nd Division, newly arrived from Istanbul, to mount a large scale attack against enemy lines during the night of 18/19 May – without adequate artillery softening up beforehand. Later, in a rare, frank admission, he acknowledged his mistake:

'But the British capacity for close combat and the reserves were so strong that a decisive result could not be gained. On both sides the losses were so great—our brave 2nd Division lost nearly 9,000 in killed and wounded—that the local British commander requested a brief suspension of hostilities to bury his dead, which I granted for the 23rd of May. This is the only instance where battle action in the Dardanelles was suspended for a brief space of time.

I feel that the attack was an error on my part, based on an underestimation of the enemy. Its preparation by our artillery, weak in numbers and deficient in ammunition, was bound to be insufficient for the purpose.'[409]

This telling insight also provides an explanation for the brusqueness of the Commander-in-Chief of the Fifth Army towards von der Goltz at their next encounter:

'When the Field Marshal took leave from His Majesty during the second half of September so that he could inspect his front at Gallipoli, the Sultan charged him to present his Imperial greetings to the adjacent 5th Army. We drove into the grove, where the 5th Army headquarters was located. The German Military Attaché, Colonel von Leipzig, was present there[410] and, on receiving us, advised the Field Marshal to forego the meeting. However, shortly afterwards, Liman von Sanders stepped out of his tent; the Field Marshal approached him quickly and said saluting: "My dear Marshal, I bring you the gr ..." These last words [remained] stuck in his throat, as Liman von Sanders snarled: "Have no time, must go to the front". Then he turned to the right and got into his car. Admiral Usedom Pasha, commander of the fortresses on both sides of the Straits, reported this regrettable incident to German Headquarters, which recommended that the two German commanders of Turkish armies should be kept apart. The Field Marshal therefore took command of the Sixth Army in Iraq.'[411]

Both sides began to concentrate on positional warfare after the first two battles for Krithia, without either side undertaking any further substantial attacks until the end of May. The effort was now to extend and strengthen defensive positions and try to hinder each other by artillery and harassing fire. The lack of ammunition forced the Turkish artillery to restrict itself to a few opportunistic or occasional targets. Colonel Kannengiesser, who had great respect for Turkish gunners, remarked that 'the battery commanders had on average considerably higher education and intelligence than their comrades in the infantry' and made an observation as to just how powerless their own artillery was:

'All were seriously worried by the very great scarcity of ammunition. [...] They clenched their fists, as I did, when they saw the most wonderful targets and dared not shoot. [...] When ammunition was allowed for a particular shoot it was regarded as a holiday and it was heartily refreshing to see how direct hits on the target were applauded.'[412]

A Turkish trench with dugout at Kanli Sirt.

Each pause in the fighting was exploited to widen trenches and thereby conceal their own movements from enemy observation. Deep saps, as wide as roads, were dug. Connecting trenches and dugouts with loopholes were constructed, though means were very often makeshift and, wherever possible, the field of fire improved for the front lines. Although these measures were to serve as protection for themselves, Turkish soldiers were not inclined in the slightest to do this sort of work voluntarily. Kannengiesser reported on the commander's non-stop efforts to motivate the Turkish troops:

> 'Actually it was a daily battle to force the Turks to do that which was necessary for their own protection. Those who know the Turkish ideas of comfort, their fatalism, their placidity, will understand. The reader must not, however, regard these qualities from the ordinary European standpoint and blame or disparage accordingly. They were much more a result of the Oriental psychology, or due to religion and climate and the low standard of education, because the ordinary Turkish soldier can neither read nor write.'[413]

Overall the situation on the battlefields remained tense. The entry in the War Diary of the MMD for 11 May had a pessimistic note: 'The intelligence from Seddulbahr is less favourable; enemy seems to be gaining ground there. As things stand, the Turks cannot hold on to unsecured terrain lying in the crossfire of the enemy ships.'[414]

On 12 May Lieutenant von Thomsen arrived at the Southern Group with replacement personnel and weapons. Because of his wound, Lieutenant Boltz had to leave for Istanbul but returned to the Peninsula on 19 May, with a newly-formed Detachment and, of great importance, with new machine guns.[415] In the meantime, the Detachment had been relocated to the left flank of the 9th Division and there even seems to have been time for great improvements to the hitherto primitive living conditions. The German contingent had made itself quite at home in a dugout: 'From a distance, I made out the sign on a board, saying "Bismarckstand" [Bismarck Post]. Inside, pictures, post cards, etc., as in non-commissioned officers' quarters in barracks.'

Kannengiesser considered that this German enclave not only had an important tactical benefit, but it also had an uplifting effect on morale:

> 'I naturally put the German Naval Section in this important but heavily threatened advanced position. The whole position between the two streams [Zığın Dere (Gully Ravine) and Kirte Dere] was thus exceptionally strengthened', and further 'This German cell in the front trenches acted like a firm anchorage on the whole position and gave all of us, Turks and Germans, moral support.'[416]

Not surprisingly, Kannengiesser also had a further reason for liking this particular dug-out:

> 'And then the smell of German food! How many times did it waft by my nose, and how much I would like to have eaten with them, even if it was simply just *Speckerbsen* [bacon with peas] in this intense heat.'

The machine guns of the German Naval Shore Detachment were again used to reinforce the foremost positions on both sides of the Zığındere ("Gully Ravine"). In addition, a second Naval officer, Lieutenant von Rabenau, was assigned to the Detachment.

General von Sanders realised that the fronts were beginning to harden and that both sides were evidently preparing themselves for positional warfare like that on the Western Front. As a consequence, on 22 May he pointed out to Germany that there was an urgent need for

The German Naval Shore Detachment's dugout. (*Bundesarchiv Koblenz*)

'... the very speedy deployment of 200 mainly fully-trained [German] Army engineers who would act as advisors to the Turkish army engineers, who had little experience in preparing and pushing forward trenches against enemy positions, for the Southern Group's battles on the Gallipoli Peninsula.'[417]

The situation was considered critical, as emerged from an entry in the War Diary of the MMD for 26 May 1915:

Torgut returns from the Dardanelles in the morning. Commander Rohde briefs me on the current situation. In his view, the Allies are so firmly entrenched on Gallipoli that they cannot be thrown out with Turkish resources. The Turkish casualties at Ari Burnu are immense. The Commanding General, Essad Pasha, is not up to the task and has no German officer with him.'[418]

On the Allied side and despite the failure of the Second Battle of Krithia, General Hamilton was still convinced that he could reach his objective; but for this, he required reinforcements in the shape of at least two more infantry divisions. Only one, however, the 52nd (Lowland) Division, was placed at Hamilton's disposal.

Hunter-Weston was determined to continue attacking Achi Baba and still anticipated success, as he was hoping for fresh reinforcements by the end of May 1915. General Gouraud, the commander of the French Expeditionary Force, supported Hunter-Weston's optimism. During May Hunter-Weston had been able to achieve small territorial gains through minor attacks. Furthermore, the British troops in the south had been reorganised and reformed on 24 May as VIII Corps, which was placed under the command of the newly promoted Lieutenant General Hunter-Weston. Both commanders, Hunter-Weston and Gouraud, tried to convince General

Hamilton to launch another major attack, to which Hamilton finally agreed on 31 May. This time, however, the target for the first day was not to reach the hill of Achi Baba but rather to fight their way, trench by trench, across the whole Turkish line right across the peninsula.

Two days later the date for the advance was fixed for 4 June. A new tactic had apparently been planned for this battle. The attack was to go forward in two waves. The first wave was to take the front lines of the Turkish defence, whereupon the second, stronger, wave was to leap frog over the first wave and attack the Turkish positions in depth. In addition, there were units designated to overcome any Turkish forces that had been left behind on ground already taken. Extensive artillery support for the attack would be provided by seventy-eight British field guns, six more batteries of the French Expeditionary Corps and, of course, by the Royal Navy lying off the coast.

On the morning of 4 June a barrage of fire rained down on the forward Turkish trenches and this lasted for over two hours. It was the overture to the attack, which was later called the Third Battle of Krithia. As usual, the Turkish troops waited out this bombardment in their dugouts and then returned to their trenches after the shelling had ceased. Kannengiesser wrote of it:

> 'On Friday, the 4th June, about 11 o'clock in the morning, a barrage suddenly descended on the front Turkish trenches from land batteries and from cruisers and destroyers lying off the southern shores. […] There was no doubt that this bombardment was the preparation for a heavy enemy infantry attack.'[419]

The situation for Kannengiesser in the 9th Division had become difficult because communications between him and Sami Bey were fraught. Sami Bey did not want to listen to the advice of the German Colonel and took little part in commanding this battle. Kannengiesser even had to complain to General Weber, as Sami Bey issued orders during the battle that had not been agreed by Kannengiesser. Thereupon Weber issued clear instructions to Sami Bey, but the latter was not about to change his obstinate behaviour. When the artillery shells began to fall on their forward positions and Kannengiesser was awaiting Sami Bey's arrival at Division headquarters for a discussion, Sami Bey did not appear; as the shells descended upon Hill 150, near the location of the Division's command post, he fled with his staff to safer ground.

The Allied attack was initially successful and the British troops in the middle and on the left flank were able to take the first Turkish trenches relatively quickly. The forward elements of the German Naval Shore Detachment also came under heavy Allied fire and the foremost trench on the left of Sigin Dere was lost, while on the right of this trench the British attack was brought to a halt by the machine guns. However, a large number of the German machine guns crews had been killed and had to be replaced by reserves.

Only on 6 June did Lieutenant Boltz received information from Leading Seaman Peters about an action which took place on the left of Sigin Dere. Peters reported that the Turkish troops in the trench had withdrawn early during the attack of 4 June and only the German machine guns were being fired, which they did until their ammunition ran out or the guns were unserviceable. In the end the men, who were now only able to defend themselves with their pistols, were taken prisoner by soldiers of the King's Own Scottish Borderers. Lieutenant von Rabenau was seriously wounded in this engagement but was fortunate enough to make a full recovery later as a prisoner of war on Malta.[420] Kannengiesser described the remarkable escape made by Leading Seaman Peters:

> 'Amongst those taken prisoner with the Naval-Lieut. von Rabenau was Leading Seaman Peters. As he was being conducted to the rear he seized a favourable moment to knock the guard senseless. He then jumped down among the English [sic] in the trench who, in wild

confusion, took him for one of themselves and wondered at his bravery as he suddenly jumped up and ran forward alone towards the Turks. But those, not recognising him greeted him as an enemy. He had to throw himself into a shell hole, where he lay for two days and two nights without food or water, and with a constant hail of bullets overhead. Owing to the heat he was almost dead of thirst when the Turkish counter-attack of 6 June freed him, more dead than alive. When praised for his coolness and bravery, Leading Seaman Peters merely answered, "I have only done my duty".'[421]

The French Corps on the right could not take their objective in the extremely difficult terrain around Kereves Dere, which meant that the British right flank was open. A Turkish counter-attack stormed in here, which brought the entire Allied attack to a halt and allowed almost all the starting positions to be recaptured on the same day. Kannengiesser described this critical phase of the fighting on the right flank of the 9th Division:

'The lost trenches had to be recovered. I had arranged an attack for the afternoon when I was called to the Southern Group, where General Weber placed five fresh battalions at my disposal including the 1st and 2nd Battalions of the 5th Infantry Regiment. I summoned all the commanding officers to Krithia and went with each of them individually to the exact road which the battalion would have to take the following morning. Even if the shrapnel continually burst over the ruins of Krithia it was still a complete explanation of the ground such as one only experiences in peace time. Doubts about the approach, deployment, development, touch, direction could not exist and actually did not exist. At 1 o'clock in the morning of the 6th June the troops began to enter Krithia and about 3.30 pm the deployed line began the attack without the enemy having noticed anything. The attack was completely successful. The excellent Bolz was the first to report, on a sheet torn from his notebook, that our old positions had been completely recaptured and the English had suffered prodigious losses. Seventeen English machine-guns, a large number of rifles and ammunition, as well as other booty had been captured.
    This attack was the saving of a very brave man who was very near death.'[422]

However, Kannengiesser said that another attack on the following day could not have been stopped in the same way: 'I felt that a further similar energetic attack of the English [sic] could have the worst results. It did not follow, however.'[423] In the days that followed there were only counter-attacks by both sides and essentially the lines had hardly changed by the end of the Third Battle of Krithia, on 8 June 1915.

    Due to the continued insertion of new units during the course of the battles for Krithia, there was serious confusion in the allocations of troops and, consequently, in the command structure of the Turkish line of defence. Of the original Turkish 9th Division, only shattered fragments were left, plus units of the 2nd, 7th, 11th, and 15th Divisions. General Weber agreed to a fundamental regrouping. The 9th Division was transferred back to Maidos to recuperate and act as a reserve, while their previous divisional front was handed over to Halil Bey, who brought in six fresh battalions. Liman von Sanders had now made up his mind to refrain from large-scale counter-attacks and to concentrate his forces on defence. This was sorely needed as the Allies launched a sweeping attack on the southern front on 20 June. In a report to Berlin on 23 June, the German Military Attaché in Istanbul stated:

'After three days of artillery preparation with enormous expenditure of ammunition, Englishmen attacked on 20, 21 and 22 the left flank of our southern section in the Dardanelles with the utmost vehemence, took our trenches three times, were thrown out three times after fierce close combat, last time this night. Casualties high. Artillery superiority of the enemy painful.'[424]

After this attack, Liman von Sanders' biggest worry was that not enough ammunition would be available and he complained about this situation on 22 June to the Military Attaché in Istanbul:

'Now I have <u>another big worry.</u> That's the <u>ammunition</u>! So much has been expended because of the <u>constant</u> attacks by the English [sic], and we have so very little for heavy artillery. What good is it to us in the long run if we repulse all attacks and [yet] finally have no more artillery <u>ammunition</u>? The whole thing is now a question of ammunition. The English [sic] will probably know that we are in short supply. That's why they always attack.'[425]

On 28 June, the German Naval Shore Detachment had to fend off another violent attack by the British, in which the last still serviceable machine guns were brought back to their own rear lines after all their ammunition had been expended. In this battle, Lieutenant Müller, who had been newly assigned to the Detachment, was seriously wounded. Since most of the Detachment's personnel were either completely exhausted or weakened by illness and they only had two serviceable machine guns, the German Naval Shore Detachment was withdrawn to Istanbul for recuperation.

With the fighting dying down somewhat, regrettably more time was left for the spread of mutual jealousies and disputes between the various senior German command figures in the Dardanelles and Gallipoli. On 30 June von Sanders wrote to Admiral von Usedom, evidently in response to one of the latter's detailed monthly reports, written directly to the Kaiser, in which the Admiral described the situation of the Fifth Army:

'To the General Government of the Straits. Regarding the very complaisant dispatch 9.88 dated 25 June 1915, I beg to differ in the following respects concerning the 5th Army: 1.) The enemy fleet has <u>not</u> been idle during the fierce battles over the past 10 days in both sectors. This is a mistake. Both sector commanders can provide greater detail. I would be very grateful if in official, written exchanges, circulated in copy, it be refrained from referring to any circumstances concerning withdrawal movements of the 5th Army. In any case, I would like to emphasise that such statements are not common practice in official documents of the German Army.
    Liman von Sanders, Royal Prussian General of Cavalry.'[426]

Despite this legitimate protest, Usedom continued his reporting beyond his direct sphere of responsibility. His motives were presumably threefold: to have some of the victorious glory of the land forces rub off on him; to play down the accomplishments achieved by Liman von Sanders; and, finally, to complain about the support measures demanded by von Sanders. In this vein, von Usedom wrote this report directly to the Kaiser on 20 July 1915:

'The battles being fought by the 5th Army against the enemy troops that have landed continue to demand great sacrifices and have not brought any advantage to the defenders. The prospects of throwing the enemy into the sea are, in my opinion, not viable at present, but the mere holding of current positions is only possible if there is a continuous ample supply of ammunition and great human effort. As I have already reported by telegram, contrary to my reservations, the Minister of War has decided that the fortress must hand over to the Army all the munitions and guns it requires. An orderly preparation for further defence, in case the army cannot hold on, was rejected as unacceptable. What the fortress has so far relinquished in ammunition and guns is listed in the attachment. [...] May your Imperial and Royal Majesty view that my endeavour here was to preserve the power of the Straits to resist, even in the event that, should there be a decline in resistance on land, it would be entirely self-reliant. [...] How long the 5th Army can contain the enemy is beyond my judgment.'[427]

Since the beginning of June 1915 the fighting on the Krithia Front had cost the Allies more than 16,000 lives and the Turkish defenders about 40,000. The Allied territorial gains, however, were meagre. The Turkish defence continued to hold firm as it had the advantage of the more favourable terrain and continuous resupply from the hinterland. The commander of VIII Corps, Lieutenant General Hunter-Weston, had a debilitating attack of sun-stroke and departed the Peninsula forever in July 1915. He left behind a legacy of heavily casualties and decimated battalions. A British corporal wrote that 'Helles looks like a midden and smells like an opened cemetery.'[428]

During the battles in the south of the Peninsula, commanders on both sides had demanded the highest sacrifices from their troops, while their respective attacks were ineffectually planned and unnecessarily pressurised, not giving their troops enough time to prepare.

Liman von Sanders finished his tactics of suicidal attacks only after the intervention by subordinate German commanders and therefore he replaced General Weber on 8 July as commander of the Southern Group. Although von Sanders did not differ in his behaviour from commanders on the Western Front, his leadership performance in this theatre should be carefully scrutinised.

In the battles for Krithia he did not adhere to his original principle of maintaining a clear point of main effort and the rash attacks by exhausted and untrained troops were doomed to failure. It is also important to remember the observations by other German officers during these battles, which confirmed that some Turkish commanders had been seriously lacking. In addition, the question remains, which operational alternatives were open to von Sanders on this front, which was scarcely seven kilometres wide and had almost no space for troop manoeuvre or even envelopment. As the field fortifications grew with each passing day, the movement of units became more and more difficult, possibly explaining the hasty attacks made by both sides. In addition, newly arriving Turkish units had not completed the preparatory training programme for night marches and attacks and were not familiar with the terrain.

In my estimation, von Sanders should have been able to hold the front line without attempting counter-attacks for a few weeks. This would have allowed him to optimise his defence fortifications, to devise and coordinate a workable counter-attack plan, to instruct the officers and troops accordingly, and to give them time for preparation and a build-up of supplies. Above all, he would then have had time to coordinate his available resources of land, sea and air power, culminating at one single point: that is, a concentrated and decisive attack.

Chapter 11

Positional Warfare and the August Landing in Suvla Bay

Although fighting still continued on both Gallipoli fronts during July, any territorial gains by either the Allies or the Turks remained minimal. The main objective for both sides was now to reinforce and expand the trench system for defence and to create favourable positions as jumping off points for counter-attacks. Indeed, opposing trenches were sometimes only metres apart. The Turks concentrated on pushing their forward trenches as close as possible to those of the Allies, so that the Allied ships could not provide artillery support, for fear of hitting their own forces. Over the months, the expansion of the trench networks made significant progress. As on the Western Font, a vicious underground war developed as both sides worked on preparing mine charges; tunnels were dug, so that explosive charges weighing several hundredweights could be laid in an attempt to breach the enemy lines.

In June 1915 Liman von Sanders put in a request for 200 trained military engineers to be sent to the Fifth Army on Gallipoli. Composed of volunteers, these sappers were to form a German engineer company, to provide expertise and support to their colleagues in the Turkish sapper units. Corporal Adolf Horaczek, a sapper then serving on the Western Front, described how he came to be selected for service in Turkey: 'On 12 June 1915, Second Lieutenant Hähnlein called for three men and an NCO from our section to go as volunteers to Turkey. Straws were drawn to decide between me and a sergeant and it fell in my favour.'[428a]

In company with other German sappers, Horaczek was sent to Berlin, where he was given 'three hundred gold francs [for safekeeping] and seventy marks for civilian clothing', as they all had to make the train journey from Berlin to Istanbul as civilians, posing as craftsmen or tourists, as their route took them through neutral Balkan States.

These sappers, under the command of Captain Zipper, had not been adequately prepared for active service in Turkey. Zipper had to be replaced in August for health reasons soon after his arrival. It seems that the personnel had simply been selected as replacements from the 2nd Engineer Replacement Battalion, but these volunteers had not been adequately examined for their medical fitness, nor were they inoculated against typhus. They were not outfitted with clothing appropriate for the climate and received no food rations of a type to which they were accustomed. After they arrived in Istanbul they were not given any time to acclimatise and were sent in support of Turkish forces as individual units directly to the Gallipoli front. Once on the Peninsula they had to live and work in a near tropical climate, where the average daytime temperature in July and August was 30°C, coupled with poor hygiene conditions and an unfamiliar diet.[429] These factors led to more than half of the original 225 men falling ill in August and ninety-seven men had to be repatriated to Germany as 'medically unfit'. Nevertheless, a corresponding number of replacements was requested, to make up for this shortfall.[430]

Despite this unpromising situation, von Sanders had praise for these men:

'This pioneer company, with a strength of 200 men, was attached to the South Group at Seddulbahr. In consequence of the torrid climate, the Turkish subsistence to which they were not used and severe losses in battle, its numbers were soon reduced to forty men. They were now distributed on both fronts to act as foremen. In this capacity they rendered valuable service.'[431]

In October smoke protection and breathing apparatus, as well as flamethrowers for trench warfare, were apparently requested for the German sapper units,[432] as well as material that was required for mining underground tunnels. Kannengiesser wrote about the efforts of trench construction and the Turkish soldiers:

'In the meantime the front line was being built – the trenches were to be narrow and two metres deep. I carried with me a stick one metre long with which I measured. In spite of this order that ensured their own safety, it took a long time before the required depth was reached. However, the troops only had their short infantry spades with, here and there, a pick to assist them. Sand bags came very sparingly from Constantinople, and those which arrived regularly disappeared, being mostly used to repair clothing. [...] The Turkish soldier, the 'Asker', was the Anatolian and Thracian, slightly educated, brave, trustworthy, of whom a large majority were Anatolians. Content with little, it never entered into his mind to dispute the authority of those above him.'[433]

The static warfare of the summer months made it particularly difficult for both sides. If the Allies' chief complaint was the lack of drinking water, the Turks complained more about the inadequate supply of ammunition and equipment. Colonel Kannengiesser reported on the difficult hygiene conditions:

'... the unfavourable climate and local conditions were made still worse by the complete indifference of the men to any hygienic methods of prevention. I have myself seen a man relieving himself into the water flowing through the Krithia Dere in May, from which the soldiers further down were forced to drink. The method of punishment that was used by the battalion commander leading them, whose attention I drew to this, I prefer not to relate. The Turk is unbelievably insensitive to corpses and their stench. I remember, for instance, that two soldiers, who sat on the extreme right flank of the front line, had laid three corpses one on top of another as cover from the sea. They sat on these and ate their bread and olives.'[434]

With justifiable concern, the Turkish Army High Command and the commander of the Fifth Army followed the development of the positional warfare now taking place. It was harder for the Turkish army to bear than for the Allies, because the numbers of reserve soldiers in Turkey were not unlimited. Since the beginning of the fighting the Dardanelles had had to be supplied with new divisions due to the high rates of casualties in that theatre. In the first half of July 1915 the four divisions of the Second Army, under General Wehib Paşa, which was standing by in Thrace for deployment to the Balkans, was subordinated to von Sanders in order to replace his battle-weary divisions in the Southern Group. Nevertheless, the strength of the Fifth Army grew to no more than 110,000 fighting troops. Personnel replacement started to become difficult; there was a lack of officers and non-commissioned officers, and all new soldiers were only barely trained.

Almost as serious as the numbers of men who had been killed, was the fact that all the equipment being used by the Turks was suffering from heavy wear and tear. While the Allies had seemingly unlimited supplies, Turkey, on the other hand, still isolated by being part of the Central Powers alliance, was forced to rely exclusively on its own very limited production and manufacturing facilities. The workshops and factories in Istanbul were only able to repair damaged or worn gun barrels and could not manufacture new field guns. Thus, the artillery of the Allies was constantly gaining superiority. In addition, the already inferior Turkish artillery could not always be extensively used due simply to a lack of ammunition. On occasions the Turks had been compelled to resort to firing blank ammunition to feign artillery support for their troops.

The ration situation was also a major problem. Neither in the theatre of operations nor in the hinterland were there any resources which could contribute provisions. This meant that all logistic support for the Army had to come from Istanbul. The sea route provided the most expeditious connection via the ports of Akbash and Maidos and there was also ample shipping space available on cargo ships. This sea route was, however, liable to disruption by British submarines that had managed to slip through the minefields in the Straits and enter the Sea of Marmara, where they had already torpedoed several cargo ships. Even if resupply by sea could not be completely prevented, it was found necessary to set up lines of communication on land, but the land route took much longer. From the railway terminus south of Adrianople, at Uzunköprü, there were still 160 kilometres - about seven days' march - to be covered along bad tracks, made almost impassable during bad weather conditions. The means of transport were biblical in nature; wagons and gun limbers were pulled by oxen, while camels and even donkeys were used as pack animals. Motor lorries only became available later. This meant that the Fifth Army was never fully supplied and the senior German Quartermaster scarcely had sufficient reserves. Lieutenant Colonel Burchardi, the Fifth Army's Quartermaster at the time, wrote in a report:

'The continually increasing strength of the army led to constantly increasing demands for rations, which finally reached 400 tons a day, and which could only be supplied by sea. In spite of hostile submarines, all transports reached their destinations, with the exception that in the harbours themselves, in the course of a month, a total of three steamers were sunk.

Owing to the lack of proper transport by land, the land columns could not properly fulfil the ration demands. The available surface transport of camel columns and supply trains was only sufficient to carry supplies from harbours to the divisions. [...] The stocks of supplies gradually grew less from day to day. Finally, even flour ran out and forced us to use maize flour for making bread. Similarly, any variety in supply gradually ceased and the rationing steadily grew worse. In spite of this, the Turkish Quartermaster General, Ismail Hacki Pasha – a particularly efficient, hard-working and clever man, deserved special recognition for the energy he had displayed in understanding how to tackle the supply problem of a land that during the time of the Dardanelles campaign was practically cut off from any appreciable import of supplies, and who made the best use of what was available for supplying the Fifth Army.'[435]

The German Naval Shore Detachment was reinforced and Lieutenant Boltz, together with three other officers, 150 men and twelve machine guns, set off from Istanbul on 27 July 1915 for the Dardanelles front. The Detachment was now no longer a purely German unit, as eighty Turkish sailors had been added to their ranks. With their equipment and supplies, the Detachment sailed on the *Reşit Paşa* to Gallipoli. From early July onwards, assistant medical officer Dr Hiltmann was assigned to provide local primary medical care to the machine-gun sections. Exactly when the German Naval Shore Detachment moved into their permanent accommodation on Kilia Tepe, a hill about 130 meters high on the European side, opposite Fort Nagara, can no longer be determined precisely, but the first buildings for this encampment of the German naval unit were probably built in July 1915.

Deutscher Unterstand nach Gallipoli.

Accommodation of the German Naval Shore Detachment on Kilia Tepe, on top of which is the monument and the German cemetery. (*Gunter Hartnagel Collection*)

The German Naval Shore Detachment dugouts on Kilia Tepe. (*Gunter Hartnagel Collection*)

Unterstände der Marine bei KiliaTepe

Not only were quarters for the men there, but a small hospital was also established. This hospital was administered from August to mid-October 1915 by (Sub Lieutenant) Dr Karl Fièvet, who was later assisted by (Lieutenant) Dr Eduard Asbeck. Both were eventually replaced by (Lieutenant Commander) Dr Ludwig Reinhold, who ran this hospital from November 1915 to October 1917. During this time personnel of the German Naval Shore Detachment who were killed in action or died from illness were buried in their own cemetery near this camp.[436] Later on, smaller buildings were put up further forward for individual sub-units of the German Naval Shore Detachment. It was intended to train the newly formed Detachment in the rear for fourteen days, but the Allied landings in early August at Suvla Bay put paid to this time of preparatory training.

Despite the preferential quarters and better provision for the German Detachment compared with other Turkish troops, they, too, had to contend with considerable health problems. Sub Lieutenant Boltz wrote in a report:

'The health of the troops was very bad during the hot season. Although it was better, thanks to better food, than for the first German sapper company that was sent out and which had been decimated by disease, the majority of officers and men have had to endure diseases such as typhus, dysentery, malaria and fever. An improvement occurred at the beginning of the cold season. At the same time, however, good quarters were made in the camps and trenches and, above all, a regular supply of food was ensured. [Note: Reinforcements or replacements to the strength came to seventy in August, forty-seven in September, thirty-two in October, nineteen in November, thirty in December and nine in January.]

The greatest concern regarding health is in the camp of Section II at Kiretch Tepe. Here there was a veritable typhus epidemic. Successively, five officers and petty officers were

The German field hospital at Bigali. (*Gunter Hartnagel Collection*)

taken ill here, suffering from typhoid fever, in September and October, among them all the section commanders, of whom Sub Lieutenant Krafft later died, and a number of men. The contaminated, old camp consisted of primitive and hastily-built earthen huts, in the middle of Turkish soldiers and near a swampy spring. The speedy relocation of the camp at the end of October to a few kilometres down the road stopped the typhoid fever at a stroke. In addition, in Kilia Tepe, Düs Tepe (Battleship Hill) and the observation posts, sporadic cases of typhoid disease have occurred. When the British withdrew the health of the troops was good. The sick who had recovered had recuperated well in Constantinople, and seemed immune to new infections, or had been declared unfit and replaced by healthy people.'[437]

Further replacements were also sought for the sapper company; for example, at the end of September, it was for 'eight, not too young, active service sapper NCOs'.[438]

From the middle of July intelligence reports indicated that the Allies would bring in more reinforcements and plan new landings in the Dardanelles: 'A report arriving via Salonika on the 16th spoke of the concentration of 50,000 to 60,000 men on the Island of Lemnos alone and gave the number of war and transport vessels assembled there as 140.'[439]

Almost all the available forces in Turkey had already been committed to the fighting in the Dardanelles. By the end of July, sixteen of the forty-five divisions of the Turkish Army had been deployed to the Dardanelles. The seven divisions that formed the First Army in Istanbul served mainly as reserves for the Gallipoli theatre. The remaining twenty-two divisions, which had much less fighting power, were spread around the Asian theatres of war.

Just as in April 1915, it could not be foreseen exactly where the Allies were going to make their landing. In defending the key points of the Gallipoli peninsula, von Sanders again seemed to favour the area around Bulair and the gap between his Northern and Southern Groups. But the Asian side of the Dardanelles also had to be secured. Three battle-worn divisions were stationed here from early August. As six divisions were allocated to the Southern and four to the Northern Group, he could still count on an army reserve of three divisions, of which he held two in readiness at Bulair and the other one between the Northern and Southern Groups.

Amid all the preparations to defend against this imminent attack, a most surprising event happened. Liman von Sanders was summoned, out of the blue, by Falkenhayn to come to Supreme Headquarters in Germany. This summons was the result of a plot against von Sanders that originated inside his own ranks to force him out of his position as the Army commander on Gallipoli. Falkenhayn had praised Liman von Sanders' achievements, when he wrote to him by telegram early in July:

'General Headquarters 8th July 1915. In receiving my report of the events on the Dardanelles, H. M. the Emperor charges me to express to Your Excellency His warmest appreciation of your work. H. M. knows that Your Excellency has fully realized the extent of the task confided to you in its relation to the course of the war and firmly relies on your superior leadership, etc. Sgd. von Falkenhayn.'

On the other hand another telegram, this time to the Military Attaché, about the impending attack suggests that, to say the least, there must have been dissonance between von Falkenhayn and von Sanders:

'General Headquarters 22nd July 1915. To the Military Attaché. From reports received here it seems probable that at the beginning of August a strong attack will be made on the

Dardanelles, perhaps in connection with a landing in the Gulf of Saros (Xeros) or on the coast of Asia Minor. It will be well to economize ammunition.
Sgd. von Falkenhayn.'[440]

Such an observation should have normally been directed at the Military Commander and Chief of the Military Mission, and not to a military–political liaison officer. The conspiracy was directly attributed to General Bronsart von Schellendorf of the Turkish General Staff. On 25 July, when Colonel von Lossow arrived as Military Attaché in Istanbul, von Schellendorf made an unequivocal report via the diplomatic reporting channel to General von Falkenhayn:

'We German officers are happy about the arrival of Colonel von Lossow. I beg Your Excellency most earnestly to request the Supreme Cabinet order Lossow's appointment as Chief of the General Staff of the High Command of the Dardanelles Army. The Army Commander would not tolerate any GS Chief who is subordinate to him, therefore it is impossible to appoint an officer from the Military Mission. But I consider a German Chief who, like Lossow, has trench war experience, to be absolutely essential, since the Army Commander has no experience in this respect, and as he had also never been in his own positions, he contradicted the views of German officers at the front and [this led to] unnecessarily high casualties. Otherwise the matter will end badly here. Lossow would also be able to replace the Army Commander in an extreme case, since he enjoys the boundless confidence of the Turks.'[441]

Marshal Liman von Sanders and General Bronsart von Schellendorf. (*Bundesarchiv Koblenz*)

The disloyalty and treachery could not be more clearly demonstrated. This also raises the question of whose information led von Bronsart to make this judgment. However, it seems that the military 'experts' in the rear were the masterminds, reinforced by General Weber, who had been replaced by von Sanders as commander of the Southern Group in July. Of course, Lossow himself was involved, and it is said that he discussed this move with Enver beforehand.

General von Falkenhayn reacted by sending a telegram to Istanbul, thus initiating the first steps towards ousting General Liman von Sanders:

> 'General Headquarters 26th July 1915. General von Falkenhayn identically [copy] to the Turkish government, Enver Pasha, and General Liman von Sanders—In order to inform the chief of staff of the German field army of the situation at the Dardanelles His Majesty the Emperor would appreciate it with thanks if the Turkish government would send General Liman von Sanders to the general headquarters. Field Marshal Freiherr von der Goltz is available to take his place in command of the Dardanelles. If desired the military attaché, Colonel von Lossow, could be designated as his chief of staff.'[442]

The proposed substitution of von Sanders with von der Goltz makes it clear that Berlin apparently intended a long term, if not a permanent, replacement for him. Von Sanders only learned a little later about the background of this intrigue, which most likely also had the blessing of Ambassador von Wangenheim: 'Soon afterwards, the whole of this Istanbul-based action, in which Enver was not involved in any way, was disclosed to me from Istanbul in full detail.'[443] He quickly realised the true intention of what lay behind his summons to Germany and therefore, on 28 July, he wrote a clearly worded letter to the German Chief of the Military Cabinet:

> 'It has been requested that I be sent to general headquarters to inform General von Falkenhayn of the situation at the Dardanelles. This instruction is issued after I have led the Fifth Army for three months in uninterrupted battles, after Enver has frequently expressed to me his thanks and confidence, at a moment when a heavy enemy attack is imminent, while General von Falkenhayn has nothing whatever to do with these operations. I stress that it is not His Majesty that has ordered me to a conference. At the same time Field Marshal Freiherr von der Goltz is suggested as my successor and as his chief of staff the military attaché, whose duty it is to render the required reports. Since my recall is certainly not requested by the Turkish government or by Enver, I ask for information whether it is the desire of His Majesty the Emperor that I request my discharge and separation from the Turkish service. Liman von Sanders'[444]

Although the relationship between Enver and Liman von Sanders was anything but cordial, the Turkish Minister of War nevertheless placed the highest value on the military capabilities of the commander of the Fifth Army. Enver entreated the relevant German authorities that von Sanders remain in post as a large scale attack on Gallipoli was imminent[445] and to order the dispatch of another German officer to Germany in place of Liman. Nevertheless, von Falkenhayn doggedly insisted that von Sanders should come to Germany, because an adequate substitute for his command could be guaranteed and the Kaiser would attach great importance to von Sanders reporting in person. This decision was only reversed after a further report from Istanbul, in which Enver had intimated to German representatives, 'that he, if Liman von Sanders had to leave, would in no case hand over the Dardanelles army to Frh. von der Goltz'.

Enver also stated that he thought von der Goltz was too old and too soft, emphasising that he would not enjoy the confidence of the Turkish Army. Enver went on to add that he would not even transfer the command of the Fifth Army to von Lossow, but would appoint a Turkish officer instead. Enver urgently asked again for Liman von Sanders to remain in post, 'for military and political reasons'.[446] Supreme Headquarters in Berlin replied that a report by Liman von Sanders in person was no longer required, but the German Army Command asked that Colonel von Lossow be attached to the staff of the Fifth Army, because of his 'wide experience in modern trench warfare'. Von Sanders commented laconically, 'He arrived shortly thereafter, but did not stay long, as I had absolutely no official work for him'.[447]

It is completely incomprehensible that the Germans could commit such a monumental error at this critical phase of the campaign. In Istanbul, there was a belief that the Peninsula could not be successfully defended any longer and some preparation was being made for the arrival of the British. Although von der Goltz claimed to have had nothing to do with these conspiratorial plans, he would have been the one to have profited most from any plot. As commander of the First Turkish Army, von der Goltz was responsible for the defence of the Greater Istanbul area, including the Marmara Region; at the same time, he had repeatedly to supply reinforcements for the Gallipoli front. In a letter to his friend Schmiterlöw, dated 8 September 1915, von der Goltz made no secret of his dislike of von Sanders, but denied any involvement in this plot:

'Just as my last divisions are now combat-ready, a number have newly come to Constantinople for training. I have to support Liman's army which, due to its already numerical superiority, should not be necessary. He [Liman] launched the 'Cabinet Question', but I did not get involved. Allah willing, upon whom all things depend, especially in Turkey, I still hope to go into battle, albeit with fewer troops. The quantity is not always supremely important! A tribute has now also been paid to me by my own Fatherland. Liman was recently recalled to Grand Headquarters for reasons which had absolutely nothing to do with me. From there [Grand Headquarters] I was nominated as a substitute for him. It came late; nevertheless, it came. But in the end nothing has transpired, and Liman will remain [in post].'[448]

This particular episode and its timing combined to cast a rather gloomy light on the characters of some of those very senior German officers and officials in Istanbul who held highly responsible positions. In pursuit of their own personal interests, they were prepared to put at risk the successful continuation of the defence of the Dardanelles.

As early as the end of June 1915, plans were underway in London for a new Allied offensive, which was now designed to bring about a decisive blow with the assistance of fresh troops. Since no major success could now be expected by further reinforcing troops in the southern part of the Peninsula, the new concentration would have to be in the north. The Allied plan of attack, which was first presented to General Hamilton on 30 May 1915, envisaged that the Ariburnu Front should be broken up, with a northern envelopment by nearly 20,000 men from the ANZAC landing point to the heights of Koja Chemen Tepe, Hill Q and Chunuk Bair. At the same time, a frontal attack on the positions in the Ariburnu sector was to tie up Turkish forces deployed there and divert them from the main thrust., The British IX Corps was to land in Suvla Bay with two divisions and attack the high terrain to the east of the Salt Lake; from there it was either to support the fight for Ariburnu in the south or to advance further to the south-east. In the south, another attack on Krithia was planned to hold down Turkish forces there and, if possible, make a breakthrough to take the heights of Achi Baba.

The envelopment of the Ariburnu Front was initially planned by General Birdwood's staff as an operation using only one fresh division and was scheduled for July. However, this was changed because now, instead of just a single division, three new ones had been made available, which delayed the planning into August. First, a fresh division had to be moved unnoticed into the very cramped bridgehead at Ariburnu and remain there a few days, although the area was already barely large enough for the existing force. Attacking north and then turning east into the various valleys in the dark with inexperienced troops brought with it a high risk of disorientation. The attack was to be made in two columns - the left one further north, enveloping Koja Chemen Tepe and Hill Q; the right one on Rhododendron Ridge, towards Chunuk Bair. However, an evaluation of the narrow nature of the terrain at Ariburnu led to the conclusion that this operation could not be carried out with three divisions, since there was only enough room for one. This led to the beginning of the planning for the operation at Suvla Bay.

For this landing, motor vessels, so-called 'beetles' were to be used, made with bulletproof hulls and which could carry up to 500 soldiers. The choice of which troops should be used and who was to take command of this operation was long debated; fresh troops from Britain were selected, since the landing was considered to be the simpler part of the operations. Lieutenant General Sir Frederick William Stopford was nominated as GOC of IX Corps; but he had had no recent experience as a battlefield commander. The plans drawn up by his staff for the landing of the 10th and 11th Divisions were quite detailed, but the orders for the attack on the surrounding heights of the Salt Lake were only vague and ambiguous, following no doubt from the *Final Instructions From GHQ to IX Corps*, which included the statement: 'Your primary objective will be to secure Suvla Bay as the base for all forces operating in the northern zone'.[449]

Therefore, from the outset, no attack by these troops ever gained momentum, nor was there any initiative demonstrated against an inferior enemy, since they were only prepared for a static securing of a bridgehead and not for a quick attacking thrust into the hinterland.

The Turkish defence of Suvla Bay was under the command of Major Wilhelm Willmer, who in mid-June 1915 had been given command of the Anafarta Group. His mission was 'to prevent any enemy landing or expansion of the existing Ariburnu Front to the north'.[450]

To cover this defensive strip that was almost ten kilometres wide, in early August, Willmer had only two *Jandarma* battalions (a paramilitary force, modelled on the French gendarmerie), an infantry battalion, a cavalry squadron, four field artillery batteries, a total of only about 2,000 soldiers. In the early phases he had no machine guns, hardly any barbed wire and his few artillery pieces were spread over a wide area. Therefore, he created dummy positions for his artillery and constantly ordered changes in their positions to deceive the enemy's observers as to his actual strength and positions. His plan was based on the assumption that he would have to hold his positions for at least thirty-six hours, until more troops could be brought from Bulair. Willmer did not expect reinforcements from the Ariburnu area of Essad Paşa, as Essad's troops would most likely come under heavy pressure in any attack on Suvla Bay or in a breakout by the Anzacs. Willmer focused his defence on three forward defence outposts: one at the top of Kiretch Tepe, one at Softa Tepe (Hill 10) and Pirnar Tepe (Chocolate Hill). Lala Baba Tepe had also been prepared with trenches and was manned by a small number of observers. He held his main forces ready in the rear, to the north, around the heights of Kavak and Tekke Tepe, and in the south, hard east on the heights around Yusufcuk Tepe (Scimitar Hill). Willmer set up his headquarters at Camli Tekke.

The battle began in the afternoon of 6 August at 2.20 pm with heavy shelling on the Helles Front as a diversionary manoeuvre. However, despite reinforcements to the 29th Division, the subsequent attack against the Turkish positions around Krithia could not be successfully pressed and were repulsed with high casualties on both sides. The fighting on the Helles Front, however, had no bearing on the progress of the fighting in the north of the Peninsula. In the evening of 6 August there was heavy shelling on the rearmost lines of the Northern Group at Ariburnu, which was soon

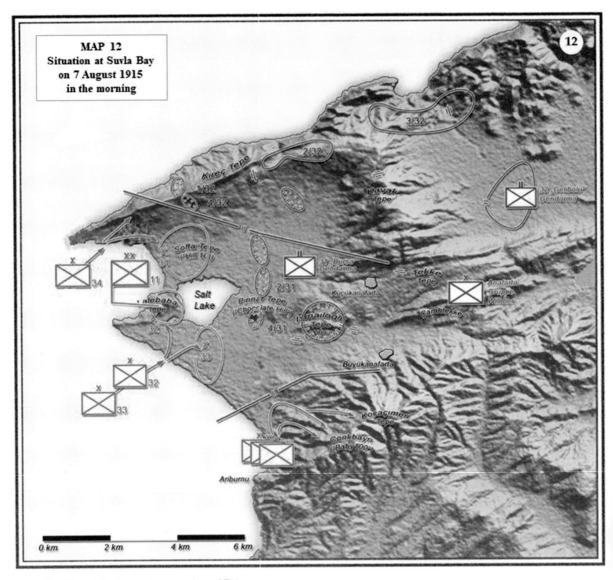

MAP 12
Situation at Suvla Bay
on 7 August 1915
in the morning

Situation at Suvla Bay, the morning of 7 August.

followed by an attack against the Group's left flank which, despite bitter fighting, brought no new territorial gains for the Allies.

At 8.30 pm the first troops, 2,000 New Zealand soldiers, started marching north from their hideouts at the ANZAC bridgehead, before they then headed east. The first attacks on the weakly defended forward Turkish posts were successful and they were quickly overwhelmed. At 9.00 pm the first reports of landings and troop movements in the area north of Ariburnu and at Suvla Bay were received at Fifth Army Headquarters. Von Sanders was well aware that there were only a few weak Turkish units where the enemy had just landed. He therefore immediately mobilised the two Turkish divisions at Bulair, as well as those units of the Southern Group that could be spared, in addition recalling units from the Asiatic side and moving them to the Suvla Front.

'Immediately upon receipt of the foregoing report I telephoned to the 7th and 12th Divisions on the upper Saros (Xeros) Gulf, ordering that they be alerted and made ready to march at once. About an hour later orders were sent to start both divisions at once in the general direction of Usun-Hisirli, east of Anafarta Sagir.'[451]

Lieutenant Colonel Kannengiesser, GOC 9th Division, which was engaged in coastal defence between the Northern and Southern Groups, was ordered by Essad Paşa at 7.00 am on 7 August to march north to Chunuk Bair and take this dominating ridge. Kannengiesser arrived ahead of his Division and just as enemy troops approached that ridge. He succeeded in holding off the oncoming enemy until his own division came up.

'From a deep valley I saw before me the steep side of the Djonk Bahir (Chunuk Bair) whose high comb eventually merged in the nearby Koja Chemen Dagh. We had to dismount from our horses and, under the already burning rays of the sun (it was 6 am), climb the sides of the Djonk Bahir, pulling ourselves slowly up by the help of small bushes and rough grass. On top was a long narrow plateau with an astonishingly far-reaching view over rough hilly country to the Aegean Sea.

Suvla Bay lay full of ships. We counted ten transports, six warships, and 'seven' hospital ships. On land we saw a confused mass of troops like a disturbed ant-heap, and across the blinding white surface of the dried salt sea we saw a battery marching in a southerly direction. With our few revolvers we could do nothing against it.

All about us was peace and quiet – not a man to be seen and no enemy in front of us in the hills. With glasses I was able to pick out bit by bit Willmer's companies north of the Asmak Dere on the east border of the flat country, and I saw English [sic] troops on Lala Baba and, on the flat, in certain places, entrenching. Nowhere was there fighting in progress. I now began a reconnaissance of the country so as to be able to receive the approaching regiments with final orders. [...] It was now only possible to occupy the Djonk Bahir as the key point of our position, with the reserves close behind, as the position had no depth. Additionally unpleasant was the fact that both wings were without support and I had no troops to protect them. It was also impossible for the moment to make contact with the neighbouring 19th Division.

During this first reconnaissance we found a Turkish battery, whose battery commander I had to awaken, as he had no idea of the altered battle front. He opened fire on the troops crossing the dried salt sea, but could only reach them with high explosive. I also found a platoon of infantry, roughly twenty men, covering the battery, which was at least something. While I now dictated reports and orders to Hunussi Bey, who had first to translate these into Turkish, Zia Bey continually swept the country in front of us with my glasses, as it was essential to keep the English [sic] as far as possible away from us.

Suddenly the enemy infantry actually appeared in front of us at about 500 yards range. The English [sic] approached slowly, in single file, splendidly equipped and with white bands on their left arms, apparently very tired, and were crossing a hill-side to our flank, emerging in continually increasing numbers from the valley below. I immediately sent an order to my infantry – this was the twenty man strong artillery-covering platoon –to open fire instantly. I received the answer: "We can only commence to fire when we receive the order from our battalion commander". This was too much for me altogether. I ran to the spot and threw myself among the troops who were lying in a small trench. What I said I cannot remember, but they began to open fire and almost immediately the English laid down without answering our fire or apparently moving in any other way. They gave the impression that they were glad to be spared further climbing.

Now I received unexpected reinforcements. From the direction of Dustepe (Battleship Hill) I suddenly saw a Turkish column coming and which was about to descend rearwards in the deep valley. It was two companies of Infantry Regiment 72. My orders to halt immediately and come under my command had to be urgently repeated before they obeyed. At the same time the commander of the 1st Battalion, Infantry Regiment 14, reached the Koja Chemen Dagh, and I took him with his companies under my orders.

Thus I was slowly able to establish a small firing front which I grouped in two wings, as the commanders of Infantry Regiments 25 and 64 reported to me that their battalions would shortly be arriving. I had been successful in keeping this exceptionally important height in our hands and bringing the forward progress of the enemy to a halt.'[452]

Kannengiesser was severely wounded in this battle:

'As I was starting back towards the left wing, which I considered endangered and which had still not found touch with the 19th Division – it was about 8 o'clock in the morning – I received from this machine gun a shot through the breast. This was most annoying. Up to date I had escaped from many other worse positions without a scratch. Now I was forced to leave my brave Division just at this most critical moment. Zia Bey and Brandl sprang to my help immediately, but had to leave me lying down as the machine gun kept this point under continuous fire. After some time the fire slackened and both carried me behind the nearby protection of a cliff. Brandl, who had studied medicine for six terms in Munich, found a bullet wound in the middle of the breast, close to the heart, and tied me up with a field dressing. [...] They laid me on a stretcher already thoroughly soaked in Turkish blood, and carried me down the steep hill, where I soon met the leading sections of my Division coming up. Below in the valley the Divisional-Surgeon, Lieutenant Colonel Nevres Bey, bandaged me up extremely well and I was then taken in a motor ambulance and put on board the *Ac Denis* at Akbash. On the way I halted at the Army Headquarters so that I could report to the Marshal on the critical position on the Koja Chemen Dagh.'[453]

The German Naval Shore Detachment of the MMD was allocated to this sector after Lieutenant Boltz had returned with about 150 men from Istanbul on 27 July. One Section, under the command of Sub Lieutenant Oskar Hildebrandt, took up position on 7 August with four machine guns in the forward Turkish trenches on the slope of Koja Chemen Tepe. The attack began in the morning after shelling by naval guns. Koja Chemen Tepe was at first overrun in close combat, but the Turks regained possession in the afternoon. However, of the sixteen men from the German Naval Shore Detachment, eleven were dead, wounded or missing. The dead included Sub Lieutenant Hildebrandt.[454]

The situation on 7 August in the area of Suvla Bay was no less critical. There, at around 10.00 pm on 6 August, three brigades of the 11th Division landed under Major General Frederick Hammersley. 32 and 33 Brigades landed just south of Kucuk Kemikli (Nibrunesi Point) and 34 Brigade further north, inside Suvla Bay. 34 Brigade was to take the Softa Tepe, which the British called Hill 10, as well as the heights of Kiretch Tepe. The two other brigades were intended to take Lala Baba Tepe and secure the right flank. These goals were realistic if the advantage of surprise had been exploited and the attack had been vigorously pressed forward. The landings were confused, at least on the left flank of 34 Brigade, as it had come ashore at the wrong place and mistook a nearby sandy hill for Softa Tepe. At 6.00 pm on 7 August, Major Willmer sent a message to General Liman von Sanders:

'The enemy landed at Nibrunesi Point about 9:30 p.m. last night. Outpost companies evacuated Lala Baba in the face of a superior enemy force and joined 1st Battalion, 31st Infantry on Chocolate Hill. The Kiretch Tepe - Chocolate Hill position is firmly in our hands. Covered by numerous men of war, the disembarkation of hostile forces continued. Am holding the position as ordered but urgently request reinforcements.'[455]

Softa Tepe (Hill 10) could be held by Willmer's forces until daybreak. At the same time the Turkish artillery opened fire, which made it difficult to disembark the 10th (Irish) Division which, under Major General Hill, landed south of Suvla Bay. During the day British troops moved up and took Pirnar Tepe (Chocolate Hill) and Green Hill in the evening. However, Ismail Oglu Tepe (W Hills) further east, were held by a company of the Bursa *Jandarma* Battalion and the 2nd Battalion, 31st Infantry Regiment. This interrupted the rapid advance to the east and gained time to bring Turkish reserves forward.

XVI Corps, under Colonel Fehsi Bey, which had been ordered by von Sanders to march the day before, was now underway and was expected in the Anafarta sector towards evening. Von Sanders wrote:

'On the afternoon of August 7th the commanding general of the Sixteenth Corps, consisting of the 7th and 12th Divisions, reported to me the arrival of the Corps, to my great surprise. He stated that the troops had made a double march on that day. I therefore in person gave this commander orders to attack in the Anafarta Plain on both banks of the Azmak Dere at daybreak on August 8.'[456]

Von Sanders realised that more and more English troops had been landed and Willmer's units were not in a position to oppose these forces. Therefore, Sanders also ordered Mehmet Ali Paşa, the commander on the Asiatic side 'to send all battalions not in the first line' across to the Suvla Front. However, on the morning of 8 August, when von Sanders rode to the assembly area before dawn, he found no troops there but only the General Staff officer of the 7th Division, who was reconnoitring positions. As the latter reported that the troops had by no means fully arrived, von Sanders ordered the attack for the evening of the same day. However, it did not take place that day:

'When toward evening I learned from Major Willmer that the troops of the Sixteenth Corps had not yet reached the assembly place designated by me, I called the commanding general to account for this; he replied that the fatigued state of the troops did not yet permit an attack.

    That evening I gave command of all the troops in the Anafarta section to Colonel Mustapha Kemal Bei, commander of the 19th Division, which was farthest north on the Ari Burnu front.'[457]

Colonel Fehsi Bey was relieved as GOC of XVI Corps because he disobeyed the order to engage the British forces at Suvla Bay immediately. Although this attack was a great challenge to the exhausted soldiers after a two-day march, it was nonetheless imperative that it take place. Willmer's troops had now fought for forty-eight hours against a much superior enemy and urgently needed to be relieved. This necessity was also recognised by Mustafa Kemal, who was the new commander, and he ordered the attack to be carried out.

On 8 August, Lieutenant General Stopford and his staff continued to remain on board the *Jonquil* and, despite the fact that the ship was equipped with limited communication facilities, he only made sporadic visits to the landing zone and therefore had no clear picture of the situation at Suvla Bay. On the beach heads his troops had made themselves comfortable, as if they were in what the Germans called an *Etappe* (a base depot in the rear); more forces were being landed and organised, trenches were being dug and those soldiers without any specific duties, bathed and drank tea. This was the front line and the number of Turkish troops on the opposite hills was clearly inferior. General Hamilton, still waiting at his headquarters on Imbros for progress reports on the attack, decided to find out for himself what was going on there. After coming ashore, Hamilton was told by Stopford that everything was going according to plan and would work out well. Hamilton, however, quickly recognised the seriousness of the situation and now stepped in personally to issue orders

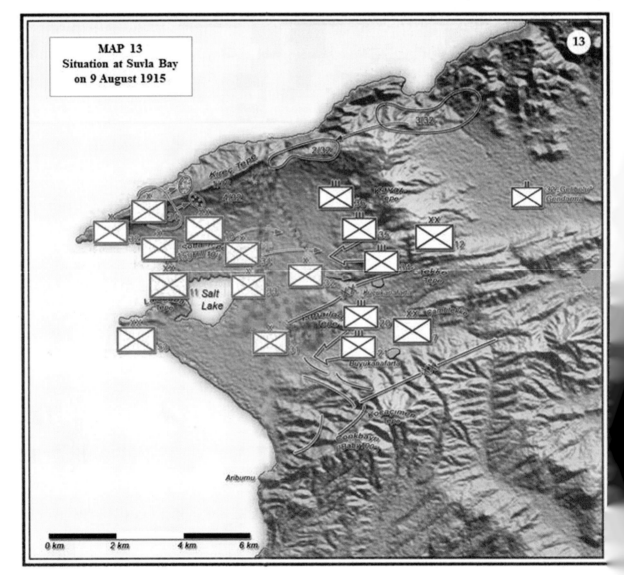

Situation at Suvla Bay, 9 August 1915.

to the 10th Division. He ordered Major General Hammersley, who had already planned an attack for 9 August, to go up against Tekke Tepe during the coming night. This interference led to great confusion. Troops already on Yusufcuk Tepe (Scimitar Hill) had to be recalled to their original positions and the attack could not begin until the morning of 9 August 1915.

On the same day, 9 August, Admiral Souchon telegraphed a report to Berlin; it not only reported the sinking of the *Barbarossa Hairedin* by a submarine in the Dardanelles the previous day but also contained another urgent call for replacement personnel for the German Naval Shore Detachment:

'At the urgent request of General Liman von Sanders, I have increased the Machine Gun Sections of the Mediterranean Division to 16 machine guns. Contribution by German Machine Gun Sections is highly appreciated by the Turkish Army Command. Corresponding increase desired. Sub Lieutenant Branconi repatriated for health reasons, Sub Lieutenant Hildebrandt, German Naval Shore Detachment, killed in action. Urgently demand replacements for Branconi, Hildebrandt and Rabenau, as well as the dispatch of three younger officers for the Machine Gun Section.'[458]

On the morning of 9 August, the counter-attack, which had already been postponed three times, began under the command of Mustafa Kemal, about whom Sanders wrote in this context:

'Mustapha Kemal, who earned his first military laurels in Cyrenaica, was a leader that delighted in responsibility. On the morning of April 25th he had attacked with the 19th Division on his own initiative, drove the advancing enemy back to the coast and then remained for three months in the Ari Burnu front, tenaciously and inflexibly resisting all attacks. I had full confidence in his energy.'[459]

With the Turkish 7th Division on the left and the 12th on the right, Mustafa Kemal now attacked Tekke Tepe. The 12th Division advanced towards the British, who, after days of agonising had finally decided, allegedly only thirty minutes before, to attack Tekke Tepe with their 32 Brigade: the 12th Division met them directly in their approach.[460] The Allied troops suffered heavy casualties and lost important high ground. In this connection, it is interesting to quote from a letter written by Lieutenant Colonel Willmer in 1927 to General Liman von Sanders. Willmer responded to the memoirs of Mustafa Kemal, in which the latter had apparently claimed to have made the essential command decisions for these battles himself.

'Straubing, 12.V.27

Dear General,

In the *Stahlhelm* [magazine] I find an article by Major Welsch about Mustafa Kemal's memoir, which Your Excellency will undoubtedly also find interesting. In Gallipoli, we were already aware that MK was not a friend of the Germans. Likewise, that he was very full of himself. It is not entirely true that on 8 August, 'with his division', that he brought the English [sic] attack to a halt on the third landing. Fehsi Bey was supposed to attack with the 7th and 12th divisions on this day but, up until the evening of 8 August, he had neither assembled the Divisions for attack, nor even considered an attack on that day. I reported this to Your Excellency, whereupon Your Excellency relieved Fehsi Bey of command that night, and ordered MK to carry out an attack, which took place on 9 August. MK launched a counter-attack on 10 August with the newly arrived 8th Division at Chunuk Bair, in which it was known that a ricocheting bullet smashed his watch, which he then presented to Your Excellency in Camli

Tekke, and through which he again came to take possession of Chunuk Bair. That MK claims the credit for the victorious Battle of Anafarta is not particularly surprising considering his great self-exaltation, although he was only the executive organ of the orders made by Your Excellency.'[461]

In retrospect Liman von Sanders was greatly offended that not only had his achievements in the operational phase not been fully recognised by the Turks, but also those of the Military Mission. He later wrote about this on 21 July 1927 to Major Mühlmann:

> For the files, I enclose a copy of a letter from Willmer as a <u>comrade in battle.</u> In view of the unbelievable presumption of the Turks – which by no means existed 12 years ago – it may perhaps transpire that the chain of command there at that time will be clarified.'[462]

Reinforced by units from the Territorial 53rd (Welsh) Division, the British attacked again on 10 August. The heights of Scimitar Hill and Ismail Oglu Tepe (W Hills) were taken by the British, but recaptured in the evening by Turkish counter-attacks and the heights were successfully defended against further attacks over the following months.

Stopford now tried to take the northern high ground around the Kiretch Tepe and thus outflank the Ariburnu front. The local Gelibolu *Jandarma* Battalion, which had held these positions on 8 and 9 August, had only two artillery pieces. On 8 August, however, a section from the German Naval Shore Detachment arrived there with four machine guns to strengthen the defences. Von Sanders had also relocated small units that could be spared from coastal defence duties at Ejelmer Bay to Kiretch Tepe and, on 10 August, appointed Major Willmer in command of these heights. With the arrival of Major Lierau, an experienced German heavy artillery officer, on the Peninsula on 11 August, General von Sanders appointed him to command all the Anafarta Group's artillery, which had previously been under the command of Mustafa Kemal.[463] Lierau quickly realised that the enemy's artillery support came primarily from the sea and that for a successful fire fight against the warships, the batteries "should be in positions immediately behind the forward infantry lines".

To this end Lierau explored valleys favourably located on both sides of Ismail Oglu Tepe (W Hills) and then ordered the change in position. The reaction of the Turkish battery commanders and gun crews was one of 'stunned faces'. Nevertheless, he was later full of praise for the splendid performance of the Turkish gunners, who had to relocate their field guns, ammunition and equipment in the searing heat and on bad or almost non–existent paths. Lierau was proved to be correct. He wrote on 12 August:

> 'At 06.00 hrs, my first shot signalled the opening of general fire. The surprise was successful. Firing was very simple thanks to easy observation. Soon effects were achieved: some ships caught fire, others began to list, a large transporter had to be taken in tow, and all ships, including the cruisers, made haste to the open sea. Even the two heavily armoured ones cleared their anchorages, but only withdrew to be out of range before anchoring again and carried on firing. But traffic to the landing sites had been stopped.'[464]

On the same day Captain Knaab arrived at the Anafarta Group, in command of a 9-cm battery from the *Goeben*, together with German naval gunners. Major Lierau had a special task for this unit:

> 'I believed that with this battery we could entrust it with something special and I positioned it on the most forward hill, directly on a steep slope, by itself and on open ground, without any

The award of the Silver Liakat Medal with Swords to Lieutenant Kleinau, an Artillery Officer serving with Major Lierau in the Anafarta Group. The original signature of Liman von Sanders and the stamp of the Military Mission. (*Gunter Hartnagel Collection*)

cover, so that it could fire directly. it would have been days before it was ready to fire if we had wanted to position it first under cover in the rocky ground.'[465]

This artillery attack was also mentioned in *Naval Operations* by Corbett:

'On 12th [August], while the Navy was working its hardest at completing landing-places and getting ashore the gear and supplies most urgently needed, and at the same time was evacuating the crowds of wounded, shrapnel began to rain on the supporting ships, and before they could get away they had suffered fifty casualties.'[466]

On 15 August the British attacked the Gelibolu *Jandarma* Battalion with two brigades, penetrating to the middle of the ridge and almost eliminating the Turkish unit completely. Its commander, Captain Kadri Bey, was killed on that day. Nevertheless, the positions were held by the *Jandarma* Battalion. On 16 August, with further reinforcements, another attack was not only repulsed but the old positions were recaptured. Von Sanders rated this Turkish victory as crucial in stopping a potential Allied breakthrough:

'If on August 15th and 16th the British had taken the Kiretch Tepe they would have outflanked the entire Fifth Army and final success might have fallen to them. The ridge of Kiretch Tepe and its southern slopes dominated the wide Anafarta plain from the north.'[467]

Kannengiesser, who was recovering from his wounds at the German hospital in Istanbul, was being kept up to date by Major Prigge, von Sanders' Adjutant, who sent him a message that arrived on 19 August:

'Since the 7th His Excellency has been literally day and night *en route*, and only by the most extreme effort have we succeeded in preventing a successful advance by the enemy, who landed four or five Divisions.[...] For the moment it has become quieter. The English [sic] have this time suffered enormous losses and the battles were far more bitter than any we have had so far.'[468]

Hamilton made another attempt to break through on the Suvla Front in a large-scale attack with his battle-tried 29th Division, which had been brought up from the Helles front, together with another infantry division. There were now six divisions under the command of Major General de Lisle (29th Division originally), the temporary successor of Lieutenant General Stopford, as well as strong ANZAC forces under Major General Herbert Cox, who was simultaneously to attack the Turkish lines on the left flank of the ANZAC front. On 21 August, after two hours of artillery preparation, the Allies attacked, but once again this attack was successfully beaten back.

On 29 August 1915, Admiral Souchon visited the Gallipoli Front and wrote home:

'Yesterday was a big day for me. I went to the Gallipoli battlefield and visited the fleet's machine-gun Detachment in the trenches. At night a strong English attack was repulsed with estimated casualties of 10,000 to the enemy. Whilst I was there, there was only weak artillery and machine-gun fire in the centre of the Ariburnu positions and in the evening, indirect bombardment of the Turkish disembarkation positions with heavy ships' guns, so I finally gained an impression of positional warfare. I would have preferred to stay in the trenches to fight through all the adventures. [...] The Turks are excellent. The 27th Regiment has been in daily combat for 4 months, without ever having been relieved, has lost 41 officers and more than 4,000 men (for whom, of course, there have always been replacements). The Turks look healthy and strong, older than our soldiers usually look. They are well dressed and almost without exception wear good English shoes. Navy Captain Rohde tells me that individual Turkish soldiers go stalking at night beyond the trenches, without their rifles, to seize the prize of English boots, rifles, money and the like. In this way, they often bring with them wounded and non-wounded prisoners. I met General v. Liman in a confident mood. He spoke of the enemy's tactical mistakes and the inferiority of his reinforcements.'[469]

During this time the forces in Ariburnu and on the Northern Front had been further reinforced by the German Naval Shore Detachment. Lieutenant Eduard Krulls wrote about the fighting in the north:

'On assignment to the German Naval Shore Detachment on Gallipoli, I travelled on 27 August 1915 to the Dardanelles and on 30 August took over the machine-gun section of Lieutenant Boltz on Düs Tepe [Battleship Hill] at Ari Burnu. There were four machine guns in position in the foremost trenches, which stretched out on the ridge of Düs Tepe, the outermost ridge to the Aegean Sea. In the lee of the ridge, about 10 minutes away from the trenches, was our camp. The English [sic] trenches lay opposite on the lower slopes, in places approaching to 20 to 30 metres to our trenches towards Ari Burnu. The distance for our machine guns was on average 300-600 metres.'[470]

The attempt by the Allies in August to force a decision with five divisions[471] on the Dardanelles had failed. Although the Entente Army now comprised thirteen divisions, it had gained nothing further than a frontal extension of about twelve kilometres.

From late August the Fifth Army was composed of the Southern, Northern and Anafarta Groups. Only weak forces remained on the Asiatic side. The Fifth Army temporarily comprised twenty-two, then later seventeen, divisions, but at the time when it was at its greatest strength, due to high casualties, the number of all ranks never exceeded more than 120,000 men. In order to relieve the Fifth Army of its defence responsibility in the rear, which was securing the Bulair Isthmus, the First Army was assigned to take over this task. At the end of August the fighting continued to ebb and the fronts hardened into a stalemate once more.

The problems of Turkish reinforcements and resupply began to increase when summer ended. The change of season to wet and cold weather called for badly needed and better accommodation and food, as well as warm clothing, all of which could not be provided in adequate quantities. Other Turkish Armies were deprived of much of their heavy artillery, because of the urgent requirements of the Gallipoli Front.

In September the front on Kiretch Tepe, the ridge in the far north, was reinforced by the German Naval Shore Detachment, for which further personnel were requested from Germany. The end of August 1915 saw the German Naval Shore Detachment divided into three sections: Section A, under Lieutenant Boltz, with four groups in the 14th Division; Section B, under Sub Lieutenant Franz Wodrig, with four groups in the 12th Division at Ismail Oglu Tepe (W Hills); and Section C, under changing commanders, at Kiretch Tepe. This organisation was changed in October 1915 to comprise only two sections. The MMD sent Berlin a message, dated 13 September 1915:

'The detached Machine Gun Sections of the Mediterranean Division of around 270 men located in 3 vulnerable positions energetically intervened with particular success in recent fighting on Gallipoli. Army command urgently requires that these stay. Replacement of numerous losses incurred through enemy action and illness in the long run not possible without undue weakening of forces afloat. Therefore please despatch, including: 15 machine-gunners, 10 petty officers, 3 ordnance mates, 97 able seamen, 3 leading seamen artillery mechanics. Field service and machine-gun training desired. Issue all men with plenty of underwear and sturdy laced boots, because not available here. Division Chief. Humann.'[472]

Lieutenant Krülls was appointed as the new Section OC of the Shore Detachment in the north.

'After a long ride without map or guide through mountains full of ravines, I finally reached the camp of the Kiretch Tepe Section in the afternoon of 18 September and took over command from Lieutenant Aliy. From the camp to our positions was a march of about three quarters of an hour, always in sight of the enemy and not protected by any sap trench against enemy fire. While I had found well-constructed trenches on Düs Tepe (Battleship Hill), there was nothing like those here but only walls of loosely piled rock, which shielded them from being seen. There were only small stretches of makeshift trenches in the ravines. The lack of proper trenches was due to the rocky soil and absence of sapper equipment. Our position ran transversely to the back of Kiretch Tepe, on the slope, then bending at right angles to the north, parallel to the coast of the Aegean Sea (Gulf of Saros).

When I arrived there were only two machine-guns in position. With the means available, I immediately had new gun positions made and then a third one forward, and one machine-gun each in the bays of Büyük Mezarlık and Kücük Mezarlık against possible attempts of an English [sic] landing and then, in the camp, set up an anti-aircraft machine gun. I received the personnel I was missing, some from Kilia Tepe, some from the Turkish 126th Regiment. Since the accommodation of the gun crews in loosely piled stone caves was inadequate, I had the off duty men start building larger huts from stone and clay. However, getting hold of any wood we needed was very difficult. For this reason the construction of splinter-proof shelters could not even be thought of. [...] In order to secure the supply of ammunition in a battle and the quick execution of small repairs, a dugout for ammunition and repairs was constructed with great difficulty directly behind the firing line, which subsequently rendered excellent services; it was in such a position that it could be quickly and safely reached by all machine-guns crews during action. Due to the complete lack of NCOs, I had my hands full to oversee the various jobs and to organise rations.

Of course the work in the front line could only be done at night because of enemy fire. Later on, after consultation with the Divisional Commander, I had two machine guns set up in front of the front line – on the one hand, to flank the enemy positions better, and on the other because it gave a morale boost to the Turks, who gained more confidence in their positions and began to continue working forward on making saps. Also here, on the extreme right flank of the Anafarta position, the enemy regularly fired four to five times a day on our positions and connecting routes. The bombardment was mostly done by batteries on land, two battleships in Suvla Bay and, from the north, a monitor and a large destroyer (in the Gulf of Saros), so we were always in a cross-fire. The enemy infantry here seemed quieter than at Ari Burnu. Action was limited to nocturnal hand-grenade attacks by our side and machine-gun duels.

As a result of the number of Turkish artillery positions located between Anafarta and Kiretsch Tepe, a lot of enemy air activity took place, during which the camp was also repeatedly bombed. The aircraft always flew at a fairly high altitude, mostly out of range of machine guns. We did not suffer as much from vermin here as on Düs Tepe (Battleship Hill); with the onset of cooler weather the plaguing by flies also began to become more bearable. In the evening of 27 September, after a grenade attack by the Turks, the English opened an extremely heavy artillery barrage on our positions, joined in by all ships at Ari Burnu, Suvla Bay and in the Gulf of Saros. On open ground en route to the front, shells and shrapnel literally flew over my head, without me being hit. This was followed by an [Allied] infantry attack all down the line from Kiretsch Tepe to Ismail Tepe (W Hills), but it was brilliantly beaten off. The English had quite a few casualties.

Through some prisoners taken by the Turks, we learned that there were already parts of the new Kitchener Army among the Englishmen [sic] who faced us. On 29 September the English repeated the hefty artillery bombardment, but did not, however, follow up with an attack afterwards. One machine-gun position and the ammunition dugout were slightly damaged by artillery hits and soon repaired again. In the days following enemy artillery activity increased more and more, and caused minor damage to the gun positions and access routes. Flying activity also increased; however, we were unable to bring down an aircraft with our machine guns. The Turks also increased their artillery activity and, supported by our machine guns, could achieve good results with their nightly hand grenade attacks.'[473]

During this phase Mustafa Kemal contracted malaria and was severely weakened by illness and physical exhaustion. When Enver Paşa inspected the troops in Gallipoli on 24 September, he left out paying a visit to Kemal's Headquarters and Kemal was so deeply upset by what he believed was a slight that three days later he submitted his letter of resignation to Liman von Sanders. With support from other Turkish senior officers, von Sanders tried at first to talk him out of it, but it was to no avail.[474] In a letter to the Minister of War, Enver Paşa, von Sanders tried to pour oil on the waters between Enver and Kemal and, on 30 September 1915, wrote a glowing testimony to Mustafa Kemal:

'Your Excellency,
I have the honour to inform you that Colonel Mustapha Kemal Bey has tendered his written resignation. I cannot endorse this request, because I recognise and appreciate Colonel Mustapha Kemal as a particularly capable, efficient and brave officer, whose services are definitely needed by the Fatherland in this Great War. Since the first landing 5 months ago, Kemal Bey has fought with distinction at the head of the 19th Division, and at the last major landing of the English in the Anafarta sector, where, at a difficult time, he had to take over command, as the designated commander of the XVI Turkish Army Corps did not carry out the repeated command to attack with the 7th and 12th Division. Colonel Mustapha Kemal Bey has also executed his task here with great bravery and with good, concise instructions, so that I felt it my duty to repeatedly express my appreciation and thanks to him. Colonel Mustapha Kemal Bey wants to resign because he believes that he does not have the confidence of your Excellency, the Vice-Generalissimo of the Imperial Army, his highest superior. He believes that this is particularly evident from the fact that Your Excellency did not call on him during Your last visit, although he was ill and still is, while Your Excellency honoured the commanders of the other three Groups. I have emphasised to Colonel Mustapha Kemal Bey that Your visit was omitted only for lack of time, and that Your Excellency is well aware of his achievement. Your Excellency, please do not accept the letter of resignation, which I do not attach for the time being, in expectation of Your Excellency's trust.
    Your Excellency, I remain, Your very loyal servant, Liman von Sanders.'[475]

Enver Paşa sent a telegram in which he sent Mustafa Kemal his best wishes for a speedy recovery and tried to explain the lack of time when he was visiting the front. Kemal replied on 4 October, saying that he would like to thank Enver for his wishes of a speedy recovery but would rather serve in another appointment, where his services could be better employed.[476]

    Kemal, however, was not offered a post that met his satisfaction and his relationship with Liman von Sanders also steadily worsened. He continued to complain to Turkish Headquarters that there were far too many Germans around him and that he once found himself obliged to send back a German officer who had been assigned to the 11th Division. In another case he refused to hand over a Turkish officer who had refused an order given by a German officer to be court-martialled by von Sanders. Major Izzettin wrote of the situation between Kemal and von Sanders: 'These incidents created misunderstandings and a coldness between the two commanders and led to the departure of Mustafa Kemal to Istanbul under cover of a medical report.'[477]

On 10 December 1915, Colonel Mustafa Kemal finally departed for Istanbul.

The fighting in the northern sector of the front continued during October, about which Lieutenant Boltz made this report:

'For MG Section I, combat intensity had been low since the end of October. The Turkish trenches, in which our machine guns were individually placed and often set up at long distances from each other, were 200 to 800 metres away from the English [sic] trenches. [...] The troops in the trenches mainly had to suffer from howitzer fire and daily, almost regularly, half an hour of shellfire from the ships. Casualties were not high unless a trench received a direct hit by accident. Quite frequently the enemy fired numerous machine guns. Our guns responded as soon as a worthwhile target came up. Each of our guns loosed off a few boxes of ammunition daily, mostly during the dark. The enemy also made themselves unpleasant with their mountain guns, which were very cleverly placed in the mountainous terrain. As soon as one of our MGs had betrayed its position when firing, a few shots dropped on us as fast as lightning, which were usually well aimed but only had an effect if they scored a direct hit. In November and December the 19th Infantry Division had daily casualties of 40-50 men caused by enemy fire and in the forward trenches, which in places were only 5 metres away from the English [sic], also through bombs. Thanks to being well protected, our German MG crews were lucky to only have a few lightly wounded. The situation was different at Section II in Kiretch Tepe, in the sector of the 11th Turkish Infantry Division, immediately on the right flank of the Turkish position. Due to the lack of naval officers, the OC was at first Lieutenant Keiner, an artillery officer detached from the Fifth Army, who was later replaced by Lieutenant Karl Raspel from *SMS Goeben*. Serving with him was Dr. Hiltmann as medical officer.

The enemy maintained constant fire here and during the night pushed his trenches closer and closer to the Turkish ones, remaining unnoticed because they could not be seen from the terrain of the Turkish trenches. So he kept gaining ground. The Turkish trenches here were quite poor as, on the one hand, they were not constructed before the English [sic] landed on 6 August and, on the other, penetrating the rocky ground was often only made possible by blasting with dynamite. The latter, of course, as with all supplies in Turkey, was not available until the fleet helped out. There was also a lack of material to expand the MG positions and dugouts. The 11th Infantry Division did not even have enough for its own needs. The base station at Kilia-Tepe was 6-7 hours march away from the Section and just during the period of expanding the positions there was a lack of transport, so that only a small amount of help from here was possible. It was often difficult to even send the food rations required to the front. Every day several boxes of ammunition were fired here from each machine-gun. Reply was always fierce enemy MG fire, which usually came from the flank. Apart from that, the gun crews in the trenches had much to suffer from heavy ships' fire from the monitors, the Juno Class cruisers and English [sic] destroyers, as well as from the shells of the land-based batteries. The casualties of the 11th Infantry Division were greater than those of the 19th Division. MG Section II lost 5 men dead and 6 men wounded in November and in early December. At the suggestion of the German Division Commander, Lieutenant Colonel Willmer, who helped us in every way as much as he could and who considered the German MGs irreplaceable in his defence plans, the Section used the time to train Turkish infantrymen on the machine guns.

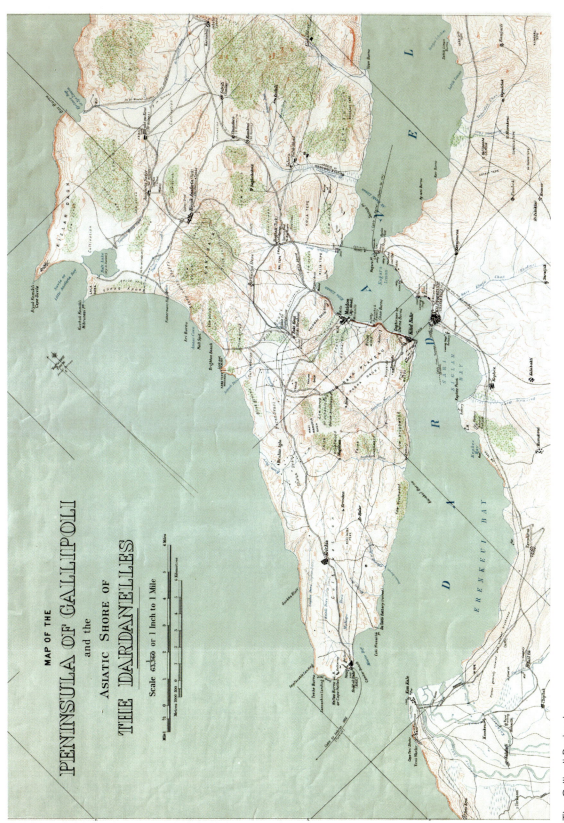

The Gallipoli Peninsula.

Wir halten fest und treu zusammen.

Above left: The German-Ottoman Alliance as illustrated through wartime propaganda postcards. (*S Chambers*)

Above right: A contemporary propaganda postcard depicting the unity and strength of the Central Powers.

Below: The German Embassy in Istanbul c.1880. (*German Archaeological Institute*)

Above: A German produced postcard showing the defence of the Dardanelles. (*S Chambers*)

Below: The Narrows of the Dardanelles. (*T Iredale*)

Above: An impressive monument of the Turkish defence of the Dardanelles, prominently depicting Corporal Seyit heaving a shell. (*T Iredale*)

Below: Fort Hamidie II (Fort No 16) at Kilidbahr. (*T Iredale*)

Above: Mines! A replica of the *Nusret*, today moored in the Dardanelles. (*S. Chambers*)

Below: The sinking of the battleship *Bouvet*, painted by Tahsin Siret, 1874-1937. (*Wikimedia Commons*)

Above: The Anzac battlefield: the landing beaches on 25 April 1915, dominated by the Sphinx. (*T Iredale*).

Below: The Suvla battlefield. Ottoman front line trenches looking towards the Salt Lake and Lala Baba. Scimitar Hill is to the left. (*S Chambers*)

An den Dardanellen.

Liman von Sanders

Above left: 'On the Dardanelles.' An advertising image by Asbach, the famous Germany brandy company.

Above right: A contemporary postcard of Liman von Sanders dated c.1916.

Below: An Ottoman Red Crescent illustration, showing a nurse tending a wounded Turkish soldier. (*S Chambers*)

Above: The central section of Tarabya German Military Cemetery today. (*T Iredale*)

Below: Remembrance Sunday 2019: the international commemoration ceremony at the Tarabya German Military Cemetery. (*T Iredale*)

For this purpose, intelligent candidates were selected from the 3 Regiments of the Division, trained and equipped with captured English machine guns. Thus two new Turkish MG companies with 6 guns each were created so that, together with the 6 German guns, each of the three Infantry Regiments could be assigned one MG Company. All three MG Companies were to be subordinated to the OC of the German MG Section. Although this organisation was not fully implemented until the British were withdrawn, the new MG's made a very valuable addition to the defence.'[478]

Boltz also reported further on the progress of housing construction for the German Naval Shore Detachment. Directly behind the front, stone houses were built and, above all, hygiene conditions were improved in order to ameliorate the questionable state of health of the German soldiers. However, this work was very limited due to the lack of building materials and transport.

In contrast, on Kilia Tepe a larger camp for the German Naval Shore Detachment was built; Boltz commented on the construction:

'Naturally, the expansion of Kilia Tepe itself was much easier compared to the camps located directly on the front and here, too, a small colony has gradually emerged. Under Navy Captain Rohde, the construction of stone houses with the few materials available had already been started in the summer. This work now had to be continued eagerly and quickly. Naturally, the main activity could only begin after the building materials necessary had been shipped out from Constantinople.

Only the stones, rocks or bricks from Maidos were available. Originally Kilia Tepe consisted of 2 stone-built houses, the remains of an ancient fortification, which were used as a galley

The port of Kilia. In the background is Kilia Tepe. (*Collection Soytürk*)

and stables. A subterranean cellar, probably the old powder chamber, served as a food store, an old cistern as a wine cellar. Officers and men at first lived in tents. In the first half of December, these were gone. In their place, an officers' mess emerged, consisting of 4 officer's quarters, 2 guest rooms, a mess, officers' kitchen, pantry and office. A little further up, within shouting distance, were the batmen's and interpreters' quarters for 8-10 men, next to it the telephone station. Still further up, 200 metres away, were NCOs' and other ranks' quarters for about 40 men. The hospital, 100 metres below the officer's mess, was equipped for 20 patients. Next to it was a second room for other ranks, which had been built first, but then proved too small. As quarters for reserves, especially during the move to the Southern Group, it did good service. Special care had been devoted to the construction of a stable for the horses; it was located some 100m away from the staff building on the other side of the radio/telegraph station. Separate stalls, a paved stable lane, saddle and feed chamber, room for the stable guard – all gave the impression of a cavalry stable at home. Gradually the development of the camp had progressed to the point that one could already think of artistic decoration and gardens, indeed the beginning of which had been made at the officers' quarters.'[479]

Today, the foundations of this settlement on the eastern slope of Kilia Tepe can only be guessed at and the remains are no longer to be found. An important role was played by the natural harbour in the Bay of Kilia, the defence of which was also assigned to the German Naval Shore Detachment:

'In the port of Kilia, steamers with provisions for the Fifth Army were often unloaded. Since the port could easily be overlooked from Kilia Tepe, the commander of the depot repeatedly approached the German Naval Shore Detachment with a request to protect these valuable steamer ships against submarines. For this purpose, apart from an SK gun (*Schnelladekanone* – a quick-firing gun) taken over from the fortress, his Excellency von Liman provided the German Naval Shore Detachment with field guns and a searchlight. One of them was designated as an anti-aircraft gun and scored almost daily.'[480]

Although speculation about the withdrawal of the Allies was already in circulation during the November of 1915, the Turkish did not want to wait for such a time and planned an offensive. The Army command and the Army commanders agreed that this counter-attack was to be carried out as soon as possible. When von Falkenhayn met Enver Paşa in Orsova on 24 November, he described the 'cleansing' of Gallipoli as the next and most urgent objective. This attack should be thoroughly prepared and supported, above all by enough artillery and ammunition. Army technical units and twenty heavy batteries were sought, in addition to considerable amounts of ammunition for the artillery already in place, confirmed by the Supreme Army Command. Reinforcements were also needed for the German Naval Shore Detachment, as can be seen from a telegram sent to Berlin on 26 November 1915: 'It is indispensable that our machine guns are used for the forthcoming battles on Gallipoli. If possible, request 2 fit and able officers for German Naval Shore Detachment because of frequent casualties. If necessary, suitable reserve officers will do.'[481]

Senior artillery and sapper officers had arrived from Germany to familiarise themselves with the peculiarities of this theatre of war. In mid-November and early December, two Austro-Hungarian heavy batteries arrived. The first German ammunition deliveries also reached Istanbul, as surface transport was finally available following the successful Serbian campaign.[482] However, the difficult connection through Serbia meant that it took weeks until all the units requested were relocated to Turkey. Meanwhile, several divisions of the Turkish Fifth Army were successively withdrawn from the front in order to undergo special training for their new task.

Chapter 12

German support in the formation of the Turkish Air Arm and air operations at Gallipoli

Turkish military aviation also played a role in the battles for Gallipoli. Its build up began shortly before the First World War.

Towards the end of November 1914 the Turkish government asked for German help to set up their own flying training school.[483] Although the main focus of the German High Command for air power was on the Western Front, von Falkenhayn made a small group of pilots, technicians and aircraft available to Turkey. Lieutenant Erich Serno, who had served in the German Air Force since 1911, was ordered to report to the German Military Mission in Istanbul 'for founding and commanding a Turkish Air Arm'.[484] The aircraft and equipment required were transported by land through neutral Romania and Bulgaria disguised as circus equipment or Red Cross packages. Each of these shipments was accompanied by pilots and mechanics in civilian clothes. When he first arrived in Turkey and like all German officers of the Military Mission, Serno was promoted to the next higher rank and now was officially the commander of the Turkish flying training school in San Stefano [485], on the Sea of Marmara.

His task was to develop the formation and organisation of Turkish military aviation and the establishment of squadrons fit for serving the front lines in the Turkish Army's different theatres of war. Not only had Serno to concentrate on various aspects of flying training, he also had to organise supplies and technical equipment. Several Turkish mechanics, blacksmiths, carpenters and drivers were trained there as aircraft mechanics and pilots. Serno also received financial support from German companies, such as the Turkish branch of Deutsche Bank, which paid for the translation and clerical services of this unit.

During the course of the war Captain Serno not only continuously expanded the flying training school but also managed to set up a weather service in Turkey. For this latter task, in 1916 he obtained the meteorological services and expertise of Professor Weichmann from Leipzig University. He also started manufacturing aircraft parts locally in Turkey, benefitting from cooperation with the *Benz-Motorenwerke* (Benz Engine Works) in Istanbul. Finally, he also designed the Turkish pilots' badge, the wings with crescent and star, which was worn on the uniform and cap. Despite Serno's ceaseless activity, when the famous German fighter ace,

Captain Erich Serno. (*Collection Bülent Yilmazer*)

Oswald Boelcke, paid a visit in mid-1916, he described conditions in the Turkish flying training school as 'poor' but also praised Serno's achievements:

> We were driving through Stambul [Istanbul], passing several barracks and through a rather desolate area, to St. Stefano, where we visited the air base there. Serno has created quite a nice empire all from scratch – but they experience great difficulties in getting supplies for lack of a local manufacturing industry, which for the time being is nothing more than a pipe dream.'[486]

It was no longer possible to bring in equipment through Romania and Bulgaria after the camouflaged shipments for the airmen were discovered, despite large bribes. This led to the formation of the German-Turkish Air Auxiliary Command in Czernèheviz, in Hungary. It was a small supply unit with an airfield near the local railway station. The aircraft to be shipped to Turkey were first disassembled and then transported by rail, re-assembled in Czernèheviz, where additional fuel tanks were installed, and then were flown over enemy (Serbia) and neutral (Bulgaria) territory across the Turkish border to Edirne. There they were refuelled and then flew the last 200 kilometres leg to the delivery location at San Stefano. The first aircraft to be ferried in this way for Turkish military aviation was a Rumpler B.I, flown by Frank Seidler (sometimes spelled as Seydler), who later served as a lieutenant in the Turkish Air Force.

This means of transportation was expensive, stretched over 500 kilometres, took over four hours and was therefore quite risky and not very reliable. Until March 1915 only four aircraft were ferried in this way. After Bulgaria joined the war on the side of the Central Powers, from November 1915 supplies were routed via the River Danube to the Bulgarian Danube port of Ruschuk and from there moved by train to Istanbul. The first aircraft were unarmed and only suitable for observation tasks. They were underpowered and therefore could neither fly especially high nor fast. Nevertheless, three of these four aircraft were assigned by Serno to the Gallipoli theatre.

In February 1915 an advance party had been sent to Gallipoli for reconnoitring the construction of an airfield with associated support facilities. The airfield was established about three kilometres from Canakkale on the Asiatic side, just south of Fort Hamidiye. The airfield was well camouflaged

A Rumpler B.I observation and training aircraft with Turkish insignia. (*Collection Bülent Yilmazer*)

and the pilots had to take off and land under a telegraph wire, which stretched across it. A small hangar was built for maintenance of a single aircraft. Serno himself supervised the transport of the first aircraft on a torpedo boat and reported on 17 March 1915 to the commander of the Straits, Admiral von Usedom. He was warmly welcomed, as the appearance of the first aircraft there represented a great boost to the troops' morale, as they had only previously seen enemy aircraft in the skies. Colonel Kannengiesser wrote:

> 'It was a happy day when the first German aircraft with the Iron Cross appeared above our heads. That was to the credit of the Chief of the Turkish Air Arm, the admirable Captain Serno. Until now, the British had ruled the skies, which gave them an incredible sense of arrogance, which was a sign of how safe they felt.'[487]

The first aerial sortie took place in the early morning of March 18, as already described, to reconnoitre the Allied fleet attack. As the fleet withdrew in defeat, Lieutenant Seidler took off in the Rumpler B.I on another sortie in the afternoon, with Turkish Lieutenant Hüseyin Sedat as observer, to recce Imbros and Mudros Bay. Over the British positions they came under anti-aircraft fire but, suffering no damage or injury, they were able to observe the withdrawal of the enemy fleet.

As the situation after the Entente naval attack quietened down somewhat, Serno returned to Istanbul and on the way back explored the ground on the European side to locate a site where an airfield could be built. He came back to the capital on 24 March 1915 and was awarded the Turkish War Medal and the Silver Liakat Medal by the Minister of War. The squadron in Gallipoli was assigned two more aircraft, the more powerful Albatros B.I, but these stayed mainly on the ground due to technical problems. Therefore the main task of observation flights and limited sorties as light bombers were carried out by the three Rumpler aircraft. The first squadron commander was Ludwig Preussner, who had arrived as a civilian in Turkey and now had the rank of a Turkish officer. It was similar in the case of technicians from Germany, who generally served in the ranks as non-commissioned officers.

The squadron soon discovered the Allied troops concentrating on Imbros and Tenedos on their reconnaissance flights, which indicated a forthcoming landing operation. Enemy facilities continued to be bombed. The British noted that 'the Turkish airmen [...] do a very good job of bombing the airfields'.[488] During the Allied landings in late April it was practically impossible for the pilots to report their reconnaissance results in good time to Fifth Army headquarters. The reason for this lay in the chain of command and correspondingly longer reporting channels, which were also hampered by the frequent destruction of communication facilities. Therefore von Sanders ordered the squadron to be placed under the direct command of the Fifth Army and the squadron was designated No 1 Air Squadron in May. To improve the connection further, the squadron was relocated at the end of June 1915 near the town of Galata, on the European side. Only dummy aircraft remained on the old airfield (near Canakkale), which ensured that it continued to be bombed, as was the intention.

A request for seaplanes from Germany had already been made in May 1915 by the Special Command (SoKo). The High Command of the Imperial Navy approved it and in June despatched to Turkey the first of the Gotha WD 1 seaplanes powered by a 100 hp engine, complete with three pilots, three observers and six mechanics, under the command of Lieutenant Ernst Liebmann. Like the land-based aircraft mentioned earlier in this chapter, they were transported by rail and air to San Stefano, where one machine remained for training purposes while the other two were moved to Canakkale. There was only a small hangar available to begin with, which was enlarged

No 1 Squadron on Gallipoli. (*Bundesarchiv Koblenz*)

Officers of No 1 Squadron in readiness. From left to right: Lieutenant Fünfhausen, Captain Körner, Lieutenant Preussner[489] and Lieutenant von Schlichting. (*Bundesarchiv Koblenz*)

sufficiently to house one aircraft. A second hangar was erected near Nagara.[490] The three Gotha WD 1 seaplanes then formed the Seaplane Detachment and was subordinate to Admiral von Usedom, who commanded in the Dardanelles. In mid-July the first sorties to Mudros, Tenedos and Imbros were launched. However, flight operations could only be carried out on moonlit nights and in the early hours of the morning as the slow, 100-horsepower and unarmoured German aircraft were clearly inferior to the faster Allied fighters. Nevertheless, more than fifty flights were carried out over enemy territory and they even undertook occasional bombing runs. In good weather submarine reconnaissance flights were conducted over the Sea of Marmara. The approaching August offensive by the Allies was revealed by the Seaplane Detachment's recce missions during the moonlit night of 27/28 July 1915, which discovered eighty-seven ships in Mudros Bay. One of the three aircraft was lost at the end of August 1915 as the result of a crash landing.

In response to further requests, a fourth and fifth WD 1 and three 150-horsepower Gotha WD 2 and a further 150 hp Gotha WD 2, armed with a machine gun, were assigned to the Seaplane Detachment in September 1915. Two more hangars were built in Canakkale to accommodate them. Although these hangars were within range of the guns of Allied ships, they had not been discovered by Allied aerial reconnaissance because they were well camouflaged. With the new, more powerful, aircraft, reconnaissance flights and attacks on enemy positions, ships and facilities could now be carried out in all but very bad weather. For this purpose, additional resupply facilities were set up to increase their range. An airfield was established in Rodosto and a refuelling depot installed on the island of Kutali, in the Sea of Marmara. From here flights were made to search for submarines and to protect Turkish resupply transports to the Dardanelles.

A Gotha WD 2 taking off at Nagara; Kilia Tepe in the background. (*Deniz Kitabevli*)

A third airfield was built at Kawak, on the Bosphorus. The aircraft permanently stationed there undertook reconnaissance flights over the Black Sea and safeguarded incoming and outgoing ships against enemy submarines. Except for bombs, the aircraft there had no armament to attack submarines from the air. Therefore a heavy aircraft with a sufficiently large payload capacity was to be procured, which could also carry a torpedo. Such an aircraft had been in the course of flight testing in Germany since July 1915, but apparently technical problems had not yet been fully ironed out. Nevertheless, everything was prepared in Istanbul for the arrival of this aircraft. For this purpose, Navy Lieutenant Rasch travelled to the Bosphorus and the Dardanelles to check on organisational measures and infrastructure.[491] Since the development of the Gotha biplane, which had a wing-span of twenty-one metres, two 160 hp engines and was designed to carry a 35 cm torpedo, was not completed – not even by the end of the war, so this never materialised.

Even with the allocation of replacement aircraft made available, jealousies once again flared up between the land based flying units, subordinate to Captain Serno and the Fifth Army, and the Seaplane Detachment, assigned to the Dardanelles Command and thus Admiral von Usedom. The latter not only raged against replacement aircraft from Germany being delivered to No 1 Squadron but protested to Berlin that it was obviously intending to incorporate the Seaplane Detachment into No 1 Squadron. This dispute explains why von Usedom wrote on 10 September:

'The guarantee for the full operational exploitation of these seaplanes lies in the close connection of the German Seaplane Detachment with the German commander in the Dardanelles, and the local German authorities. [...] I cannot find a good reason to transfer these five aircraft to the Turkish government and thus to the Air Arm Inspectorate, with the large numbers of army aircraft available there.'[492]

On 31 October, von Usedom went on to praise the successful work of the Seaplane Detachment:

'The formation of a special German Seaplane Detachment turned out to be very fit for purpose, because trained German naval aviation personnel are superior to those flying the land-based aircraft, both in long-distance reconnaissance over the islands as well as in submarine attacks, because of their naval expertise. The aircraft apparently were successful in bombing the French aircraft tent hangars on Tenedos and the English balloon shed on Imbros, as well as carrying out valuable reconnaissance on enemy naval forces. On 9 August - as mentioned above - an enemy submarine was destroyed by the bomb dropped by a seaplane.'[493]

After the withdrawal of the Allied troops at Ariburnu, the aircraft of the Seaplane Detachment flew almost daily over the southern tip of the Peninsula and were able to report evidence indicating an early Allied withdrawal from there. However, for reasons unknown, these reports were not forwarded and thus could not be incorporated in the tactical planning of the Fifth Army.

By the end of the year the Seaplane Detachment had lost four aircraft due to forced landings or damage by high winds but was fortunate not to have suffered any personnel losses. The full complement at the time consisted of three officers, a midshipman, twelve pilots and forty-eight Turkish sailors for the operation of a total of five aircraft. The supply of replacement aircraft, however, also created problems in Germany, since every serviceable aircraft was needed there. There was a continuous dispute between the Imperial German Navy and the Army as to which would have to hand over the aircraft required for Turkey.

The pilots of the Seaplane Detachment showed themselves to be both intrepid and resourceful, as shown by following accounts. On 25 January 1916 Petty Officer Stenzel reported that, as an observer, along with Chief Petty Officer Schuetz, he carried out a night flight in aircraft tail number 237 to bomb aircraft hangars on Tenedos:

'Gliding down from an altitude of 800 m over Tenedos down to 600 m. 3 bombs dropped on tent hangars. Several close to the tents exploded. Then a new run. Fourth bomb dropped over the first shed, which fell into a larger tent belonging to the flight station, where it immediately caused a blazing fire. During the whole time experienced very lively shrapnel and gunfire from all parts of the island, marked by the muzzle flashes. Prior to a new run my pilot, Schuetz, was shot through the left thigh, which resulted in a large loss of blood. As a result of his increasing weakness, made emergency landing at Seddulbahr. Then I lifted Schuetz into the observer's seat, bandaged the wound provisionally and taxied [the aircraft] across [the water] to Fort Hamidiye, where I immediately organised more medical attention.'[494]

A report by Petty Officer Meuser described a flight he took to deliver fuel to one of his unit's aircraft, which had needed to make an emergency landing on the water. During the flight he also had to ditch, as the ignition of his engine failed. He was flying solo and landed about 400 metres from the shore:

'After cleaning a few spark plugs, I tried to start again, but the engine would not start. I would have had to spin the prop and operate the starter myself. Since there was no help from land, I jumped into the water and pushed the aircraft 80 – 100 m in front of me until I had solid ground under my feet and could push the aircraft ashore. After I had cleaned all the spark plugs, six Turkish soldiers came along. I explained that this was a German aircraft and ordered them to undress and positioned two of them on the tail and one to hold on to each wing unit, because the beach was very stony and the floats could be seriously damaged. The other two soldiers had to spin the propeller while I operated switches and starters. After approx. 20 minutes the engine fired and, as a safety measure, I took the one Turk with me and took off to rendezvous with aircraft tail number 573. After 15 minutes, I arrived and could carry out my mission.'[495]

By mid 1916, the Seaplane Detachment had nine aircraft and two in reserve. Until then it was a purely German unit, as the formation of a corresponding Turkish wing obviously caused problems, as was shown in a report by Admiral von Usedom:

'The question of creating its own Seaplane Detachment creates difficulties in higher Turkish circles. The Ministry of Marine has procured three such aircraft in Germany and has had three officers trained as pilots. Three more seaplanes are on the way. Observers and fitters are still missing. So when, some time ago, the Ministry of Marine, together with the Fleet (Mediterranean Division), approached me with the view of annexing these new aircraft to the German Seaplane Detachment while maintaining their identity as Turkish, and to take care of their training, I had agreed – so long as it only concerned a few aircraft – but only under certain conditions.'[496]

The use of seaplanes as combat aircraft beyond reconnaissance or bomber roles, however, was not possible. Von Usedom noted this in April 1917:

'No major air battles came about. Among the German seaplanes, only one was equipped with a machine gun, but it was not suitable as a fighter aircraft because of its poor flight and climbing characteristics; the other seaplanes could only carry bombs. The lack of naval single-seat combat fighters has made this particularly noticeable.'[497]

Captain Serno was constantly trying to get additional support from Germany. In particular there was a lack of combat-capable aircraft, the consequence of which he had experienced in an incident himself. Together with his observer, Lieutenant Martin Körner, Serno took off on 8 May 1915 on a mission in the course of which they had to beat off an enemy aircraft attack with just their pistols, for which he was awarded the Iron Cross First Class. Finally Berlin prepared and despatched some Albatros C type aircraft. This model was more effective than the unarmed B type models they already had, as the observer now sat behind the pilot and was armed with a machine gun mounted on a turntable.

The first aerial combat for the Turkish side happened on 27 September 1915 and was credited to Lieutenant Karl Kettembeil, who had been an artillery officer on the Gallipoli front before being reassigned to No 1 Air Squadron. He was on a flight with Lieutenant Ludwig Preussner as his observer when they discovered an enemy aircraft over the Gulf of Saros and successfully engaged it.

After Serno had demanded the best aircraft in Germany for the Gallipoli theatre, at the end of December 1915 the first Fokker E.III aircraft were delivered to the Turkish Air Arm. The E.III was a very manoeuvrable monoplane and its machine gun fired forward through the synchronized propeller.

These aircraft were assigned to the newly created No 6 Squadron, which was also called the 'Fokker Squadron'. Lieutenant Joachim Buddecke (in Turkish service as a captain) was the Commanding Officer and the pilots were, without exception, German officers and NCOs. Buddecke described his arrival at Gallipoli, where he not only experienced the peculiarities of army life but also Turkish conditions:

'The senior commanders of armies usually look different. Here we descended a staircase to the dugout in a low, pine-covered gorge. [...] the one end of the gorge forms the German quarters, the other the Turkish. [...] Serno introduced me to Major Prigge, the aide-de-camp of the Marshal [von Sanders] and together with him we climbed higher into the ravine and waited outside a fence surrounding the Commander-in-Chief's cabin. Soon he came out and I stood before an army commander who had just rendered the English [sic] one of the greatest

A Fokker E.III at Gallipoli - note the two different national emblems. (*Bülent Yilmazer Collection*)

Above: An Albatros D.III on the airfield at Gallipoli.[498] (*Bülent Yilmazer Collection*)

Right: Captain Hans-Joachim Buddecke (right) and Major Max Schueler von Krieken. (*Bülent Yilmazer Collection*)

defeats of the war, which was unforeseeable. [...] The afternoon I spent over a map in the officers' mess. [...] Incidentally, I met a depot commander, who only complained about one fact. The thing was so bizarre that I mention it here. The man lacked any means to punish his subordinates. Detention would be as pleasant for them as free time. Birching is allowed, but he didn't want to use it every day. So he came up with another devilish remedy. In the bay of Akbash Harbour, which was bombed almost daily by the enemy, he had erected three clearly visible white tents. The given aim was that now he could impose detention. The time was then served in these tents. Nothing was easier than that.'[499]

Some of the aerial engagements fought by No 6 Squadron with their Fokker E.III aircraft included: 6 January 1916 - Lieutenant Buddecke shoots down 2 aircraft. One was flown by Busk of the RNAS; the other by Lecomte of Escadrille MF 98 T. Both Allied pilots were killed in action; 7 January – Croneiss one kill; 8 January – Theodor Croneiss shoots down an RNAS aircraft piloted by Bremner & Burnaby, which made a forced landing. The Allied pilots burnt their aircraft and were evacuated on morning of 9 Jan from Helles; 9 January – Buddecke shot down a further Allied aircraft, but this could not be confirmed as a kill; 11 January – Hans Schütz scored his first victory against RNAS pilots Brinsmead & Boles in aerial combat over Helles; 12 January – Buddecke shot down another Allied aircraft, flown by Boles (killed) and Branson, who was wounded and taken prisoner. This was his sixth in total and his third on Gallipoli. For his actions, Buddecke was awarded the Golden Liakat Medal by Enver and promoted to captain; 25 January – Buddecke with one kill; 26 January – one [kill] which could not be confirmed; 27 January – Buddecke shot down a Farman; this was his eighth confirmed kill. The Fokker Squadron chalked up an impressive number of confirmed kills in one month, without suffering any losses themselves.

During the Allied withdrawal, further reconnaissance flights were carried out. The seaplanes were tasked with bombing ANZAC camps and artillery positions. After the Allies had withdrawn, the entire air defence was transferred to No 1 Air Squadron at Galata, which

Lieutenant Theodor Croneiss.
(*Bülent Yilmazer Collection*)

2nd Lieutenant Emil Meinecke.
(*Bülent Yilmazer Collection*)

Warrant Officer Kurt Haaring.
(*Bülent Yilmazer Collection*)

covered the Gulf of Enos up to Smyrna and the Gulf of Alexandretta. Turkish squadrons still continued to fly combat, reconnaissance and bombing missions.

On 4 February, Theodor Croneiss scored a kill; more kills were claimed by Buddecke at the end of March and on 4 April, but these remained unconfirmed. On 14 April 1916 Captain Buddecke was awarded the *Pour le Mérite*. He described his last air victory over Gallipoli:

'I might have been about twenty yards from him when the huge bird rose vertically in front of me. Immediately I threw my aircraft to the left, then to the right, so as not to let him fall on me and thus to see me. The mighty craft lay halfway on his back and dropped. Next to me something whistled past, shuddering in front of me, stone-like in the open air – then a white cloud of smoke shot out, immediately afterwards it caught fire and, like a comet, the burning machine plummeted down. After a few hundred metres it recovered again and suddenly went into level flight. The fire went out, the wings collapsed upwards, and like a shuttlecock it became smaller and smaller, six kilometres from the airport. I landed. As my bird taxied, there was a popping jolt. The soldiers in their haste to get out of the way had left behind the chocks that I needed for take-off. One such chock had ripped through a main wing. I saw immediately that I would be out of action for days [...] [and] the people came running to kiss my hands, clothes and shoes. "Allah can do many things", they said, "and so can the Germans."'[500]

In July 1916 the airmen on Gallipoli received a VIP visit by German flying ace, Captain Oswald Boelcke, who at that time already had nineteen confirmed kills to his credit and thus also was a recipient of the *Pour le Mérite*. He was picked up by his fellow airmen at the station in Istanbul-Sirkedji on his arrival on 14 July and was very well looked after by both the Military Mission and comrades in the Navy. Boelcke wrote in his diary:

'At lunchtime I was a guest of the Navy on the *General* and in the afternoon I drove with Captain Deckert and other gentlemen through the Bosphorus to Therapia, where the German cemetery is located. Then we drove to *Goeben* and *Breslau*, where I was really well looked after. After a tour of the two ships and dinner afterwards, there was a wonderful summer evening concert on deck. Captain Ackermann, commander of the *Goeben*, organised the men to give me three cheers and the sailors took me on their shoulders. What they get up to - who could have imagined this earlier!'[501]

In addition to official matters, Boelcke enjoyed some holiday leisure, such as during a trip to Izmir.

'20.7. Noon with Excellency Liman v. Sanders, who was very nice and had himself photographed with Buddecke and me. [...] 22.7. In the morning we had a swim with some ladies and gentlemen in Kordilo, from where Buddecke picked us up with a yacht. That was wonderful! The view from the gulf to the mountains all around and to Smyrna itself is wonderful. In the evening we went to tea with the Austrian consul, where all sorts of people [were] met and many languages were spoken.'[502]

Boelcke also visited Gallipoli, although he was very disappointed that he was not allowed to fly there but had to go overland.

25.7. Now I have to go the long way via Bandirma-Istanbul to the Dardanelles. In a plane I could be there in 2½ hours, but Buddecke absolutely refuses to give me one. He mentions a thousand reasons against this, but I believe that he has orders from the airfield commandant, or even from headquarters, that I am not allowed to fly here either.'[503]

According to some sources, Boelcke did not fly any solo sorties at Gallipoli, only as a passenger on a flight with Meinecke on 29 July 1916: 'Then in a biplane with 2nd Lieutenant Meinecke, who had come over from Galata. I made a very nice flight over Troy, Kum Kale, to Seddulbahr, to the former English positions at the Dardanelles.'

However, Meinecke noted in his memoirs:

'In 1916 the *Pour le Mérite* flyer, Captain Oswald Boelcke, came on an inspection visit to our *Jagdstaffel* and remained two to four days with us. Above all, he observed for himself what enemy observation flights involved. Since Lieutenant Croneiss was not present, Captain Boelcke and I flew together, each in a Fokker E.III, and made reconnaissance flights over the islands of Imbros, Tenedos, and Mitylene ... these islands were occupied

Flying aces bathing near Izmir. 3rd right - Buddecke, 5th right - Boelcke, far left - Major Schueler von Krieken. (*Author's Collection*)

by the English [sic] and they had their flying fields there. We flew every day as long as Captain Boelcke was with us; however, we did not see a single Englishman [sic] in the air.'[503a]

Boelcke's return journey to Istanbul was by air, courtesy of Meinecke in the LVG Baby:

'After a quick breakfast I flew with Meinecke, who picked me up, first to Chanak and then on the north coast of the Marmara Sea back to St. Stefano.'[504.]

While the Gallipoli land battles were completely over, the Turkish Air Arm and the Turkish Navy continued to fight on in this area of operations. On 27 January 1917 Lieutenant Emil Meinecke took off in a Fokker E III from the airfield of the No 6 Squadron in Galata to fly a 'lap of honour' on the occasion of the Emperor's birthday over Fort Hamidié. There he was attacked by six British aircraft, which for lack of ammunition, used pistols to try and to bring him down. In the subsequent dogfight, he shot down two aircraft, one of which made an emergency landing in the sea, whilst the others hightailed it back to Imbros. He could not fire at more aircraft because his gun jammed. This was said to be the first aerial combat victory for the Turkish Air Arm, but there are always discrepancies in victory claims, because British records note the combat but say that the Allied planes got away.

Liman von Sanders (middle) with Captain Buddecke (left) and Captain Boelcke (right) near Gallipoli. (*Bundesarchiv Koblenz*)

Emil Meinecke was transferred in autumn 1915 to No 1 Squadron in Gallipoli after a spell as a flight instructor in San Stefano. He flew mostly reconnaissance flights at the front with an Albatros C.III; Prince Hohenlohe von Öhringen acted as his observer. In April 1916 he returned to flying training duties again, before taking over the command of No 1 Squadron from Theodor Croneiss. He flew a Fokker E.III from then on, with which he also scored his aerial victories in 1917.

In his own words, Meinecke describes another dogfight and personal encounter with the downed Allied pilot:

'On 17 February 1917, I had quite an air battle with a Bristol Bullet single seater. We had a tail chase of about fifteen minutes, neither of us being able to get in a shot. He made an attempt to attack me and as he pulled away over me, I was able to give him a short burst, without supposing that I had hit him. I could hardly believe my eyes as he went down in a glide, always in front of my machine. I kept my hand on the trigger and planned that at the least movement to turn the wrong way I would shoot. This was not necessary and he made a belly landing close to our hangar, without knowing, however, that he was so close to our field as it was so small and so well camouflaged that a strange pilot would never take it for a flying field. The English [sic] pilot was named Lieutenant Gordon Bysshe and he also was unwounded. As I took him prisoner, I offered to shake hands, but he was extremely angry. […] His Bristol Scout had two machine guns fixed to the side of the fuselage, close behind the engine. A thin steel cable passed through the fuselage and connected to the two trigger levers. Pulling this wire would fire the machine guns. They were to be used only in an emergency. The two Lewis guns each had a 25-round drum and they could not be adjusted in flight. At the place where the bullets had to pass through the propeller arc, small steel protectors had been fitted to the propeller blades and taped over with strips of linen. In spite of these steel protectors, we saw, as it lay before us, that there were five holes in one propeller blade and four in the other one. I believe that if the fight had lasted longer, he would have shot off his own propeller.'[504a]

Meinecke made the first test flight with the repaired aircraft himself, but on another flight, a few days later, the engine failed and the Bristol crash-landed, without Meinecke suffering any injury.

Another personal encounter with an Allied pilot was noted by Meinecke:

'In October 1917, an English [sic] pilot was brought to us. On his return flight from Constantinople, where he had dropped bombs, he had to make an emergency landing in the Gulf of Saros because the propeller and gears of one engine had torn off and it seemed that the machine could not be kept in the air (I believe it was a Handley-Page). He had set it down in the water a very short distance from his home port. The name of the pilot was Alcock; I believe he was a captain and he was later very famous as the first pilot to fly across the Atlantic non-stop. […] The name of the observer I have forgotten. Captain Alcock was with us for only one day. He was asked the usual questions about the number of aircraft and men, but he did not divulge very much. He was a pleasant person to chat with. The following day, he was taken to a PoW camp.'[504b]

In mid-October 1917 the Air Arm in Istanbul and Gallipoli were significantly strengthened to provide a mobile reserve for the visit of Kaiser Wilhelm II. Lieutenant Rudolph von Eschwege, also known as the 'Eagle of the Aegean', since he already had sixteen confirmed kills at that time, came to Gallipoli with two more squadrons, but they did not have to fly any combat missions.

Lieutenant Meinecke
(right) with Lieutenant
Bysshe in front of the
downed Bristol Scout D.
(*Bülent Yilmazer Collection*)

On 20 October 1917, the Turkish fleet, now under the command of Admiral Hubert von Rebeur-Paschwitz, attempted to break out of the Dardanelles and attack the Allied fleet. The *Goeben* struck so many mines that she had to break off the attack and came under attack by enemy aircraft. The *Breslau*, which was also attacked from the air, drew alongside the *Goeben* to shelter under their anti-aircraft umbrella. *Breslau* ran into a minefield and sank after striking several mines. The *Goeben* hit another mine and was almost unable to manoeuvre in the mouth of the Dardanelles. To ward off the enemy air attacks, all available air squadrons were scrambled to defend the *Goeben*.

Lieutenant Meinecke, who deputised for Croneiss as Squadron Commander, was briefed by Admiral Merten's headquarters. Only he and Erich Muhra were available at the Squadron, which now flew around the clock to protect the damaged cruiser. The *Goeben* made its way slowly to Nagara, where she ran aground. After recognising her predicament, the Allied air forces immediately launched one of the largest air offensives of the First World War against a battleship. On 23 January 1918, Meinecke shot down his fifth enemy aircraft and, a day later, Theodor Croneiss, now returned from Istanbul, chalked up another kill. On 26 January the *Goeben* could finally be made ready to get underway and made for the docks in Istinye. The ship had been attacked by approximately 60 aircraft flying over 250 missions and dropping around 15 tons of bombs which, however, caused no significant damage to the warship.

On 29 January 1918 Meinecke notched up his sixth and final victory over Gallipoli against a Sopwith Camel. On 23 May Theodor Croneiss shot down his fifth enemy aircraft. In the course of that year new aircraft were delivered from Germany, mainly through the good offices of Major Serno. These included some AEG C.IV, Albatros D.III and seven Fokker D.VII, four of which were transferred to Gallipoli in October 1918. At the beginning of August Emil Meinecke and Warrant Officer Kurt Haaring were scrambled and engaged in aerial combat. While Meinecke shook off his opponent, Haaring suffered a bullet wound in the stomach. He was still able to land his aircraft, but succumbed to his injuries on 17 August 1918. He was, as far as is known, the only fatal casualty of No 1 Squadron. In early October Erich Muhra was seriously wounded by five bullets in a dogfight but survived.

As the war progressed there were more and more confrontations between German and Turkish soldiers; the following example shows how far these conflicts could go. On 15 August 1918 Vice-Admiral Merten wrote to Admiral Usedom of an incident in which a German warrant officer, a pilot in No 1 Squadron from Galata, was tied up and beaten by a Turkish captain and demanded that 'the Group's Chief of Staff, Lieutenant Colonel Shefik Awni, a well-known German hater, should be removed from his position'. The squadron commander reported the incident, involving the handing over of a captured British aircraft but which, contrary to higher orders, was not released by the Turkish guards:

> 'After the English [sic] aircraft took off, ten guards with fixed bayonets stormed on the aircraft left behind. The pilot, Schlüter, resisted and was tied up. Zsihau, a mechanic, and Schlüter, still tied up, were brought to Kuludag. The duty officer there, a Captain Mehmed, slapped Warrant Officer Schlüter in the face. Then the flight crew was pushed in a dark old donkey stable and Schlüter was released from his bonds. The captain did not show himself anymore. He only let it be said that they should be tied up by order of Group, but he would refrain from doing so. In the evening the crew was taken to a barred room with wooden benches. As food they were given bread and water. [...] The difficulties encountered stem from the Chief of Staff, Lieutenant-Colonel Shefik Awni, known to be anti-German.'[505]

On the Gallipoli front the enemy was often treated with consideration. Lieutenant Franz Eicke, an air observer in No 1 Squadron, reported in his records that it was common between enemy squadrons to exchange information about crashed aircrews and to airdrop letters and personal kit for prisoners:

> 'The airman who had been shot down wrote a letter to his comrades in which, apart from informing his relatives, asked for his kit to be air dropped at a certain place at such and such a time. This letter is dropped from the air above the enemy's airfield, and the prisoner's comrades promptly get what is wanted. A special signal flare is arranged for the aircraft that fly such a mission, which prevents an attack by an opponent.'[506]

Eicke, who conducted such a supply flight in September 1918 (as an observer) to drop letters from two captured enemy airmen, a Greek and a Frenchman, on the island of Imbros, reported:

> 'The courier bag is already overboard, another look down, to see the bag with the black-and-white pennant slowly approaching the ground. Now you can see all sorts of people running towards the spot, the aircraft now slowly gaining altitude and heading northeast.'

He was, however, attacked by two enemy aircraft.

> 'What does that mean, our agreements are no longer respected? [...]and then it starts, the first rounds crash in our ears. [...] It's just fortunate that the two of them are such bad marksmen, because it's not much different than when an old, fat bumble-bee messes around with two mosquitoes. In any case, as dreary as this morning is, I have never ever felt the inferiority of our Turkish brother-allies' equipment [so greatly]. But what's the point, as all the good aircraft are needed more in the West.'[507]

The aircraft showed twenty-three hits after landing, and the German crew was very angry about this attack, which was contrary to agreements made. But the very next day a British aircraft flew over the German airfield and dropped a bag containing a letter:

'Royal Flying Corps, Imbros, 28 September 1918

Today we received a bag of letters that one of your machines dropped, for which I thank you very much. One of your officers (a pilot) who was shot down at Chios in July, was killed, but the observer was rescued and he's doing well. If you want to drop his kit, I will make sure that he gets it. We are sorry that our fighter pilots pursued you this morning, but the red flare was not seen in time. I think it would be better if your aircraft dropped letters at Cape Kephalos, and then fired the red flare before you reach the shore. That would be safer. Can you use a bag or a box that floats, in case the letters fall into the water? Do you have any message from one of our officers, Lieutenant Houghton? My officers entreat me to add that we all appreciate the decent way in which our dog-fights are conducted. When the war is over, would you like to join us for lunch?

Best regards to 'our friend the enemy',
Graham Donald, Captain, Royal Flying Corps.'[508]

It seems that not all Turkish troops agreed with or were informed of this 'chivalrous' behaviour and the squadron commander complained that items from the captured pilots' kit were sometimes stolen by Turkish authorities:

On 1 August, a mailbag of clothing for the two captured flying officers was dropped here by us. The clothing was checked and re-packaged under my personal supervision and sent to Group. According to the receipt of the British flying officers, about half is missing.'[509]

These and similar incidents may have been common for flying personnel but that must not disguise the fact that in this theatre of war the air battles fought were relentless. There is no reason to talk about a 'Gentleman's War' in the air in relation to the Battle of Gallipoli, as is sometimes found in Turkish circles today.

By late 1915, there were a total of seven flying squadrons in the Turkish Air Arm at the following stations: Gallipoli - No 1 and No 6 Squadrons; Mesopotamia - No 2 Squadron; Uzunköprü (Western Thrace) - No 3 Squadron; Adana - No 4 Squadron; Constantinople (Second Army) – No 5 Squadron; Caucasus – No 7 Squadron.

By the end of the war Germany had supplied Turkey with a total of 296 aircraft of various types, including: Albatros B.I, C.I, C.III; Rumpler B.I; LVG B.I; Fokker E.I, E.III; Gotha LD.2, WD.I, WD.2; and Pfalz AII. A number of captured enemy aircraft also found their way into the Turkish Air Arm.

Chapter 13

German Involvement in Naval Operations at Gallipoli

The defence of Gallipoli could only be successfully conducted in close cooperation with the Turkish Fleet and the Çanakkale Fortress Command. The Fifth Army was supported during the fighting by the fortress artillery, which was subordinated to the Navy, as well as on occasion by the ships of the Fleet itself. As a substitute for heavy artillery, the two warships *Haireddin Barbarossa* and the *Torgut Reis*, the former German Brandenburg-class battleships *Kurfürst Friedrich Wilhelm* and *Weissenburg,* were in action. They provided indirect fire from the Dardanelles against enemy ships that lay off Ariburnu and Seddulbahr. In the absence of an observation balloon, their fire control was located on the heights of Koja Chemen Tepe. Under Admiral von Usedom, the Fortress Command artillery brought the enemy's right flank, as well as the landing sites at Seddulbahr, under effective fire from the Asiatic shore.

However, the Special Command (SoKo) needed further support from the MMD, and this was provided. Admiral Souchon, the Fleet Commander, noted on 12 May 1915 in the KTB (*Kriegstagebuch* – War Diary):

> 'Since Admiral v. Usedom urgently needs guns in the Dardanelles in order to bring the Seddulbahr position under fire. After consulting artillery expert Navy Captain Pieper, who considers it a good idea, I decide to transfer 2 of the 15cm guns from the *Goeben*, together with 1,000 shells.'[510]

On 22 May 1915 another entry reads:

> 'Now that we have to do everything to strengthen the Dardanelles, I am furthermore providing light guns and ammunition from the ships.'[511]

The Fifth Army, fighting the land battles on Gallipoli, asked for additional direct support from the MMD. The ships sent for this task had only limited success - despite special fire control by observation officers. The war diary of the MMD for 18 May 1915 noted:

> 'At the request of General v. Liman, who plans an attack on Ari Burnu on the morning of 19 May and wants to be supported by our naval artillery, I despatched *Torgut* to the Dardanelles in the evening, although both ships can barely fire at the same time, and only a protective steamer is available.'[512]

On 1 June, General von Sanders once again asked for support for 'the decisive attack on Seddulbahr', in which 'participation by the fleet would be of great value'.[513] He suggested steaming out from the Dardanelles in force in order to engage the Allied fleet at Seddulbahr and in Morto Bay and requested the use of submarines. The timing of this important attack, however, he made dependent on the availability of his own artillery ammunition and therefore could not state a precise date for it. As mentioned in earlier chapters, the German Naval Shore Detachment had

The commanders of the destroyer *Muavenet*, Lieutenant Commander Firle (left), Lieutenant Commander Ahmet Saffet Bey (right) and and Lieutenant Commander Riza (centre). (*Author's Collection*)

been transferred from the Fleet to serve with their machine guns in units of the Fifth Army, which meant a significant strengthening of the Turks, as they were not exactly well equipped with such weapons. In addition the Fleet provided ammunition and heavy guns, dismantled from the ships and then installed directly into coastal defence emplacements at the Dardanelles.

Two notable operations of the Navy deserve to be described here. On 13 May 1915 the Turkish destroyer *Muavenet*, under the command of German Lieutenant Commander Firle and Turkish Lieutenant Commander Ahmet Saffet, sank the English pre-dreadnought battleship HMS *Goliath* in the Dardanelles. After the Allies had gained a foothold on the Peninsula for two weeks and the fighting slowly turned into positional warfare, it was principally the British naval guns that kept hammering the Turks. General Weber, who had taken command of the Southern Group on the Peninsula at the beginning of May, therefore sought assistance from the SoKo. Only a torpedo attack on the Allied battleships would settle the matter and Admiral Merten came up with the idea of using the small, albeit outdated, 'Italian' torpedo boats, so called because they had been built in Italy. The Naval Staff in Istanbul had taken note of Lieutenant Commander Firle, who in Canakkale a few days earlier had given a presentation to Admiral von Usedom and Admiral Merten on the formation of a submarine hunting group in the Dardanelles. Thus, Lieutenant Commander Firle was selected for a corresponding operation and received a telegram on 9 May 1915: 'Situation makes imperative night attack on enemy battleship Morto Bay. If instructions allow, come immediately, bring along German commanders and torpedo experts for 3 small vessels here.'[514]

Firle arrived on board the German-built destroyer, *Muavenet*, on 11 May in Çanakkale, where a meeting with the SoKo staff took place:

'In a meeting with the Governor-General of the Straits, Admiral v. Usedom, His Excellency explained that the Turkish positions at Seddulbahr [...] were severely harassed by flanking fire from British warships lying at night in Morto Bay and the army urgently requests diverting the enemy's attention in some way away from these points. Admiral v. Usedom asked me for my opinion on the possibility and manner of carrying out a torpedo boat attack on the ships lying there. I explained that only after I had been down the minefields' safe channels, prepared for the warships, could I judge the navigational feasibility of the attack; but that in my opinion only a destroyer, not a small torpedo boat, would be suitable for this military exercise.'[515]

Afterwards, Firle went to the command post of Colonel Wehrle to discuss with him the needs from the perspective of the Turkish troops on the ground and from there to form an impression of the situation in Morto Bay.

Until 02.00 hrs I was in the observation post of the howitzer battery in Erenkeui on the Asian shore, almost opposite the shore of Morto Bay, from whence one has an excellent overview of the night activity at the entrance of the Dardanelles, as it has been every night since 25 April. In front of the entrance of the Dardanelles one could see in a sea of lights, as in the port of Kiel, the combined Anglo-French fleet with their transports. [...] Two battleships were anchored in the Dardanelles, in Morto Bay, that night, which illuminated the positions on land with their searchlights and maintained a continuous fire of heavy and medium guns on these positions. [...] From Hissarlik Point across to Erenkeui Bay, according to the permanently-stationed observation officer, Sub Lieutenant Krieger, the destroyer escort had been regularly identified operating six to eight B-class destroyers in pairs. On this evening one saw the right wing boat steam off below the observation post of Erenkeui Bay. An unnoticed passage through this security belt, with a reasonable chance of success, was therefore only possible close to the European coast.'[516]

On the evening of 12 May the *Muavenet* dropped anchor. Minister of War Enver Paşa, who had just returned from a tour of the front, even paid her a personal visit and departed with his best wishes for this assignment.[517]

The leadership style of Firle was notable, as he always took especial care to ensure good cooperation between Turkish and German members of the crew. The German officers under his command were Sub Lieutenants Andreae and Sebelin. He did not regard his Turkish comrades-in-arms as inferior and shared responsibility with the Turkish commander Ahmet Saffet, with whom he had a close friendship and with whom, even years later, he still corresponded regularly. The battle report detailed the action: 'Decide to schedule the attack after midnight, counting mainly on fatigue [of the Allied crews] after the bombardment and likelihood of lower vigilance in the [Allied] ships and, above all, their protective destroyers'.

Crew of the Muavenet. Standing in front of the torpedo tube, from right to left: Lieutenant Commander Ahmet Saffet Bey, Lieutenant Commander Firle and Boatswains Mate Stamm, who launched the first torpedo. (*Sammlung Soytürk*)

The Turkish destroyer *Muavenet*. (*Bahattin Öztuncay*)

On 13 May, the *Muavenet* raised anchor at 0.15 am and began its mission with the approach through the minefields. Manning the three torpedo tubes were the German torpedo men Stamm, Buskohl and Eggers.[518] At 1.15 am they launched three torpedoes in quick intervals and which did not miss their target: '3 clear detonations, torpedo tracks to bridge, aft funnel and stern. Ship keels over to starboard after the first hit, wrapped in dense black clouds, stern mast a red flame of fire. No shouting or yelling to be heard.[519]

At 2.00 am the *Muavenet* arrived back in Suandere Bay and Firle sent this radio message to the Fleet Commander: 'An English battleship [*Goliath*] sunk by 3 torpedo hits in Morto Bay. Firle.'[520] 'To *Muavenet*. Well done. Fleet Commander',[521] came the reply at 10.15 am.

In the KTB (War Diary) of the MMD, the following entry was made:

'[This is] A wonderful testimony to the deliberation, the skill and the daring of the half flotilla commander [Firle]. I express my highest appreciation to him and to the whole flotilla that they were able to achieve such success through their infinitely laborious hard work with Turkish equipment and personnel. Since Commander Pfeiffer has taken over the flotilla this has made great progress. It surpasses my earlier long-cherished expectations that now all ships can be used for operations extending several days.'[522]

Lieutenant Commander Firle's assessment of his crew is also worth quoting, as it underlines the undivided respect he showed to his German and Turkish crew members:

'The conduct of the German crew members among our destroyer personnel was to be taken for granted as the fruit of years of warlike exercises. Everyone, from torpedo-man to stoker, worked with exemplary calm and reliability, as though on exercise, and everyone was watching with the enthusiasm born of being able to launch the beloved weapon at the enemy for the first time in a real night attack. When the third torpedo hit its target, the German officers and crew cheered and waved their caps. In the same way, I can only say the best about the Turkish crew, about the commandant, officers and men, about their conduct during the attack. Calmly and with confidence, they followed German directions - the Commandant had explicitly asked me beforehand to give all the commands personally - each performed their best at their posts and rejoiced in sincere, almost incredulous, enthusiasm, at their success.'[523]

It is a sobering thought that during the sinking of HMS *Goliath*, of the crew of approximately 750, the Captain (T.L. Shelford RN), together with 570 officers and men, lost their lives.

The success of the *Muavenet* was justly celebrated when the ship, with a new coat of paint, entered Istinye Bay, near Istanbul, on 14 May:

'Wild hurrahs from the *Goeben, Olga* and all the other ships, the Turkish helmsman's tears ran down his cheeks. The three empty torpedo tubes were swung to port. It really was the best reward and thanks you can get as a soldier. Touching welcome from the Flotilla Commander and all acquaintances. Reported to the Fleet Commander in the afternoon. He was very nice to me, thanked me in the name of the Fleet, Germany etc.'[524]

Many years later, in June 1935, Firle had an unexpected encounter with a relic of this successful attack, as he wrote from South Africa to his former shipmate, Andreae:

'Yesterday we were in Port Elizabeth in Schlangenpark. A kind of naval museum is there. As I was harmlessly looking at sharks and stuff like that, hanging on the wall there's a buoy, a life-belt [from] HMS *Goliath*. Underneath a label read: 'Sunk in the Great War, in the Dardanelles'. I would like to have written below: "By German Capt. Firle and one of the visitors to the Marine Hall".'[525]

The first successful attack of a German submarine at Gallipoli was another spectacular success of the Navy. An early request in 1915 by Admiral Souchon to the Austrian fleet commander for the assignment of Austrian submarines to Istanbul had been turned down. He therefore telegraphed an urgent request to the Admiralty Staff in Berlin on 1 March 1915: 'Submarine involvement in Dardanelles defence would be very promising and valuable. Austrian Admiral has rejected my request for assigning submarines because unsuitable and necessary in the Adriatic. [...] Supply can be made in Asia Minor.'[526]

Ambassador von Wangenheim telegraphed the Foreign Office on 2 March:

'According to the Admiralty, the Dardanelles situation would change in one fell swoop if two submarines came. Admiral Souchon's appeal to Austria has been rejected. It must gradually dawn on Austria that forcing the Dardanelles, in its effect on the neutrals, could give the whole war an unfavourable turn for us.'[527]

After Austria repeated its refusal, the German Admiralty Staff responded and on 10 March ordered the Commander of the High Seas Fleet to provide a submarine to protect the Dardanelles. Admiral Souchon was informed on 10 March that two smaller submarines would be ready for despatch on 22 March - one of them was UB 8, which arrived on 25 March in Pola. An important Austro-Hungarian naval port at the southern tip of the Istrian peninsula, it was assembled there and, under the command of Lieutenant Voigt, made its way towards Turkey.

On 25 April, under the command of Lieutenant Commander Hersing, U 21 left Wilhelmshaven for the Mediterranean Sea. The voyage was preceded by a comprehensive and secretive logistical preparation to supply the submarine with fuel and food whilst it was underway, mainly by merchant ships. On 13 May U 21 entered Cattaro, then one of the main bases of the Austro-Hungarian fleet on the Adriatic coast of Montenegro, where it underwent an overhaul. On 20 May Hersing was underway again and expected to arrive off Gallipoli four days later. Hersing sighted the Russian cruiser *Askold* on 24 May but did not attack it, in order that he could slip by unnoticed directly off the coast of Gallipoli and there provide relief to his countrymen and their Turkish allies.

A day later U 21 reached the Dardanelles and noticed that the Allied fleet was not – as expected – at Kaba Tepe but at Cape Helles. Therefore the submarine could not attack in the morning but had to wait for a more favourable time.[528] It was soon to come: on 25 May, U 21 sank HMS *Triumph*, an action that Lieutenant-Commander Hersing described:

'At about 12 o'clock I suddenly discovered an enemy warship just below the coast of Gallipoli; it was the English ship of the line *Triumph*. I immediately downed my periscope and headed for the ship, for I had discovered that landwards enemy observation was considerably weaker. After about 45 minutes, I came back up to 10m to make my attack. The British warship had poured flanking fire on the Turkish trenches during the morning and all on board were now having lunch. With torpedo protection nets deployed, the ship steamed about 5–6 nm/hr back

The German submarine U21 on its voyage through the Mediterranean.

HMS Triumph. (*Stephen Chambers*)

and forth under the coast. The whole crew was lying on the upper deck and sunning themselves, only the lookout posts, heavily armed [sic] with binoculars, watching for submarines. [...] I look out of the periscope, the battleship 400m ahead of me. I had deviated from the aiming line, had to turn hard. Forward with increased speed. 300m ... 200m ... then I launch the fish! Through the torpedo net! Notice, before I steer the only possible course diving under the battleship, that all guns are aimed at me... Massive salvos. Terrible buffeting occurs... The submarine is thrown around like a ball ... we are flung against the walls... It was a scare that was worth it: the battleship capsized and in 9 minutes disappeared into the blue tide.'[529]

Colonel Kannengiesser witnessed this torpedo attack from the shore:

'I had visited these battalions on 25th May and towards noon was returning to the staff of the 9th Division when I saw the English armoured cruiser *Triumph* lying close to the coast below. She was apparently quite comfortably making herself ready to shoot in the direction of Ariburnu. I had scarcely reached my tent when I heard, at roughly 12.30 pm, a terrific explosion, and not long after my interpreter, Major Zia Bey, burst into my tent and announced that the *Triumph* had just been sunk.'

Kannengiesser continued,

'The result showed itself in an astonishing manner. Next morning all the ships had disappeared as if God had taken a broom and swept the sea clear. They had all fled to the harbours of Imbros and Lemnos, ... No more ship-shelling of our trenches ... The joy of the brave Turks can scarcely be described. They danced in their trenches and cried, "Allah büjük, Allemano büjük" (Allah is great, Germany is great).'[530]

Even Navy Lieutenant Hörder, employed as an observation officer, reported on the action:

'This ship in particular had frequently bombarded Maidos, Kilia, Mal Tepe and the Turkish positions and batteries with her 19cm as well as with lighter guns during the last few days. It was almost the same programme every morning, noon and evening. At noon I heard a dull bang. Great excitement in the trenches. Destroyers, trawlers and ships' boats hurried to the rescue, while all the big ships steamed off at full speed. [...] After twelve minutes the ship capsized, 21 minutes later the stern reared up and the ship sank bow first into the depths, leaving behind a sad field of debris. In the trenches, great joy and loud cheers, shooting fell silent, friend and enemy stared at the water, conscious of experiencing an unforgettable moment.'[531]

Most of the crew were saved in the sinking of the *Triumph*, but seventy-three sailors lost their lives.
After this successful action, Hersing sailed to Istanbul with U 21, but was under way again on 26 May for the waters around Gallipoli. A day later, shielded between countless smaller ships, he saw the outlines of HMS *Majestic*, against which he also carried out an attack:

'In silhouette, this was the *Majestic* that was in these waters and now had anchored close to shore so that in the event of a torpedo hit she would not fare like her sister, the battleship *Triumph*, two days ago. The captain hoped that if he was hit his ship would soon drop to the seabed and the superstructure would stick out of the water so that the crew could still save themselves. However, it was difficult to test whether this surmise was correct: as often as I sailed up and down the vessels, I discovered no gap to launch my torpedo into the Englishman's [sic] hull. Once again I sailed along the whole nest of them, and I eventually discovered a gap. It was not big, 20m at the most. But I tried it. Aimed exactly with my whole boat, maybe... Now I was heading exactly aft of the *Majestic*. I pressed the electric button ... the boat shuddered: the fish was gone. The torpedo created its wake of fine bubbles, through the many vessels... If nothing comes in between, if none of these motor barges comes in between... Nothing came in between: a world-shaking detonation... I had obviously hit the boiler room... All at once I saw the ship move ... strange ... head-down, as the sailor says ... it seemed to want to capsize ... dropped ... a minute passed, a second, third, fourth. Then the ship turned like a whale, whipping itself over, waves roaring over the other small vessels and out of the chaos, out of nameless panic, the fore-ship of the *Majestic*, keel up ... the remainder of the battleship had disappeared. It had taken four and a half minutes to destroy the 15,000-ton warship.'[532]

The effects of these two torpedo attacks were significant for the Allied forces on land, as the *Queen Elizabeth*, the other battleships and the *Ark Royal* (a seaplane carrier) were completely withdrawn for a few weeks from the operational area to the secure ports on Imbros and Lemno because of the threat of submarine attacks. The Allied forces on land, however, suddenly found themselves left alone on the hostile coast. Compton Mackenzie commented, 'It is certain that the Royal Navy never executed a more demoralizing manoeuvre in the whole of its history'.[533]

Although, at least in the short term, their artillery support eased, the Allies tried to protect their fleet better by new means of defence against submarines and thus were able to renew support for the troops on the ground. Shallow-draught boats with heavy-calibre guns – monitors – were particularly useful. Although a larger number of German submarines now operated in the waters around Gallipoli, they could only sink enemy transport ships. General von Sanders did not appreciate the circumstances of the more difficult nature of submarine missions and demanded further naval support from the Fleet Commander:

'As early as June 16 I had to telegraph to the naval chief, Admiral Souchon in Constantinople, that the enemy was again using his large transports unhindered in transferring and relieving his troops. On June 20 I telegraphed him that the enemy war vessels had begun the same activity with their artillery as before the success of the submarines. On June 29 I informed him that in a large attack on the preceding day against the right flank of the south front they had strongly cooperated with their fire and were doing the same on June 29 in the still continuing battle on the south front.'[534]

The sinking of *HMS* Majestic. (*From* 'U 21 rettet die Dardanelles', *p.64.*)

Although the bulk of the fighting on Gallipoli was conducted by troops on the ground, naval support did at least relieve to a certain extent the pressure of enemy artillery fire. If one looks at the numbers of German soldiers on this battlefield, far more German specialists were used in the naval forces and air arms than with the Fifth Army directly. Liman von Sanders had deemed the possibilities of specific cooperation of the different services to be necessary, but mainly made complaints to the Fleet Commander and hardly considered joint planning or even arranging appropriate inter-service meetings. Indeed, in collaboration he saw rather an annoying competition that could detract from his fame. He wrote in his notes:

'To understand the following brief description of the battles of the Gallipoli campaign, it must be said that they were almost entirely led by the troops of the Fifth Army, and that the participation of the Turkish–German navy could naturally only be a limited one. In Germany, I came across quite erroneous views. It has often been said in Germany and written that the campaign on Gallipoli, which was so important for the war's outcome, was fought equally by the army and the navy on the Turkish side.'[535]

Lieutenant Commander Hersing. (*Author's Collection*)

Elsewhere he noted:

'The idea expressed in German papers that the cooperation of the submarines had broken the backbone of the attack against the Fifth Army on the Gallipoli Peninsula was, therefore, quite mistaken. At home such erroneous statements led to a false estimation of the efficiency of the submarines.'

Even in a personal interview with the Emperor, he noted the need to put the role of the Navy into clear perspective and thus brought himself disfavour with William II, which Liman described:

'Between the two reports in Pless[535a] I was ordered to report in person to H.M. the Emperor in the New Palace in Potsdam. During this interview I had not much to say, for H.M. the Emperor spoke of the Gallipoli Campaign and the excellent conduct of the Turkish troops in Galicia. H.M. was not well informed about Gallipoli and assumed a much more extensive participation of the submarines than had been possible under then existing conditions. After the long exposition of H.M., I stated the limited period within which the submarines had gained results and furnished the exact dates; the Emperor seemed displeased at such a correction of former reports. He ended the conversation curtly, while on all other occasions he had shown me his good will.'[536]

As much as Army commander von Sanders lacked a vision for joint force operations, it is also understandable that he was more than upset at the flowery reports from Admiral von Usedom or, for example, popular books of 'derring do', such as were written by Lieutenant Commander Hersing.[537]

Chapter 14

The Allied Withdrawal from Gallipoli

A total of thirteen Allied divisions were deployed on Gallipoli since the beginning of August 1915 and yet Hamilton had asked for further reinforcements of another 100,000 soldiers. Given the overall situation of the war, however, the British government did not approve this. Lord Kitchener had already considered the evacuation of the Peninsula at the end of August. The French proposal to carry out a decisive attack on the Asiatic side of the Dardanelles with six of their divisions was soon abandoned, since all forces were needed for a new offensive on the Western Front. At the end of October, after the French view prevailed that the Gallipoli theatre should no longer receive reinforcements, the strategic goal of the attack on the Dardanelles, namely the seizure of Istanbul, was at last abandoned. All that was left to do was to clarify whether the land gains on the peninsula should be kept or whether all troops should be withdrawn. Although the British and the French had basically decided to withdraw from Gallipoli on 8 December 1915 (Salonika beckoned), the British did not want to give up their position on the important maritime route and considered holding on to the Helles enclave for as long as possible.

The Turks were also assessing the possible options open to the Entente. Although a withdrawal was thought possible, they did not believe so and argued that only a massive attack would drive out the Allied forces. However, on 31 October Admiral von Usedom considered a possible withdrawal of Allied troops:

'But I do not think it likely that the enemy abandons his positions without a hard attack. In order to be able to throw them out, very thorough artillery preparation is required first of all, but there is not sufficient ammunition available, nor can it be produced here.'[538]

Kannengiesser noted:

'Rumours and suggestions that the enemy were going to evacuate Gallipoli naturally swarmed round us on Gallipoli. I, personally, did not believe in such a possibility because, taking into account the English character, I considered it out of the question that they would give up such a hostage of their own free will and without a fight.'[539]

Kannengiesser was constantly seeking information about a possible withdrawal and used officers on special patrols for reconnaissance. On 20 December it was reported by the 25th Regiment that a huge fire was burning on the beach at Salt Lake and at the mouth of Asmak Dere. There were also increased ship movements but due to dense fog it could not be determined if it was a withdrawal or a reinforcement of the troops on land. All uncertainty was cleared up for Kannengiesser the next morning:

'Then – about 6 in the morning – I rode myself to the Corps battle command post on Tekke Tepe, so that with the approaching dawn I could immediately see for myself what was the exact position. […] All my doubt, however, disappeared, as with the growing dawn from the command post I recognised, through the mist, fires burning on the enemy's side. That could only be his depots and material which he begrudged us […] Now forward, after them. Catch them before they are all on their ships […] I issued the necessary orders to carry through on the Divisional fronts to the coast with the artillery in close support: the many mines to be rendered useless; the English [sic] trenches to be consolidated facing the sea; divided the routes forward; and ordered new telephone wires to be laid down.'[540]

But the Turkish follow-up came too late and the Allied troops had already completely cleared the Ariburnu section and Suvla Bay. The subsequent exploration of the former No Man's Land and the British positions and trenches revealed not only vast amounts of equipment and supplies but also many dead bodies that could not be recovered during the fighting.

'A Turk and an Englishman must have suddenly met one another there, and in the hand-to-hand fighting the Englishman had driven his knife into the back of the Turk from above, while the Turk had simultaneously driven his dagger into his enemy's vitals. There we found the two skeletons, locked together, lying against the side of the trench – a typical picture of the stubborn fighting on Gallipoli.'[541]

The withdrawal of the Allied troops in the northern area of the peninsula was observed at the II. MG group of the Naval Shore Detachment by Surgeon Koch:

'At 3.30 am the enemy set off two mines. The infantry fire of the Turks was not answered. Therefore, at 3.45 pm an assault on the enemy trenches was made. The trenches were clear of the enemy, except for two wounded and one unwounded Hindu. Very large quantities of provisions, ammunition wagons, equipment, a gun, a number of rifles, infinite quantities of medical supplies and tents fell into our hands. At 4.45 pm the first and second machine guns advanced. Lieutenant Schmidt took over the first MG, which took up position on the last hill in front of the beach. The second MG, under Chief Petty Officer de Birgnis, was also put into position to cover the Ari Burnu landing site. I was with 2nd MG with medical supplies. Since it was futile to shoot, we concealed the guns against the fire of the cruisers and monitors and inspected the camps. In the shelters we found tables set with lamps burning. A bowl of macaroni was ready to be eaten. Spilled ammunition, bombs, flares, telephone and telegraph equipment were found in large quantities by us. Lieutenant Schmidt, Chief Petty Officer de Birgnis and I were the first to go to the tented storage on the beach, where we found tons of ammunition, provisions, drinks, various live horses (most of the horses were shot by the enemy), donkeys and goats. While we were searching we were surprised by a fierce fire of the cruisers and monitors and forced to shelter in the inadequate dugouts. With longer breaks, the firing lasted until the evening. But that did not stop us from increasing our abundant haul.'[542]

A Corps command initiated tactical and administrative measures on the exploitation of what the Allies had left behind. For example, each division was to appoint a special 'commissioner of captured goods' to distribute the spoils of war equitably and also to let the troops left behind to share in it. For understandable reasons, certain supplies were reserved for Germans:

'I will only just mention the enormous amount of splendid sides of bacon, each beautifully packed in a clean white bag. The Turks greatly detest anything to do with the *domus* (pig), so that the Germans received untouched the whole of these supplies. Two days later I was able to despatch two wagons loaded with bacon to the Germans in the Southern Group.'[543]

After this successful withdrawal, the remaining Allied forces in the south experienced a less serene withdrawal scenario – or, at least, this was the intention of General von Sanders, who now had almost all non-essential troops transferred to the Southern Group. For this purpose the 12th Division and the bulk of the heavy artillery were moved to the Helles front on 22 December. The remaining units in the north were reorganised, the Anafarta Group was dissolved and XVI Corps was made directly subordinate to the Army High Command. Von Sanders now commissioned Kannengiesser with training the remaining divisions, especially in attack procedures, which were rehearsed on the specially created training grounds at Tursht-en-Keui and Greater Anafarta. The units of the German Naval Shore Detachment deployed in the north were also immediately reassigned to the south, of which Lieutenant Boltz wrote in a report:

'On 22 December, MG Section I marched directly, and MG Section II via Kilia Tepe, where they stayed overnight, to the southern front. Meeting point of the Sections was the landing pier of Soghanli Dere. Thanks to the horses and wagons now available and thanks to the possibility of using a small steamer, the heavy stuff – MGs, ammunition, kitbags, hammocks – were able to be transported directly to this jetty on the beach. The march was undertaken in a very short time and without any rush. The MGs were joyfully welcomed by the Group Commander, His Excellency Cevar Pasha. Up to now only 13 MGs had been available to him on the entire southern front, 4 each in each of the 3 divisions! The united MG Sections moved into a camp near Aly-Bey Chiftlik. Five MGs under Sub Lieutenant Count Deym were then sent to the left flank Division (the 15th), five other MGs under Sub Lieutenant Schmidt sent to the centre Division (the 20th). On 24 December, five machine guns were reported as placed in position on the front line of the Fifth Army. Another five MGs followed in the late evening.

The number of MGs would soon be increased to 14 and later to 20. For Sub Lieutenant Count Deym's Section, the Turkish Division had prepared excellent MG emplacements and bombproof accommodation quarters. Two of the MGs flanked one of the craters blown by the French, who were opposite us, and where an enemy break through was feared. They were only 20 metres away from the enemy trench, but they were well protected against bombs, which were extensively lobbed here. The Section did not fire in action and suffered no losses. The MGs of Schmidt's Section had been positioned in the vicinity to the east of the village of Krithia, which had been hotly contested for months. Here, the MG emplacements had to be newly selected and constructed, and here the German sappers readily assisted. On the night of 30 December the English set off a mine under the Turkish trenches and immediately stormed into attack. They managed to take two parts of a forked trench and to occupy it. One man was killed, another missing since then and two people wounded. The MGs were installed in a better location. Otherwise, the MGs no longer saw action here.'[544]

On 26 December 1915, the War Office in London had already given the order to clear the Helles Front before 10 January 1916. This was achieved after careful preparation during the night of 8 to 9 January; but this time the Turks noticed the procedure. Major Senftleben wrote on 4 January 1916 to his former CO, Lieutenant Colonel Kannengiesser:

'I am now commander of the heavy artillery of the southern portion, from Krithia Dere to the shores of the Dardanelles, and have two old and ten new batteries under my command, among which is the Austrian 24-cm. howitzer battery with 1200 rounds. I also have ample ammunition for the other batteries, so that we are shooting from early till late and somewhat facilitating with German shells the retreat of the enemy. The many Red Cross cars which we see on the enemy's side are not only carrying ammunition! In order to stir up things a bit I have brought my 15-cm. quick-firing howitzer battery so far forward that from early morn we can also treat Seddulbahr to some of our good ammunition. I await each dawn with impatience to be able to reopen firing and you, Colonel, can very easily imagine what joy such artillery activity with such good observation affords us and with what zest we sit from 7 in the morning till dusk in our observation posts. […] In my opinion the enemy is withdrawing slowly but certainly. I deduce that from the daily reports of the batteries and from my own observations. Many batteries are now only firing with one or two guns. […] I personally believe that in 8-14 days the enemy will have retired, if not earlier, but I am satisfied that this time he will not get away quite undisturbed or undamaged. Unfortunately the infantry cannot be induced to attack.'[545]

The German *Luftwaffe* sent Major Siegert as delegate to make an inspection of the Gallipoli Front. On 5 January 1916 Major Serno of the Turkish Air Arm, took Siegert, along with the pilot, Second Lieutenant Faller, on a reconnaissance flight. In the after-flight briefing, Siegert agreed that the Allied forces would withdraw from Gallipoli within the next 2-3 days. Siegert commented in his memoirs that Turkey could have taken several thousand prisoners in this favourable situation. He himself had returned to Istanbul on 6 January 1916 to make his report there, but neither Enver Paşa nor Major Feldmann, the chief of operations, believed him. As late as 7 January 1916, the freshly arrived 12th Division attacked on the extreme right flank to straighten the front for a planned large-scale attack. The Allies resisted bitterly. Although the artillery could still cause damage and disrupted the withdrawal, Allied soldiers were able to withdraw completely even from this sector of the front. The embarkations had again been carried out at various points and thus time was gained. The advance of the Turks into the enemy's area was hampered both by extensive minefields and continuous shelling from the naval guns, during which Major Welsch was wounded whilst investigating the enemy positions. The German Naval Shore Detachment reported the withdrawal of the Allies:

'Since the evacuation of the Anafarta position, there have been increasing indications among the Southern Group that the enemy intends to evacuate the Peninsula. On the Turkish side more ammunition arrived daily and the enemy positions and camps were increasingly brought under fire. The Austrian motorised mortars also took an active part in the bombardment. During the night of 8 to 9 January the Turkish artillery was particularly busy, without any significant return fire being inflicted on it. The Turkish infantry regiments at the front, which until recently had experienced casualties of 40-50 men a day and had suffered severely, had not been able to make a strong enough attack, the Turkish commanders apparently hesitating so as not to sacrifice any more men than necessary. They could see that the enemy would evacuate Gallipoli even without a bayonet attack! At the southern tip, too, the enemy has left behind large quantities of war material of all kinds, the recovery and evaluation of which took place in a manner similar to that of Anafarta. The German Naval Shore Detachment was again able to provide itself with plenty of bacon and canned food. The sailors also managed to increase their transport section by catching half a dozen horses and valuable English mules left behind. Many beautiful animals had been shot by the enemy and lay in rows as they had been tethered there. Looking at the cemeteries, some with mass graves, an estimate could be made about the great losses suffered by the enemy. Even if, unfortunately, it was not possible to deal the enemy a last devastating blow, the officers and men were delighted that the enemy had been finally expelled after long months of bitter fighting and the attempt, made with such huge resources, to conquer the capital, has been finally given up.'[546]

As late as mid-1916, Gallipoli still resembled a battlefield, albeit abandoned. The German Engineer Unit was tasked to assist in the clean-up work and to repair communication roads. Schweder reported on the amount of reclamation:

'In contrast, little had been done for salvaging the immense booty left behind here by the British and French, as well as collecting wire, wood, iron and other building materials, of which friend and foe had so little in the months of fighting, that we could still form a very clear overview of the material value stored on the peninsula. So far only food and ammunition, guns and rifles have been collected and brought to safety. But the building materials, machines, equipment, tools and especially empty cans on Gallipoli still lying around today, was estimated by an expert accompanying us to be worth about 120 million marks. And this statement probably refutes best the assertion of the enemy that they would leave Gallipoli calmly and take with them everything of value. [...] Paths and footbridges are still protected by barbed wire, laid all around trenches, mine entrances and saps, so that the first task is to clear the most important roads. For this purpose, about the middle of the Peninsula, there is a large sapper

An abandoned Allied landing place and living quarters near Seddulbahr. (*Bundesarchiv Koblenz*)

unit, whose magnificent camp in the midst of the heath, even down here deep in Turkey, bears witness to the German love of order, adaptability, efficiency, and diligence.'[547]

Many messages of special thanks were sent to the German Naval Shore Detachment after the battles, amongst which were these:

'On 9 January 1916, the following telegrams [FT] arrived:
FT to Kilia Tepe on 9.1.16.
I express my greatest appreciation to the German Naval Shore Detachment for their exemplary bold and tough actions in the midst of the brave troops of the Fifth Army. It has brought about the great and well-deserved success today and will be a glorious epic of the German-Turkish fleet. Fleet Commander
FT from 5th Army. To Admiral Souchon.
I beg, Your Excellency and the Fleet, to express the sincerest thanks of the Fifth Army for the excellent support we have always had from the fleet and throughout the fierce battles from the German Naval Shore Detachment through all the eight and a half months. Liman v. Sanders.'[548]

After the battles at Gallipoli were all over, there was no heroes' welcome awaiting the German officers and men on their return to Istanbul. Their coming was barely registered and their accomplishments little appreciated. Lieutenant Field Marshal Joseph Pomiankowski, the Austro-Hungarian military plenipotentiary to the Ottoman Empire, wrote down his reflections on this sad fact:

'There can be no doubt that the main credit for the successful defence of the Straits is due to Marshal Liman. His military knowledge, energy, spirit, and stamina had proved incomparably superior to those of his English [sic - indeed Hamilton was Scottish] opposite number. However, as has been the case with many deserving men, Liman found neither due recognition nor reward for his services. He just simply had too many enemies and begrudgers, both among the Turks and the Germans. His arrival in Constantinople was quite without pomp and unnoticed; only Enver Paşa and some official personalities were at the station [...] to welcome him. My feeling was that for a man who at that time should almost have been regarded as the saviour of the Ottoman Empire, should have received a very different reception.'[549]

General Liman von Sanders received only scant recognition from Germany for his great success. That may have been because he had made many enemies with his, brusque undiplomatic style and his military pragmatism. It was different for Admiral von Usedom, on the other hand, who through his regular reports had always maintained close and good relations with Berlin and directly with Wilhelm II, even though his reports had often covered topics beyond his areas of direct competence. This may explain why he received a congratulatory telegram from Berlin immediately after the withdrawal of the Allies with the following wording:

'After the final expulsion of our enemies from the Gallipoli peninsula has become reality, I remember gladly and gratefully that in March last year your determined and purposeful leadership succeeded in thwarting the great Anglo-French attempt to break through the Straits. Signed Wilhelm.'[550]

The doubts about Turkish gratitude and the sustainability of German support became apparent in many quarters. The newly-found self-confidence of the Turks after the victory of Gallipoli was viewed suspiciously by the Germans, which underlines an assessment written by Admiral von Usedom:

> 'The life forces that the compulsion of war in Turkey has awakened will fall asleep again after peace. If the military performance and ability of personnel and [standards of] material are to be maintained, German influence in key positions is necessary. [...] However, foreigners in command positions are already embarrassed by Turkish national pride aroused by the war, and after the war they will find it intolerable.'[551]

In another report he complained about the fact that the Turkish allies with their new self-confidence would no longer pay enough respect to the superior role played by German soldiers:

> 'It cannot be denied that the self-esteem of the Turks rises as the threat to the Straits is reduced, and this is most evident in a semi-educated middle class of officers and civil servants who consider themselves as competent as Germans and to be freed from the necessity to learn. The absolute inability to deal with constructive criticism, especially to deal with self-criticism, is a prominent characteristic of the Turks. It will sometimes be necessary to put an end to the presumptuousness of individuals and it will be necessary, despite all the concessions, to emphasise the fact that without German help neither the Straits nor Turkey could have been held in this war, wherever Turkish national pride attempts to reverse this relationship. I should not fail to point out that the real men in power, such as Enver Paşa and Talaat Bey, do not express such views, but moreover remain loyal.'[552]

On the other hand, Lieutenant Commander Humann showed a great deal of understanding for the Turkish viewpoint:

> 'The Turks know by themselves that they are not able to do anything or at least not much; but they are far from delighted, if you more or less try to rub their noses in it. [...] Added to this is the natural mistrust of the weak against the much stronger, against those successful everywhere; and the cautious prickling by the Entente supporters, pointing out that we are supporting Turkey only to be able to gobble up all the country on our own afterwards. And we ourselves add more fuel to the creeping fire of slander, when our officers conduct themselves as if they are in a country they have just conquered.'[553]

There are several different and often conflicting records concerning casualties of the battles at Gallipoli. Alas, it is not possible to find numbers which completely agree. One reason for this was the permanent replacement of personnel in the units at the front. As an example, in XVI Corps, a major formation that was assigned to the Anafarta front in the north, for the period from 14 October to 9 December 1915, the losses were 509 dead, 2,158 wounded, 3,386 sick and 2,159 so-called 'teptil hava' (climate changers),[554] which suggests a total loss of 8,212 men in just two months in a Corps with three divisions of around 12,000 men each. The missing personnel were, as far as possible, replaced from units belonging to the Turkish First Army in Istanbul. Therefore, the high numbers seem to be quite plausible.

Fighting alongside the Turks in Gallipoli, there were around 700 German soldiers of all ranks on active service in December 1915. In the Anafarta Group there were fifty-one German officers and about a hundred NCOs and other ranks; in the Northern Group (ANZAC) there were eight Germans, but the other ranks' strength can no longer be established. In the Southern Group (Helles), there were about thirty-five German officers on active duty.[555] However, to these numbers should be added the German personnel of the Military Mission in Istanbul, the crews of the ships belonging to the Mediterranean Division and the Special Command (SoKo), together with a large number of specialists who were seconded to Turkey for the production of weapons and ammunition, as well as medical staff and replacements. Overall, between 2,500 and 3,000 German military personnel were directly or indirectly engaged in the fighting on Gallipoli, of whom more than 530 were killed or died of wounds or sickness. The number of sick or wounded can no longer be ascertained, but it would seem to have been more than 1,000.

Altogether, various figures suggest that on the Allied side more than 58,000 soldiers fell and around 196,000 were wounded or sick. On the Turkish side the consensus suggests over 87,000 died and over 250,000 were wounded or sick.

Chapter 15

The Time after the Battles of Gallipoli

The deployment of German soldiers on the Gallipoli Peninsula did not end with the withdrawal of the Allied troops in January 1916. Since this sector of the front was still under enemy surveillance and a renewed landing could not be completely ruled out, some units remained with supply, observation and security missions – a total of around 11,000 Turkish soldiers. As for the Germans, there remained about ten to twelve German officers in artillery units of the Fifth Army. The German naval crews of the coastal fortifications under the command of Admiral Merten, the German Naval Shore Detachment, the flying squadrons at Gallipoli and Nagara and the staff of the field hospital at Bigali all remained until the end of 1918. The observation of enemy naval forces and the pilotage and *Etappe* service for incoming and outgoing German U boats were all carried out by the German Naval Shore Detachment. In addition to the Detachment commander, his adjutant and a doctor, between about 1916 and 1918 this unit comprised approximately fifty German NCOs and men and just as many Turkish soldiers. The headquarters and the living quarters, as well as their own cemetery were still at Kilia Tepe. The food was provided by the Fleet Command, but the German Naval Shore Detachment had also set up a small farm with livestock and some cultivation. In addition, until the withdrawal in 1918, they were still feeding off the supplies left by the Allied forces during the evacuation. Nevertheless, the men sometimes felt that the food was inadequate and tried to get more funds from Istanbul to buy meat occasionally from the surrounding farmers.[556] In addition to the cattle sheds, stables were built in which sixteen riding and draught horses were accommodated. There was also an observation post and a radio station.

In order to allow the most complete observation possible of enemy forces operating around the Peninsula, fully-constructed observation posts were set up at four different locations along the coastline. Each of these posts was usually staffed by an NCO and six men. These groups also lived in self-built, permanent quarters in the immediate vicinity of the posts. There, too, farming took place on a small scale for self-sufficiency and the men maintained good relations with the local population. These outposts were provided with food and mail twice a week. Every morning, noon and evening, all observations were reported to Kilia Tepe and summaries relayed to the Fleet Command by radio. The southernmost observation point was at Cape Tekke (Helles), then northwards to the second at Gaba Tepe, at the former ANZAC landing zone, a third at Cape Suvla, and the fourth at Varila Tepe. This northernmost post was also called 'Hersing Post' because it was built on the advice of Lieutenant Commander Hersing, who was the skipper of U21.

All the submarines that wanted to enter the Dardanelles headed for this position in order to take on board the commander of the German Naval Shore Detachment as a pilot. This was necessary because the Allied forces had made the entire coastal area difficult to navigate by the use of nets and mine fields and tried to expand these obstacles whenever possible. The approximate time of a submarine's arrival was communicated by the Fleet Command to the Shore Detachment by radio. The Detachment in turn notified the HQ Fifth Army, to prevent Turkish artillery firing at the submarines by mistake. After the boat's arrival, the commander of the German Naval Shore Detachment was notified; he then had a four hour ride to Hersing Post, where he went on board the submarine. The voyage around the coast of the Peninsula to the Dardanelles, which only took place in the dark, took eight to nine hours and ended in the Bay of Maidos. There the submarines remained for one or two days to give the crew, above all, the chance of rest on terra firma. The German Naval Shore Detachment had not only built extra living quarters for the visiting submarine crews, but also provided opportunities for sports and leisure. For the submarine's departure from the Dardanelles, the commander of the Shore Detachment went back on board and, after passing through the minefields, disembarked at Suvla Bay.

The life of the German Naval Shore Detachment was considered rather monotonous. Variety was only provided by mail calls, visitors from other commands, the submarine crews, or the flying visits of the Mediterranean Division's pastor, Navy Chaplain Ludwig Müller, who was very popular with the men. An important event in October 1917 was the visit of Kaiser Wilhelm II to the Dardanelles, during which he inspected the fortifications and troop units.

The winter of early 1918 was bitter and cold, so the German Naval Shore Detachment had to suffer heavy snowfall and a biting wind, though at least they lived – in contrast to the Turkish soldiers – in solid stone houses. Eventually, even the 'half-frozen' Turks were dug out of their snow-covered tented quarters and lodged in the camp at Kilia Tepe.[557]

In early 1918 General Liman von Sanders was given command of the Army Group in Palestine, and the Fifth Army returned to Turkish command. This worsened the hitherto good contact between the Army and the units led by Germans. Turkish language leaflets were dropped from British aircraft in the summer of 1918, calling for them to desert, which also contributed to the Turks turning their backs on German soldiers. The hitherto frugal Turkish soldiers, because of a

Visit of Kaiser Wilhelm II to the Dardanelles 1917: first row, far left, Admiral v. Usedom, Wilhelm II, an adjutant, Admiral Merten. (*Archäologisches Institut Istanbul*)

continuing poor supply situation, showed themselves open to the exhortations of ringleaders and there were the first signs of giving up, desertion and betrayal, all of which had an effect even on the German Naval Shore Detachment. The Turks were sometimes physically violent towards German soldiers and Turkish officers more or less blatantly showed their aversion to the influence of German officers. In addition, German officers were gradually assigned to other fronts, thereby not only reducing their numbers but also their influence.

By the armistice agreement between Russia and Turkey of 16 December 1917, the maritime war in the Black Sea was virtually ended. After the sinking of the *Breslau* on 20 January 1918 in the Aegean Sea off the Dardanelles, in which 336 German sailors were killed,[558] as well as the severe damage sustained by the *Goeben* in the course of this same operation, the Mediterranean Division, and thus the heart of the Turkish fleet, had ceased to exist.

When Bulgaria signed a truce with the Entente on 29 September 1918 this also had a significant impact on the supply line to Istanbul and Turkey. A hostile atmosphere clearly directed against the Germans had to be prevented from breaking out in Turkey. On 7 October 1918 the Military Mission and the MMD commanders began planning for the evacuation of German troops from Turkey. A day later the decision was made that Talat Paşa's Cabinet would resign and a new government under Ahmet Izzet Paşa would commence peace negotiations with the Entente. A ceasefire agreement concluded at Port Mudros also determined what would happen to German soldiers still present in Turkey. The ceasefire came into force at noon local time on Thursday, 31 October 1918, and the new government tried to obtain from the German Fleet Commander, who was now no longer in command of the Turkish Navy, the whereabouts of German ships and submarines currently in Istanbul and Turkish waters.

After the collapse of the Bulgarian front, a general withdrawal of German troops was also expected in Gallipoli. As early as 28 October, Vice Admiral Merten told Headquarters:

> 'With the departure of the Bulgarians, the general order changes. New Turkish government engaged with the enemy in ceasefire negotiations. Therefore, the withdrawal of the 21-man German mission from Canakkale is being prepared. The withdrawal is to be kept secret. From now on, Turkish officers and men will take over the tasks of the German mission.'[559]

The withdrawal was prepared and all expendable material, as well as cattle and horses, handed over to the Turkish commander, Hilmi Paşa, who provided support for the departure as best he could. On 31 October 1918 the last German soldiers left the Peninsula. That morning, the *Loreley* and *Iskenderun* cast off from Canakkale. Both ships were loaded with the remaining movable equipment, including the Austro-Hungarian howitzer battery. The Naval Aviation Base was handed over completely; however, the seaplanes had previously been ferried to Sevastopol or had been burned as a result of an Allied bombing raid at the end of May 1918.

From 1 November the withdrawal of German troops from Istanbul began. About 1,000 men embarked on the *Fleiss*, en route to Nikolayev in the Ukraine, from whence a safe train journey to Germany seemed a likely prospect. In the completely overcrowded ship were also the leaders of the old regime, Talat Paşa, Cemal Paşa and Enver Paşa, who feared retribution from the approaching victorious powers. More ships followed in the next few days and the last, the *Corcovado*, cast off on 3 November after the *Goeben* had been officially handed over to the Turkish Navy and the previously selected and well-trained Turkish crew had boarded the ship. The *Goeben* was used for many years by the Turkish Navy (as the *Yavuz*) until she was finally scrapped between 1973-1976 in Gölcük, near Istanbul, after being laid up for many years. Allegedly, the Federal Republic of Germany endeavoured to buy the *Goeben*, but was outbid by a Turkish salvage company. Parts of the bridge, gunnery instruments, the ship's bell and the Imperial war ensign of the *Goeben* were saved, however, and are still to be seen today in the Naval Museum in Beşiktaş, Istanbul.

The aircraft in Çanakkale, Izmir and Istanbul were all consolidated at the airfield in San Stefano and later transferred to Maltepe, on the Asiatic side. Some Turkish pilots tried to smuggle aircraft to Anatolia and thus reach the Turkish forces of the Revolutionary War. The Allies, who meanwhile had occupied Istanbul, recognised the attempt, however, and as a result all flying equipment was completely destroyed.

Not all of the Germans managed to get away from Istanbul on time however. By order of the British High Commissioner, Vice Admiral the Hon. Sir Somerset A. Gough-Calthorpe, those remaining were detained by British troops. For the German other ranks this took place in a detention camp near Scutari, which had served as a hospital and reception centre after the withdrawal of German troops from Palestine in September 1918. German officers were interned on Princes' Islands. In their respective locations, both officers and men were to await their planned repatriation by ship. Internment could be regarded as tolerable, especially, for example, for the officers on Princes' Islands. These officers were hardly restricted in their freedom of movement. One of the Turkish officers assigned to guard the inmates, Captain Akoemer,[560] who had previously served in the Hanoverian Uhlans, asserted that he had never regarded his German comrades as prisoners, much less treated them as such.

At the end of January 1919 the remaining 10,000 men (about 9,000 Germans and 1,000 Austro-Hungarians) were embarked on five German-crewed ships and taken to Hamburg.

Liman von Sanders, who barely escaped capture at Nazareth, in Palestine, in September 1918, returned to Istanbul after the ceasefire, and oversaw the repatriation of German forces. He was taken

The German internment camp near Haidar Pasha, outside Scutari Cemetery. (*Bundesarchiv Koblenz*)

Liman von Sanders in retirement in Munich.
(*Bundesarchiv Koblenz*)

prisoner by the British in February 1919, charged with alleged war crimes, and released in August. He then went into retirement and died on 22 August 1929 in Munich, aged seventy-four.

Field Marshal Freiherr von der Goltz assumed command of the Sixth Army in Mesopotamia in October 1915, though his mission was also to have a political character:

> 'Field Marshal Freiherr von der Goltz is entrusted with the execution of those missions, the purpose of which is to utilise Persian forces in the interests of the Central Powers and Turkey in the present war and at the same time to secure the future freedom and independence of Persia.'[561]

This was the means by which Liman von Sanders and von der Goltz were to be separated from each other and Goltz awarded an appointment 'without offending him'. As a field commander, he successfully planned the battle of Kut el Amara, the victorious outcome of which, however, he did not live to see. During a visit to his soldiers in a military hospital he caught typhoid fever and died in Baghdad on 19 April 1916 and was buried with full military honours in Istanbul in June 1916.

Great pressure by the Turks led to Admiral Souchon being relieved of his post on 24 August 1917 and he was replaced by Vice Admiral von Rebeur-Paschwitz. Souchon experienced the end of the war and the Kiel sailors' revolt as Station Chief in that German port. In March 1919 the Admiral asked to retire from active service and, at the age of 81, he died on 13 January 1946 in Bremen.

Chapter 16

The German Military Cemetery in Tarabya

The German Military Cemetery in Tarabya is the sole remaining 'monument' to the German forces' participation in defence of the Ottoman homeland. Both the Turkish defenders and the Allied invasion forces all have monuments on the Peninsula to commemorate their fallen during the Gallipoli campaign. The one monument to fallen German soldiers, which was on Kilia Tepe, was taken down when the bodies from the adjoining cemetery were reinterred in Tarabya in the 1930s.

After the steady expansion of the German military presence in Turkey from 1913 and the intensive military training programmes, the first serious illnesses and deaths of German soldiers in Istanbul soon started to occur, due to the unfamiliar climate and especially the lack of vaccines against tropical diseases. A part of the park surrounding the summer residence of the German Ambassador in Tarabya was to be turned into a cemetery to bury Germans who had either died of their illness or had been killed. When ready, any German soldiers,who died in the hospitals in and around Istanbul or had been killed in combat operations were to be buried here. In Istanbul there were already other cemeteries for German soldiers in Skutari, Feriköy and Kuruçeşme.[562]

The history of the Military Cemetery in Tarabya[563] is thus closely linked to the fighting on Gallipoli. It originally started when Sultan Abdul Hamid II (1876 – 1909) donated a park on the shores of the Bosphorous at Tarabya to Emperor Wilhelm I in 1879. The site was intended to give the German diplomatic representative the option to build a summer residence. This is where the embassy staff would be better able to live and work during the hot months of the year than at their Embassy building in Pera, which is still in the Taksim district of Istanbul. Measuring exactly 17.66 hectares, this property had a real estate value estimated at that time of around half a million gold marks. The grounds were formally handed over to the German Reich on 7 June 1880 to the Ambassador, Prince Heinrich VII Reuss. In a telegram from Berlin dated 22 May 1880, the pleasure of receiving this property by the German Reich was rather terse: 'His Majesty regards it as renewed proof of the Sultan's friendship and accepts this gift with special thanks'.[564]

Funds were granted by the German Reichstag in 1885 to put up representative Embassy buildings on the site. Between 1897 and 1901 it was developed according to the original plans made by the architect Cingriyan and revised by the German master builder Dörpfeld. These buildings and the idyllic park surrounds, now owned by the Federal Republic of Germany, are beautifully preserved and are still in use today.

The first bodies to be interred in Tarabya were three sailors of the Mediterranean Division. Whilst bunkering coal in May 1914 in Istanbul, the crew of the visiting *Goeben* responded to a large fire that had broken out in a barracks in Pera. Hundreds of sailors from the MMD volunteered to help with the firefighting work, which led to casualties among the sailors:

'However, some of the men next to a sudden furious jet of flame were so severely injured by it that they could only be rescued from the blazing element by the effort and sacrifice of their comrades. They had suffered such severe external and internal burns that all the efforts of the doctors could not avert their death. Of five seriously wounded, three died in the German hospital from their burns.'[565]

The first officer to be buried in Tarabya was Lieutenant Commander Fritz Hilgendorff, who committed suicide on 8 March 1915 in a hotel in Istanbul.

The fighting on the Dardanelles saw the first casualties of the German soldiers in action. During the bombardment of the outer Dardanelles forts on 19 February 1915, two German soldiers were killed, but only Sub Lieutenant Woermann was actually named; the name of the other German soldier continues to remain unknown. Because it was too far from the Peninsula to Istanbul to be convenient, those killed in action were buried directly on site. This was also the case for Woermann, whose funeral was attended by Colonel Kannengiesser:

'Sub Lieutenant Woermann was killed at the Orhanié Battery. Underneath a Turkish flag, his face turned towards Mecca, he was laid to rest by a *hoca*. A dead and yet graphic testimony of German-Turkish brotherhood in arms.'[566]

Just a few weeks later, on 18 March 1915, in the wake of the Allied fleet attack on the Dardanelles, four other German sailors who were assigned as artillery crew at Fort Hamidié were killed, together with Turkish soldiers. Von Usedom wrote about the casualties:

'Despite the heaviest bombardment so far, losses were low. Three Turkish officers and twenty-one men, among them three Germans; wounded were one German and one Turkish officer, as well as eighteen German and fifty-nine Turkish other ranks. [...] In the evening the dead from the German detachment at Hamidié, one NCO, two men, were buried. [...] Among the wounded, meanwhile, a German NCO has died.'[567]

Three German naval ratings: Paul Sommerfeld, Erich Schildhauer and August Brilla, were killed by a direct hit, which wounded another, Wilhelm Radau, who succumbed to his wounds two days later.

The funeral in Tarabya of the three German naval ratings from the Goeben, killed fighting the fire in a Turkish barracks. (*Sammlung Soytürk*)

The German sailors were buried with their dead Turkish comrades in a common grave. At first the grave was adorned with a wooden cross on top of which was written: 'Suffered a hero's death for the Fatherland on 18 March 1915', followed by the names and at the bottom 'The German Detachment'. The cross was replaced a year later by a marble gravestone. This small burial ground at Hamidié was the only cemetery that was preserved later and only these four German sailors were reburied in Istanbul.

A German war correspondent, Paul Schweder, wrote about the first commemoration in honour of those who fell at Fort Hamidié on 18 March 1916:

> 'The first solemn anniversary remembrance ceremony of the fierce Dardanelles battle was on 18 March. We march across a marshy meadow to the quiet burial ground at the foot of the Dardanos Ridge, where four German and three Turkish heroes of the memorable day have found their final resting place. When I saw the graves for the first time a few weeks ago, they were still surrounded by a mysterious fence, behind which German and Turkish stonemasons in uniform were working with hammer and chisel. Today, next to that, loving hands had also placed tree and flower decorations and spring flowers sprouted from both the German and the Turkish communal grave. On both stood magnificent marble gravestones, the inscriptions of which list the names and deeds of these March casualties. For the first time we saw the cross and crescent in a joint German–Turkish cemetery. [...] And then the gnarled Vice-Admiral from far-away German East Prussia, who laid down two wreaths of simple cypress and pine

Graves of the fallen German and Turkish soldiers of the attack on Fort Hamidié, 18 March 1915. (*Collection Goossen*)

branches on the two tombs on behalf of all the funeral guests, movingly commemorating his men, whom he himself had buried in the cool earth a year ago. [...] The German and Turkish units from the Dardanelles forts were paraded all around. Speaking first from a black-and-white field pulpit, Navy Chaplain Müller from Wilhelmshaven, who had just come over from the [German] Navy Corps in Flanders, and here together with Bavarian Catholic chaplain, Father Hieronymus, doing pastoral care for the German naval forces in Turkey, commemorated the heroes of 18 March. [...] The Turkish soldiers raised their hands in prayer, and the German comrades followed their example by putting their elbows to the side and opening their hands upwards. After reading some verses from the Koran, the *hoca* praised the close relations between Germany, Austria–Hungary and the Turkish Empire, whose sons had sealed with their blood on 18 March. [...] A joint parade of the two units under Turkish command concluded the celebration in the fort, where later the combatants of 18 March sat together for a convivial meal in the modest canteen.'[568]

The first grave stones were large pieces of shrapnel on the graves, which were later replaced by ones made of marble. The graveyard was later edged with a wall and was the only German cemetery to be preserved after the war. The mortal remains of the four German soldiers were reinterred in 1936 in Tarabya. The cemetery at Fort Hamidié remains a Turkish memorial today.

Headstone of Lieutenant Woermann. (*Author's Collection*)

Headstone at Fort Hamidié. (*Author's Collection*)

Over the course of the next year, headstones made of marble or stone were erected for the grave of Sub Lieutenant Woermann and for other German casualties buried in various places around Gallipoli.

With the Allied landings on 25 April 1915, German soldiers were also directly involved in the fighting on land, especially the Naval Shore Detachment of the Mediterranean Division. With its two machine gun sections, the Detachment was in action from 3 May 1915 in the south of the Peninsula and suffered the highest losses.[569] Anyone killed initially had to be buried directly on the battlefield in simple graves, always providing that the dead bodies could be recovered. Already on their first day in action on 3 May, Leading Seamen Gerhard Prüntges and Werner Dathe were killed around Kereves Dere whilst resisting the French attack. On 4 May, Able Seaman Reinhold Drechsler was killed and two days later, Leading Seaman Hinrich Kutnik died as a result of a head shot. Able Seamen Johann Haase and Gerhard Flesner were killed on 4 June,

Headstone at Kumkale. (*Gebhard Bieg Collection*)

as well as Leading Seamen Eduard Gorzelski and Paul Hoheisel of the Naval Shore Detachment, killed by an artillery hit at Sigindere and who all were probably buried in two double graves. Oddly enough, of these seven men killed in the early battles for Krithia, only Hinrich Kutnik was recorded by name during the later interment in Istanbul, while the other names were lost.

On 9 June 1915, Ordnance Mate Robert Lass and the Able Seaman Paul Schirrmacher were killed at Kumkale. It is suspected that these two were killed during the bombardment of the fort at Kumkale or in a mine explosion, since at that time there was no fighting on land on the Asiatic side. While the loss of both soldiers was confirmed in the reports of the Special Commission, the grave locations were lost. It was only by chance that the gravestone was found by a farmer under cypress trees about 200-300 metres from the east end of Kumkale village on the road to Canakkale. In 1993 the gravestone was handed over to the Troy excavation facility, where it is still in the local excavation house.[570] It can be assumed that the grave of the two sailors was also located where the stone was found.

On 28 June 1915, during the heavy fighting on the southern front near Krithia, Leading Seaman Peter Brückers was killed. Elements of the Naval Shore Detachment were relocated on 6 August to the Anafarta Front to reinforce the defence against the landing at Suvla Bay. Sub Lieutenant Oskar Hildebrandt, the platoon commander of the machine-gun section there, was killed on 8 August on Koja Chemen Tepe. He was first buried in the nearby valley of Deniz Dere and later reburied in the cemetery of the Naval Shore Detachment on Kilia Tepe. Also killed on that day were Able Seaman Matthias Dank, who was buried on Ismail Oglu Tepe, and Fritz Klaus, who was first buried in Kurt Dere. Leading Seaman Ernst Buchmüller died of his wounds on 10 August 1915. Presumably these soldiers were later reburied at Kilia Tepe. The Naval Shore Detachment had its permanent quarters and established its own cemetery there. While the stone buildings for the accommodation were on a plateau on the southern slope of the approximately 130 metres high hill, the cemetery was situated on the hilltop itself. The German war correspondent, Paul Schweder, who visited the Gallipoli battlefields in 1916, wrote of this cemetery:

'Already today, where the flags of victory flutter over Gallipoli and the Straits, a mighty monument rises on the dominant height of Kilia Tepe for a number of German combatants killed in the long battle of Gallipoli. [...] On the highest point of the mountain [sic], the heroes of our Naval Shore Detachment who fell in the battles at Ari Burnu, Anafarta and Seddulbahr and were buried by their comrades up here, have their final resting place in one of the most beautiful landscapes in the world. I saw the graves of Sub Lieutenant Hildebrandt, four leading seamen, one petty officer, and two sailors who were there from July to the end of 1915. Above their heads a mighty granite pedestal, topped by an old ship's anchor, rises up. The [men of the] machine-gun section hauled it up the mountain, together with a few dozen heavy old Turkish stone cannonballs, to make a lasting memorial to the dead comrades. It is all quiet and peaceful around this last resting place for the lads in sailor blue.'[571]

The end of 1915 saw only sporadic battles taking place on Gallipoli. The Naval Shore Detachment, which had been divided into two sections, at Ariburnu and Kiretch Tepe, mourned the loss of Leading Seaman Wilhelm Peters, killed on 7 September. On 4 June Peters had heroically escaped from British captivity by knocking his guard down, then spent two days in a shell hole and, dying of thirst, was almost shot whilst making his way back to his own lines.

Cemetery of the Naval Shore Detachment on Kilia Tepe. (*Gunter Hartnagel Collection*)

He was buried on Kilia Tepe. On October 17, another marine, Leading Seaman Christian Rathert, died of typhus and was buried in the cemetery of the Naval Shore Detachment. On 8 November, Leading Seaman Hinrich Kaufhold was killed, followed by Able Seamen Wilfried Hecht on 12 December and Emil Reinicke on 29 December; all were buried in the Military Cemetery on Kilia Tepe.[572]

The list of the Naval Shore Detachment's casualties for the period 3 May to 29 December 1915 records a total of thirty-two killed, of whom, however, only a few appeared to have been laid to rest on Kilia Tepe. No exact casualty figures are known about the volunteer Sapper Company, which was employed on Gallipoli from July 1915. This voluntary unit was formed in Germany specifically for trench warfare and mine laying and suffered high casualties within a short time, mainly due to illness. There is only a record of unit losses in 1919 at the 'Old Turkish Hospital at Cham Burnu'. In the Turkish cemetery there were some German graves, marked with crosses for three 'German Sappers'[573], as well as Sapper Bierwagen, who died of wounds in the military hospital of Aga Dere on 20 August 1915. A casualty list dated 23 September 1915 recorded at this time three sappers killed and two who died of illness.[574]

At the suggestion of the Naval Attaché, Lieutenant Commander Humann, a Cemetery Commission was formed in Istanbul in August 1915. The Ambassador approved as its members the Military Chaplain (Count von Lüttichau), the Naval Attaché (Lieutenant Commander Humann) and the Military Adviser (Colonel von Lossow). However, General von Sanders had not been informed of this decision, 'because Marshal Liman von Sanders at that time was down at the Dardanelles almost all the time'.[575] The Commission set itself the task of carrying out dignified military funerals and to unify the development and administration of the military cemetery in Tarabya. In addition, a detail for the work in Tarabya was drawn from the

The band of the Breslau plays at a burial in Tarabya Cemetery. (*Bundesarchiv Koblenz*)

Sculpture by Georg Kolbe in the German Military Cemetery, Tarabya. (*Thomas Iredale Collection*)

contingent of the Mediterranean Division. At the beginning of April 1916, this detail numbered twenty-men men, under the watchful eye of a Chief Petty Officer.[576] The money to buy the materials and plants required for the cemetery came from donations and special funds.[577]

After the death of Baron von Wangenheim,[578] Richard von Kühlmann became Ambassador. Von Kühlmann knew the sculptor Georg Kolbe, who had already created a relief sculpture for a German-Belgian Military cemetery in Belgium. At the instigation of the Cemetery Commission, Kolbe was brought to Istanbul for the artistic design of the Military Cemetery in Tarabya. In the meantime, Kaiser Wilhelm had personally approved 'the cemetery in the grounds of the Embassy Park in Tarabya'.[579]

The choice of the motif of the sculpture was controversial even during the planning phase, since Kolbe did not, as usual, wish to depict a heroic soldier but to expand the theme of loss. It unclear whether he also wanted to take into consideration those soldiers and civilians who died of illness or disease in hospitals, or whether he wanted to distance himself from the typical portrayal of battlefield heroics. In any case, his design of an angel in the form of a mother, protectively holding a dying warrior, was endorsed by the Cemetery Commission. When the Kaiser came to Turkey in October 1917 for a short visit, he also visited the cemetery he had authorised. He examined Kolbe's work, which was still in progress.[580] The Kaiser did not like the sculpture at all, since he would have preferred a more heroic presentation and Wilhelm's harsh criticism wounded the sculptor deeply. Ambassador Kühlmann described this moment in his memories:

'In Therapia [sic], my friend, the sculptor Georg Kolbe, was working on a monument to the German warriors killed in the war of the Orient. Unfortunately, his design did not have the good fortune to please the Emperor. I soothed the downcast artist and told him that the Emperor was very impulsive and often expressed himself in an outspoken manner; one should not take this so tragically, but adapt the details which he had criticized somewhat, but for the rest carry on quietly. Wilhelm II never saw the finished monument on the upper slopes of the Embassy parkland.'[581]

In addition to this work of art, which he sculpted out of a five-ton block of limestone, Kolbe created the architectural layout for the cemetery. His concept was to have the graves in terraces on the slopes above the Bosphorus.

Kaiser Wilhelm II lays flowers on the grave of Field Marshal von der Goltz in October 1917. Also pictured are Naval Attaché Humann and Essad Paşa. (*Federal Archives, Koblenz*)

The most dramatic loss experienced by the German forces in Turkey was through the sinking of the light cruiser *Breslau* after she hit five mines on 20 January 1918 in the Aegean Sea. In total, 336 sailors died on that day. Only 56 bodies were subsequently recovered and buried by British troops on Imbros and Lemnos. There is a moving account about the sinking, written by Petty Officer de Grignis, who survived and sent it to one of his former superiors, Lieutenant Commander von Knorr:

'Finally all members of the crew, as far as they were still alive, were in the water, and now came the greatest moment, which proved that German sailors showed themselves worthy of their great country in the face of death. The ship rose up and down then, with the bow up, stood still for a few seconds and, with a great hurrah for the proud ship and the German homeland, she disappeared, in battle undefeated, into the depths of the sea. Now songs of the homeland began to be sung, and everything collapsed about us. The water was a little over 6 degrees, and gradually most started to succumb. Captain, they all died quietly and devotedly, almost no moaning to be heard, only here and there a head sinking down into the water, and one more brave comrade had given his country all that he could give.'[582]

In 1918 Dr Siegfried Emmo Neulen was assigned as Graves Officer to Turkey.[583] Since the cemetery in Tarabya was not yet finished, he put the graves for the German fallen of the German Asiatic Corps in what is now the International Protestant cemetery in Skutari.

He began preparations for interring the dead who were scattered along the Anatolian Railway, as well as those who fell in Syria and Palestine, in this collective cemetery. German soldiers who died

The monument in the German Military Cemetery in Skutari, 1918. (*Bundesarchiv Koblenz*)

in the internment camp in Constantinople during the winter of 1918/1919 were buried there. The cemetery in the Skutari district, now Üsküdar, was probably close to today's CWGC cemetery at Haidar Pasha, in which mostly Allied soldiers of both World Wars are buried.

With the expulsion of the German forces in October 1918 and the end of the war, work was discontinued at the cemetery in Tarabya, although according to Article 225 of the Treaty of Versailles Germany was still responsible for the continuing care of German military graves in Turkey.[584] The dead soldiers in Turkey had not been completely forgotten at home. For example, after the sinking the *Breslau*, Gustav Stresemann, a prominent German politician, had immediately initiated a collection in Germany for a stone monument in honour of those killed on the *Goeben* and *Breslau* and wanted to know in a letter he wrote in 1922 'whether the monument has actually been erected'.[585] However, such a monument was never built, as in 1918 the Cemetery Commission had already misappropriated the donation of 25,000 marks collected by Stresemann for the development of the cemetery in Tarabya, which in fact cost a total of approximately130,000 marks.

After the war the German cemeteries were initially without special care since Germany did not have its own diplomatic representation and only one German representative was present at the Swedish Embassy in Istanbul. In 1921 forty-eight German soldiers had to be transferred from the German cemetery in Ferikoy to Tarabya, since the land, already leased in 1914 to Germany, had been sold without the knowledge of the tenants to a French monastery. The new owners now demanded immediate clearance of the property, for which the former owner, because of his fraudulent action, should pay the cost of the reburial.[586] Thus by early 1925 there were in Istanbul only the military cemeteries in Tarabya, with 198 grave sites and Skutari, with eighty-eight graves. The cemetery in Tarabya was still unfinished, but there were already five terraces and the retaining walls, while about

125 metres remained without gravestones. It was only in 1924, when Rudolf Nadolny[587] took up the duties as Ambassador in Istanbul, that the cemetery in Tarabya would no longer remain forgotten. Nadolny paid great attention to the care of the graves and described the work he had had done at the cemetery:

'The Cemetery to our heroes was high above the Bosphorus and needed special care. I had the whole complex thoroughly restored. [...] In the lowest part, a relief had been created by the sculptor Kolbe.[588] Facing towards the Bosphorus, a forecourt with balustrade and cedars was made, from which the view swept over the Bosphorus to Bujukdere and the Black Sea. A new pathway gave direct access to the road. The graves were distributed on three terraces. The middle one contained only three graves, that of Field Marshal v. d. Goltz, Ambassador Baron v. Wangenheim and Military Attaché Colonel v. Leipzig. Each was covered with a marble slab. I had a stylized iron cross of black marble put at the heads of each of these three graves. The remaining 201 graves of soldiers and nurses had wooden crosses that were covered with climbing roses. Finally I had a motor installed down at a spring in the park, which provided the cemetery with water. Every year, on the birthday of Field Marshal v. d. Goltz, the Turks held a funeral [sic] service at his grave and were very satisfied with the good condition of the grave and its surroundings. Once a German father appeared before me, to exhume the body of his son and transfer it to Germany. We went to the cemetery together. When the father stood at the grave of his son and then looked over to the Bosphorus, he said after a long moment of silence: "No, I'll leave him here. At home, he cannot have it like he has here with his comrades". In Skutari was another German heroes' cemetery. After it had been put in order, I later had the bones of the German soldiers who were killed and buried in the Dardanelles reburied in Skutari.'[589]

There are no longer any relevant documents about the graves on Gallipoli and their condition. No consistent registration took place during the war, as the different commands, such as the Special Command (SoKo), the Naval Shore Detachment or the Engineers Company all had different collective grave sites and sometimes there were individual graves of German soldiers. Where no marble gravestones with inscriptions were made for the graves at a later date and over time both the wooden crosses and graves fell victim to the weather, they could not be attributed to any particular soldier and they were finally forgotten. In a letter from Ambassador Nadolny, who in 1925 took stock of all German war graves in Turkey, it is clear that in the Canakkale district a total of seventeen German soldiers were buried, six of them near Fort Hamidié, four in Topçamlar, one in Chevketié, and two in Najakçeşme, near Çatkaltepe. One soldier was buried at Sairid and eighteen were buried in the Kiliana district, near Maidos and Ali Bey Chiflik.[590]

In a compilation from 1936 of all the graves around Gallipoli, the following are mentioned: two in Aga Dere, one in Anafarta, fifteen at Gallipoli, sixteen at Hamidiè, five on Imbros, five at Kilia Tepe, two at Krithia, one at Chevketié, twenty-four at Seddulbahr, four at Çalkaltepe, one at Çurşumköy, two east of Kumkale and four near Topçamlar.[591] These completely different statements show the poor quality of the information about the graves and even their location was not marked on any maps. The number of presumed dead disagree with the documentation available today; most of the names must have already been lost in the first years after the war. This situation was very clearly recognised by Ambassador Nadolny in 1925 and he therefore requested the posting of a Commissioner, 'to timely rectify the imminent total blurring of traces of our war cemeteries' and 'to receive reports on the situation and the – mostly desolate – state of cemeteries scattered across the country'.[592]

To have the grave sites around Gallipoli inspected, Nadolny sent Legation Counsellor Braun von Stumm to participate in a tour by Turkish officers and politicians, who wanted to commemorate the defensive battle on the Peninsula. His report made it clear that the Allies had 'strewn the battlefields in the most luxurious, indeed almost obtrusive, manner, with cemeteries and monuments, all of which are in perfect condition[593] but Turkish grave sites, apart from the grave of a Turkish corporal and a Turkish battle monument, were 'in dismal condition' and there was nothing to see. This did not escape the attention of the rest of the travelling party and it was decided that in future 'the commemoration of Turkish soldiers, who were, moreover, the victors, would be visibly honoured'.

According to the local gendarmes and some residents, no German graves were known. Only in Maidos were there supposedly still some German grave sites. Braun von Stumm suggested, as a consequence, to find first a Turkish-speaking trusted representative who would be capable of identifying all the old burial places, then to provide a solid and visible enclosure around the grave sites and ultimately to seek assistance from the local authorities to prevent grave robberies.

Whether the reburial from Gallipoli to Skutari mentioned by Ambassador Nadolny in his own memoirs actually took place cannot be verified. However, there is evidence that such an action under his direction was never carried out. There is no longer any documentation about such a transfer and in 1932 and 1935 further attempts were made to recover or maintain the war graves on Gallipoli, i.e. up to 1935 no reburials took place in Istanbul.

In October 1931, the Chancellor of the German Embassy took a trip to Canakkale, to see the condition of the cemetery at Hamidiè and to assess on the ground whether it would be possible to build a memorial to fallen German soldiers at Cape Kephes. The cemetery, although very run down, measured 361 square metres and was considered to be large enough to be used for 'the reburial of German soldiers from the surrounding areas, as far as remains are still to be found'.[594] At the time there were still four German and two Turkish soldiers buried there. On the question of a monument, there was a very pessimistic assessment from Istanbul, whose reasoning remains valid today. A permit by the Turkish government for such a monument would not be likely to be granted, 'as resistance against lessening one's own exploits by setting up a visible sign remembering German military assistance would be difficult for the Turks to accept'. Therefore it was suggested that the small cemetery at Hamidiè be developed 'into a single dignified memorial to Germany's participation in the Turkish theatre of war' and that all German graves in the area should be relocated there.

These ideas seem to have been pursued for years but were never implemented. In June 1935 there was a re-examination of the cemetery at Hamidiè. Its condition had worsened further. The photographs in the German Political Archives reveal that there were also some graves of other German soldiers in addition to the four graves mentioned so far. It is likely that their graves had been abandoned and only the headstones were transferred to Hamidiè. In the meantime, even the Imperial War Graves Commission agreed to 'support a fitting resting place for German soldiers',[595] a position that was immediately communicated to the Turkish authorities, showing that such support from an erstwhile foe was indeed in 'the spirit of the brotherhood-of-arms'.

In July 1936 it was finally decided to abandon the cemetery at Hamidié and to rebury the mortal remnants of German soldiers in Tarabya. This measure was justified by the imminent fortification of the Dardanelles and the resulting structural hazard to the cemetery. The reburial transfer should be by sea route and take place in 'the most solemn form possible'. The effort and costs would be justified because, 'In their dignity, they have not yet strayed from the prevailing idea of a symbolic total transfer of all [soldiers] from their original graves, especially corpses scattered throughout Asia Minor'.[596]

This statement is important because it proves that from the entire area from Gallipoli-Canakkale, of the more than eighty known graves of German soldiers, actually only four were reburied in Tarabya.

The transfer from Canakkale was coordinated by the visit of the cruiser *Emden* in Istanbul. On 30 and 31October 1936, the bodies were exhumed and on 1 November 1936 the remains of those who fell in the Dardanelles were transferred by a hired steamboat to Tarabya. At the ceremony in honour of the war dead on 8 November 1936, the Cultural Attaché, Baron von Mirbach, and the crew of the *Emden* took part. In records from Turkey dating from the years before the Second World War, it is stated: 'November 1936 – in the presence of General Ali Fuad Erdem, the funeral of fifty-two German warriors who fought in the Dardanelles took place in Tarabya'.[597] The number mentioned was, therefore, purely symbolic, as de facto only the remains of four soldiers were reburied. The small cemetery in Hamidié continues to exist as a purely Turkish memorial.

The cemetery of Tarabya was further developed with considerable resources, not least financial. The German War Graves Commission had been supporting the renovation work in Tarabya since 1926 with an annual sum of 4,000 Reichsmarks. The Association of German Iron Foundries wanted to provide 196 cast-iron crosses. The provision of permanent grave markers, however, did not materialise and in 1932, the wooden crosses were still on the graves. In November 1935 staff of the German War Graves Commission's construction department visited the site on the Bosphorus to make proposals for a central memorial to all the fallen in Turkey. Despite preparatory work, such as surveying the terrain, this project was not implemented. Instead, the Commission's construction department planned a design for Tarabya that was to be elaborated to relocate the soldiers' graves from the Dardanelles to Istanbul. The idea for this merger had already existed during the Great War, as can be deduced from a statement by Schweder in 1916:

'One even considers, that all the remains of German officers and men who fell on Ottoman soil in the Great War should be brought here later on, where German soil can cover them and German hands decorate their graves uniformly, regardless of whether they come from victoriously famed Gallipoli, from the Trojan plain, from the hot Iraqi front, from the ice fields of the Caucasus or the Sinai Desert. The same blue sky will be there to greet them, the same tropical floral splendour of Tarabya's peaceful Embassy garden will encircle their hills, the same soft waves of the Bosphorus tide at their feet will be their dream.'[598]

A commemoration ceremony in Tarabya in 1941, with members of the Hitler Youth and SA Istanbul in attendance. (*Bundesarchiv Koblenz*)

Tarabya was incorporated in the training and heroic glorification of the Nazi movement during the Second World War, which also had been established with some of the German population in Istanbul. A wooden cross was erected with the inscription 'Faithful to death' in the cemetery and, on various occasions, members of the Hitler Youth and SA provided a Guard of Honour there. On the back of the picture of such a ceremony, pictured above, it was noted:

> 'German Hero Memorial Hour on the Bosphorus. On the gloriously located German Heroes' Cemetery in Istanbul, from where you can enjoy a sweeping view of the Bosphorus, an emotionally charged memorial service was held in connection with the donation collection day for the German War Graves Commission. This day saw a Guard of Honour provided by members of the German SA of Istanbul parading at the cemetery and the graves were magnificently decorated. – our picture shows the centre of the German cemetery on the Bosphorus with the SA Guard of Honour.'

Today this wooden cross, overgrown and lying amongst old lumber, remains as a forgotten relic on the site in Tarabya. In 1958 the graves of German soldiers from the Second World War and found by Turkish fishermen on the Black Sea coast, of which 124 could be identified and five were unknown, were exhumed from their makeshift graves and transferred to Tarabya.

The German military cemetery in Skutari was given up in 1962 because it was both difficult and costly to maintain; the graves were transferred to Tarabya. This meant that a number of marble

Old wooden cross in Tarabya, pictured in 2007. (*Author's Collection*)

headstones were brought to Tarabya, which now lie in the extension part of the cemetery. The remaining headstones from Gallipoli were mounted on a side wall - although they no longer mark any actual graves. In 1979 the German War Graves Commission decided to consolidate into Tarabya all the fallen within Turkey and whose graves were threatened by loss. For this purpose the cemetery was surveyed anew in the spring of 1980 and extension areas created on the steep slopes; reburials from various grave sites in Turkey took place in 1981. In total, with this last significant measure of the German War Graves Commission, the remains of 220 soldiers, including the remaining German dead in the international cemetery in Ferikoy, were reburied in Tarabya, which is now the only remaining German military cemetery. On 10 October 1982 the now extended cemetery in Tarabya was inaugurated by a major ceremony.

In addition to the German Ambassador and officials of the German War Graves Commission, high-ranking officers of the Turkish Armed Forces were also represented at this inauguration, which included the commander of the First Army, Orgeneral (General) Haydar Saltik, and the commander of III Corps from Maslak, Korgeneral (Lieutenant General) Doğan Güres, as well as many guests who came from Germany. Only two marble tablets, at graves 162 and 163, now commemorate the German soldiers who fell in Gallipoli, but no mention of the connection to Gallipoli is apparent. Many of the forty-one unknown soldiers inscribed on the panels appear by name in Appendix 2. All German officers serving between 1914-1916 with units of the Ottoman Army, Navy and Air Arm engaged in the Gallipoli, Dardanelles and Black Sea theatres of war or in support of Ottoman war materiel production and logistics, as well as German casualties in this campaign, are included in Appendices 2 and 3. These lists indicate that at least 534 German soldiers were killed - a figure that previously could not even be guessed at.

Amongst the notable people buried in Tarabya are:

Field Marshal Colmar Baron von der Goltz

Probably the most famous grave in the military cemetery in Tarabya is that of Field Marshal Colmar von der Goltz, who died from typhus in Baghdad on 19 April 1916 and was first buried there and later transferred to Istanbul. There is still an annual tribute paid to him, with a wreath laying ceremony by a Turkish Military Delegation on Remembrance Day, to commemorate his understanding nature and achievements in Turkey. His old professional rival, Liman von Sanders, wrote of von der Goltz:

'Field Marshal von der Goltz died of typhus on 19 April 1916 in Baghdad. It was a tragic fate that he could no longer savour the prize of the last months. The mourning of this revered leader and teacher was prevalent throughout the Turkish officer corps. On 24 June 1916 a great funeral service for the Field Marshal took place in Constantinople, followed by his solemn burial in the Memorial Cemetery in Tarabya, where the Field Marshal found his resting place in one of the most beautiful spots on earth.'[599]

An article about his memorial service appeared in Istanbul on 25 June 1916 in the German language newspaper, the *Osmanischer Lloyd*:

'On the picturesque squares, surrounded by historical memories, in front of the Ministry of War, under the mighty acacia trees next to the *Kommandantur*, the coffin containing the remains of Field Marshal Freiherr von der Goltz laid in state. Between two field guns stood

Grave of Baron von der Goltz. (*Author's Collection*)   Grave of Baron von Wangenheim. (*Author's Collection*)

the coffin, covered by the Ottoman and German war flags, on which were the helmet, *Kalpak* and sword of the deceased, amidst magnificent wreaths and flowers… Then the coffin with the earthly remains of the Marshal of two Empires disappeared from view and drove to that place in the park of Tarabya where already many a brave man dear to our hearts rests near the Moltke monument.'[600]

Ambassador Baron von Wangenheim

One of the few non-military burials in the cemetery was that of Ambassador Baron Hans von Wangenheim, who died of a stroke in Istanbul on 25 October 1915. Obviously Admiral Souchon was little bothered by his demise; he wrote to his wife the same day:

'Wangenheim died this morning after lying unconscious for two days. I was there this morning, but only spoke to the children, who are still uncomprehending of their loss. [...] Tomorrow I'm on the *Goeben*, we are very curious who will be Ambassador here.'[601]

However, Ambassador Henry Morgenthau, the harshest critic but apparently also one of Wangenheim's secret admirers, wrote of his last meeting and the funeral:

'Wangenheim rose to leave. As he did so he gave a gasp, and his legs suddenly shot from under him. I jumped and caught the man just as he was falling. For a minute he seemed utterly dazed; he looked at me in a bewildered way, then suddenly collected himself and regained his poise. I took the Ambassador by the arm, piloted him down stairs, and put him into his auto. By this time he had apparently recovered from his dizzy spell and he reached home safely. Two days afterwards, while sitting at his dinner table, he had a stroke of apoplexy; he was carried upstairs to his bed but never regained consciousness.

On October 24th I was officially informed that Wangenheim. was dead. [...] A few days afterwards official Turkey and the diplomatic force paid their last tribute to this perfect embodiment of the Prussian system. The funeral was held in the garden of the German Embassy at Pera. The enclosure was filled with flowers. Practically the whole gathering, excepting the family and the ambassadors and the Sultan's representatives, remained standing during the simple but impressive ceremonies. Then the procession formed; German sailors carried the bier upon their shoulders, other German sailors carried the huge bunches of flowers, and all members of the diplomatic corps and the officials of the Turkish Government followed on foot.

The Grand Vizier led the procession; I walked the whole way with Enver. All the officers of the *Goeben* and the *Breslau,* and all the German generals, dressed in full uniform, followed. It seemed as though the whole of Constantinople lined the streets, and the atmosphere had some of the quality of a holiday. We walked to the grounds of Dolma Bagtche, the Sultan's Palace, passing through the gate that the ambassadors enter when presenting their credentials. At the dock a steam launch lay awaiting our arrival, and in this stood Neurath, the German *Conseiller*, ready to receive the body of his dead chieftain. The coffin, entirely covered with flowers, was placed in the boat. As the launch sailed out into the stream, Neurath, a six-foot Prussian, dressed in his military uniform, his helmet a waving mass of white plumes, stood erect and silent. Wangenheim was buried in the park of the summer embassy at Therapia, by the side of his comrade Colonel Leipzig. No final resting-place would have been more appropriate, for this had been the scene of his diplomatic successes and it was from this place that, a little more than two years before, he had directed by wireless the *Goeben* and the *Breslau,* and safely brought them into Constantinople, thus making it inevitable that Turkey should join forces with Germany, and paving the way for all the triumphs and all the horrors that have necessarily followed that event.'[602]

Second Lieutenant Ludwig Preussner, Turkish Air Arm

The solemnity and magnificence of the military honours that were paid, especially by the Turkish military, is illustrated by the funeral of Ludwig Preussner.

On 16 May 1916, German pilot and flying instructor Ludwig Preussner crashed at the Turkish flying training school in San Stefano whilst on a training flight. Allegedly, the student pilot with him in the aircraft blocked the joystick in panic. Sergeant Ludwig 'Louis' Preussner, serving in Turkey as a Turkish second lieutenant, died of his injuries on 29 May 1916 in the German hospital and was then buried with full military honours in the military cemetery in Tarabya. His gravestone lies modestly and unobtrusively between the graves of his other comrades. War correspondent Schweder filed this report of Preussner's funeral:

'He was definitely the best aviator down here and so, even after the happy end of the Dardanelles adventure, he was quickly assigned as a flying instructor in San Stefano. There he crashed on a training flight and died after two days of painful suffering. The mortal remains of the bold German conqueror of the skies we have today taken to the grave.

At the front they carried the broken and half-burned propeller of his aircraft, wreathed with flowers in Turkish colours: for Preussner died as a pilot in Turkish service, and his Turkish comrades almost jealously ensured that he was to be granted full Turkish military honours. The band of the Turkish Fire Brigade of the Imperial Capital led the coffin to the sound of Chopin's funeral march, and every Turkish sentry and passing officer and soldier saluted the coffin. Even on the roof of the German Embassy the mighty black-and-white-and-red flag was hoisted at half-mast as we passed. On the jetty of the Imperial Palace of Dolmabahçe the volleys of the salute fired by the Turkish infantry detachment resounded, as the German aircrew officers in Turkish uniform carried the coffin on the pinnace of the *Goeben*. And all the Turkish officers and men who had accompanied the coffin to here also participated in the crossing to Tarabya. [...] It's like one fairy tale when we arrive. The Embassy palace lies lonely and enclosed for,

despite the summer [heat], its owner carries on his offices in Constantinople. The big, much-praised, garden dreams quietly to itself. But then, as the coffin approaches containing the dead pilot, the wide gates, moved by an invisible hand, open wide and we step into the earthly paradise, which the whim of a sultan gave away with a royal gesture. You enter as going into an old German cathedral, among the trees and shrubs brought from all over the world into the garden of Tarabya. [...] Germans and Turks vie with each other for the honour of carrying the dead airman along the winding paths.'[603]

The only German grave that is still preserved on Gallipoli was made for Nurse Erika and lies, somewhat hidden and overgrown, above a Turkish cemetery south of Kumköy.

Left: Second Lieutenant Ludwig Preussner in Gallipoli. (*Bülent Yilmazer Collection*)

Below left: Propeller of Preussner's aircraft as a temporary grave marker in Tarabya. (*Collection Bülent Yilmazer*)

Below right: A recent photograph of Second Lieutenant Ludwig Preussner's tombstone in Tarabya. (*Author's Collection*)

She was married to a Turkish medical officer, Ragip Bey, and worked with him in a Turkish hospital. During an artillery bombardment on 26 September 1915 she was killed by shrapnel and her husband erected a marble grave according to Muslim custom. On the grave stone is inscribed: 'While helping to care for wounded Turkish soldiers, Erika, a German nurse, wife of Captain Ragip Bey, lost her life through a shell. 26 September 1915'.

Above: The grave of Sister Erika at Kumköy on Gallipoli, 2007. (*Author's Collection*)

Right: Hamidié Cemetery, 2007. (*Author's Collection*)

Epilogue

These chapters on German-Turkish cooperation in the First World War are not intended to evoke a heroic epic – even though many contemporary commentaries seem to speak such a different language. The great number of contemporary quotations that I have used capture the prevailing *zeitgeist*, which sowed the seeds of German enthusiasm, which made the war possible in the first place. The national identity of Germany and its soldiers was shaped by the Wilhelmine bourgeoisie, strict Prussian education and the determining militarism of the country at that time. From this emerged the excessive role of the military in society and would probably explain the expression of a national sense of superiority towards other nations and cultures, culminating in the somewhat arrogant motto *Am Deutschen Wesen soll die Welt genesen*, which can be roughly translated as: The German way will be the world's salvation.[604] This sense of mission was to influence many German soldiers serving in Turkey and largely determine their conduct. In common with the majority of soldiers in other foreign armies, they had had little or no experience of other cultures, especially Muslim culture. The German colonial adventures in South West Africa, Tangyanika and China are unlikely to have contributed to any improvement in intercultural competence. Thus it is understandable that throughout the years of the Military Mission in the Ottoman Empire that very few soldiers developed any special empathy for the Turkish way of life and their Muslim comrades.

Coupled with an unfounded criticism of foreign customs, this national arrogance often upset, insulted and annoyed the Turks. Despite a certain understanding of the special cultural aspects of the host country, which grew as time went by, the Turks could hardly have gained the impression that they were regarded as being of equal status with the Germans. However, one of the essential prerequisites for gaining the recognition and respect of others is to feel that you are on equal terms. This lack of understanding, coupled with mutual distrust and disrespect, caused unnecessary problems and quarrels in too many places and situations. Of course, even then, clear thinking Turkish politicians and military leaders were aware that the war did not much involve Turkish interests, but they had to make do with a situation created by several Turkish politicians working in cooperation with the Germans. Nevertheless, defending Gallipoli was perceived as a Turkish national endeavour and was vigorously fought. The Turks could have spared themselves these battles were they to have joined forces with another ally at a suitable moment.

Apart from these cultural differences, however, it is clearly documented that Germany had a significant share in the development of Turkey's military capabilities at that time. This covered not only training but also the supply of weapons, ammunition and equipment. In 1912 the Turkish Army and Navy were both in a very poor condition and their subsequent rapid reform bore the German stamp. Despite what has been written in this book, the dispute over what part German leadership and equipment had in the battles on Gallipoli may never reach a balanced, equitable conclusion. Nevertheless it is clear to me that a victory for the Turks, including at Gallipoli, would have been unthinkable without German support in artillery training on land and sea, the reorganisation of munitions production, the regulation of supply and, last but far from least, the leadership capabilities of individual officers, such as Kannengiesser, Wehrle, Boltz and Lierau – to name but four. German military 'development aid' not only laid the foundations for producing modern weapons and munitions in Turkey, but the large number of German medical officers helped to reorganise and update the Turkish health services.

Although German advice was politically desirable at that time, it was hardly wanted at an executive level and had little lasting influence. This was not only due to Turkish inertia but was often due to the lack of empathy of the German training instructors as well. Many Turkish officers felt themselves undermined by German influence and offended in their national pride and military ethos. Nonetheless, training by German officers did provide rapid, superficial achievements that instilled new pride in Turkish leaders.

Liman von Sanders had a major part to play in the reform of the Turkish armed forces as the Head of the Military Mission. In particular he was able to achieve improvements in overall military capability by his very hard and disciplined training regime. He worked pragmatically towards this goal, without acting politically but, unfortunately, also without paying enough attention to 'the Turkish way of doing things'. His ability to prevail, even against considerable resistance, did eventually lead to the indisputable fact that he was given the Supreme Command for the defence of Gallipoli. His planning and assertiveness in this campaign was responsible for the successful, but also very costly, defence. All unemotional and unbiased analyses allows for no other conclusion.

Mainly due to the myths surrounding Mustafa Kemal Atatürk, the battlefields of Gallipoli today are pilgrimage sites for Turkish tour groups from all over the country. The infrastructure on the Peninsula has been continually improved and developed in recent years, not only to satisfy the flow of visitors on public holidays and weekends but also to fulfil the need for tangible testimony of that era. In the 1990s 'show' trenches were dug at prominent places and fortified as in the war. These are also tourist attractions, like the continuing renovation of the fort in Seddulbahr, or the small privately owned museums in the area. The battlefields of Gallipoli, especially the sites marked by huge monuments commemorating the deeds of Mustafa Kemal, are today viewed as the birthplace of modern Turkey and are therefore regarded with special interest and great national affection.

Another particularly strong link with Gallipoli is that of the Australians and New Zealanders, whose soldiers had to suffer tremendous losses, especially in Ariburnu, later renamed Anzac Cove. These soldiers stood under British command and were there to enable a victory for the British Empire. The Australian and New Zealand Army Corps triggered national solidarity, not only in Australia, but also in New Zealand, which fuelled a growing feeling of independence from British rule. Every year Australians and New Zealanders travel to the Peninsula, especially on 25 April, when thousands spend the early hours of the morning on North Beach to commemorate the landings of 1915. For the British, this campaign was a bitter defeat, but strategically had no long-lasting negative consequences. It serves as a model from which to study military mistakes and Gallipoli is still an inportant battlefield study for serving British officers.

Gallipoli has little if any national significance for Germany. The passing years mean that veterans and those present in other capacities in Turkey are no longer alive. The German engagement in this campaign is nowhere commemorated with a monument, although some 3,000 military personnel were involved, of whom over 530 were killed and many more were wounded or fell ill with disease. In particular, all the German soldiers and sailors who were killed and whose bodies could not be recovered from the battlefield or from the sea, deserve to be honourably commemorated. However, this commemoration, it appears to me, was neglected by Germany itself. Both the preservation of the German graves and the construction of a memorial would have been possible and would most likely have been supported by the Turks. But there was never a really decisive initiative from Germany and finally, with the decision to relocate the fallen German soldiers from Hamidié in the 1930s, they symbolically tried to forget the other German grave sites on Gallipoli and thus close the chapter about German soldiers on Gallipoli. A memorial monument could have been erected at any time in Tarabya to commemorate those who fell on Gallipoli, but to this day awareness seems to be missing.

Every year on Remembrance Day the spirit of the old brotherhood-in-arms is revived. This is when the area Turkish commander, accompanied by a small honour guard, lays a wreath in Tarabya and visits the grave of Field Marshal von der Goltz. The bond with Germany, which is still positive in Turkey, does not, however, emanate from brotherhood-in-arms during the joint battles fought in the Dardanelles, but commemorates Marshal von der Goltz and Hauptmann von Moltke for their services in reforming the Turkish military forces. These officers were obviously enamoured with Turkey, understood the culture without, however, wanting or being able to exercise political influence in the state. Only in this way can it be explained that the relatively small influence of these two German officers has so significantly outweighed the much more significant German military involvement in Gallipoli or in other Turkish theatres of war. In a country attaching great importance to symbols and traditions, the names von der Goltz and Moltke are synonymous with friendship with Germany. This tradition is still proudly maintained. If current, bilateral political decisions overlook this emotional attachment and the Moltke or von der Goltz connections are not even remembered in Germany, the Turks often find this difficult to understand.

Strategically, the victory on Gallipoli had neither lasting importance for Germany nor for Turkey. Allied forces were kept away from the Western Front and used in this theatre of war; and supplying Russia had only limited possibilities. The British 29th Division and the Australian and New Zealand forces originally intended to reinforce the Western Front were diverted to Gallipoli. The aims intended by Germany could be achieved with relatively little manpower and, compared to the material battles on the Western and Eastern Fronts, with limited use of materiel and ammunition. However, the strategic advantages of the Gallipoli victory were soon eaten away. Turkish operations in Palestine, now had to be supported by much stronger German forces and which finally led to the deployment of the approximately 25,000 strong 'Asia Corps' from Germany, significant forces that otherwise would have been available for the Western Front. These troops in the Middle East required complex logistics, which led to an additional material burden on the already exhausted German war economy. Despite this deployment of troops and material, the front could not be held in Sinai and there was a costly retreat, which for many German soldiers lasted until the end of the war in Istanbul.

But if Gallipoli is viewed from a historical and technical point of view, it takes on a major significance. Never before had naval, land and air forces been used on such a limited battlefield. Even though this cooperation only arose when it was a matter of 'needs must' arising from particular situations and not planned as a long term joint operation, there were cooperative actions at all levels. Even though there was no single or joint leadership, the different arms achieved a common or at least mutually supportive effect on the battlefield. The experiences of this 'new' type of warfare, positive and negative, were not evaluated, lessons learned and findings implemented, at least not by the Germans. Opportunities, requirements and problems of joint military operations, as experienced in Gallipoli, could have led to important conclusions and thus influenced subsequent battles. Investigating such evidence is not a part of this book, but should be carefully considered. The same applies to the challenge of a multinational operation, especially in the context of the cooperation of armed forces from completely different cultural backgrounds.

What would have happened if Turkey had not sided with the Central Powers? Turkey would probably have made the Allies pay dearly for any termination of the military alliance with Germany in the shape of extensive security guarantees and political and economic support. This, in turn, would probably have led not only to concessions in the Middle East, but also to a ceasefire in the Caucasus, ultimately guaranteeing Turkey a considerably expanded territory after the World War.

That would have been probable even without an active participation of the Turkish army on the Allied side. Greece and Romania might have joined the Allies as early as 1915; whilst presumably Bulgaria would not have joined Germany's side in the war, which outcome, combined with the Allies' much desired supply route to Russia through the Black Sea, would have led to much greater pressure on the Central Powers in the south and east. The Allied battle fleets would now have been deployed against Germany in the Atlantic, as well as in the North and Baltic Seas, and troops originally assigned to the Western Front but tied to Gallipoli might have made a new offensive possible there – not to mention the manpower deployed to defend the Suez Canal. Had this development begun at the end of 1914, it is possible that the First World War could have been decided for the Allies at the end of 1915. A similar outcome, albeit delayed by at least a year, seems to me to have been possible if Gallipoli had been lost to the Turks and the British troops had invaded Istanbul not in October 1918 but in 1915.

In my view, the Imperial Germany of 1914 was guilty of manoeuvring its Turkish ally into the war. The government was deceived, many unsuspecting and innocent people were sent to their deaths by ruthless orders, and soldiers were treated with disrespect and arrogance. Imperial Germany's political manoeuvrings in Turkey were shameful. It may sound strange, but I am convinced that a plea for forgiveness for suffering caused by Germany in that era is long overdue.

Since there is no one, particular, responsible body to deliver such an apology in today's Germany, on their behalf I would like to apologise, also with this book, and ask forgiveness for the suffering that has been caused.

Alphabetical list of German officers serving between 1914-1916 with units of the Ottoman Army, Navy and Air Arm engaged in the Gallipoli, Dardanelles and Black Sea theatres of war or in support of Ottoman war *materiel* production and logistics

EK I = Iron Cross First Class; EK II = Iron Cross Second Class; OPM = Order 'Pour le Mérite'.

Name	Rank	Branch	Time	Assignment/Function/Awards/Notes
Abel, Hein	Sub Lieutenant	Navy	1915/1917	Commander of a Turkish torpedo boat; then navigation officer on *Hamidiye* and *Goeben*
Ackermann, Richard	Captain	Navy	1914/1918	Commander of the *Goeben* *Awarded Liakat Medal in Gold with Swords, Medjidie–Order 2nd Class, Cross of the Knight of the Royal Order of the House of Hohenzollern with Swords; retired 1919 as Rear Admiral*
Adelmann, Dr. Edgar	Second Lieutenant (Assistenzarzt	Army (Medical)	1916	Special Command (SoKo)
Adle	Second Lieutenant	Army	1914/1918	Adjutant to Lieutenant Colonel Wehrle
Adriano, Alfred	Commander	Navy	1915	Mediterranean Division (MMD), served on *Hamidiye;* German Commander of *Turgut Reis*
Agrell, Friedrich	Sub Lieutenant (Marine-Ingenieur)	Navy (Engineer)	1915/1916	Engineer on *U-14*
Ahrens, Dr.	Lieutenant	Army	1914/1918	Army Legal Services
Akermann	Captain	Army	1915/1916	Commanding Officer of Territorial Forces
Albrecht	Major	Prussian Army	1914/1916	As Turkish Lieutenant Colonel, in peace-time Corps Commander in Aleppo; In war-time, Chief of Staff of 5th Army Corps *After returning from Turkey, Lieutenant Colonel then on General Staff of Kowac Government. Ret'd as Lieutenant Colonel. Died 1921*

Allinge, d' Hans	Sub Lieutenant	Navy	1915/1916 1917	*Goeben;* Port Commander in Derince, later Adjutant
Althaus	Captain	Prussian Army	1915/1916	As Turkish Major in the Military Mission and Commanding Officer of a Turkish Engineer Battalion in 6th Turkish Army. *Died 1918 as CO Engineer Bn 376 in Boult aux Bois*
Altmann, Ulrich	Sub Lieutenant	Navy	1915/1918	*Goeben*
Aly, Gerhard	Lieutenant	Army	1915	Artillery Command, *Treated in September 1915 in the German hospital in Istanbul for typhus*
Anderheggen, Ernst	Second Lieutenant	Army	1915/1918	Responsible for coal supplies
Anderten, von	Second Lieutenant	Prussian Army	1916/1918	In Military Mission as Turkish Lieutenant and Adjutant to von Schellendorf, Chief of the Turkish General Staff *Ret'd as Lieutenant*
Andreae, Brami	Sub Lieutenant	Navy	1914/1916	1914 Crew member of *Goeben,* Commander of a Turkish torpedo boat; took part as Watch Officer on *Muavenet* in the attack on HMS *Goliath* on 12 May 1915, during which he supported the torpedo crew during launch. *Awarded EK I on 15 January 1916*
Andreae, Prof. Dr.	Captain	Army		Surveying engineer
Andriano, Ruprecht	Lieutenant Commander	Navy	1916/1918	German Commander of *Torgut Reis,* then in the rank of Commander, was the German Commander of *Hamidiye* *Awarded Osmanie Order 4ᵗʰ Class with Sabres, Liakat Medal in Silver with Swords*
Ankarcrona, Stieg	Sub Lieutenant	Navy	1914/1916	Crew member of *Goeben* as Watch Officer *Silver Liakat Medal 27.12.1915*
Anschütz, Oskar	Lieutenant	Army (Aircrew)	1915/1918	Observation Officer in No 1 Flying Squadron in the Dardanelles

Name	Rank	Branch	Time	Assignment/Function/Awards/Notes
Apel, Kuno	Lieutenant	Navy	1914	Naval Shore Detachment officer on the *Breslau*
Arendt, Franz	Engineer Officer Candidate		1915/1916	Weapons Inspectorate *Died 7.11.1916, buried in Tarabya*
Arendt, Franz	Captain (Stabsarzt)	Army (Medical)	1915/1916	Hospital ship *Reşid Paşa* *Died 7.1.1916, buried in Tarabya; (name on gravestone spelled incorrectly)*
Arimond, Fritz	Sub Lieutenant	Navy	1915/1917	*Goeben*
Arnim, Joachim von	Commander	Navy	1913/1915	Admiral's Staff Officer 1 of Mediterranean Division, German Commander of *Loreley*, *Barbaros Hayrettin* and *Mesudiye*. *EK II May 1915, Osmanie Order 4th Class, Liakat Medal in Gold, Medjidie Order 3rd Class*
Arnold, Ernst	Commander	Navy	1917/1918	As Turkish Lieutenant Colonel, Chief of Staff of Dardanelles Headquarters *Retired in 1920 as Commander*
Arnoldi, Dr. Henrich	Lieutenant	Army		Chemist
Asbeck, Dr. Eduard	Major (Oberstabsarzt)	Army (Medical)	1915/1917	Worked in the main camp of the Naval Shore Detachment on Kilia Tepe from 29.9.15 – 9.11.15; then at the Military Hospital in Istanbul-Harbiye
Aye, Karl	Captain	Army	1915/1918	On the staff for Coastal Defence of the Dardanelles, Commander of Fort Hamidié
Baare	Captain (General Staff)	Prussian Army	1915/1918	Attached Military Mission and worked in the Army and Replacement Departments of the Turkish War Ministry. *Retired as Major*
Babinger, Franz	Second Lieutenant	Army	1914	Orientalist
Bachert	Captain	Army (Territorials)	1915/1916	Employed as metal casting engineer in the Ordnance Department in Constantinople.

Back, Ulrich (Pasha)	Major	Prussian Army	1910/1917	Until 1913, CO of an Officers' Training Camp, then as Turkish Colonel, Commanding Officer of the Turkish War School, from 1914 part of Military Mission; during the fighting on Gallipoli, as a Turkish Major General, Commanding Officer of XVII Army Corps on the Bay of Saros. *In February 1915, treated for a fractured elbow in the German hospital in Istanbul.* *After returning from Turkey, served as a Colonel, he commanded the 16th Infantry Brigade. Ret'd 1920 as a Major General.*
Baden, Friedrich	Sub Lieutenant	Navy	1914/1915	Served on *Breslau*
Bader, Ludwig	Second Lieutenant	Army		Employed in the Weapons Factory in Gülhane (Istanbul)
Baedke, Johannes	Second Lieutenant	Army	1915/1916	Special Command (SoKo), as Turkish Lieutenant, was a section leader in the Anatoli-Kawak battery *Silver Liakat Medal 12.10.1915*
Bahlinger, Johannes	Sub Lieutenant	Navy	1914/1916	Navigation and Signal Officer in Bodrum and Fethiye, served later on the *Goeben*
Baier, Hans	Paymaster	Navy	1916/1917	Special Command (SoKo)
Ballas, Dr. Max	Lieutenant Commander (Marine-Stabsarzt)	Navy (Medical)	1916	Surgeon on the *Breslau*
Baltzer, Hermann	Lieutenant Commander	Navy	1917/1918	Torpedo boat Commander
Bantleon, Ernst	Lieutenant (Marine-Oberingenieur)	Navy (Engineer)	1914/1918	Special Command (SoKo), Engineer working in the Ministry of Marine
Bauer, Cäsar	Lieutenant Commander	Navy	1915/1916	Commander of *UB 46*, on 7 November 1916 sank the sailing ship *Melani* *Born 02.05.1886, died 07.12.1916 on UB 46 in the Black Sea at the entrance to the Bosphorus after hitting a mine. Memorial plaque in Tarabya, Istanbul. The remains of the wreck are displayed in the Naval Museum in Canakkale.*

Name	Rank	Branch	Time	Assignment/Function/Awards/Notes
Baumann, Reinhard	Sub Lieutenant (Marine-Ingenieur)	Navy (Engineer)	1915/1916	Served on *Goeben*
Becker, Franz	Lieutenant	Navy	1916/1917	Commander of *UC 20*
Becker, Gustav	Lieutenant (Marine-Oberingenieur)	Navy (Engineer)	1915/1918	Engineer on the *Goeben*
Becker, Henry	Lieutenant	Army (Aircrew)	1916/1918	No 1 Hydroplane Squadron
Becker, Paul	Lieutenant	Navy (Ordnance)		Ordnance officer on the *Breslau*
Behm, Gustav	Lieutenant	Navy	1916/1918	Naval Shore Detachment of the Mediterranean Division
Bennecke	Lieutenant	Army		Forestry engineer
Bentheim, Egon von	Lieutenant	Navy	1915/1917	As Turkish Lieutenant Commander, Commander of Turkish torpedo boat *Muavenet*. Admirals' Staff Officer 2, Mediterranean Division *EK I 15 January 1916*
Bentmann, Dr. Eugen	Major (Oberstabsarzt)	Army (Medical)	1916/1917	Responsible for all laboratory equipment
Berg, Waldemar	Sub Lieutenant	Navy	1915	From 30.1.1915 Intelligence Officer and special duties in the Military Mission for Balkan countries *EK II August 1915*
Berndt, Kurt	Sub Lieutenant	Navy	1914/1915 1917/1918	I. Lieutenant *Goeben* *Liakat-Medal* Syria
Berndt, Paul	Lieutenant (Marine-Oberingenieur)	Navy	1915/1916	Engineer on *Breslau*, later for the torpedo boot flotilla *EK I 15 January 1916*
Berner, Bruno	Sub Lieutenant	Navy	1914/1916	*Goeben*, then SoKo
Berthold, Karl	Major	Army	1915/1916	On the staff of 5th Army, later Area Commander in Toroslar
Bettaque, Rudolf	Offizierstellvertreter (Acting Commissioned Officer)	Navy	1915/1916	Torpedo specialist, sailed aboard the *Nusret* *EK II April 1915* *died 07.05.1916, buried in Gallipoli, gravestone in Tarabya*
Beutner, Henry	Lieutenant	Ordnance	1915	Special Command (SoKo) *EK II June 1915, returned to Germany in July 1915 due to ill health*
Biedenweg	Lieutenant	Army	1915	Sapper detachment Gallipoli

Biedermann, Paul	Lieutenant (Marine-Oberingenieur)	Navy	1914/1915	*Goeben*
Bieler, Max	Sub Lieutenant	Navy	1914/1915	Crew member of *Goeben*, as Lieutenant special duties in Asia Minor, Commander of the *General*, as Lieutenant Commander, was the German Commander of the torpedo cruiser *Peyk-i Savket* *Medjidie Order 4th Class, Liakat Medal in Silver with Swords*
Bindernagel	Lieutenant	Army	1916/1917	*Seriously injured in a traffic accident on 17 June*
Binhold, Theodor	Captain	Prussian Army	1909/1912	From mid-October 1909, as Turkish Major, Commanding Officer of a model field artillery regiment in Erzincan.
			1914/1915	Attached Military Mission; during the fighting on Gallipoli, Commanding Officer of 3rd Field Artillery Regiment, later in charge of the Southern Group's artillery. Finally as Turkish Lieutenant Colonel, Commanding Officer of the Turkish Field Artillery Firing School, *Treated for influenza in April 1916 in the German hospital in Istanbul.* *Born 24.8.70 in Neheim, entered service 12.3.90, after returning from Turkey with serious heart problems, served in the rank of Captain as Battery Commander of the 59th Field Artillery Regiment. Ret'd as Major; died 1919*
Birk, Erwin	Lieutenant	Army		Engineer
Birn, von	Lieutenant Colonel	Army	1909/1915	Commanding Officer of the Turkish Infantry School
Bischof (Pasha)	Lieutenant Colonel	Prussian Army	1910/1918	Until 1913, latterly, as a Turkish Colonel, Inspector of the Turkish Supply Train; from 1914, attached Military Mission and employed as Major General in Turkish Supreme Headquarters. *Ret'd as Major General; died in 1938*

Name	Rank	Branch	Time	Assignment/Function/Awards/Notes
Bischoff, Josef	Major	Prussian Army	1912/1916	Attached Military Mission; as Turkish Lieutenant Colonel, took part in the Balkan War in charge of the Supply Train; as Colonel, in charge of supply for the 5th Army and later, Commanding Officer of 1st Turkish Camel Regiment in Palestine. *After the War, Commanding Officer of the Baltic "Iron Division"; awarded OPM. Ret'd as Major*
Bischoff, Wegmann	Commander	Navy	1914	Served as an artillery officer in the Dardanelles; relieved due to kidney problems
Blaschke, Ernst	Lieutenant	Army		Engineer
Blell	Captain	Prussian Army	1916/1917	As Turkish Major, on staff of Military Mission and Commanding Officer of a Turkish Depot Regiment in Adana. *Ret'd as Major*
Blume, Dr.	Lieutenant Commander (Marine-Stabsarzt)	Navy (Medical)	1914/1915	*Goeben*
Blumenau, Hermann	War Advisor		1916/1917	Mining Department in the Ministry of War, Istanbul *Died 7.3.1917, buried in Tarabya*
Bluth, Ernst	Sub Lieutenant	Navy	1915/1916	*Goeben*
Bodenstein, Alwin	Lieutenant (Marine-Oberingenieur)	Navy (Engineer)	1914/1916	Crew member of *Goeben;* left Constantinople on 11 December 1915 to build up the Iraq Flotilla under Lieutenant Commander Ney.
Boehringer, Julius	Sub Lieutenant	Navy	1915/1916	Engineer in the Mediterranean Division
Boelcke, Oswald	Captain	Army	1916	Renowned German flying ace paid a morale-boosting visit to Istanbul, Gallipoli and Izmir in July 1916
Boerner, Hans	Sub Lieutenant	Navy	1915/1917	Served aboard *Goeben* und *Breslau*
Böhme, Fritz	Sub Lieutenant	Navy	1915/1918	*Goeben*, later Canakkale und in Syria at Hamadan, then in Istanbul on *UC 75*
Böhmer, Johannes	Paymaster	Navy	1917/1918	*Goeben*

Boltz, Wilhelm	Lieutenant	Navy	1914/1915	Commanded the Naval Shore Detachment in Gallipoli, wounded at Kereves Dere; later in action at Krithia and Ariburnu
			1917	Commanding Officer of Navy Academy at Heybeliada
			1918	As Lieutenant Commander, Commanding Officer of the Euphrates River Detachment
				Ret'd 1920 as Lieutenant Commander
Böning, August	Paymaster	Navy	1915/1918	*Breslau*, then with the Euphrates River Detachment
Borggräfe, Wilhelm	Lieutenant		1915/1918	Special Command (SoKo); artillery officer
Bormann, Fritz	Sub Lieutenant	Navy	1915/1917	Navigation Officer on the torpedo boats *Yadigar* and *Bafra*
			1918	Turkish torpedo boat at Sevastopol
Bormann, Wilhelm	Lieutenant	Army (Aircrew)	1915/1917	Turkish Air Arm
			1917/1918	In Iraq, Flight Commander of the 6th Army
Böttrich, Sylvester	Major	Prussian Army	1914/1917	In peace-time, as Turkish Lieutenant Colonel, Head of the Railway Department of the Turkish General Staff, In war-time, Head of Turkish Field Railways
				After returning from Turkey, Battalion Commander of 30th Infantry Regiment. Ret'd as Lieutenant Colonel; died in 1940
Bötzow, Willi	Captain	Prussian Army	1916/1918	Attached Military Mission; as Turkish Major and Adjutant to General Bischof (Pasha)
				Imperial Army, Air Force Colonel
Boyne	Engineer Officer Candidate (Marine-Ingenieur Aspirant)	Navy	1915/1916	Senior *Aspirant* on *UB 23*
Branconi, Friedrich von	Lieutenant	Navy	1914/1915	Served as Navigation Officer on the *Goeben*
Brandt, Wilhelm	Sub Lieutenant	Navy	1914/1916	1914 Crew member of *Goeben*, as Turkish Lieutenant in the Dardanelles attached mine-sweeping squadron and Battery Officer of the 'Usedom-Battery'.
				EK II 26.7.1915, Silver Liakat Medal 12.10.1915; July 1916 EK I

Name	Rank	Branch	Time	Assignment/Function/Awards/Notes
Brasch, Ernst	Lieutenant Lieutenant Commander	Navy	1914/1915 1916	On staff of mine-laying flotilla; laid minefield in the Gulf of Aqaba. Suez Canal pilot. IV. Watch Officer *Goeben* and with 8th Section of the 1st Sinai Expeditionary Corps *EK II April 1915, EK I August 1916*
Braunert, Dr. Maximillian	Lieutenant (Oberassistenzarzt) Lieutenant Commander (Marine-Stabsarzt)	Navy (Medical)	1915/1916 1917/1918	Ship's doctor on *Goeben* Doctor at the Navy Garrison
Bressel	Sub Lieutenant	Navy	1915	Detachment Officer on *Torgut Reis*
Breuer, Carl	Commander (Marine-Oberstabsingenieur)	Navy (Engineer)	1914/1917	Engineer on the *Goeben*, then Group Engineer for the Mediterranean Division (MMD) *Demob 1919 as Captain (Eng.)*
Brimberg, Franz	Paymaster	Prussian Army	1914/1918	As Turkish Senior Paymaster, served at the Commissariat of the Military Mission and the 1st and 5th Turkish Armies *Demob 1920.*
Brinkmann, Franz	Sub Lieutenant	Navy	1914/1916 1916/1918	Served on *Breslau*, *Barbaros Hayrettin* and *Turgut Reis* Permanent staff of U-Boat Flotilla Iraq and Palestine as Adjutant
Brodosotti, Hermann	Major	Army	1915/1916	Field Railway Inspectorate Istanbul, *Treated during January/February 1916 in the German hospital for lung catarrh.* *Born 9.8.68 in Löwenberg/Schlesien, commissioned 1.4.1889*
Bronner, Rudolf	Sub Lieutenant (Marine-Ingenieur)	Navy (Engineer)	1916	*Breslau*
Brümmer-Städt, Bruno	Sub Lieutenant (Marine-Ingenieur)	Navy (Engineer)	1915	*Breslau*
Brüning, Fritz Prof. Dr.	Major (Oberstabsarzt)	Army (Medical)	1916/1917	Military Mission, Lecturer in Gülhane
Brünn, W. Dr.	Major (Oberstabsarzt)	Army (Medical)	1915/1917	Often detailed to Military Mission as bacteriologist in a laboratory
Buchardi, Theodor	Lieutenant Colonel	Army	1915	

Büchsel, Ernst	Commander	Navy	1914/1918	2. Admiral Staff Officer Mediterranean Division (MMD), German Commander of *Mecidiye*, latterly in the Personnel Department of the Turkish Ministry of Marine *Demob. 1919 as Captain*
Buddecke, Hans Joachim	Lieutenant	Army (Aircrew)	1915/1917	As Turkish Captain, CO of No 1 Flying Squadron on Gallipoli *Born 1890, 8 kills in the territory of the Ottoman Empire and thus the most successful fighter pilot, nicknamed "El Sahin", (the "Hawk"). Killed 10 March 1918 near Lille, buried in Berlin, Liakat Medal, OPM* *Book: "El Schahin – Der Jagdfalke"*
Buddenbrock, Friedrich Wilhelm Freiherr von	Lieutenant	Navy	1917/1918	Special Command (SoKo), No 1 Hydroplane Flight on Gallipoli
Buhlan, Willy	Captain	Army	1916/1918	Special Command (SoKo); Naval Shore Detachment, later Adjutant to Admiral v. Usedom
Bultmann, Johannes	Lieutenant		1914/1918	Special Command (SoKo) Artillery officer
Bünte, Walter	Lieutenant	Army		Building engineer
Buntebardt, Hans	Sub Lieutenant	Navy	1914/1916	Navigation Officer on *U21*
Burchardi	Preuß. Intendanturrat		1913/1918	Military Mission, In peace-time as Turkish Lieutenant Colonel with the Turkish General Commissariat, In war-time, assigned to the 5th Army Commissariat in the Dardanelles. *Demob 1919*
Bürklein, Reinhold	Sub Lieutenant	Navy	1918	*Goeben*
Busse, Wilhelm	Commander	Navy	1914/1915	1st Admiral Staff Officer Mediterranean Division und Head of the Iraq Naval Detachment *Medjidie-Order 3. Class, Imtiaz Medal in Silver with Swords. Demob. 1920 as Captain*
Bydekarken, Rudolf	Sub Lieutenant (Marine-Ingenieur)	Navy (Engineer)	1915/1917	*Breslau*

Name	Rank	Branch	Time	Assignment/Function/Awards/Notes
Carls, Rolf	Lieutenant Commander	Navy	1914/1916	1st Gunnery and Watch Officer *Breslau*, took part in the fighting on the Gallipoli Peninsula *Born 1885, EK I- 15.5.1915, Osmanie-Order 4. Class, later Imperial Navy, Grand Admiral Knight's Cross to EK. Died 1945*
Carmer, Graf von	Major	Army	1915/1917	Military Mission und later with the 5th Army
Cederholm, Swen	Lieutenant Commander	Navy	1914	Commander of auxiliary cruiser *Corcovado* and Turkish mine layer *Nilüfer* *Killed in 1914 when the Nilüfer sank.*
Chelius, Oskar von	Lieutenant General	Army	1916	Adjutant General, visited Istanbul in 1916, to present the Sultan with a sabre of honour as a gift from Kaiser Wilhelm II. *Gest. 1923*
Christoph	Acting Commissioned Officer (Offiziersstellvertreter)		1915/1916	Special Command (SoKo) *Awarded Silver Liakat Medal 12.10.1915*
Collin, Rudolf Prof. Dr.	Captain (Oberstabsarzt)	Prussian Army (Medical)	1915/1918	As Turkish Lieutenant Colonel, attached Military Mission and Senior Sanitation Officer of the Military Mission. *Treated in July 1916 in the German hospital in Istanbul. Born 28.9.1873 in Danzig, commissioned 1.4.1892.*
Conn, Bruno	Commander	Navy	1914/1916	Commanded the minesweeper *Taschos* during the fleet action against Russia in October 1914; CO of the 2nd Turkish torpedo boat Half flotilla; then as Turkish Lieutenant Colonel, Commanding Officer of German Navy Department in the Dardanelles *Silver Imtiaz Medal 12.10.1915, EK I. March 1916* *Demob. 1920 as Captain*
Conrad, Alfred	Lieutenant		1915/1917 1918	Straits Command Canakkale Special Command (SoKo)

Cramer, Hubert Graf von	Major	Prussian Army	1915/1916	Military Mission as Turkish Lieutenant Colonel and 5th Army High Command. *Was treated in November 1915 in the German hospital in Istanbul.* *Born 12.7.65 in Potsdam, commissioned 1.9.15*
Crienitz	Captain	Army	1915/1916	CO of 2nd Turkish 15cm Howitzer Battery, as successor to Major Mannert. *He also came down with typhus*
Croneiss, Carl	Lieutenant	Army (Aircrew)	1915/1918	Croneiss was posted to the German Military Mission in Constantinople in 1915: In the subsequent war years, served as a pilot in the Ottoman Air Arm, first as a Captain of the Turkish Flying Squadron in Chernahevicz, later with No 1 Squadron at the Dardanelles. Posted in 1916 to No 2 Squadron in Bagdad and Persia. In 1918, appointed Commanding Officer of the Turkish Flying School in San Stefano near Constantinople *Born 9 January 1891 in Bad Dürkheim; died 31 July 1973 in Nürnberg. Awarded Imtiaz, Liakat & Mecidiye Medals.*
Croneiss, Theodor Jakob	Lieutenant	Army (Aircrew)	1915/1918	Pilot with No 1 Squadron at the Dardanelles *Credited with 5 kills on Ottoman Territory, Liakat Medal*
Cummerow	Captain	Prussian Army	1915/1916	Inspector of the *Etappe* (LoC) with the 6th Turkish Army *Reichswehr, Ret'd as Colonel*
Danz, Kurt	Senior Navy Paymaster (Marine Stabszahlmeister)	Navy	1914/1918	Administration Special Command (SoKo) and Turkish Ministry of Marine
Deckert	Captain	Navy	1916/1918	
Deckert, Karl	Sub Lieutenant	Navy	1915/1918	*Goeben* and *Breslau*, later Syria
Deetjen, Hermann	Sub Lieutenant	Navy	1917/1918	*Breslau* *Killed 20 January 1918 during the sinking of the Breslau near Imbros*
Dekerr	Deputy Lieutenant Commander (Hilfskapitänleutnant)	Navy	1915	Mediterranean Division; coal supplies and transportation

Name	Rank	Branch	Time	Assignment/Function/Awards/Notes
Detleffsen	Captain	Army	1915	Commanding Officer of heavy artillery in the Northern Group
Detten, von	Captain	Prussian Army	1915/1916	As Turkish Major, Military Mission and Commanding Officer of a Turkish Depot Regiment near Istanbul *Later Colonel*
Deveroff	Lieutenant	Army		Railway Liaison Command in Mardin
Dewitz, Albrecht von	Lieutenant	Navy	1915/1916	Commander of *UC 15* und *UC 25* *Missing November 1916 on UC 25*
Deym, Graf von	Sub Lieutenant	Navy	1915/1916	Attached Naval Shore Detachment as observation officer
Diesinger	Lieutenant	Army	1915/1919	Artillery Officer with XVI Army corps, under Major Willmer on Gallipoli as OC of the 614th Howitzer Battery (12cm) part of 1st Artillery Battalion. Commanded the *Ethna Rickmers* during the German evacuation of Istanbul in 1919
Dinnendahl, Gustav	Sub Lieutenant (Marine-Ingenieur)	Navy (Engineer)	1915/1918	IV. Watch Engineer *Goeben*
Dohrn, Rudolf	Sub Lieutenant	Navy	1915/1918	Mine Command
Domeier, Wilhelm	Paymaster		1914/1917	Special Command (SoKo), later in Canakkale
Döninghaus, Friedrich	Lieutenant	Army	1916	Agricultural school in Burgas. *Treated during August/September 1916 in the German hospital in Istanbul for dysentery. Born 5.9.1869 in Barmen, commissioned 1.10.91*
Dönitz, Karl	Sub Lieutenant	Navy	1914/1916	Officer on the *Breslau* and Navy Flying Squadron, *EK I. 5 May 1916. Born 1891, married the daughter of General Weber in Istanbul. Later Grand Admiral who signed unconditional surrender on 8 May 1945. Died 1980* *Book: "Die Kreuzerfahrten der Goeben und Breslau"*

Dörflein	Lieutenant	Navy	1915/1917	Inspectorate of Arms and Munitions in Constantinople, responsible for accounting and procurement. *Killed when the Halic sank on 27 May 1917.*
Dorndeck, Willi	Lieutenant	Navy (Torpedos)	1916/1918	Special Command (SoKo); Mines and Torpedo Officer
Dressel, Hans	Sub Lieutenant	Navy	1914/1915	Served on *Goeben* and *Turgut Reis* *Awarded EK II in April 1915*
Dümmel, Dr. Paul	Lieutenant Commander (Marine-Stabsarzt)	Navy (Medical)	1917/1918	Worked in the main camp of the Naval Shore Detachment on Kilia Tepe from October 1917 to 7 May 1918
Eberhard, Simon	Captain	Army (Aircrew)	1915/1916	Turkish Air Arm
Ebert, Georg	Lieutenant	Army	1915/1916	Field railways. *Treated during February 1916 in the German hospital in Istanbul.* *Born 24.2.84 in Stettin, commissioned 17.4.1901*
Eccardt, Hans	Paymaster	Navy	1917/1918	*Goeben*
Eckerlein, Adolf	Lieutenant Commander (Marine-Stabsingenieur)	Navy (Engineer)	1915/1916	German Engineer on board *Turgut Reis*
Effnert, Alexander	Captain	Prussian Army	1914/1918	As Turkish Major, in peace-time Commanding Officer of an Engineer Battalion in Istanbul; in war-time, Commanding Officer of the Engineers in the Southern Group in the Dardanelles. Served later in Palestine. *Ret'd 1920 as Major*
Eggert	Captain	Prussian Army	1914/1918	In peace-time, as Turkish Major, instructor at the Turkish War Academy; in war-time, as Major, Corps Chief of General Staff, then Commanding Officer of the 25th Turkish Infantry Division in Romania. *After returning from Turkey as Major, then Chief of General Staff 51ˢᵗ Command. Ret'd as Lieutenant Colonel, died 1939*

Name	Rank	Branch	Time	Assignment/Function/Awards/Notes
Eggert, Karl Hans	Lieutenant	Army	1915/1916	16th Foot Artillery Regiment, Anafarta Group (Ismail Tepe). *Treated during November/December 1915 in the German hospital in Istanbul for dysentery. Born 9.1.87 in Kiel, commissioned 1.8.14*
Ehlers, Erich	Lieutenant (Marine-Oberingenieur)	Navy (Engineer)	1914/1917	Engineer on the *Goeben*
Ehrensberger	Lieutenant	Navy	1916	Mediterranean Division (MMD)
Ehringer	Lieutenant	Army	1915	Pilot during fighting on the Suez canal
Ehringhaus	Major	Army	1915/1916	OC Engineer Battalion on Gallipoli
Eicke, Franz	Lieutenant	Army (Aircrew)	1917/1918	Observer in No 1 Squadron at Gallipoli
Eiffe, Peter Ernst	Lieutenant Commander	Navy	1915/1916	Commander of *UB 42*
Ellendt, Renatus	Lieutenant Commander	Navy	1915/1916	Commander of the gunboat *Taschküpru*, *Court-martialled for collision with the pilot boat Kicabet on 4 May 1915, which sank. Acquitted. EK II August 1915, Silver Imtiaz Medal 27.12.1915*
Endres, Franz Carl	Captain	Bavarian Army	1912/1918	Until 1913, as Turkish Major, instructor at the Turkish War Academy; from 1914 Military Mission, then as Turkish Lieutenant Colonel, Departmental Head in the General Staff *Born 1878, Liakat Medal, Medjidie Order, demob1920 as Major. As a journalist, wrote over 40 books especially about Freemasons. Died in 1954. Book: "Die Türkei. Bilder und Skizzen von Land und Volk"*
Endruck	Lieutenant	Bavarian Army	1915/1917	Adjutant to Lieutenant Colonel Hans von Kiesling
Engelbrecht, John	Sub Lieutenant (Marine-Ingenieur)	Navy (Engineer)	1917/1918	*Breslau*
Engelking, Oskar	Lieutenant Commander	Navy	1915/1916	Special Command (SoKo); later Commander of the gunboat *Doghan* on the Tigris *EK II June 1915*

Eschenbrenner, Dr. Hugo	Lieutenant (Marine-Oberassistenzarzt)	Navy (Medical)	1918	*Breslau* *Killed 20.1.1918 off Imbros on board the Breslau*
Essig, Dr. Karl	Lieutenant (Marine-Oberassistenzarzt)	Navy (Medical)	1915	*Breslau*, later worked in Joseph Hospital in Istanbul
Falkenberg, Werner von	Major	Prussian Army (on General Staff)	1914/1915	As Turkish Lieutenant Colonel; in war-time Chief of the General Staff of the 4th Army
Falkenhausen, Alexander von	Major	Prussian Army (on General Staff)	1916/1918	As Turkish Lieutenant Colonel, Military Mission and then as Colonel, Chief of the General Staff 7th Turkish Army. At the end of the war, on the Embassy staff in Istanbul. *Born 29.10.1878 in Silesia, before the War, Military Attaché in Japan, later awarded OPM. Died 1966.*
Faller	Lieutenant	Army (Aircrew)	1915/1916	As Turkish Captain, served as a pilot on Gallipoli und Izmir *In 1914, former flying teacher of Oswald Boelcke in Darmstadt*
Fanger	Lieutenant	Navy	1916	*Breslau*
Fehlandt, Dr.	Captain (Stabsarzt)	Army (Medical)	1915/1917	Surgeon
Feldbausch, Hans	Sub Lieutenant	Navy	1914/1915	II. Lieutenant *Goeben*
Feldmann, Otto von	Major	Prussian Army	1913/1918	As Turkish Lieutenant Colonel, in peace-time Chief of the Mobilisation Dept; member on the staff of Admiral von Usedom. In war-time, Chief of General Staff of the 1st Army, latterly Operations Dept of Turkish General Staff. *Did not believe the estimation made after a reconnaissance flight by Major Siegert, that the Allies were withdrawing from Gallipoli.* *After returning from Turkey as Lieutenant Colonel, served as Commanding Officer of an Infantry Battalion on the Western Front. Demob 1920 as Lieutenant Colonel.*
Fenner, Arthur	Lieutenant Commander (Marine-Stabsingenieur)	Navy (Engineer)	1915	Senior Engineer on *Hamidiye*

Name	Rank	Branch	Time	Assignment/Function/Awards/Notes
Fenski	Captain	Army	1915/1916	Artillery Commander in XVI Army Corps. *Treated during October 1915 in the German hospital in Istanbul for dysentery.*
Fièvet, Dr. Karl	Lieutenant Commander (Marine-Stabsarzt)	Navy (Medical)	1914/1917	Doctor on *Breslau;* worked from 2.8.15 – 13.10.15 in the main camp of the Naval Shore Detachment on Kilia Tepe; later at the Joseph Hospital in Istanbul. *EK II May 1915*
Fircks, Wilhelm Freiherr von	Lieutenant Commander	Navy	1915	Mediterranean Division (MMD), as Commander of the torpedo boat *Timur Hissar* conducted an independent six-week sortie during March/April 1915 in the enemy-held Aegean Sea., Assigned on 27 November 1915 as courier to Berlin. *Turkish War Medal, killed May 1917*
Firle, Rudolph	Lieutenant Commander	Navy	1914/1915	Commander of the 1st Turkish Torpedo Boat Half Flotilla, Commander of the Turkish torpedo boat *Muavenet Millie*; on 13 May 1915, as Commander torpedoed and sank the English battleship HMS *Goliath* in Morto Bay. Later assigned special duties in Bulgaria. *Gold Liakat Medal with Sabres, Silver Imtiaz Medal with Sabres, EK I. Born 14.12.188; married in Istanbul, demob. 1920 as Commander, later Chairman of Norddeutscher Lloyd.*
Fischer	Captain	Prussian Army	1914/1916	As Turkish Major, Military Mission and later on staff of General v. Kress in Palestine.
Fischer	Lieutenant	Wuerttemberg Army	1914/1918	Latterly as Turkish Major. Adjutant to the Chief of the General Staff of the 5th Army *After returning from Turkey, served as Lieutenant General and Division Commander in the Reichsheer. Died 1938.*

Flaccus, Ludwig	Lieutenant	Navy	1915/1916	Special Command (SoKo); Naval Shore Detachment *Killed 14.7.1916 in Mosul*
Flebbe, Dr. Johannes	Captain (Stabsarzt)	Army (Medical)	1915/1916	MO on Gallipoli
Flecken, G.	Lieutenant	Navy (Legal Service)		Navy Lawyer aboard *Goeben*
Flegel, Dr.	Marine-Kriegsgerichtsrat	Navy	1914/1915	1. Magistrate of the Mediterranean Division (MMD)
Fleischhauer, Max	Senior Navy Paymaster	Navy	1915/1918	Senior accountant to Mediterranean Division (MMD)
Fränkel	Lieutenant	Army (Aircrew)	1916/1917	Pilot in Diyarbakir
Franz, Wolf	Lieutenant Commander	Navy	1915/1916	As III. Gunnery Officer on the *Goeben*
Freese, Johann	(Deputy) Lieutenant	Navy	1915/1916	Coal supplies and transportation *EK II 23.1.1916, EK I 11.7.1916, died on 29.8.1916 in Cerablus after a short illness.*
Frege, Konrad	Lieutenant	Navy		Commander of a Turkish torpedo boat, then in Canakkale Artillery Commander in the forts at Ertrogul and Hamidié *Was shot at on 27 September 1914 by English ships, which led to the closing of the Dardanelles; EK II 20.9.1915*
Freudenberg, Walther	Lieutenant Commander	Navy	1914/1918	Navigation Officer *Goeben* *Liakat Medal*
Freund, Alfred	Second Lieutenant	Army	1916/1918	Special Command (SoKo); Artillery Officer in the forts Hamidié, Seddulbahr and Canakkale
Freutel, Johann	Second Lieutenant	Army (Ordnance)	1915/1916	As Turkish Lieutenant in the Armaments Office *EK II 27.1.1916*
Freyberg, Freiherr von	Commander	Navy	1914	Instructor on *Hamidije*
Freye	Lieutenant	Navy	1914	Artillery Officer in the Special Command (SoKo); was so severely wounded on the lower arm from a shot by another German soldier whilst unloading, that he had to be relieved.
Fricks, Wilhelm Freiherr von	Lieutenant Commander	Navy	1914/1915	Commander of Turkish Torpedo Boat Flotilla *Killed in 1917 at Hornsriff on U 54*

Name	Rank	Branch	Time	Assignment/Function/Awards/Notes
Fries, Franz	Captain	Army	1916/1918	Accountant
Fritzsche	Captain	Army	1916/1918	Engineer responsible for controlling ore deliveries to Germany.
Froese, Martin	Lieutenant	Army	1915/1916	Coastal Inspectorate *EK II. January 1916*
Fugger, Dr. Graf zu Glött	Marine-Kriegsgerichtsrat	Navy (Legal)	1914/1915	2. Magistrate of the Mediterranean Division (MMD)
Fünfhausen	Lieutenant	Army (Aircrew)	1916/1918	Pilot in the Hydroplane Squadron on Gallipoli.
Gabler	Lieutenant	Army	1914	Military Mission
Gäckle, Immanuel	Sub Lieutenant (Marine-Ingenieur)	Navy (Engineer)	1914/1917	Engineer on the *Breslau* *EK I August 1916*
Galen, Maximilian Graf von	Lieutenant	Army	1914/1916	Garrison Command Istanbul, later Adjutant to Lieutenant Colonel Falkenhausen in Palestine. *Treated during June 1916 in the German hospital in Istanbul for intestinal catarrh. Born 30.4.92 in Bevesundern, commissioned 30.9.1911, died 13.2.1960*
Gansser, Konrad	Lieutenant Commander	Navy	1914/1917	Commander of *U 33* *Demob 1919 as Lieutenant Commander*
Garber	Lieutenant	Army (Aircrew)		Air Arm Pilot at Canakkale
Garke, Rudolf	Captain	Prussian Army	1916/1917	OC Railway Special Command 2 *Born 23.10.1874, died. 02.05.1917 in Istanbul, buried in Tarabya*
Gebler, Theodor	Lieutenant	Navy	1914/1915	Special Command (SoKo); Platoon Leader of Naval Shore Detachment
Gehl, Paul	Lieutenant Commander (Torpedo-Kapitän)	Navy (Ordnance)	1915/1916	As Turkish Lieutenant Colonel attached Engineer Corps in the High Command of the Straits as specialist for underwater weapons and mines. Was aboard the *Nusret* on 7 March 1915 *Turkish War Medal 9.11.1915, Silver Imtiaz Medal 27.12.1915, repatriated in September 1916 due to wife's illness, demob. 1918*
Georgi, Dr.	Lieutenant	Army	1915/1916	Attached to No 1 Flying Squadron on Gallipoli; afterwards as meteorologist with Flying Detachment 300 "Pasha" of the German Asia Corps in Palestine.

| Gerdts, Johannes | Lieutenant | Navy | 1915/1917 1917/1918 | Commander of Turkish torpedo boot

Sea command Derince, afterwards Commander of torpedo boat *Bafra*, later Sevastopol |
|---|---|---|---|---|
| Gerlach, Johannes | Lieutenant | Navy | 1914/1915 | *Goeben* |
| Gerlach, Johannes | Lieutenant | Prussian Army | 1914/1918 | In peace-time, as Turkish captain, company commander of a Turkish Engineer Battalion. In war-time, Intelligence Officer for III. Reconnaissance Regiment in 3rd Corps

Finally, Commanding Officer of 307 Engineer Bn. 1920 Demob as major. |
| Gesche, Hans | Paymaster | Navy | 1914/1916 | *Goeben* and *Breslau* |
| Giebeler, Werner | Lieutenant Commander | Navy | 1915/1917 | Navigation Officer *Goeben* |
| Gies, Jacob | Sub Lieutenant (Marine-Ingenieur) | Navy (Engineer) | 1914/1915 1915/1917 1918 | Engineer on the *Goeben*

On Engine Training Ship *Muin-i-Zafer* and *Tiri-Müjgan*

Instructor |
| Giese, Dietrich | Sub Lieutenant (Marine-Ingenieur) | Navy (Engineer) | 1915/1917 1918 | *Goeben* and Turkish torpedo boat

Euphrates River Detachment |
| Giese, Max | Lieutenant | Army (Ordnance) | 1915/1918 | As Turkish lieutenant colonel, Military Mission and Munitions Directorate.

Treated during October/ November 1915 and 1916 for stomach problems in the German hospital in Istanbul. Born 25.5.76 in Memel/ East Prussia, Commissioned 14.10.1897, Demob as Lieutenant Colonel |
Giloi, Fritz	Sub Lieutenant (Marine-Ingenieur)	Navy (Engineer)	1914/1915	*Goeben*
Glahn, Walter	Sub Lieutenant	Navy	1914/1918	Civil servant in Canakkale; Minesweeper Squadron in Istanbul, then Torpedo Boat Flotilla
Gloger, Max	Lieutenant Commander (Marine-Oberzahlmeister)	Navy	1914/1915	Paymaster *Goeben*
Göebel, Dr. Alfons	Captain (Stabsarzt)		1915/1917	Mediterranean Division (MMD), assigned in Canakkale

Name	Rank	Branch	Time	Assignment/Function/Awards/Notes
Goltz, Colmar Freiherr von der (Pasha)	Lieutenant Colonel	Prussian Army	1883/1893	As Turkish major general and lieutenant general, Inspector General of Turkish Military Training and Education; as Turkish Marshal, successor to Kähler Pasha as Head of Mission and Deputy Head of the Turkish General Staff. After returning from Turkey, command 6th Infantry Division as lieutenant general.
	Colonel General		1909/1913	As Turkish Marshal, Head of the German Army Reformation Officers sent to Turkey, 1908/1909 and 1910 in a special mission to oversee manoeuvers in Turkey,
	General Field Marshal		1915/1916	Supreme Commander of the 6th Turkish Army
				Born 1843, Osmanie-Order, Medjidie-Order, died 19.04.1916 from typhus in Bagdad.
				Buried in Istanbul-Tarabya
				Books: "Der Thessalische Krieg and die türkische Army"; "Denkwürdigkeiten"; "Anatolische Ausflüge"; "Bilder aus der türkischen Army"
Görth, Wilhelm	Paymaster	Navy	1914/1916	*Breslau* and *General*
Gössel, Konrad	Sub Lieutenant	Navy	1914/1916	Special Command (SoKo), as Turkish lieutenant, Section Chief in the Dardanelles at Seddulbahr
				Silver Liakat Medal 12.10.1915,
				EK I July 1916
Goullon, Kurt	Second Lieutnant	Army (Ordnance)	1915/1918	Special Command (SoKo); later Armaments Bureau
Grabau, Karl August	Lieutenant Commander	Navy	1914/1915	1. Officer *Breslau*, German Commander of *Mecidiye*, Commander of *Breslau*
				Demob 1920 as commander
Grabe, Hans	Marine-Stabsingenieur (Lieutenant Commander)	Navy (Engineer)	1915/1918	Senior Engineer *Breslau*
				EK I 27. August 1915, killed 20.1.1918 at Imbros when Breslau sank
Graetz	Major	Army (Aircrew)	1916/1918	Head of flying training at the Flying School in San Stefano.

Greßmann, Oscar (Pasha)	Colonel	Prussian Army	1915/1917	As Turkish Major General, Military Mission and Artillery Commander of the 5th Army in the Dardanelles. Then as Prussian major general, in command of the German Iraq Forces in the Sixth Army, as well as the LoC Inspectorate in Aleppo. *Ret'd as lieutenant general*
Griesinger, Alfred	Lieutenant Commander	Navy	1915/1918	As Turkish major of Heavy Artillery; 2. Admirals Staff Officer with Admiral von Usedom's Coastal Inspectorate *Turkish War Medal, EK II 12.1.1916*
Grimm Eberhard	Lieutenant	Army	1915/1916	Military Mission, 3rd Turkish Field Howitzer Battery. *Treated during June/July 1916 in the German hospital in Istanbul for a gunshot wound on his left forearm, received on 16 June 1916 in Eskishir. Born 26.4.94 in Berlin, Commissioned 11.3.14*
Grimm, Anton	Lieutenant	Army	1915/1916	Military Mission, later German Asia Corps Palestine; Transportation Command at Kunetra
Gröger, Wilhelm	Second Lieutenant	Army (Aircrew)	1914/1917	Special Command (SoKo); No 1 Hydroplane Flight *EK I September 1916, drowned in the Bosphorus on 8.9.1917 near Istanbul.*
Gronemann, Alfred	Sub Lieutenant (Marine-Ingenieur)	Navy (Engineer)	1914/1915 / 1915/1918	*Breslau* / Director of a Turkish rifle and ammunition factory
Grundner, Wilhelm	Lieutenant	Army		Military Mission, 16th Turkish Engineer Battalion. *Treated during August/September 1916 in the German hospital in Istanbul. Born 9.4.1887 in Kempten, Commissioned July 1907*
Grüter, Paul	Sub Lieutenant (Marine-Ingenieur)	Navy (Engineer)	1915/1916	*UB 7* *Killed on 27.10.1916 in the Black Sea*
Grützmacher	Kriegsgerichtsrat	Army (Legal)	1915/1918	Judge Advocate, conducted courts-martial on behalf of the Head of the Military Mission.
Gülpen, von	Captain	Prussian Army	1915/1917	As Turkish major, Military Mission and LoC Inspector for Third Turkish Army.

Name	Rank	Branch	Time	Assignment/Function/Awards/ Notes
Günther	Major	Prussian Army	1916/1917	As Turkish lieutenant colonel, Military Mission and Commanding Officer of a Turkish Engineer battalion. *Ret'd as major*
Günther, Albin	Sub Lieutenant	Navy (Ordnance)	1916/1917	Special Command (SoKo), specialist for mines and torpedoes.
Haaring, Kurt	Officer Candidate (Offizierstellvertreter)	Army (Aircrew)	1915/1918	Air Arm pilot in Gallipoli *Died on 17 August 1918 as a result of a gunshot wound received during aerial combat.*
Haas, Arthur von	Lieutenant Commander	Navy	1914/1918	Intelligence Officer Mediterranean Division and LoC Command. *EK II August 1915*
Haber	Captain	Army		Worked for the Commission for Coal and Raw Materials Procurement in Istanbul.
Haehnert, Fjador	Captain	Army	1915	Commanding Officer of 1st Artillery Battalion of XVI. Army Corps on Gallipoli. *Treated for dysentery in October 1915 in the German hospital in Istanbul. Born 1887, 5 Batteries with German COs*
Haentjens, Peter	Lieutenant	Army	1915/1916	Special Command (SoKo), as Turkish captain, Battery Commander of the *Goeben's* 8,8cm SK battery at In Tepe/Dardanelles *Silver Liakat-Medal 12.10.1915, contracted rheumatism and transferred to a sanatorium in Germany.*
Hagen, Karl Wilhelm von dem	Lieutenant	Prussian Army	1914/1915	As Turkish captain, in peace-time Commanding Officer of the Turkish Gymnastic Centre, war-time post as Intelligence Officer with the 1st reconnaissance regiment in the Dardanelles, then served in Palestine. *Killed in February 1915 on the Suez Canal. The British buried him on the banks of the Canal.*
Hagendorf, Otto	Lieutenant Commander	Navy	1915/1918	Commander of Turkish mine-sweeper on the Bosphorus.
Hahn	Lieutenant	Army		Engineer in Istanbul.
Hajessen, Richard	Lieutenant	Army	1915/1917	Special Command (SoKo), artillery officer.

Hammer	Captain	Army		Artillery officer in the Dardanelles, CO of 614 Art Batt.
Hammerstein-Eduard, Karl von	Lieutenant	Army		Engineer.
Hannemann, Ludwig	Sub Lieutenant (Marine-Ingenieur)	Navy (Engineer)	1916/1918	*Breslau* *Became a British PoW after the Breslau went down.*
Harbuval gen. Charmaré, Archibald Graf von	Lieutenant Commander	Navy	1915	Commander of U-Boat trap *Dere* and Jan 1916, platoon commander in the Naval Shore Detachment. *Born 3 July 1882 in Stolz, died from dysentery on 12 August 1916 in Beirut, EK II December 1915,*
Hashagen, Eduard	Sub Lieutenant	Navy	1915/1916 1917	Assigned to the Dardanelles and in the mine-sweeping Division took part in the search for *UB 46* Adjutant to Commander of the Mine-sweeping Flotilla. *EK II April 1916*
Hauck, Karl Walter	Lieutenant	Army	1916/1917	1916 on the staff of von der Goltz, later air observer with Flight Detachment 304b *Treated for recurrent fever during April 1916 in the German hospital in Istanbul. Born 5.6.88 in Steinau, commissioned 16.8.14. On 29.1.1918, he was on a flying sortie as observer, he landed the aircraft successfully after the pilot was killed. Subsequently British PoW in Egypt.*
Havik	Colonel	Army	1915	GOC of 13th Division.
Heiberg	Captain	Army	1915	German Military Mission Istanbul.
Heibey	Second Lieutenant	Prussian Army	1914/1918	In peace-time, as Turkish captain, battery commander of a model battalion of Turkish Heavy Artillery; in war-time, as Turkish major, artillery commanding officer of a Turkish Division in Palestine. *Demob 1920 as major.*
Heidler, Otto	Paymaster	Navy	1914/1917 1918	Special Command (SoKo). Torpedo boat flotilla.
Heilige	Lieutenant Commander	Navy	1915/1917	Commander of *UB 7*.
Heiling, Peter	Sub Lieutenant	Navy	1915/1916	*U 46* *Died 7.12.1916, buried in Tarabya.*

Name	Rank	Branch	Time	Assignment/Function/Awards/Notes
Heilingbrunner, Friedrich	Second Lieutenant	Bavarian Army	1915/1917	As Turkish captain, Military Mission and commander of a heavy Turkish artillery battery on Gallipoli, later on the Caucasus front. *Born 5.10.1891 in Bamberg, later Reichswehr, General of Flak Artillery, died 1977 in Edling-Wasserburg.*
Heimburg, Heino von	Lieutenant	Navy	1915/1916	Commander of *UB 14*
			1916/1917	Commander of *UC 22*
			1917/1918	Commander of *UB 68*
			1918	Commander of *U 35* *Born 1879, OPM 1917, 1933 fortress commander of Cuxhaven, Vice Admiral, died 1945 in Stalingrad; Book: 'U-Boot gegen U-Boot'.*
Heine, Hans	Lieutenant (Marine-Ingenieur)	Navy (Engineer)	1914/1916	Chief engineer on *U 21*.
Heinemann-Gründer, Dr. Curt	Major (Oberstabsarzt)	Army (Medical)	1916/1918	Fifth Army
Heinke, Curt von	Lieutenant	Navy	1914/1916	Signals Officer on the staff of *Goeben*, later on *UB 7* and radio station Black Sea. *EK I. November 1915, presumed killed near Sevastopol when UB 7 was sunk.*
Heinrich, Max	Captain	Prussian Army	1916/1917	Commanding Officer of Motor Transport Unit 500. *Ret'd as major.*
Heintze, Baron von	Major	Prussian Army	1916/1917	As Turkish lieutenant colonel, Military Mission and High Command of Fifth Army. *Liakat-Medal*
Heller, Bruno von	Lieutenant	Navy	1915/1916	Commander of *UC 38* and *UC 15* During his visit in 1917, Boelcke reported that he was accompanied by a Lt Heller in Constantinople. *Missing on UC 15 in the Black Sea in 1916.*

Heller, Hans, Georg, Wilhelm	Lieutenant	Army	1915	On the staff of the Fifth Army on Gallipoli *Born 20.12.1892 in Wolfenbüttel, EK II, died of dysentery and meningitis on 18.07.1915 in the German hospital in Istanbul, buried in Tarabya.*
Helling, Karl	Lieutenant Commander	Navy	1915	*Killed 28.5.1915, buried in Tarabya.*
Hendricks, Wilhelm	Second Lieutenant			Engineer
Henkelburg, Hans	Lieutenant	Army (Aircrew)	1915	Pilot during the fighting at the Suez Canal.
Hensel, Hans	Major	Army	1915/1918	Responsible for Forces Postal Services in Istanbul.
Hepp, Wilhelm	Sub Lieutenant (Marine-Ingenieur)	Navy (Engineer)	1914/1917	*Breslau*, then engineer for the Torpedo Boat Flotilla. Dockyard chief in Istiniye (Stenia). *Died on 9.10.1917*
Hering, Adolf	Lieutenant (Marine-Ingenieur)	Navy (Engineer)	1915/1917	Engineer for the Torpedo Boat Flotilla, later *Goeben*.
Hermann, Johannes	Second Lieutenant	Army	1915/1916	Special Command (SoKo), as Turkish lieutenant of Heavy Artillery; Head of the Staff Division and Chairman of the Personnel Office. *EK I 15 January 1916*
Hermann, Peter	Lieutenant Commander	Navy	1914	Commander of the Turkish mine-layer *Samsun*
			1915	III. Watch Officer *Goeben* and as Duty Watch Officer, averted being torpedoed on 14 November 1915. *EK II 1915*
Herschel, Heinrich	Second Lieutenant	Army	1915/1918	As Turkish captain, Company Commander and 2 I/C of the Training Battery of Fort Hamidié. *EK II 26.3.1915, Silver Liakat Medal, 31.3.1915, Silver Imtiaz Medal 12.10.1915, EK I 14.10.1915*
Hersing, Otto	Lieutenant Commander	Navy	1915/1918	Commander of *U 21*. *Born 1885; on 25 May 1915 torpedoed and sank the battleship HMS Triumph and HMS Majestic on 27 May 1915.* *Liakat-Medal in Silver with Sabres, OPM 5.6.1915, demob 1918 as commander. Died 1960. Book: 'U 21 rettet die Dardanelles'.*

Name	Rank	Branch	Time	Assignment/Function/Awards/Notes
Herz, Franz	Captain	Army		Military judge
Hesselberger	Lieutenant	Army (Aircrew)	1915/1918	Aircraft pilot.
Heuck, Albert (Pasha)	Lieutenant Colonel	Prussian Army	1914/1918	In peace-time, as Turkish colonel, Commanding Officer of Turkish 13th Infantry Division; in war-time latterly, as Turkish major general, Commanding Officer of the 12th Division on Gallipoli and Anafarta. *Osmanie Order, Medjidie Order, after returning from Turkey, as a colonel, commanded 237 Infantry Brigade. 1918 OPM, Demob 1919 as major general.*
Heuermann, Johannes	Paymaster	Navy	1916/1918	*Goeben* and service in the Turkish Ministry of Marine.
Heydebreck, Kurt von	Lieutenant Commander	Navy	1916/1918	German Commander of *Hamidiye*, then on the *Breslau*. *Rescued when the Breslau sank; died 1928 in Istanbul as lieutenant commander.*
Heydecke, Paul	Judge Advocate (Kriegsgerichtsrat)	Navy	1915/1917	Senior judge for the Navy Court of the Mediterranean Division (MMD). *Killed or died on 28.12.1917 in Istanbul, buried in Tarabya.*
Hildebrandt, Oskar	Sub Lieutenant	Navy	1914/1915	*Breslau*, later commander of a machine gun platoon with the Naval Shore Detachment on Gallipoli. *Killed on 8 August 1915 on Hill 971 on Gallipoli, later buried at Kilia Tepe and presumably re-interred as an unknown soldier in Tarabya.*
Hildemann, Fritz	Captain	Army	1915	First commander of Engineers Company on Gallipoli. *Born 1889.*
Hilgenberg, Karl	Sub Lieutenant (Marine-Ingenieur)	Navy (Engineer)	1914/1916	VII. Watch engineer *Goeben*.
Hilgendorff, Fritz	Lieutenant Commander	Navy	1914/1915	Watch Officer on *Goeben*, was renowned for his inappropriate treatment of Turkish subordinates. *Born 24.04.1883, Osmanie Order 4th Class, Liakat Medal,* *Committed suicide on 8 March 1915 in a hotel in Istanbul, buried in Tarabya.*

Hiltmann, Dr.	Sub Lieutenant (Hilfsassistenzarzt)	Navy (Medical)	1915/1916	Doctor for the machine gun units of the Naval Shore Detachment on Gallipoli, 3 July 1915 – 20 January 1916, *EK II August 1915*
Hintersatz, Wilhelm	Captain	Army	1916/1918	Turkish General Staff and Adjutant to Enver Pasha.
Hochberg, Graf von	Captain (Stabsarzt)	Army (Medical)	1915	In the Dardanelles and Syria; relieved of duties due to misunderstandings with the Turks.
Hoebel	Captain	Army	1916	Artillery officer.
Hoensbroech, Graf von	Lieutenant	Army		Commander of a pack animal company.
Höfer, Alfred	Lieutenant Commander	Navy	1914/1918	Head of the Coaling Office; later Barrier Commander on the Dardanelles and OC Naval Shore Detachment from 18.2.1917 *Turkish War Medal 12.10.1915, Silver Imtiaz Medal 27.12.1915*
Hoffmeister, Hans	Captain	Army	1916/1917 1917/1918	Military Mission. Artillery officer in Canakkale.
Högemann, Gerhard	Captain	Army	1915	Assigned for one month to the Military Mission
Hohenberg, Graf von	Oberstabsarzt (Major)	Army (Medical)	1915/1917	Surgeon
Hohenlohe, Prinz von				
Höhne, Rudolf Rupert	Lieutenant	Army	1916	13th Foot Artillery Regiment *Treated during August to October 1916 for typhus in the German hospital in Istanbul. Born 6.4.1892 in Metz, commissioned 15.7.1910.*
Hölder, Adolf	Second Lieutenant	Army	1915/1918	Special Command (SoKo); Armaments Inspector
Holy-Ponienzietz, Franz von	Captain	Army	1916/1918	Commander of the Musketry School in Bigali on Gallipoli. *Treated during February 1916 in the German hospital in Istanbul for tracheal catarrh. Born 30.12.88 in Stralsund, Commissioned 2.5.1904.*

Name	Rank	Branch	Time	Assignment/Function/Awards/Notes
Homeyer, Otto	Lieutenant Commander	Navy	1915	Navigation Officer *Breslau*.
			1916/1918	1st Officer *Breslau;* in October / November 1917 he was Deputy Commanding Officer of *Breslau* and in early December 1917 was awarded the Turkish Recue Medal for conducting rescue operations after an ammunition dump exploded in 'Haydar Pasha'. *Born 31.12.1882 in Cologne, Liakat Medal with Sabres, EK II June 1915, EK I on 5 May 1916, Turkish Recue Medal; killed on 20 January 1918 at Imbros when the Breslau went down.*
Hommel, Adolf	Lieutenant Commander	Navy	1915/1918	Attached to the Coastal/Survey Inspectorate, responsible for fitting telescopic sights on the 35cm and 24cm guns; later the Liaison Officer for the Mediterranean Division to the Fifth Army; then as Turkish Captain, assigned as factory manager and draughtsman in the Armaments Inspectorate. *EK II October 1915, Turkish War Medal 23.12.1915*
Hommel, Wilhelm	Lieutenant	Army	1915/1917	Later captain in the Armaments Inspectorate. *EK II July 1916*
Hootz, Werner	Midshipman	Navy	1917/1918	*Goeben,* later *Breslau.* *Rescued after the Breslau went down.*
Hopffgarten, Graf von	Major	Prussian Army	1914/1915	In peace-time, as Turkish lieutenant colonel, Inspector General of Cavalry; in war-time, intelligence officer in a Turkish general command. *After returning from Turkey, commanded as a lieutenant colonel, the 471st Infantry Regiment. Demob 1919 as Colonel.*
Höpfner, Fritz	Sub Lieutenant	Navy	1916/1918	Special Command (SoKo); artillery officer.

Hopmann, Albert	Vice Admiral	Navy	1915/1916	Assigned to personally assist Djemal Pasha in the reformation of the Ministry of Marine. Later, in Syria, felt his services were pointless and did not like being in Turkey. He coined the phrase: 'Better to break stones in Germany' [...than to see service in Turkey. Author's comment.] *Born 1865, died in 1942.*
Hopp, Wilhelm	Lieutenant (Marine-Ingenieur)	Navy (Engineer)	1915/1917	Turkish workshop vessel *Tirimuchdjan* *Killed 09.10.1917, buried in Tarabya.*
Hörder, Otto	Lieutenant	Navy	1915 1915/1916	II. Watch Officer *Breslau*, as observer and supply officer in the Dardanelles, reported the sinking of HMS *Triumph*. *EK II June 1915.*
Huber, Karl Otto	Captain	Bavarian Army	1916/1918	As Turkish major, Military Mission; Railway Inspector and in charge of transhipment for the Head of the Turkish Field Railways.
Hülst, von	Captain	Prussian Army	1916/1918	As Turkish major, Military Mission and Adjutant to the Quartermaster-General in the Turkish Supreme Headquarters. *Ret'd as major.*
Humann, Hans	Commander	Navy	1913/1917	Commander of the station ship *Loreley*, Liaison Officer to the Mediterranean Division (MMD), Head of Intelligence Section and Naval Attaché of the Embassy in Istanbul. Grew up in Turkey, spoke fluent Turkish and knew the Turkish mentality. He was a very trusted adviser and friend to both Enver Pasha and Ambassador von Wangenheim. *Born in Turkey, son of Pergamon Archaeologist Carl Humann; Imtiaz Medal in Silver, Liakat Medal in Gold, Medjidie Order 4th Class; Demob 1920 as captain.*
Hummel, Rudolf	Sub Lieutenant	Navy	1915/1918	Special Command (SoKo), artillery officer.

Name	Rank	Branch	Time	Assignment/Function/Awards/Notes
Hunger, Waldemar	Captain	Prussian Army	1914/1918	In peace-time, as Turkish major, CO of an infantry regiment in Izmir; in war-time, as Turkish lieutenant colonel, Commanding Officer of the 28th Infantry Regiment, latterly Commanding Officer of the 34th Infantry Division in Palestine. *Treated for a gunshot wound during August/September 1915 in the German hospital in Istanbul. Born 1875, demob 1920 as major.*
Huttner, Dr.	Lieutenant (Stabsapotheker)	Bavarian Army (Medical)	1914/1918	In peace-time, as Turkish major, Inspector of Turkish Medical Supplies; in war-time, apothecary with the First and Fifth Armies. *After demob, Under Secretary at the Air Ministry.*
Ippen, P.	Second Lieutenant	Army	1915/1916	Mining engineer
Ittmann	Captain	Army	1915/1917	At Gallipoli on the staff of the 8th Heavy Artillery Regiment with Colonel Wehrle, later in Syria with the Seventh Army. *Killed 1918 near Aleppo.*
Jäckle	Sub Lieutenant (Marine-Ingenieur)	Navy (Engineer)	1915	III. Watch engineer *Breslau*.
Jaeger, Waldemar	Second Lieutenant	Army	1915/1918	Special Command (SoKo), artillery officer in Istanbul and Canakkale.
Jaenicke	Lieutenant	Prussian Army (Ordnance)	1914/1918	In peace-time, as Turkish ordnance lieutenant assigned artillery in Edirne; In war-time, Straits Command. *Demob 1919 as Lieutenant.*
Jakobsen, Werner	Sub Lieutenant	Navy	1918	*Goeben*
Jamme, P.	Lieutenant	Army		Engineer
Jansen	Major	Army	1915/1916	Arms and Munitions Inspectorate in Constantinople, responsible for munition transport and firing trials.
Janson, Gerhard von	Commander	Navy	1914/1916	As Turkish Lieutenant Colonel, Chief of Staff of Special Command (SoKo), Turkey, under Admiral v. Usedom.
			1917/1918	Commanding Officer of the Naval Detachment of the 'Yildirim' Army Group. *Silver Imtiaz Medal 31.3.1915, 15.5.1915 EK I, Golden Liakat-Medal 21.11.1915. Demob 1919 as commander.*

Joerss, Karl	Sub Lieutenant	Navy	1914/1916	Gun Commander of *Hamidiye* and *Goeben*, Special Command (SoKo), Deputy Battery Commander.
			1916/1917	Adjutant Straits Command Canakkale.
			1917/1918	Straits Command Istanbul.
				EK II 26.3.1915, Silver Liakat-Medal 31.3.1915, Silver Imtiaz-Medal 12.10.1915, EK I – 14.10.1915.
Jordan	Lieutenant	Army	1915/1916	Arms and Munitions Inspectorate in Constantinople, responsible for the Artillery Depot in Karagatch, Field Artillery.
Jung, Heinz	Sub Lieutenant	Navy	1915/1918	First on *Muavenet*, later on *Tasoz* and *Samsun*.
Jungels, Dr.	Captain (Stabsarzt)	Prussian Army (Medical)	1916/1918	As Turkish major, Military Mission and Chief of Staff to the Commander of Turkish Field Medical Services. *Ret'd as major.*
Jürgens, Emil	Sub Lieutenant	Navy (Ordnance)	1915/1916	As Turkish lieutenant with the Armaments Office *EK II July 1916*
Kabant	Lieutenant	Army	1915/1916	Special Command (SoKo), sent home because of economic problems with his pharmacy.
Kagerah, Alfred	Lieutenant Commander	Navy	1915/1918	Commander of the 1st Turkish Torpedo Boat Half-Flotilla. *Turkish War Medal*
Kahl, Dr. von	Captain	Army		In Istanbul with the Commission for Coal Mining and Raw Materials
Kahle	Major	Prussian Army	1915/1918	As Turkish lieutenant colonel, Military Mission and Turkish Armaments Office and Deputy Inspector of the Armaments Inspectorate. *EK II 18.11.1915, after the war served in Reichsheer as lieutenant colonel. Demob 1927 as Colonel.*
Kähler	Sub Lieutenant (Marine-Ingenieur)	Navy (Engineer)	1915/1916	Senior candidate *UB 18*
Kähler, Clemens	Lieutenant	Navy	1915/1916	Adjutant on the Bosphorus, Transport Officer, later the Salvage Officer in Seddulbahr. *EK II April 1916*

Name	Rank	Branch	Time	Assignment/Function/Awards/Notes
Kaisenberg, Heinrich von	Sub Lieutenant	Navy	1915/1917	*Hamidiye*, artillery officer *Goeben*, later Adjutant at Gallipoli *EK II July 1916*
Kaiser, Johann	Lieutenant Commander	Navy (Ordnance)	1915/1916	As Turkish major, with the Arms and Munitions Inspectorate in Constantinople, responsible for shell acceptance and quality control. *EK II 26.9.1915*
Kaltenborn-Stachau, von	Lieutenant	Army	1915	Engineer Detachment on Gallipoli. *Repatriated to Germany due to chronic intestinal and heart problems.*
Kandler	Marine-Ingenieur		1915/1916	Senior engineer officer candidate *UB 17*
Kannengiesser, Hans (Pasha)	Major	Prussian Army	1914/1918	As Turkish colonel, in peace-time Departmental Head on the Turkish General Staff; in war-time, as Turkish major general, commanded the 9th Division on Gallipoli, where he was wounded in August 1915 and treated for it in Istanbul. Later Deputy Commanding General of XVI Army Corps, Commanding General of XIV Army Corps and Commanding General of XXV Turkish Army Corps at Edirne.
				Born 25.6.68 in Görlitz, commissioned 22.3.86, demob 1920 as major general, Osmanie Order, Medjidie-Order, died 1945 *Book: 'Gallipoli'.*
Karkowski, Wilhelm	Officer Candidate (Marine-Ingenieur)	Navy (Engineer)	1915/1916	*UB 46* *Killed when UB-46 sank on 7.12.1916, buried in Tarabya.*
Kastner, Felix	Lieutenant (Marine-Oberzahlmeister)	Navy	1914/1916	Crew member of *Goeben*, later Divisional Secretary of the Mediterranean Division (MMD).
Katschmann, Dr. Erich	Lieutenant (Marine-Oberassistenzarzt)	Navy (Medical)	1915/1917	Naval Garrison Hospital.
Keiner	Lieutenant	Army	1915	Artillery officer with Fifth Army on Gallipoli, also assigned as Platoon Commander of the Naval Shore Detachment at Kiretch Tepe.

Keiper, Ludwig	Lieutenant	Army (Aircrew)	1915/1916 1916	No 1 Squadron. No 2 Squadron, Adjutant to Head of Air Arm.
			1916/1918	Flying instructor at the Flying Training School in San Stefano Commanding Officer of No 15 Squadron in Trakya. *Later lieutenant general of the Air Force*
Keller, Dr.	Captain (Stabsarzt)	Army (Medical)	1915/1917	Surgeon
Keller, Hans von	Lieutenant Commander	Navy	1915/1918	Navigation Officer *Breslau*. *Rescued after the Breslau went down.*
Kerruth, Richard	Lieutenant Commander	Navy (Ordnance)	1916	Special Command (SoKo).
Kersting, Herman	Captain	Army	1916/1917	Turkish War Ministry.
Kertscher	Lieutenant	Army (Aircrew)		Pilot in No 6 Squadron.
Kessel, Walter	Lieutenant	Navy	1916	No 1 Hydroplane Flight.
Kettembeil, Karl	Lieutenant	Army	1915/1917	Served first as artillery officer on the Gallipoli front, later transferred to No 1 Squadron as an observer. During a sortie in an aircraft piloted by 2nd Lieutenant Ludwig Preussner, Kettembeil, shot down the first enemy aircraft for the Turks on 27 September 1915. Transferred in January 1916 to Flight Detachment 300 with the German Asia Corps in Palestine.
Kettner, Paul	Commander	Navy	1914/1915	Commander of *Breslau*.
			1917/1918	As Captain, Chief of Staff Special Command (SoKo), Turkey. *Medjidie Order 3rd Class, Osmanie Order 3rd Class, Liakat-Medal Gold with Swords, Medjidie Order 2nd Class with Sabres, Osmanie-Order 2nd Class with Sabres. Demob 1920 as rear admiral.*
Keyserlingk, Albin Karl Freiherr von	Lieutenant	Navy	1915/1916	Special Command (SoKo), Platoon leader in the Naval Shore Detachment.

Name	Rank	Branch	Time	Assignment/Function/Awards/Notes
Keyserlingk, Harald Freiherr von	Lieutenant	Navy	1914/1915	Commander of *Gayret* during the fleet action against Russia; October 1914, Military Mission, interned in Athens and on 27 November 1915 assigned as courier to Berlin. *EK I on 15 January 1915*
Kiecker, Eduard	Lieutenant			Special Command (SoKo), weapons officer.
Kiesling auf Kieslingstein, Edler Hans von	Major	Bavarian Army (General Staff)	1915/1918	As Turkish lieutenant colonel, Military Mission and Chief of General Staff of the Sixth Turkish Army. German Military Mission in Iran, latterly Head of LoC Mission 'Yildirim'. *Imtiaz Medal, Medjidie Order, Ret'd as Lieutenant Colonel. Books: 'Mit Feldmarschall von der Goltz Pascha in Mesopotamien und Persien'; 'Soldat in drei Weltteilen'.*
Kinscher, Dr.	Marine-Stabsapotheker	Navy	1915/1917	Naval apothecary depot.
Kirchhoff, Robert	Sub Lieutenant	Navy	1915/1916	With Naval Shore Detachment Canakkale, then *Goeben*.
Kirchner, Johannes	Lieutenant	Navy	1915/1916	Commander of *UC 13* and *UB 23*.
Kirsten	Major	Saxon Army	1914/1916	As Turkish lieutenant colonel, in peace-time CO of 1st Turkish Cavalry Regiment. In war-time Caucasus front and in the Dardanelles, CO of a Cavalry Regiment. *After returning from Turkey, commanded as major, the 177th Infantry Regiment, where he was killed at Warneton in 1917.*
Klaas, P.	Lieutenant	Army		Engineer
Klagemann	Commander (Marine-Baurat)	Navy (Technical)	1915/1916	Responsible for mechanical engineering in the Mediterranean Division (MMD).
Klages, Dr.	Lieutenant (Marine-Oberassistenzarzt)	Navy (Medical)	1915/1916	Worked aboard the *General*.
Kleinau	Lieutenant	Army	1915	Artillery officer with XVI Army Corps as OC 15cm Gun Battery with the 1st Artillery Battalion on Gallipoli. *Turkish War Medal*

Klein, Dr. Bruno	Lieutenant (Oberassistenzarzt)	Army (Medical)	1915/1917	As Turkish captain, with the Coastal Inspectorate; sector medical officer at the In Tepe section, later with the Bosphorus-Anatolian Hospital. *EK II 23.1.1916*
Kleinke	Captain	Army	1915/1916	With the Arms and Munitions Inspectorate in Constantinople, responsible for small arms and machine guns. *Relieved in August 1916 but seems to have been later assigned to field weapons maintenance.*
Kleuckert	Captain	Army	1915/1916	With the Arms and Munitions Inspectorate in Constantinople, responsible for light artillery.
Klingenbeil	Lieutenant	Army (Aircrew)	1916/1918	Aircraft pilot with the Hydroplane Detachment on Gallipoli.
Klitzing, Freiherr Lebrecht von	Captain	Navy	1915	Commander of *Breslau* from 17 February 1915 – 30 August 1915 *EK II Mai 1915, Medjidie Order 3rd Class, Osmanie Order 3rd Class, Liakat Medal in Silver with Sabres, Turkish Rescue Medal, Demob in 1920 as rear admiral.*
Klocksien, Paul	Lieutenant	Army	1915/1916	With the Arms and Munitions Inspectorate in Constantinople, responsible for transportation of weapons and equipment from Germany.
Klose, Richard	Lieutenant	Army	1915/1916 1918	Artillery officer in Canakkale. Palestine.
Knaab	Captain	Army	1915	Commander of a *Goeben* 9 cm gun battery, later CO of the 2nd Artillery Battalion of the XVI Army Corps.
Kneife, Dr. Otto	Captain (Stabsarzt)	Army (Medical)	1915/1917	Hospital in Cukurbostan (Istanbul).
Knispel, Arnold	Commander	Navy	1914/1915	Gunnery Officer of the *Goeben*, Commander of the German-Turkish mine-sweeping group. *EK I. 15 January 1916*
Knorr, Paul	Sub Lieutenant (Marine-Ingenieur)	Navy (Engineer)	1915/1916	I. Watch engineer, *Breslau* *EK II Mai 1915*
Knorr, Wolfram von	Commander	Navy	1915/1917	Commander of *Breslau* from 16 September 1915 – 9 July 1917 *Order of the Knight's Cross of the Royal House of Hohenzollern with Swords. Demob 1919 as Captain.*

Name	Rank	Branch	Time	Assignment/Function/Awards/Notes
Koch, Robert	Feldunterarzt	Army (Medical)	1915	Medical officer for the machine gun units of the Naval Shore Detachment on Gallipoli from 16 October1915 – 13 January 1916.
			1916/1917	IV. Army Turkish field hospital.
Koch, Theodor	Lieutenant Commander	Navy	1915/1918	Responsible for bridges in the High Command of the Straits. *Silver Imtiaz Medal 27.12.1915, EK I July 1916*
Köhler	Second Lieutenant	Army	1915/1916	Tethered balloon section. *EK II on 15.11.1915*
Köhler, Franz	Lieutenant (Marine-Ingenieur)	Navy (Engineer)	1915/1916	Engineer on *U 18*. *EK II June 1915*
Köhler, Wilhelm	Bauinspektor Meister		1916	*Died 20.8.1916, buried in Tarabya.*
Köllner, Otto	Sub Lieutenant (Marine-Ingenieur)	Navy (Engineer)	1916/1917	*Goeben*
König, Friedrich Karl	Second Lieutenant	Army (Aircrew)	1915	Flying squadron on Gallipoli. *Born 10.4.83 in Berlin, died 11.11.1915 in the German hospital in Istanbul.*
König, von	Captain	Prussian Army	1913/1917	Staff Military Mission, on the staff of the First Army. *After returning from Turkey, served as captain in the Military Administration in Romania. 1920 Demob as major. Died 1941 as colonel in the Reichsheer.*
Königs	Oberingenieur		1915/1916	Special Command (SoKo). *EK II 27.1.1916*
Kophamel, Waldemar	Lieutenant Commander	Navy	1915/1916	Commander of *U 35*. *Born 1880, OPM 1917, died in 1934.*
Koritzki, Siegfried	Lieutenant	Navy	1914/1916	As Turkish captain, a company commander in the Bosphorus fort units and OC of the Anatolian-Kawak Battery. *EK II June 1915, Silver Liakat Medal 27.12.1915*
Körner, Martin	Lieutenant	Army (Aircrew)	1915/1918	Aircraft observer on No 1 Flying Squadron on Gallipoli. *Silver Liakat Medal, on 8. May flew with Captain Serno and both engaged an enemy aircraft with pistols.*
Kortmann, Johannes	Sub Lieutenant	Navy	1917	Special Command (SoKo), Artillery officer.

Kottwitz, Egon Freiherr von	Commander	Navy	1914/1916	German Commander of *Hamidiye*, latterly Commanding Officer of the Naval Shore Detachment on Gallipoli. *Demob 1916 as commander.*
Kraft	Second Lieutenant	Army		Fortress Officer with the Sixth Army
Kraft, Werner	Sub Lieutenant	Navy	1914/1915	Navigation Officer in the Torpedo Boat Flotilla, then *Goeben*, afterwards Naval Shore Detachment on Gallipoli; died from typhus. *Died 6.11.1915, buried in Tarabya although his father, Rear Admiral Kraft, wanted his body brought back to Germany.*
Krämer, Erich	Sub Lieutenant	Navy	1915/1918	Special Command (SoKo), with the Mine-Sweeping Squadron in Canakkale and Istanbul.
Kraus, Theodor	Sub Lieutenant	Navy	1914/1915	IV. Lieutenant *Goeben*.
Krause	Lieutenant Commander	Navy	1915	*EK II August 1915*
Krause, Georg	Lieutenant (Marine-Ingenieur)	Navy (Engineer)	1914/1916 1917	II. Watch engineer *Goeben*. Successor to Hepp in charge of the wharf in Istiniye (Stenia). *Due to illness, repatriated November 1915 for 45 days to Germany.*
Krause, Hellmut	Second Lieutenant	Army	1915/1918	Intelligence officer with the Military Mission in Istanbul, served later in Bagdad.
Kremp, Otto	Lieutenant (Marine-Oberingenieur)	Navy (Engineer)	1916/1917	Weapons engineer.
Kress von Kressenstein, Friedrich Freiherr (Pasha)	Major	Bavarian Army	1914/1918	In peace-time, as Turkish lieutenant colonel, Commanding Officer of the Field Artillery Firing School and Departmental Head in the General Staff. In war-time, Departmental Head of Operations in Supreme Headquarters and then, as Turkish major general, commander of the Eighth Turkish Army in Palestine. *Born 24.4.1870, after returning from Turkey, served as a colonel as Head of the German Delegation in Caucasus. Golden Imtiaz Medal with Sabres, Osmanie Order 2nd Class with Sabres, Medschidie-Order 2nd Class with Sabres, OPM, died in 1948. Book: 'Mit den Türken zum Suezkanal'.*

Name	Rank	Branch	Time	Assignment/Function/Awards/Notes
Kretzschmer, Hans-Wilhelm	Major	Saxon Army	1916/1917	As Turkish lieutenant colonel, Military Mission and Chief of the General Staff of the Second and then Sixth Turkish Armies as successor to Colonel von Gleich. *Treated for tracheal inflammation during July 1916 in the German hospital in Istanbul. Born 26.6.1871 in Possendorf near Dresden, commissioned 2.4.1891, Reichsheer, died as major general ret'd.*
Krieger, Ernst	Sub Lieutenant	Navy	1914/1916	*Breslau* and Turkish torpedo boat *Drac*, later as Turkish lieutenant with the Coastal Inspectorate
			1916/1918	Lecturer at the Navy Academy in Canakkale *Imtiaz Medal with Sabres, Silver Liakat Medal 12.10.1915, Osmanie Order 4th Class, EK I on 14.6.1915.*
Krüger	Officer Candidate (Marine-Ingenieur Aspirant)	Navy	1915/1916	Senior engineer officer candidate *UC 25*.
Krüger, Bernhard	Lieutenant Commander	Navy	1914/1915	II. Watch Officer *Goeben*.
			1917	3. Admiral's Staff Officer Mediterranean Division (MMD), then commander of a U-Boat Half-Flotilla in Constantinople. *EK I August 1916, Turkish War Medal, demob 1919 as commander.*
Krülls, Eduard	Lieutenant	Navy	1915/1916	Navigation Officer Hamidiye and *Goeben*, then from 30 August 1915, platoon commander with the Naval Shore Detachment on Gallipoli.
	Lieutenant Commander		1917/1918	Commander of a U-Boat Half-Flotilla in Constantinople. *EK II in April 1915; on 19.10.15 brought to hospital in Istanbul for typhus treatment.*
Krümmer, Ewald	Lieutenant	Army	1915	*Treated during September 1915 in the German hospital in Istanbul. Born 1886 in Bonn.*

Kübel, Theodor	Major	Bavarian Army	1914	Adviser for railway construction for the Military Mission. *Killed in August 1918 as CO of an Infantry Regiment on the Western Front.*
Kühlwetter, Friedrich von (Pasha)	Captain	Navy	1914/1915	As Turkish major general, latterly Chief of Staff of the Straits High Command. *Medjidie Order 2nd Class 5.11.1915, Demob 1919 as rear admiral.*
Kühne	Second Lieutenant	Army	1915/1916	Served under Major Willmer on Kiretch Tepe.
Kuhne, Max	Lieutenant Commander	Navy	1914/1915 1916/1917	Personnel Office of the Mediterranean Division and Ministry of Marine. *Breslau* and *Goeben.*
Kümmerling	Offiziersstellvertreter		1915/1916	Special Command (SoKo). *Silver Liakat Medal 12.10.1915*
Kümpel, Otto	Commander	Navy	1914/1917	Adjutant and Watch Officer on *Goeben.* *EK I August 1916, Medjidie Order*
Küssner, Lothar	Sub Lieutenant	Navy	1915/1918	Special Command (SoKo); 1st Mine-Sweeping Squadron in Istanbul.
Küster	Lieutenant (Oberassistenzarzt)	Army (Medical)	1915/1916	As Turkish captain with the Coastal Inspectorate. *Silver Liakat Medal 12.10.1915*
Küster, Erich	Lieutenant (Marine-Ingenieur)	Navy (Engineer)	1914/1915	III. Watch engineer *Goeben*, responsible for the boilers. *Due to illness, repatriated to Germany in November 1915.*
Laffert, Karl von	Major (General Staff)	Prussian Army	1914/1915	From 6.1.1914 as Military Attaché at the German Embassy in Istanbul. *After returning from Turkey as lieutenant colonel, to the General Staff of the 7th Cavalry Division in Strasbourg, then CO of the 83rd Territorial Infantry Regiment. 1920 demob as lieutenant colonel.*
Lampe, Heinrich	Commander	Navy	1914/1918	1. Officer *Goeben.* *EK I August 1916, died 1928 as Commander*
Landmann, Gustav	Lieutenant	Army	1916/1917	Special Command (SoKo), Artillery Officer

Name	Rank	Branch	Time	Assignment/Function/Awards/Notes
Landsberg	Lieutenant Commander	Navy	1915/1918	Pilot with No 1 Squadron, Gallipoli.
Lange	Captain	Army	1915	General Staff Officer of the 9th Division. *Relieved due to ill-health and repatriated to Germany.*
Lange	Captain	Prussian Army	1914/1915	As Turkish major, in peace-time lecturer at the Turkish War Academy; in war-time Chief of the General Staff of X Army Corps in Erzerum. *After returning from Turkey served as major on General Staff of the Ninth Army High Command, died 1942 as major*
Lange, Paul	Captain	Army	1915/1917	As Turkish major, Head of the Turkish Navy Music Corps.
Langenn–Steinkeller, Franz Helmut von	Lieutenant	Army	1915/1918	As Turkish captain, Military Mission and 1st Adjutant to v. Kress in Palestine *Captain (Ret'd).*
Langfeld, Walter	Lieutenant Commander	Navy (Aircrew?)	1915/1916	1st No 1 Squadron, Straits High Command. *Demob 1919 as lieutenant commander.*
Lass, Robert August Ludwig	Sub Lieutenant	Navy (Ordnance)	1915	Special Command (SoKo), 3./III. Naval Artillery Detachment. *Born 1880, commissioned 1.4.1913, killed on 9.6.1915 in the Dardanelles, gravestone found at Kum Kale and today to be seen in the excavation house in Troy.*
Lauffer	Major	Wuerttemberg Army	1914/1918	As Turkish lieutenant colonel, in peace-time Commanding Officer of the Turkish Cavalry Officers Riding School; in war-time Intelligence Officer in the II. Reconnaissance Regiment, later in Palestine. *After returning from Turkey, served as a major commanding the 236th Reserve Infantry Regiment. Died 1940 as lieutenant colonel `(Ret'd).*

Legat, Wilhelm von	Major	Prussian Army	1914	As Turkish lieutenant colonel, Commanding Officer of the Turkish War Academy *Died 21.08.1914 in Istanbul, buried in Tarabya.*
Lehmann	Second Lieutenant	Army	1916	Pilot with the No 1 Squadron, Dardanelles.
Lehmann	Captain	Prussian Army	1911/1918	CO of Model Artillery Regiment, latterly as Turkish lieutenant colonel; in war, CO of a Turkish Field Artillery unit. *Died 1939 as lieutenant colonel(Ret'd).*
Leipzig, Erich von	Major (General Staff)	Prussian Army	1901/1908 1915	From 19 September 1901, Military Attaché at the German Embassy Istanbul. On 21 May1906, promoted lieutenant colonel. On 18 August 1906, he was relieved of his post. As colonel, from 11 January 1915, again served as Military Attaché in Istanbul *On return from Turkey, served as Regimental CO of the 12th 'Lithuanian' Uhlan Regiment in Insterburg.* *Died 28.06.1915 in Uzunköprü, buried in Tarabya, Istanbul (shot himself with his own revolver in a train, probably suicide).*
Lichtschlag	Major	Army	1916/1918	As Turkish lieutenant colonel, director of a rifle factory.
Liebeskind, Hans Albrecht	Sub Lieutenant	Navy	1914/1916	Crew member of *Goeben*, took part on the minelayer *Nilüfer* in the fleet action against Russia in October 1914, later commander of a Turkish torpedo boat. *EK I 15 January 1916*
Liebmann, Ernst	Lieutenant Commander	Navy (Aircrew)	1915/1916	1st No 1 Squadron in Gallipoli. *EK II August 1915, Turkish War Medal12.10.1915,* *EK I 8 February 1916.*
Lienau, Hermann	Lieutenant Commander	Navy	1914/1916	Commander of the *General*.

Name	Rank	Branch	Time	Assignment/Function/Awards/Notes
Lierau	Major	Prussian Army	1914/1918	As Turkish lieutenant colonel, Military Mission and CO of the Heavy Artillery in the Anafarta Group in the Dardanelles and in the Army Group Yildirim in Palestine. *Lieutenant Colonel*
Liesching, Ernst	Second Lieutenant	Army	1916	Radio Unit 151, treated for dysentery during August and September 1916 in the German hospital in Istanbul. *Born 4.2.1882 in Stuttgart, Commissioned 1.10.1907.*
Lindau	Lieutenant	Army		
Linke, Kurt	Sub Lieutenant (Marine-Ingenieur)	Navy (Engineer)	1914/1915	*Breslau.*
Linnenkamp, August	Lieutenant Commander	Navy	1914/1915	*Breslau.*
Linnenkopp	Lieutenant	Navy	1915	IV. Watch Officer, *Breslau.*
Lodder, Gustav	Lieutenant / Captain	Army	1915 / 1916	Assigned to arms and munitions production in Constantinople, responsible for ships' and coastal guns. / *EK II 27.1.1916*
Lorenz	Captain	Prussian Army	1915/1918	As Turkish major, Military Mission and latterly as Adjutant Military Mission. *Reichsheer, Major General*
Lorenzen, Fritz	Paymaster	Navy	1914/1917	*Goeben.*
Lorey, Hermann	'Commander'	Navy	1915/1918	German commander of *Torgut Reis;* German commander of *Barbaros Hayrettin* when she was sunk on 8 September 1915 by the British submarine HMS *E 11;* latterly commander of the Turkish Torpedo Boat Flotilla. *Born 1877, Reichsmarine, demob 1924 as rear admiral; later Director of the Army Museums; died 1954.* *Books: 'Die German Landungsabteilung auf Gallipoli', 'Der Krieg in den türkischen Gewässern'. First volume: 'Die Mittelmeerdivision' Second volume: 'Der Kampf um die Meerengen.'*

Lossow, Otto von	Major	Bavarian Army	1911/1913	As Turkish lieutenant colonel, instructor at the Turkish War Academy. During the Balkan War of 1912/1913, commanded a Turkish infantry division at Catalca.
	Colonel (General Staff)		1915/1918	Military Attaché 19 July1915; from 19 April 1916 'German Plenipotentiary at the Imperial Embassy in Constantinople'.
				Promoted on 1 April 1916 to major general (Bavarian Army).
				After returning from Turkey, served as lieutenant colonel on the General Staff of the Bavarian Army. In the Great War, latterly as major general, died as lieutenant general (Ret'd).
Lothes, Paul	Lieutenant Commander (Marine-Oberingenieurrat)	Navy (Engineer)	1914/1916	Mediterranean Division (MMD), responsible for coal supplies in Tekirdağ.
			1917/1918	Oil Supply Command in Iraq and Syria.
Lotze, Dr. Konrad	Marine-Stabsarzt (Lieutenant Commander)	Navy (Medical)	1916/1918	Mediterranean Division (MMD), MO in Canakkale.
Lübbe	Lieutenant Commander	Navy	1915/1916	Commander of *UB 42* and *UC 23*.
Lübben, Theodor	Sub Lieutenant (Marine-Ingenieur)	Navy (Engineer)	1915/1916	*Goeben.*
Lüders, Wilhelm	Sub Lieutenant (Marine-Ingenieur)	Navy (Engineer)	1915	VI. Watch Engineer *Goeben*.
Lukranka, Johannes	Commander (Marine-Stabsingenieur)	Navy (Engineer)	1915/1918	I. Watch and Electrics Engineer *Goeben*.
Lustig, Dr. Max	Lieutenant	Army		Financial specialist.
Lüttge, Fritz	Sub Lieutenant (Marine-Ingenieur)	Navy (Engineer)	1914/1915	*Goeben.*
Lüttichau, Siegfried Graf von	Chaplain	Army Chaplain	1915/1918	Embassy Chaplain in Constantinople, later with Army Group Yildirim.
				EK II, stayed in Turkey after the War, conducted the first service in the Embassy Chapel in Tarabya in 1924 after it was reopened.
Lüttjohann, Hans	Lieutenant	Navy	1916	Watch Officer, later Commander of *UB 7*.
				Missing in Sevastopol after UB 7 sank.

Name	Rank	Branch	Time	Assignment/Function/Awards/Notes
Mackensen, Erich	Lieutenant (Marine-Oberingenieur)	Navy (Engineer)	1914/1915	Engineer *Breslau*.
Madlung, Rudolf	Commander	Navy	1914/1915	I. Officer *Goeben*, Commander of the Turkish Torpedo boat Flotilla; German Commander of *Mecidiye;* German Commander of *Peyk-i Sevke;* from 23 January – 3 July 1915 Commander of *Breslau*. *Demob 1920 as captain.*
Mahlstedt, Stefan	Feldmagazin Inspektor		1915/1918	Inspector with the Provisions Office in Constantinople.
Majewski, Georg von	Captain	Prussian Army	1916/1918	As Turkish major, OC Engineers of XI Army Corps; latterly OC Engineers of the XXII Army Corps in Palestine. *Born 1888, later Reichsheer as major general; suicide in May 1945 when Town Commandant of Pilsen.*
Martinengo, Carlos	Lieutenant	Army	1916	In Turkish Ministry of War, then Area Commandant in Iraq.
Matthiesen, Ernst	Lieutenant Commander	Navy	1914/1916	CO of Shore Battery, II. Mine-Sweeping Squadron at Zunguldak *EK II 26.3.1915*
Matz, Karl	Sub Lieutenant (Marine-Ingenieur)	Navy (Engineer)	1916/1917	*Goeben.*
Mayer, Prof. Dr. Georg	Major (Oberstabsarzt)	Bavarian Army	1913/1916	As Turkish lieutenant colonel, in peace-time Medical Department in the Turkish Ministry of War; in war-time, Deputy Medical Inspector and Medical Officer of the Fifth Turkish Army.
			1917/1918	On the Advisory Board of the Senior Medical Officer of the Military Mission. *After returning from Turkey, latterly Corps Medical Officer of the 1ˢᵗ Bavarian Army Corps, died 1936 as Generaloberarzt a.D.*
Meerscheidt-Hüllessen, Wilhelm Freiherr von	Captain	Navy	1914	German Commander of *Torgut Reis*.
Meier	Second Lieutenant	Prussian Army (Ordnance)	1914/1918	As Turkish lieutenant, in peace-time artillery officer in Edirne; in war-time with General Weber in the Straits High Command. *Captain in the Reichsheer.*

Meineke, Emil	Second Lieutenant	Army (Aircrew)	1915/1918	Flying instructor in St. Stefano, later as aircraft pilot on Gallipoli from autumn 1915. *Total of six confirmed kills on Gallipoli. After the Great War test pilot with Fokker and flew more than 1000 aircraft produced by Fokker during the Second World War. Afterwards as mechanic during the Berlin Airlift on the US Airbase in Frankfurt, then emigrated to Canada.*
Meinke	Second Lieutenant	Prussian Army (Fortifications)	1914/1918	As Turkish lieutenant, fortifications work in peace-time for General Weber Pasha, in war-time in the Dardanelles. *After returning from Turkey, died in 1918.*
Meis, Albert	Lieutenant Commander	Navy	1914/1917	Commander of Turkish torpedo boat *Samsun* and cargo ship *Loreley.*
Meisner, Erich	Marine-Baumeister	Navy	1915/1916	Responsible for ships' engines in the Mediterranean Division (MMD).
Mellenthin, Hans-Joachim von	Lieutenant	Navy	1914/1916	Until December 1914, German Commander of *Berk-I Satvet*; from January 1915, Commander of the Turkish torpedo boat *Samsun*, then took part in a special mission on the torpedo boat *Timur Hissar* in the Aegean Sea and, until April 1916, pilot for the German U-Boats in the Dardanelles. *Born 25. 03 1887. After the War, businessman in Colombia, returned to Germany before WW2, partly serving in the German Navy and partly on the estate of his brother-in-law, Field Marshall Fedor von Bock. Mellenthin died on 12.06.1971 in Kiel.*
Merkel, Hans Gotthard	Captain	Prussian Army	1915/1918	1915 on the staff of von der Goltz (83rd Infantry Regiment), German Iraq Group; and on the Staff of the LoC Inspectorate in Aleppo and Damascus. He was treated in December 1915 in the German hospital in Istanbul, *Born 8.3.1885, later colonel, killed on 29.4.1945 as Commanding Officer of the Frankfurt an der Oder Military District.*

Name	Rank	Branch	Time	Assignment/Function/Awards/Notes
Merten, Johannes (Pasha)	Vice Admiral	Navy	1914/1918	Special Command (SoKo), as Turkish lieutenant general, Commander of the Dardanelles Fortifications and Delegate to Turkish Supreme Headquarters. *Golden Liakat Medal 31.3.1915, Medjidie Order 1st Class 5.11.1915, Imtiaz Medal, died 1926.*
Mertz, Heinz	Sub Lieutenant	Navy	1915/1918	*Goeben* and Mine-Sweeping Squadron as Signals Officer, October 1916 – October 1917 *Goeben* as 1. Signals Officer, then until October 1918, 1. Signals Officer for the Mine-Sweeping Squadron.
Metge, Dr. Ernst	Lieutenant (Marine-Oberassistenzarzt)	Navy (Medical)	1915/1918	Turkish Navy Hospital Taşkışla, later Euphrates River Detachment. *EK II April 1916*
Meyer	Lieutenant Commander	Navy	1916	Special Command (SoKo).
Meyer, Christian	Sub Lieutenant (Marine-Ingenieur)	Navy (Engineer)	1914/1916	*Loreley*, later *Berk-i Satvet* and *Goeben*.
Meyer, Heinrich	Paymaster	Navy	1915/1916	Special Command (SoKo), Canakkale.
Meyer, W. Georg	Stabsapotheker	Army	1916	German LoC Medical Depot. *Taken on 4.7.1916 to the German hospital in Istanbul and died at 16.30 hrs of heart failure. Born 29.11.74 in Eberswalde, buried in Tarabya.*
Meyr, Dr. Fred	Lieutenant Commander	Navy (Aircrew)	1915/1916	Aircraft observer and OC airfield Canakkale. *EK I 8 February 1916, Imtiaz Medal, Liakat Medal.*
Mielenz	Second Lieutenant	Army (Aircrew)	1916/1918	Aircraft pilot in Gallipoli.
Mielke, Emil	Senior Paymaster (Marine-Oberzahlmeister)	Navy	1914/1916	Paymaster of the Torpedo Boat Flotilla, later Euphrates River Detachment.
Mikusch-Buchberg, Dagobert von	Captain	Prussian Army	1915/1916	As Turkish major, Military Mission and latterly Ia in General Command of the VI Turkish Army Corps in Romania.
			1917/1918	Liaison officer Army Group Yildirim to the Prussian Ministry of War. *Major ret'd.*

Missuweit, Heinz	Sub Lieutenant	Navy	1914/1915	Crew member of *Goeben*, Mediterranean Division (MMD), special duties for Asia Minor.
Modrow	Major	Prussian Army	1915/1917	As Turkish lieutenant colonel, Military Mission and artillery commander in the Dardanelles and Palestine. *Died as colonel ret'd.*
Mohl, Hans von	Lieutenant Commander	Navy	1915/1916	2. Admiral's Staff Officer Mediterranean Division (MMD) and special duties for Asia Minor, later OC U–Boat Base at Kyshla Buku Orak (at Bodrum).
Moosauer, Prof. Dr. Sigmund	Marine-Oberstabsarzt (Commander)	Navy (Medical)	1914/1918	Ship's Medical Officer *Goeben*.
			1918	Senior doctor at the Navy Hospital in Istanbul. *Born 1877, EK II and EK I in 1914, Turkish Silver Imtiaz Medal, Turkish Medjidie Order 3rd Class with Sabres, Turkish War Medal, later Head of Medical Services of the Reichsmarine, then Kriegsmarine, discharged 1940, died in 1944.*
Moritz, Dr.	Stabsveterinär	Army (Veterinary)	1916/1917	Temporarily attached Military Mission, later with the Army Group Yildirim.
Mücke, Hellmuth von	Lieutenant Commander	Navy	1914/1915	1. Officer of the *Emden*, in charge of her Naval Shore Detachment. After the *Emden* was grounded off the Cocos Islands, made his way via the Arabian Peninsula to Constantinople.
			1917	OC Euphrates River Detachment *Born 1881, June 1915 repatriated to Germany due to illness, demob 1919 as commander, died in 1957.* *Books: 'Die sagenhafte Fahrt des Emdenlandungskorps'; 'Ayesha'.*
Muhl, Walter	Sub Lieutenant	Navy	1915/1918	Ministry of Marine, later *General*, Navigation Officer on the torpedo boats *Numune* and *Samsun*, latterly Adjutant.
Mühlens, Prof. Dr. Peter	Marine-Oberstabsarzt	Navy (Medical)	1915/1918	Military Mission, as hygienist with the Fourth Turkish Army on the Suez Canal, also worked in the Augusta Victoria Hospice, Jerusalem; interim service with the Bulgarian Army. *EK II May 1915, EK I 2. October 1915*

Name	Rank	Branch	Time	Assignment/Function/Awards/Notes
Mühlmann, Dr. Carl	Lieutenant	Prussian' Army	1913/1918	As personal Adjutant (together with Prigge) came with Liman von Sanders in 1913 to Istanbul; as Turkish major, Adjutant to General v. Sanders, General Staff Officer to Colonel von Sodenstern during the attacks at the beginning of May 1915 in the Southern Group on Gallipoli; later with General Weber. *After returning from Turkey, served as captain in 54th General Command. Demob 1920 as major. Kept a diary about the fighting in Gallipoli.* *Books: 'Oberste Heeresleitung und Balkan im Weltkrieg 1914/1918'; 'Der Kampf um die Dardanellen'; 'Die Deutsche Militär-Mission in der Türkei'; 'Das deutsch-türkisch Waffenbündnis im Weltkriege'.*
Muhra, Erich	Second Lieutenant	Army (Aircrew)	1915/1918	Aircraft pilot in Gallipoli.
Müller, Dr. Victor	Lieutenant Commander (Stabsarzt)	Navy (Medical)	1916/1918	MO on *Breslau*. *EK II April 1916, killed 20 January 1918 when the Breslau sank off Imbros.*
Müller, Erich von	Commander	Navy	1914/1915	1. Officer *Goeben*. *Reichsmarine, demob 1921 as captain.*
Müller, Heinrich	Sub Lieutenant (Marine-Ingenieur)	Navy (Engineer)	1915/1917	*Breslau*
Müller, Ludwig	Chaplain (Marinepfarrer)	Navy	1916/1917	Navy Chaplain Mediterranean Division (MMD). *Born 1883, Turkish War Medal, committed suicide 30.7.1945.*
Müller, Max von	Lieutenant	Army	1915/1916	Military Mission Istanbul. *Treated for dysentery in February 1916 in the German hospital in Istanbul. Born 5.7.88 in Danzig, commissioned 1.10.1908.*
Müller, Rudolf	Sub Lieutenant	Navy	1915	*Goeben*, commander of a Machine Gun Platoon of the Naval Shore Detachment. *Seriously wounded on 28 June 1915 at Krithia.*

Müller, Vincenz	Second Lieutenant	Army (Engineers)	1915/1917	As Turkish Lieutenant with the Engineers Command on Gallipoli, later Iraq campaign. *Born 5.11.1894 in Aichach, Mecediye Order 5th Class, Liakat Medal, committed suicide on 12.5.1961 in Berlin. Book: 'Ich fand das wahre Vaterland', lieutenant general of the Wehrmacht and the NVA.*
Müller, Wolf	Lieutenant	Army	1915/1916	Depot Regiment Fifth Army. *Treated for dysentery in December 1915 in the German hospital in Istanbul. Born 3.12.84 in Cologne.*
Nathusius, Peter Gottlob Engelhard von	Captain	Prussian Army	1916/1917	As Turkish major, Military Mission and CO of a Turkish Depot Regiment in Iraq. *Born 18.3.1885 in Sommerschenburg, EK I, Turkish War Medal, killed on 26.2.1917 at Kut-el-Amara.*
Natz, Emil	Second Lieutenant	Army	1914/1916 1917/1918	As Turkish lieutenant, assigned to the Coastal Artillery as platoon commander, successor to Lieutenant Woermann as Commandant of Fort Orhanié. Special Command (SoKo). *EK II 26.3.1915, Silver Liakat Medal 31.3.1915.*
Neid, Konrad	Sub Lieutenant	Navy (Torpedoes)	1914/1917	Special Command (SoKo), Mine and Torpedo Officer in the Dardanelles. *Turkish War Medal 9.11.1915, Silver Liakat Medal 27.12.1915, EK I July 1916.*
Neiling, Peter	Sub Lieutenant	Navy	1916	*U 46.* *Died or killed on 07.12.1916, buried in Tarabya.*
Neinke	Lieutenant	Army	1915/1916	Group Signals Officer of the Mediterranean Division (MMD).
Neuhaus, Gerhard	Lieutenant Commander (Marine-Stabsingenieur)	Navy (Engineer)	1915/1918	Senior Engineer *Goeben.* *EK I August 1916*
Neumann, Karl	Sub Lieutenant	Navy	1918	*Goeben*

Name	Rank	Branch	Time	Assignment/Function/Awards/Notes
Ney, Otto	Lieutenant	Navy	1914/1915	*Goeben*
	Lieutenant Commander		1916	Commander of the Iraq Flotilla.
Nickelhausen	Lieutenant	Navy	1915	Flag lieutenant of the Mediterranean Division (MMD).
Nickels, Julius	Lieutenant Commander	Navy	1916/1917	Commander of *Tasoz*.
			1918	Commander of *General*.
Nicolai	Second Lieutenant	Army		
Nicolai, August (Pasha)	Lieutenant Colonel	Saxon Army	1913/1918	In peace-time, as Turkish colonel, Commanding officer of a Turkish infantry division. In war-time, latterly as Turkish major general, GOC of the 3rd Division, later GOC of the II Turkish Army Corps and Inspector of Artillery for the Fourth Turkish Army, initially at Kum Kale; later colonel and Deputy Commander XVI Army Corps. Due to illness, he was replaced by Colonel Kannengiesser.
				After returning from Turkey, as a colonel served as an artillery CO on the Western Front, returned to Turkey after the war in 1924 to set up an Intelligence Service, died 1941 as major general (Ret'd).
Nicolaus, Karl	Commander	Navy	1914/1915	2. Admiral's Staff Officer Mediterranean Division (MMD).
Niebuhr	Lieutenant	Navy	1915/1916	Mediterranean Division and *U 21*. *EK I*
Nielsen	Second Lieutenant (Vize-Feuerwerker)	Army (Ordnance)	1915/1916	Mathematician in the Armaments Office.
Niemeyer	Lieutenant	Army	1915/1917	Artillery Observation Officer on the Gallipoli coast, later trained as an Air Observer and as Turkish captain saw service in Bagdad. *EK I 30 May 1915, killed on 17 January 1917 during an air recce sortie and buried in the German Military Cemetery in Bagdad.*
Niemöller, Max	Lieutenant	Army	1915/1918	Staff Military Mission, Personnel Department, later, as Turkish major, Head of the Coal Department in the Turkish Supreme Headquarters.

Nillrich, Dr.	Lieutenant Commander (Marine-Stabsarzt)	Navy (Medical)	1915	MO of the Torpedo Boat Flotilla, also Head of the Polyclinic and MO of *Olga*.
Niltmann, Dr.	Sub Lieutenant (Marine-Assistenzarzt)	Navy (Medical)	1915/1916	MO with Naval Shore Detachment on Gallipoli.
Nitzsche, Martin	Lieutenant Commander	Navy	1915/1917	As Turkish major, Commandant of Fort Hamidiye, later Sector Commander at In Tepe. *EK II 8.12.1915, EK I 27.1.1916*
Nostitz, Moritz Freiherr von	Captain	Army	1916	2. General Staff Officer
Obering	Sub Lieutenant	Navy	1915/1916	Left Constantinople on 11 December 1915 to set up the Iraq Flotilla in Persia under Lieutenant Commander Ney.
Ody, Edmund	Paymaster	Navy	1916/1917	*Breslau*
Oels, Paul	Paymaster	Navy	1916/1917	*Goeben*
Öhringen, Prinz Hohenlohe von	Lieutenant	Army (Aircrew)	1915/1918	Air Observer with No 1 Flying Squadron.
Oldershausen, Erich Freiherr von	Lieutenant Colonel	Army	1915/1916	Military Mission. *Treated for intestinal catarrh and cholangitis during March 1916 in the German hospital in Istanbul. Born 10.1.72 in Bielefeld.*
Olshausen, Dr.Gustav	Sub Lieutenant (Marine-Assistenzarzt)	Navy (Medical)	1915	MO *Goeben* and *U 51* *EK II June 1915*
Opitz, Wilhelm	Sub Lieutenant	Navy	1916/1917	No 1 No 1 Squadron
Oppernheimer, Emanuel	Sub Lieutenant	Navy	1914/1917	*Goeben*, then at Canakkale.
Orthmann	Second Lieutenant	Army		Officer on the staff of XVI Army Corps.
Pahlau, Paul	Second Lieutenant	Army		Special Command (SoKo), Weapons officer.
Palis, Karl	Lieutenant Commander	Navy	1915/1916	Commander of *UB 45* and *UB 46*. *Killed 1916 off Varna.*
Pankow, Luis	Paymaster	Navy	1914/1916	Crew member of *Goeben*, later Divisional Secretary of the Mediterranean Division (MMD).
Pansegrau, Erich	Sub Lieutenant	Navy	1915/1917	Special Command (SoKo) as artillery officer, later Libya/Tripoli.
Paraquin, Adolf	Captain	Army	1915	
Paulke	Major	Prussian Army	1915/1916	Professor at the Technical University in Karlsruhe; as Turkish major, Military Mission, head of Ski Training in the Third Army on the Caucasus front.
Petersen, Dr. Hellmuth	Marine-Stabsarzt	Navy (Medical)	1915/1918	Military Hospital Harbiye, later Euphrates River Detachment. *EK II on 11.11.1915*

Name	Rank	Branch	Time	Assignment/Function/Awards/Notes
Petrick, Hermann	Lieutenant	Army (Ordnance)	1915	Armaments and Munitions Inspectorate in Constantinople,
	Captain		1916	Responsible for electrical matters, supervisor of draughting office administration. *EK II 27.1.1916*
Pfannenstiel	Major (General Staff)	Prussian Army	1916/1918	As Turkish lieutenant colonel, Military Mission and Head of the Railways Department in the Turkish Supreme Headquarters. *Lieutenant Colonel(Ret'd).*
Pfeffer-Wildenbruch, Karl	Lieutenant	Prussian Army	1915/1917	Latterly German Iraq Group, Sixth Turkish Army. *Born 1888, died 1971*
Pfeiffer, Adolf	Commander	Navy	1914/1917	Commander of the Turkish Torpedo Boat Flotilla. *Turkish Service Medal, EK I 11.7.1915, Reichsmarine, demob1928 as rear admiral(Ret'd).*
Pflanz, Hans	Second Lieutenant	Army (Aircrew)	1915/1918	Special Command (SoKo), later No 1 Squadron 1.
Pfundt	Captain	Saxon Army	1916/1918	As Turkish major, Military Mission and Adjutant to General Bischof Pasha.
Pfützenreuter, Otto	Lieutenant Commander	Navy	1914/1915	I. Watch Officer *Goeben*.
Philipp	Officer Candidate (Vize-Feuerwerker)	Navy (Ordnance)	1915/1916	As Turkish officer candidate, platoon commander on the Bosphorus.
Philipp, Eugen	Sub Lieutenant	Navy (Aircrew)	1914/1918	Special Command (SoKo), aircraft pilot on No 1 Squadron at Canakkale.
Phillipi, Otto	Paymaster	Navy	1917/1918	*Goeben*
Pieper, Waldemar (Pascha)	Captain	Navy	1914/1917	As Turkish major general, Head of Turkish Armaments Office and Armaments Inspectorate Constantinople. *Born 1871, as Commander of the cruiser Yorck considered responsible for its sinking and the death of 336 seamen. Disciplinary transfer to the Mediterranean Division, where he was fully rehabilitated. EK I 26.7.1915, Osmanie Order 2nd Class 21.1.1916, demob 1919 as rear admiral, died 1945.*

Pila, Arnold	Marine-Oberzahlmeister	Navy	1915/1917	Special Command (SoKo), later Straits Command Canakkale
Plenio, E.	Lieutenant	Army		Military Police
Poggemeyer, Friedrich	Paymaster		1914/1918	Special Command (SoKo)
Pohl, Leo	Lieutenant	Prussian Army	1914/1917	As Turkish Captain, in peace-time Adjutant to the Inspector General of the Turkish Engineer and Pioneer Corps; in war-time, as Turkish major, latterly as Adjutant to the Chief of the Turkish General Staff. *After returning from Turkey, captain, latterly on Staff of 1st Reserve Division. 1920 demob as major.*
Pommeresch, Victor	Sub Lieutenant	Navy	1914/1916	Special Command (SoKo), as Turkish lieutenant served as platoon commander and gun captain in the Dardanelles *EK II 26.3.1915, Silver Liakat Medal 12.10.1915.*
Popp, Friedrich	Sub Lieutenant	Navy (Aircrew?)	1915/1917	Special Command (SoKo), No 1 Squadron at Canakkale.
Posseldt (Pasha)	Lieutenant Colonel	Prussian Army	1909/1915	From mid- October 1909 until 1913, as Turkish major general, Inspector General of the Turkish Foot Artillery; from 1914 Military Mission, latterly Commander of the Erzerum fortress until 1915. *Died 1930, as lieutenant general (Ret'd).*
Pötrih	Lieutenant Colonel	Army	1915/1916	Commanding Officer of 9th Division as successor to Kannengiesser.
Potschernik	Major	Prussian Army	1914/1918	As Turkish colonel, Inspector General of Turkish Military Transportation. *After returning from Turkey, served in the rank of lieutenant colonel in the 100th Grenadier Regiment. 1919 demob as colonel.*
Pramann, Ernst	Captain (General Staff)	Saxon Army	1915/1917	General Staff Officer to the Head of German Field Railway Systems in Istanbul. *Treated for rheumatism during January 1916 in the German hospital in Istanbul. Born 30.4.78 in Bielefeld, lieutenant colonel.*
Presse, Dr. Paul	Marine-Oberbaurat	Navy	1915	Special Command (SoKo) as shipyard specialist.

Name	Rank	Branch	Time	Assignment/Function/Awards/Notes
Preussner, Ludwig	Second Lieutenant	Army (Aircrew)	1915/1916	As Turkish lieutenant, commanded No 1 Flying Squadron in Gallipoli. *Turkish War Medal, Silver Liakat Medal, EK I; killed in an aircraft accident on 16 May 1916 on the San Stefano airfield and died of his injuries on 29 Mai 1916. Buried in Tarabya..*
Priess, H.	Stabsapotheker	Army (Medical)	1916/1917	Attached as required to the Military Mission.
Prigge, Erich R.	Captain	Prussian 'Army'	1913/1918	In peace-time, as a Turkish major, Commandant of the Turkish Cavalry NCO School; in war-time, Adjutant to General Liman von Sanders. *After returning from Turkey, served in the rank of captain on the General Staff of the 203rd Infantry Division. Demob 1920 as major. Books: 'Dardanellen Kriegstagebuch'; 'Der Kampf um die Dardanellen'.*
Prosch, Friedrich	Sub Lieutenant	Navy	1914	*Goeben*
Quaritsch, Karl	Captain	Army	1914/1915	Accounting Inspector in the Mediterranean Division (MMD).
Quast, Wilhelm	Captain	Army		Engineer.
Rabe	Second Lieutenant	Army	1915	Ferried a fighter aircraft to Gallipoli and then remained there in No 1 Flying Squadron.
Rabe, Hans	Major	Prussian Army	1909/1914	In peace-time from mid-October 1909 to 1913 as Turkish major, instructor at the Turkish War School, Military Mission.
			1914/1918	CO of a Turkish Infantry Regiment in Edirne. In war-time took part in the fighting on Gallipoli, CO of 15th Infantry Regiment, then of a combined Division in Istanbul. *After returning from Turkey, CO of 62nd Infantry Regiment. 1920 demob as lieutenant colonel.*
Rabenau, Götz Friedrich von	Sub Lieutenant	Navy	1914	*Goeben*
			1915	Naval Shore Detachment in Gallipoli. *Born 28.9.1891 in Kastel, wounded on 4 June 1915 during the 3rd Battle of Krithia and taken prisoner by the British. Evacuated to Malta, where he recovered from his wounds and remained there until 1919, left active service in 1921.*

Rabius, Heinrich	Lieutenant	Navy	1914/1915	Special Command (SoKo), platoon commander in the Naval Shore Detachment.
Raith	Captain	Prussian Army	1915/1916	As Turkish major, Military Mission, then the Sixth Turkish Army in Iraq.
	Major		1917/1918	German Asia Corps Palestine, CO of the 702nd Infantry Battalion. *Lieutenant colonel of the Luftwaffe.*
Ramsey, von	Major	Army	1916/1918	Surveyor
Rasch	Lieutenant	Navy (Aircrew)	1915	Pilot of a Gotha, was in Istanbul to examine landing and servicing possibilities of this new type of aircraft.
Raspel, Karl	Lieutenant	Navy	1915	VII. Watch Officer *Goeben* and Naval Shore Detachment on Gallipoli.
			1916	Responsible for die surveying and mapping the Euphrates.
			1918	Commanding Officer of the Euphrates Flotilla.
Raydt, Hermann	Lieutenant	Navy	1914/1915	Port Commander in Istanbul, later Commander of the Turkish torpedo boat *Yarhisar.* *Believed killed on 3 December 1915*
Recke	Second Lieutenant	Army	1916/1917	Aircraft pilot in Diyarbakir.
Reclam, Victor (Pasha)	Captain	Navy	1914/1916	As Turkish major general, latterly Inspector of Turkish Coastal Fortifications. *Born 1871, EK I 1915, Golden Liakat Medal, demob 1920 as rear admiral, died 1946.*
Redern, Claus von	Sub Lieutenant	Navy	1915/1916	Commander of a gun boat, later on *Goeben.*
Reeder, Arnholdt	Lieutenant (Marine-Oberingenieur)	Navy (Engineer)	1915/1916	Special Command (SoKo), technical adviser to Commandant Dardanelles and, among other things, as German Naval Engineer on the *Nusret.* *Responsible for laying twenty-six sea mines on 8 March 1915, EK II April 1915, Silver Liakat Medal 12.10.1915.*
Rehm, Dr. Friedrich	Second Lieutenant (Unter-Assistenzarzt)	Army (Medical)	1916	MO at Iskenderum.
Reimann, Felix	Major	Army	1915	*Treated for typhus 17.6. – 26.7.1915 in the German hospital in Istanbul.*

Name	Rank	Branch	Time	Assignment/Function/Awards/Notes
Reinhold, Dr. Ludwig	Marine-Stabsarzt (Lieutenant Commander)	Navy (Medical)	1915/1918	As MO in the main camp of the Naval Shore Detachment on Kilia Tepe from 9 November 1915 until October 1917, then with the Military Hospital Harbiye, later Euphrates River Detachment.
Restorff, von	Captain	Army	1915/1918	Adjutant to General Field Marshal von der Goltz.
Reuss, Heinrich Prinz zu XXXVIII	Lieutenant	Navy	1914/1915	On the torpedo boat *Sivri*, he successfully laid a total of nineteen mines on 21 and 28 March 1915 and was singled out for special mention in the report by Admiral v. Usedom. *Contracted typhus late 1915. Killed 1918 on the Western Front. EK II April 1915, EK I 21.09.1915, Silver Imtiaz Medal 12.10.1915.*
Rhode, Josef	Sub Lieutenant	Navy	1918	*Goeben*
Ribbentrop, Joachim von	Lieutenant	Army	1915	Assigned to the Military Mission for the German Embassy Constantinople. *Born 1893, NSDAP 1932, 1938 Foreign Minister. In the Nurnberg Trials 1946 sentenced to death and hanged.*
Richter, Friedrich	Captain	Navy	1915/1917	Initially, Chief of Staff of Special Command (SoKo) Turkey, as Turkish major general, then Mediterranean Division (MMD). *Reichsmarine, died 1922 as vice admiral (Ret'd).*
Richter, Friedrich	Lieutenant (Marine-Oberingenieur)	Navy	1914 1915/1918	Special Command (SoKo). Engineer in the Armaments Inspectorate. *EK II Juli 1916*
Riekau, Dr.	Captain (Stabsarzt)	Army (Medical)	1915/1918	MO of the Second Turkish Army in Charput.
Riemeyer, Julius	Sub Lieutenant (Marine-Ingenieur)	Navy (Engineer)	1915	Shipbuilding Engineer in the Mediterranean Division (MMD).
Rietzsch, Willy	Sub Lieutenant	Navy		Commander of a Turkish torpedo boat.
Rist, Albert	Second Lieutenant	Army	1915/1916	Fifth Army in the Dardanelles (Kum Kale). *Treated for malaria during January 1916 in the German Hospital in Istanbul. Born 16.11.87 in Ölkoven/Württb. Commissioned 5.8.14*

Ritschl, Harald	Lieutenant	Navy	1914/1915	*Breslau*
Ritter, Georg	Lieutenant	Navy	1915	Special Command (SoKo).
	(Marine-Oberingenieur)		1916	Engineer with the Armaments Inspectorate.
Ritter, Hermann	Second Lieutenant	Army	1915/1917	Special Command (SoKo), artillery officer.
Rodenwaldt, Ernst Robert Carl, Prof. Dr.	Major (Oberstabsarzt)	Army (Medical)	1915	Consulting hygienist of the Fifth Army, additionally from 1916-18, Principal German Medical Officer of the Fifth Army. *Born 1878, died 1967.*
Röder	Second Lieutenant	Army	1915/1917	Aircraft pilot at Iskenderun and Mersin.
Roenick, Arthur	Sub Lieutenant (Marine-Ingenieur)	Navy (Engineer)	1914/1915	*Breslau*
Roesner, Ernst	Lieutenant (Marine-Oberassistenzarzt)	Navy (Medical)	1916/1918	Mediterranean Division (MMD).
Rohde	Sub Lieutenant	Navy	1915/1917	Coastal Inspectorate.
Rohde, Karl Nikolaus	Commander	Navy	1914/1916	German Commander of Barbaros *Hayrettin*, then Commanding Officer of the Naval Shore Detachment on Gallipoli and initiated the building the camp on Kilia Tepe; later III. Admiral's Staff Officer of the Mediterranean Division (MMD). *EK I 11.7.1915, posted back to Berlin after illness in 1916, demob 1919 as commander (Ret'd).*
Rohdewald, 'August' Wilhelm Heinrich (Pasha)	Colonel	Prussian Army	1916/1918	As Turkish lieutenant general, Military Mission and Quartermaster General at Turkish General Headquarters *Born 1866, died as Major General (Ret'd)*
Röhlfing, Hans	Captain	Prussian Army	1915/1916	OC of the 930th Light Field Howitzer Battery of the Sixth Turkish Army *Died 11.12.1916 in Istanbul from wounds received at Kut el Amara, buried in Tarabya.*
Röhr	Lieutenant Commander	Navy	1915	
Römmich, Ludwig	Lieutenant	Army	1915/1916	Served in the 3rd Battery of the 16th Artillery Regiment. *Treated for dysentery during December 1915 and January 1916 in the German hospital. Born 5.8.89 in Münster, commissioned 2.8.14.*

Name	Rank	Branch	Time	Assignment/Function/Awards/Notes
Rosenberger, Dr. Wilhelm	Marine-Stabsarzt (Lieutenant Commander)	Navy (Medical)	1915/1916	MO on the staff of the German Commander in the Dardanelles. *EK II April 1915, Silver Imtiaz Medal 12.10.1915.*
Rosentreter, Fedor	Lieutenant Commander	Navy	1914/1915	Crew member of *Goeben*, German Commander of *Turgut* during the fleet action against Russia in October 1914, Commandant of *Barbaros Hayrettin*. *EK II April 1915, repatriated to Germany because of a serious nervous disorder on 7 August 1915.*
Roßberger, Hermann	Captain	Army	1915	*Treated during August/September 1915 in the German hospital for 'Debility after feverish cold'.*
Röttgen	Lieutenant	Army (Engineers)	1915/1916	Armaments and Munitions Inspectorate in Constantinople. Responsible for Personnel Matters.
Rüdiger	Sub Lieutenant	Navy	1915/1916	IV. Lieutenant *Breslau*. *EK II April 1916*
Ruef, Walter	Sub Lieutenant	Navy (Aircrew)	1915/1917	Flying Officer in the Dardanelles. *EK II 28.11.1915*
Rühl, Philipp	Captain	Army	1915	
Rühle	Captain	Army	1915/1916	Assigned to the Turkish General Staff.
Rümann, Arnold	Lieutenant	Navy	1914/1915	Navigation Officer *Goeben*.
Rümann, Wilhelm	Lieutenant Commander	Navy	1914/1918	Commander of a Turkish torpedo boat.
Runken, Henry	Sub Lieutenant (Marine-Ingenieur)	Navy (Engineer)	1917/1918	*Goeben*
Rusche, Hans	Lieutenant	Navy	1914/1915	V. Watch Officer *Goeben*
Ruschhaupt, Dr. Erich	Marine-Stabsarzt (Lieutenant Commander)	Navy (Medical)	1915/1917	MO on Gallipoli, later with the Sixth Army in Bagdad and the Eighth Army.
Sägler	Sub Lieutenant (Marine-Ingenieur)	Navy (Engineer)	1915	IV. Watch Engineer *Breslau*.
Saling, Paul	Sub Lieutenant	Navy	1914/1915	*Goeben* and *Breslau*, later in Anatolia.
Salzwedel, Gerhard	Second Lieutenant	Navy	1914/1917 / 1918	Special Command (SoKo), OC machine gun unit at Ariburnu; later Adjutant with Coastal Inspectorate. Army Group Yildirim and later Syria and Mesopotamia. *Lightly wounded on 12.8.1915 in Gallipoli Silver Liakat Medal 12.10.1915.*

Sanders, Otto Liman von (Pasha)	General of Cavalry	Prussian Army	1913/1918	As Turkish Marshal, Head of the Military Mission; in peace-time Commanding General Turkish I Army Corps, then Inspector General of the Turkish Army. In war-time, Commander in Chief of the First and later the Fifth Turkish Army and Army Group Yildirim. *Born 18.2.1855 in Stolp, OPM with Oak Leaves, Golden Imtiaz Medal, died 22.8.1929 in München as general of cavalry (Ret'd)* *Book: 'Fünf Jahre Türkei'.*
Sandrock, Dr. Wilhelm	Lieutenant (Marine-Oberassistenzarzt)	Navy (Medical)	1915 1916	Medical Officer *Goeben*. Left Constantinople on 11 December 1915 for Persia to build up the Iraq Flotilla under Lieutenant Commander Ney.
Sarraxin	Sub Lieutenant	Navy	1915/1916	V. Lieutenant *Goeben*. *EK I on 19. 04. 1916*
Schack	Vice Admiral	Navy	1914	Adviser for the improvement of the Dardanelles fortifications. Had to work in civilian clothes, but was relieved of post after six months due to his relationship with the British Royal Navy Mission being too close.
Schack, Walter	Paymaster	Navy	1914/1916	*Goeben*
Schade, Johannes	Sub Lieutenant (Marine-Ingenieur)	Navy (Engineer)	1915/1916	II. Watch Engineer *Breslau*. *EK II April 1916*
Schade, Werner	Lieutenant	Navy	1914/1915	VIII. Watch Officer *Goeben* and *Peyk-i Savket*. *From 1941 Assistant Naval Attaché Istanbul.*
Schäfer, Albert	Second Lieutenant	Army (Aircrew)	1915	Air Arm Istanbul.. *Treated for scabies during October 1915 in the German hospital in Istanbul. Born 1880,*
Schäfer, Rupert	Sub Lieutenant	Navy	1915/1917	Special Command (SoKo), commander of a torpedo boat. *Killed on 02.07.1917 during minesweeping in the Dardanelles, buried in a mass grave in Tarabya, gravestone put up in a different location.*
Schäfer, Wilhelm	Lieutenant	Navy	1915/1916	I. Lieutenant Breslau. *EK II April 1916, wounded on 22.7.1916 during a battle with Russian naval forces.*

Name	Rank	Branch	Time	Assignment/Function/Awards/Notes
Schaller, Friedrich	Sub Lieutenant	Navy	1915	
Schätzlein, Dr. Paul	Second Lieutenant	Army	1916/1917	Special Command (SoKo) *Killed on 27.05.1917 in the Black Sea, buried in Tarabya.*
Schaumburg-Lippe, Prinz Moritz zu	Captain	Army	1915/1917	As Turkish major, served in the High Command of the Fifth Turkish Army. *Died 1920 as Rittmeister (Ret'd).*
Scheele, Dr. K.	Lieutenant Commander (Marine-Stabsarzt)	Navy (Medical)	1916/1918	*Later Professor in Essen.*
Schelle, Martin	Sub Lieutenant	Navy	1914/1915	Torpedo specialist, *Breslau*, later commanded a torpedo boat.
Schellendorf, Friedrich Wilhelm Bronsart von (Pasha)	Colonel	Prussian Army	1913/1917	As Turkish lieutenant general, Chief of the General Staff of the Turkish Third Army in the Caucasus. *Born 1864. After returning from Turkey as Major General GOC of 4th Replacement Division, 1920, discharged as lieutenant general (Ret'd), died 1950.* *Book: 'Ankara und Enver Pascha'*
Schelling, Karl	Lieutenant Commander	Navy	1914/1915	
Schenk, Friedrich	Lieutenant	Navy	1916/1918	OC Navy Labour Detachment Istanbul, later Adjutant to Lieutenant Commander Baltzer, transportation officer for German soldiers.
Scherz, Gustav	Sub Lieutenant	Navy	1914/1916	III. Lieutenant Goeben, later in Canakkale as observer on the Bay of Saros; later with the Fourth Army.
Scheubner-Richter, von	Major	Army	1914/1916	Attached to German Consulate in Erzerum, later in Iran and Caucasus.
Schierholz, Rudolf	Captain	Saxon Army	1914/1917	In peace-time as Turkish major, instructor at a Turkish Staff Officers' Training Camp; in war-time, first responsible for the coastal defence of the 3rd Division; then as Turkish lieutenant colonel, CO of the 9th Infantry Regiment in the Dardanelles and in Palestine as Turkish lieutenant colonel, CO of a Regiment, for securing the Hejaz railway. *Died 8.12.1917 from typhus in Maan, re-interred 1932 in Nazareth.*

Schierhorn, Otto	Sub Lieutenant (Marine-Ingenieur)	Navy (Engineer)	1914/1915	*Breslau*
Schierstädt, von	Lieutenant Colonel	Prussian Army	1915/1918	As Turkish colonel, Detachment OC with the Fifth Turkish Army, Commanding Officer of Cavalry Brigade. *Died 1919 as lieutenant colonel (Ret'd).*
Schlee, Hans	Major	Army	1915/1918	Formerly of the 3rd Telegraph Battalion, in Turkey responsible for signals and radio, head of the tracking station 'Osmanie'.
Schlee, Max (Pasha)	Major	Wuerttem-berg Army	1914/1918	Latterly as Turkish major general, Inspector General of the Turkish Field Artillery. *Osmanie Order, Medjidie Order, After returning from Turkey, artillery commander of XIII Corps. Discharged 1919 as major general (Ret'd).*
Schleip, Prof. Dr.	(Colonel) Oberstarzt	Army	1915/1916	Chief Medical Officer German Hospital in Istanbul.
Schlette	Technischer Sekretär	Navy	1915/1916	Mediterranean Division (MMD). *EK II April 1916*
Schlichting, von	Lieutenant	Army (Aircrew)	1915/1916	Aircraft pilot on No 1 Squadron at Gallipoli. *Son of Major v. Schlichting, deceased 1911,*
Schlubach, Erich	Commander	Navy	1915/1917	1. Admiral's Staff Officer Mediterranean Division (MMD), Commander U-Boat Half Flotilla, Constantinople. *Put forward for EK I on 7.11.15 for destroying HMS U 20, but turned down. EK I August 1916.*
Schmidt, Arthur	Sub Lieutenant (Marine-Ingenieur)	Navy (Engineer)	1914/1916	V. Watch Engineer *Goeben* und *Peik*.
Schmidt, Hans Martin	Sub Lieutenant	Navy	1915/1916	*Breslau*, later VI. Lieutenant *Goeben*, later platoon commander in machine gun unit in Canakkale. *EK II on 30.11.1915.*
Schmidt, Kurt	Sub Lieutenant (Marine-Ingenieur)	Navy (Engineer)	1914/1916	Engineer in the Torpedo Boat Flotilla.
Schmidt, Siegfried	Lieutenant	Navy	1914/1915	*Breslau.* *Killed 29.05.1915 in the Mediterranean.*

Name	Rank	Branch	Time	Assignment/Function/Awards/Notes
Schmidt-Kolbow	Major	Prussian Army	1915/1919	Latterly as Turkish lieutenant colonel, Military Mission Artillery Sector Commander in the Southern Group of the Fifth Turkish Army and in Army Group Yildirim. *Reichsheer, colonel.*
Schmiedicke, Erich	Sub Lieutenant	Navy	1914/1918	Crew member of *Goeben*, later *General und Breslau*; later Naval Shore Detachment as observation officer.
Schmitz, Kurt	Sub Lieutenant	Navy	1915/1918	*Goeben* as Adjutant to Commandant, also saw action in Canakkale.
Schmücker, F.	Assistenzarzt	Army (Medical)	1916/1918	Medical Officer in Istanbul.
Schneider, Carl	Lieutenant Commander	Navy	1915/1918	As Turkish major II. Admiral's Staff Officer and I. Adjutant Straits High Command. Flew as observer with Captain Serno on 18 March on the first flight over Gallipoli and discovered the approaching Allied fleet. *EK II 26.3.1915, Silver Liakat–Medal 31.3.1915, EK II 4.6.1915, Silver Imtiaz Medal 27.12.1915, discharged 1920 as commander (Ret'd).*
Schneider, Friedrich	Marinebaurat	Navy	1914/1918	Responsible for shipbuilding in the Mediterranean Division (MMD).
Schoede	Lieutenant (Oberassistenzarzt)	Navy (Medical)	1916	Mediterranean Division (MMD).
Scholle	Lieutenant	Navy	1915	III. Watch Officer *Breslau*.
Scholz, Emil von	Lieutenant	Navy (Ordinance)	1915	Searchlight and Ordinance Officer in the Dardanelles. Also assigned for weapons and munitions production in Constantinople; as captain in 1916, responsible for ships' and coastal artillery guns. *Silver Liakat–Medal 12.10.1915.*
Schrader, Otto von	Lieutenant	Navy	1914/1915	Intelligence officer in Istanbul, later commander of the Turkish torpedo boat *Yadigar*, commander of the Turkish Torpedo Boat Flotilla, U-Boat commander in the Black Sea. *Born 18.3.1888, Turkish Service Medal, EK I on 15 January 1916, later admiral in WW2, committed suicide on 19 July 1945 in Bergen/Norway.*

Schraudenbach, Ludwig	Major	Bavarian Army	1916/1917	As Turkish lieutenant colonel, Military Mission and latterly commander of 14th Infantry Division Caucasus and Iraq. *Died as colonel.*
Schröder	Captain	Prussian Army	1914/1917	As Turkish major, in peace-time CO of 1st Model Army Train Battalion in Istanbul; in war-time, latterly Inspector Army Trains in the Aleppo and Mersina LoCs. *Treated for malaria in September 1915 in the German Hospital in Istanbul. 1920 Discharged as major (Ret'd).*
Schubert, Wilhelm	Second Lieutenant	Army (Aircrew)	1915/1918	Special Command (SoKo), aircraft pilot in No 1 Squadron.
Schuch	Preuß. Rechnungsrat	Prussian Army	1914/1915	As Turkish major, in the Army Replacement Department of the Turkish Ministry of War. *After returning from Turkey, Army Manning Office.*
Schueler von Krieken, Max	Captain	Army (Aircrew)	1915/1918	Aircraft pilot and commander of No 5 Squadron in Izmir (Smyrna).
Schuh, Martin	Lieutenant	Army	1916	As Turkish captain with the Military Mission in Istanbul, later with Army Group Yildirim. *Born 11.7.1882 in Landshut, died on 23.8.1916 from cholera.*
Schulbach	Commander	Navy	1915/1918	Mediterranean Division (MMD).
Schultz, Hans Ernst	Sub Lieutenant	Navy	1915/1916 / 1917	Watch Officer in the L.M.S.D., commander of a minesweeper. Instructor at the Navy Academy. *EK II 27.1.1916*
Schulze	Second Lieutenant	Army (Aircrew)	1915/1916	Aircraft pilot in Gallipoli and Iraq.
Schum, Dr.	Lieutenant (Oberassistenzarzt)	Navy (Medical)	1915	Mediterranean Division (MMD), detached to Bulgaria.
Schütz	Sub Lieutenant	Navy	1916/1917	Watch Officer *UB 45*.
Schütze, Arnold	Commander	Navy	1918	1. Officer *Goeben*. *Discharged 1919 as commander (Ret'd).*
Schüz, Hans	Lieutenant	Army (Aircrew)	1916/1917	Aircraft pilot in Gallipoli in No 6 Squadron and later in Palestine with the Sixth Army as a Turkish captain. *Ten confirmed kills on Ottoman territory and was the most successful fighter pilot in the Turkish Army.*

Name	Rank	Branch	Time	Assignment/Function/Awards/Notes
Schwab, Martin	Sub Lieutenant	Navy	1914/1916	1914 Crew member of *Goeben*, Det. Officer *Torgut Reis* and *Hamidie*. Left Constantinople on 11 December 1915 for Persia, to build up the Iraq Flotilla under Lieutenant Commander Ney. *EK I November 1915*
Schwabe, Fritz	Lieutenant	Army		Engineer
Schwabe, Kurt	Major	Army	1915/1917	Mediterranean Division (MMD), then German Asia Corps Palestine as divisional commander.
Schwager, Ottmar	Second Lieutenant	Army	1915/1917	Telegraph section.
Schwarz	Lieutenant	Navy	1915/1916	Watch Officer *UB 42* and *UB 14*.
Schwießelmann, Hans	Lieutenant	Navy (Ordinance)	1914	Special Command (SoKo) as torpedo and mine specialist. *Killed when the Nilüfer sank on 22.11.1914.*
Sebelin, Erwin	Lieutenant	Navy	1915/1916	Commander of a Turkish torpedo boat; on 12 May 1915 sailed aboard the *Muavenet* under the command of Firle and took part in the attack on HMS *Goliath*. *EK I on 15. January 1916*
Seckendorff-Aberdar, Freiherr von	Captain	Army	1915	Served in the Turkish Ministry of War, as Turkish major.
Seelinger, Dr. Arthur	Captain	Army	1916	Representative of the Prussian Ministry of War. *Treated in August 1916 in the German Hospital in Istanbul. Born 9.7.1870 in Reichenbach/Silesia, commissioned 1.10.1892*
Seidl, Fritz	Lieutenant	Army	1915/1916	On the staff of von der Goltz. *Treated in January 1916 in the German Hospital in Istanbul. Born 3.10.80 in Breslau, commissioned 2.8.14.*
Seidler, Frank	Second Lieutenant	Army (Aircrew)	1915/1917	Ferried the first German aircraft (Rumpler B I) from Germany via Bulgaria to Adrianople and later took part in the battles on Gallipoli as a pilot (as a Turkish lieutenant). *Liakat-Medal*
Sell, Friedrich Freiherr von	Lieutenant Commander	Navy	1916/1918	*Breslau* *Killed when the Breslau went down on 20 January 1918 off Imbros.*

Semmler, Anton	Sub Lieutenant	Navy	1915/1918	Special Command (SoKo), Barrier and mine pilot in the Dardanelles. *EK II March 1916.*
Senftleben	Captain	Prussian Army	1915/1917	As Turkish major, Military Mission, then Artillery Sector Commander of XVI Army Corps and Southern Front in the Dardanelles; later served in Iraq. *Colonel.*
Serno, Erich	Second Lieutenant	Army (Aircrew)	1914/1918	As Turkish captain, built up the Turkish Air Arm and organised the Flying Training School in San Stefano, latterly as Turkish major, Inspector the Turkish Air Arm and Commander of No 1 Squadron on Gallipoli. *Imtiaz–Medal with Sabres, Turkish Lifesaving Medal, Medjidie Order with Sabres, After returning from Turkey as Captain, served in the Reichsheer. Discharged 1921 as major (Ret'd).*
Seyffert, Hermann	Paymaster	Navy	1915/1916 1917/1918	Fleet paymaster. Service with the Ministry of Marine.
Siebeler	Lieutenant	Navy	1915	VI. Watch Officer *Goeben.*
Siegert	Major	Army (Aircrew)	1915	Representative of the Air Arm. *After a recce flight on 5 January 1916, piloted by Second Lieutenant Faller, he predicted the withdrawal of the Allied forces; later Inspector of the Air Arm.*
Sievert	Major	Prussian Army	1916/1918	As Turkish lieutenant colonel, Military Mission and Intelligence Section in Turkish Supreme Headquarters. *Lieutenant Colonel (Ret'd).*
Sodenstern, Eduard von (Pasha)	Lieutenant Colonel	Prussian Army	1914/1916	In peace-time as CO of the Turkish Infantry Musketry School; in war-time as Turkish major general, Commanding Officer of 14th Division in the Dardanelles; later Commanding Officer of 25th Division.

Name	Rank	Branch	Time	Assignment/Function/Awards/Notes
				Treated in February 1916 for dysentery in the German Hospital in Istanbul. Born 12.11.66, commissioned 14.4.85. On 5 May 1915, due to a knee injury, handed over command to General Weber, discharged 1918 as major general (Ret'd).
Soleski, Wilhelm	Second Lieutenant	Army (Aircrew)		Aircraft pilot in the Flying Training School in San Stefano.
Soller	Captain	Army	1915/1916	As Turkish major, assigned to the Armaments and Munitions Inspectorate in Constantinople, responsible for quality control of deliveries from the private sector and for allocation of orders to same.
Sommer, Otto	Sub Lieutenant	Navy	1915/1917	Commander of the Turkish torpedo boat *Numune-i Hami*
Souchon, Wilhelm (Pasha)	Vice Admiral	Navy	1913/1917	From 23 October 1913, commander of the Mediterranean Division and later the Commander in Chief of the Turkish Fleet. Pushed for the attack on the Russian ports and so brought Turkey into the war on the side of the Central Powers. *Born 1864, 1904/05 Chief of Staff of German Cruiser Squadron in East Asia, October 1916 OPM, Osmanie Order, Medjidie Order. Discharged 1919 as Admiral (Ret'd), died of heart failure on 13 January 1946 in Bremen.*
Spetzler	Oberingenieur		1915	Armaments Inspectorate.
Sporleder	Sub Lieutenant (Marine-Ingenieur)	Navy (Engineer)	1915	Engineer as torpedo specialist with the Torpedo Boat Flotilla.
Sprengel, Friedrich	Lieutenant Commander	Navy (Ordinance)	1915	As Turkish captain with the Armaments Office. *Relieved of post due to lack of diligence and sent back to Germany.*
Staczewski, von	Captain	Prussian Army	1914/1918	As Turkish major, in peace-time engineer officer in Edirne; in war-time, assigned to General Weber; latterly OC Engineers Company in the Caucasus and Palestine. *Died 1930 as major (Ret'd).*

Stade, Karl	Lieutenant Commander (Marine-Stabsarzt)	Navy (Medical)	1916/1918	Naval garrison MO.
Stadler	Second Lieutenant	Army (Aircrew)	1915	Aircraft pilot on the Suez Canal.
Stadler, Dr.	Lieutenant Commander (Marine-Stabsarzt)	Navy (Medical)	1915	Mediterranean Division (MMD), assigned to Bulgaria.
Stange	Captain	Prussian Army	1914/1918	In peace-time as Turkish major, artillery officer in Edirne; in war-time, Artillery Commander Officer in the Caucasus and Erzerum, but fell seriously ill there; later Dardanelles and, finally, as Turkish lieutenant colonel commanding the Foot Artillery Firing School. *After returning from Turkey, as major in the 8th Foot Artillery Regiment. Discharged 1920 as lieutenant colonel (Ret'd).*
Stange, Christian August	Major	Prussian Army	1914/1917	As Turkish lieutenant colonel, in peace-time Commanding Officer of the 8th Infantry Regiment; in war-time, as Turkish Colonel, latterly Inspector of Replacement Troops Istanbul, took part in the attack on Ardahan. *After returning from Turkey as the Lieutenant Colonel Commanding Officer of the 59th Infantry Regiment. Died 1918 from gas poisoning in the field.*
Staszewski, Karl von	Major	Army	1915/1917	Engineers officer in the Caucasus at Erzerum, in Edirne and under the command of General Weber in Gallipoli.
Stein, Gustav	Lieutenant	Army	1915/1916	15th Engineers Section of the 1st Regiment, Military Mission. *Treated in December1915 for an injured hand in the German Hospital. Born 4.10.89 in Dedelsheim/ Hofgeismar, Commissioned 31.3.1908.*
Steinbauer, Wolfgang	Lieutenant	Navy	1915/1916	Watch Officer on *U-35* under Lieutenant Commander Kophamel. *Born 6.5.1888 in Strasbourg, EK IIand EK I, OPM in 1918, 1942 captain.*

Name	Rank	Branch	Time	Assignment/Function/Awards/Notes
Steinmann, Albert	Sub Lieutenant	Navy	1918	*Goeben*
Sterke	Commissariat Secretary	Prussian Army	1914/1918	As Turkish captain, in peace-time with the Turkish General Commissariat; in war-time assigned to Army Commissariat of the First Army, latterly Palestine.
Stoeckicht, Otto	Sub Lieutenant	Navy	1917/1918	*Goeben*, later *Breslau*.
Streithorst, Martin	Paymaster	Navy	1914/1918	Assigned to the Turkish Ministry of Marine.
Strempel, Walter von (Pasha)	Major (General Staff)	Prussian Army	1906/1914	On 28 September 1906, Military Attaché at the German Embassy in Istanbul, then as Turkish lieutenant colonel, Chief of Staff Military Mission, but relieved on orders from General von Sanders for apparently being too familiar with the Turks. *Discharged 1914 and as Turkish major general, military escort for Turkish Princes. Osmanie Order, Liakat Medal, died 10.4.1935 in Jena as colonel (Ret'd).*
Stritez, Friedrich Deym Graf von	Lieutenant	Navy	1914/1915	Istanbul.
			1915	Machine gun unit on Gallipoli.
			1916/1918	Anatolia and Euphrates River Detachment.
Stübel, Heinrich	Lieutenant Commander	Navy	1915/1917	As major (General Staff) Admiral's Staff Officer in the Coastal Inspectorate in the Dardanelles. *EK II September 1915, Turkish War Medal 9.11.1915*
Stutzin, Dr. Joachim	Major (Oberstabsarzt)	Army	1915/1917	Surgeon. *Treated for exhaustion in September 1915 in the German Hospital. Born 1868 in Memel.*
Tacke, Dr. Friedrich	Commander (Marine-Stabsarzt)	Navy (Medical)	1914/1915	*Goeben*
Tägert, Wilhelm	Captain	Navy	1915/1918	1. Admiral's Staff Officer, Mediterranean Division. *Born 1871, EK I on 19 April 1916* *Reichsmarine, discharged 1921 as vice admiral (Ret'd), died 1950*
Tautz, Arthur	Lieutenant	Navy	1916/1918	Navigation Officer *Goeben*. *Was rescued when the Breslau went down.*

Telek	Hilfsleutnant	Army	1915	Coal supplies and transportation.
Tewes, Karl	Lieutenant	Navy (Ordinance)	1915/1916	Special Command (SoKo), ordinance officer in the Dardanelles. *EK II 23.1.1916*
Thauvenay, Etienne Perrinet von	Major	Prussian Army	1913/1916	As Turkish lieutenant colonel, in peace-time Departmental Head in Turkish General Staff; in war-time, General Staff Officer to Colonel Sodenstern in the Southern Group, later relieved by Liman v. Sanders. *After returning from Turkey as lieutenant colonel, latterly Commanding Officer of 33rd Territorial Infantry Regiment. Died 1929 as major general (Ret'd).*
Thieme, Dr.	Preuß. Oberveterinär	Prussian Army (Veterinary)	1914/1918	In peace-time as Turkish captain, advisor to the Turkish Veterinary Inspector; in war-time as Turkish major, Veterinary Officer of the First Army, latterly Principal Veterinary Officer with the Army Group Yildirim', Palestine. *General Staff Veterinary and Commanding Officer of the Army Veterinary Academy in the Reichsheer.*
Thierry	Lieutenant Colonel (General Staff)	Prussian Army	1915/1916	Plenipotentiary General Staff Officer to the Chief of German Field Railways in Istanbul. *Died as major general (Ret'd).*
Thomsen, Waldmar von	Lieutenant	Navy	1915 1915/1918	Platoon Commander in the Hamidié Battery. From 12 May, Commander of a machine gun platoon of the Naval Shore Detachment. Special Command (SoKo), Armaments and Munitions Inspectorate in Constantinople, Adjutant to Colonel Pieper. *EK II April 1915, Turkish War Medal 9.11.1915, Silver Liakat Medal 27.12.1915, died of heart failure in Zonguldak (Black Sea coast) and buried there with full military honours.*
Tiedemann, Bruno	Lieutenant	Army		Engineer.

Name	Rank	Branch	Time	Assignment/Function/Awards/Notes
Tippelskirch, Ulrich von	Lieutenant Commander	Navy	1915/1916	German Commander of *Torgut Reis*, and then *Hamidiye*, latterly Naval Liaison Officer to the Fourth Turkish Army. *EK II June 1915, discharged 1919 as commander (Ret'd).*
Todenwarth, Freiherr von	Lieutenant	Navy	1915/1916	*U 21*, later in charge of the Landing Group for Libya.
Tolki	Sub Lieutenant	Navy	1915/1917	Responsible for coal supplies in the Mediterranean Division (MMD).
Töpfer, August	Oberingenieur		1916	*Killed 11.10.1916, buried in Tarabya.*
Torbahn, Ernst	Feuerwerks-Leutnant	Army (Ordinance)	1915/1916	As Turkish lieutenant, assigned to the Armaments and Munitions Inspectorate in Constantinople, responsible for the Artillery Depot in Karagatch, Heavy Artillery. *EK II 27.1.1916.*
Trabitzsch, Arthur	Second Lieutenant	Army	1915/1918	Special Command (SoKo), artillery officer.
Trachbrod, Gerhard	Sub Lieutenant	Navy	1918	*Goeben*
Trales	Hilfsleutnant	Army	1915	Coal supplies and transportation.
Trembur, Dr.Heinrich	Captain (Navy) (Marine-Gen.-Oberarzt)	Navy (Medical)	1914/1918	Senior Naval Medical Officer in Turkey. *EK II May 1915, discharged 1921 as Marine-Generalarzt.*
Trommer, Bruno Traugott Karl (Pascha)	Lieutenant Colonel	Prussian Army	1914/1918	In peace-time as Turkish colonel, Commanding Officer of 10th Turkish Infantry Division; in war-time latterly as Turkish major general, Commanding General of the Turkish XIV Army Corps in the Dardanelles and Coastal Defence of Izmir. *Treated for typhus from September to October 1915 in the German Hospital. Born 1865 in Hohensalza, after returning from Turkey as colonel latterly Commanding Officer of 237th Infantry Brigade. Discharged 1920 as major general (Ret'd).*
Trützschler, von Falkenstein	Major (Oberstabsarzt)	Army	1915	Head of the German Medical Mission, served as medical officer in the fighting on Gallipoli as a surgeon.

uarters	Second Lieutenant	Army	1915/1916	Armaments Inspectorate Istanbul. *Treated in January 1916 in the German Hospital in Istanbul. Born 15.8.89 in Halle, commissioned 18.10.1907.*
Ullrich	Lieutenant	Navy	1915/1917	Watch Officer *UB 14*.
Unger, Hermann	Lieutenant	Army		Editor of the soldiers' newspaper 'Am Bosporus' in Istanbul.
Usedom, Hans Leo von	Sub Lieutenant	Navy	1915/1917	From mid-October 1915 with the Special Command (SoKo). Observation officer in Yeni Shehr (Dardanelles). *Son of Admiral von Usedom, EK II 21.12.1915, EK I 8. 02. 1916.*
Usedom, von Guido (Pasha)	Admiral	Navy	1914/1918	As Turkish Marshal, Head of the Special Command (SoKo) Turkey and Commander in Chief of the Dardanelles Straits. *Born 1854, OPM with Oak Leaves, Golden Imtiaz Medal 31.3.1915, Liakat Medal, Medjidie Order II. Class, died 1925 as admiral (Ret'd).*
Valentiner, Max	Lieutenant Commander	Navy	1917	Commander of *U 38* *Born 1883, discharged 1920 as commander (Ret'd), OPM, Liakat Medal, died 1949. Book: 'U 38 – Wikingerfahrten eines German U-Bootes'.*
Voigt, Carl	Lieutenant Commander (Marine-Stabsarzt)	Navy (Medical)	1915/1917	MO in the Russian Hospital in Istanbul, Field Hospital in Cukurbostan (Istanbul).
Voigt, Dr. Walter	Captain (Stabsarzt)	Army (Medical)	1915/1917	Field Hospital in Cukurbostan (Istanbul).
Voigt, Ernst von	Lieutenant	Navy	1915/1916	As Turkish lieutenant commander, Commander of *UB 8*, which was brought by rail to Pola and was thus the first German U-Boat in Turkish waters.
Vollmer, Hans	Captain der Matrosen Artillery d. Res.	Army?	1915/1916	As Turkish captain, battery commander of an 8.8cm Quick Firing Battery handed over to the Army in the 1st Artillery Battalion on Gallipoli, the 'Usedom-Battery'. *Turkish War Medal 22.9.1915, EK II 2. September 1915, Silver Liakat Medal 10.10.1915.*

Name	Rank	Branch	Time	Assignment/Function/Awards/Notes
Vollmer, Harry August	Lieutenant (Marine-Oberingenieur)	Navy (Engineer)	1915/1916	Engineer on the *Breslau*. *EK II May 1915.*
Vonberg	Captain	Prussian Army	1914/1916	In peace-time as Turkish major, CO of a Field Artillery Regiment in Sivas; in war-time, in the Dardanelles as Turkish lieutenant colonel, CO of the 30th Field Artillery Regiment with the Anafarta Group and latterly in the Caucasus. *Died 1916 from typhus in Bitlis (Eastern Turkey).*
Voß, Rudolf	Lieutenant (Marine-Oberingenieur)	Navy (Engineer)	1914/1916	Engineer on the *Goeben*, later *Barbaros Hayrettin*. *EK II May 1915.*
Wachs, Gustav	Lieutenant Commander (Marine-Stabsarzt)	Navy (Medical)	1914/1917	Medical accounts section *Breslau*.
Wagenblast, Kurt	Sub Lieutenant	Navy	1915	Special Command (SoKo), artillery officer in Canakkale, then on *General* and assigned to Straits Command in Istanbul.
Wagner, Paul	Midshipman	Navy		Secretary in Supreme Headquarters.
Wahle	Colonel	Army		As Turkish major general.
Wahlen, Willy	Lieutenant	Army	1914/1916	1914 Crew member of *Goeben*, torpedo boat *Bafra*, took over command of the gun boat *Tasküpru* from Lieutenant Commander Ellendt. *Turkish War Medal 9.11.1915, Silver Liakat Medal 27.12.1915.*
Walter, Ulrich	Second Lieutenant	Army		Engineer.
Walther, Hans	Lieutenant	Army	1915/1918	As Turkish captain, Battery Commander of the Rumeli-Kawak Battery, later in Palestine. *EK II June 1915*
Warsow	Captain	Army	1916/1918	Commander of the aircraft park.
Weber, Erich Paul (Pasha)	Colonel	Prussian Army	1913/1917	As Turkish major general, in peace-time Inspector General of the Turkish Engineers and Pioneer Corps and Fortifications. In war-time, Commanding General in the Dardanelles, first of the XV Corps on the Asiatic side und later the Southern Group, relieved on 8 July 1915 after dispute with General von Sanders.

				Born 1860. After returning from Turkey as major general in the Reichsheer, Commanding Officer of 2nd Division, died 1928 as general of the infantry. Weber's daughter married Karl Dönitz in Istanbul.
Wegner	Lieutenant	Navy	1915	Commander of *UB 44*
Wehowski, Hellmuth	Lieutenant	Army	1916/1917	Special Command (SoKo) as artillery officer.
Wehrle	Second Lieutenant	Army	1914/1915	On the staff of his father's 8th Heavy Artillery Regiment on Gallipoli. *Son of Major Wehrle (Pasha).*
Wehrle (Pasha), Heinrich	Major	Prussian Army	1914/1918	In peace-time as Turkish lieutenant colonel, Commanding Officer of the Turkish Foot Artillery Firing School; in war-time, as Turkish colonel, CO of the 8th Field Howitzer Regiment and latterly, as Turkish major general, Inspector General of Turkish Heavy Artillery in the Fifth Army. *Before coming to Turkey, with the Firing School in Jüterbog. After returning from Turkey as colonel, commanded the 4th Artillery Depot Directorate. Discharged 1920 as major general (Ret'd). Book: 'Aus meinem Turkish Tagebuch'.*
Weichbrodt, Ernst	Torpedo–Ober– Ingenieur	Navy	1915/1916	Engineer in the Torpedo Boat Flotilla. *Born 1882. 1939 Commander (Eng.), 1941/42 with Torpedo Command Pillau/East Prussia, died 1954.*
Weickmann, Ludwig Prof.	Captain	Army	1915/1918	Chief meteorologist of the Turkish Air Arm; set up the Turkish weather service.
Weidanz, Dr.	Captain (Stabsarzt)	Army (Medical)	1915/1917	Surgeon.
Weidtmann, Eduard Hubert (Pasha)	Colonel	Prussian Army	1911/1913	From January 1911 until 1913, first as Turkish colonel, CO of a Turkish Officers' Training Camp and Head of Training Courses for Turkish Infantry Officers, Military Mission, latterly as Turkish major general, Head of the Turkish Army Replacement Service.

Name	Rank	Branch	Time	Assignment/Function/Awards/Notes
			1914/1917	*Treated for inflammation of the iris in May/June 1916 in the German Hospital in Istanbul. Born 11.5.1860 in Elberfeld. Osmanie Order, Medjidie Order. After returning from Turkey as major general, Commanding Officer of 171st Infantry Brigade. Died 1934 as lieutenant general (Ret'd).*
Weimann–Bischoff, Julius	Major	Army	1915/1916	Commander of the Bosphorus fortifications.
Weis	Second Lieutenant	Prussian Army	1914/1916	As Turkish lieutenant and fortifications specialist, in peace-time, assigned to General Weber (Pasha); in war-time, fortifications on the Bosporus and Dardanelles. *Discharged 1916.*
Weißenbruch, Adolf	Second Lieutenant	Army	1916	Military Mission. *Treated in September 1916 in the German Hospital in Istanbul. Born 19.1.1894 in Mainz, commissioned 10.7.1911.*
Wellmann, Franz	Sub Lieutenant	Navy	1915/1916	Special Command (SoKo), II. Lieutenant *Breslau*, later *Goeben*
Welsch, Otto	Captain	Bavarian Army	1914/1917	As Turkish Major, in peace-time Instructor at the Turkish Cavalry Officers' Riding School; in war-time latterly as Turkish lieutenant colonel in Palestine and the Dardanelles, Adjutant to Colonel Kannengiesser in XVI Army Corps then until 1918 as major in the German Asia Corps, Palestine. *Was an instructor at the Military Riding School in Munich, died 1939 as major (Ret'd).*
Wendenburg, von	Marine-Baurat	Navy	1916/1917	Mediterranean Division (MMD).
Wendlandt	Lieutenant	Navy	1915	Commander of *UC 38*.
Wendrich, Max	Second Lieutenant	Army	1916/1918	Special Command (SoKo), aircraft engineer.
Werner	Lieutenant	Navy	1915/1916	Commander of *UB 7*. *EK II June 1915.*
Werner, Arnold	Sub Lieutenant	Navy	1914	Special Command (SoKo) *Goeben*, artillery officer in the Straits Command.

Wernicke, Fritz	Lieutenant Commander	Navy	1916/1918 1918	Commander of *UB 42*. Commander of *UB 66*. *Killed 15.1.1918 in the Aegean Sea on UB 66.*
Westernhagen, von, Thilo	Captain	Army	1915	Adjutant to Colonel Kannengiesser. *Treated for exhaustion in the German Hospital in Istanbul from 15. – 24.8.1915.*
Wichelhausen, Alfons	Lieutenant	Navy	1914/1916	Flag Lieutenant (Adjutant) *Goeben*. *EK I November 1915*
Widermann	Captain	Navy	1915	From 8 August 1915, Commander of the *Breslau*.
Wiesend, Alfred	Lieutenant	Navy (Ordinance)	1915	Special Command (SoKo), Arms und Munitions Inspectorate.
Wiesmann	Lieutenant	Army (Ordinance)	1915/1916	As Turkish captain, Arms and Munitions Inspectorate in Constantinople, responsible for trench weapons. *EK II 14.10.1915, Turkish War Medal 31.1.1916.*
Wiesner, Rudolf	Paymaster	Navy	1915/1918	Fleet Paymaster.
Wilhelm	Lieutenant	Army	1916/1918	Arms and Munitions Inspectorate in Constantinople, responsible for the transportation of munitions and equipment from Germany.
Wilhelmi	Captain	Prussian Army	1914/1916	As Turkish major, in peace-time CO of the Model Battalion of Turkish Heavy Artillery; in war-time commander of a Heavy Howitzer Battalion in the Dardanelles and later in Kut el Amara. *After returning from Turkey as major, CO of the 116th Foot Artillery Regiment Staff. Died 1920 as lieutenant colonel (Ret'd).*
Wilken, Karl	Paymaster	Navy	1915/1917	*Breslau*
Wille, Dr. Hermann	Lieutenant Commander (Marine-Stabsarzt)	Navy (Medical)	1915/1916	Medical Officer with the Coastal Inspectorate.
Willmer, Wilhelm	Major	Bavarian Army	1915/1918	As Turkish lieutenant colonel, Military Mission and commander of the Turkish 11th Infantry Division on Kiretch Tepe, Commander of the Coastal Defence Group on Suvla Bay, then commander of the 5th Division at Suvla, later Palestine. *Lieutenant Colonel.*

Name	Rank	Branch	Time	Assignment/Function/Awards/Notes
Willrich, Dr. Georg	Lieutenant Commander (Marine-Stabsarzt)	Navy (Medical)	1914/1916	Crew member of *Goeben*, hospital and depot ship *Olga*, Head of the Polyclinic in Emirgan.
Wodarz	Captain	Navy	1914/1918	Negotiating officer of the MMD for the hand-over of the Russian Fleet.
Wodrig, Franz	Sub Lieutenant	Navy	1914/1915	*Breslau* and later platoon commander with the Naval Shore Detachment on Gallipoli. *EK I August 1916*
Woermann, Hans	Sub Lieutenant	Navy	1914/1915	Battery Commander of Fort Orhanié. *Killed on 19.02.1915 during the bombardment of the forts in Orhanié in the Dardanelles, buried in Canakkale, headstone und commemoration stone in Tarabya.*
Wolff, Dr. Walter	Oberarzt	Army	1916	Military Mission. *Treated for dysentery during June/July 1916 in the German Hospital in Istanbul.17.5.82 in Berlin, commissioned 1.10.1902.*
Wolfram, Joachim	Sub Lieutenant	Navy	1915/1916	III. Lieutenant *Breslau*, Observation officer in the Dardanelles, temporarily detached from the Fleet to the Special Command (SoKo). *EK II 14.10.1915*
Wolfskeel, Eberhard Graf von Reichenberg	Captain	Prussian Army	1915/1917	As Turkish major, Military Mission and artillery commander in the Dardanelles, later in Diyarbakir and Iraq with XII Army Corps. *Born 1875. In charge of the artillery, which fired on the Armenian forts in Urfa and was adviser to General Fakhri Pasha.* *Reichsheer colonel, died1954.*
Wolpmann, Kurt	Major (General Staff)	Prussian Army	1916	Representative of the military plenipotentiary at the German Embassy in Constantinople. *Treated for respiratory disorder in May 1916 in the German Hospital in Istanbul. Born 7.9.78 in Cologne, commissioned 17.3.1897, lieutenant colonel (Ret'd).*

Wossidlo, Fritz	Commander	Navy	1914/1915 1918	As Turkish lieutenant colonel, 1. General Staff Officer of the Straits High Command (Bosphorus) and commander of Fort Hamidiè; then Navy Liaison Command in Istanbul. Later commander of the Navy Command Syria-Iraq. *EK II 26.3.1915, Silver Imtiaz Medal 31.3.1915, Reichsmarine, discharged 1923 as rear admiral (Ret'd).*
Wrochem, von	Second Lieutenant	Prussian Army	1914/1916	In peace-time, latterly instructor in a Turkish Staff Officers' Training Camp; in war-time, Adjutant to Colonel Kannengiesser, then Deputy LoC Inspector of the Second Turkish Army. *After returning from Turkey, served as captain in the 2nd Guards Regiment. Discharged 1920 as major (Ret'd).*
Wunderlich, Dr. Hans	Major (Oberstabsarzt)	Army	1914/1917	*Breslau,* later Military Hospital Harbiye.
Wurmb, von	Lieutenant	Navy	1915/1916	As Turkish captain, gunnery officer in the Dardanelles. *EK II June 1915, Turkish War Medal 9.11.1915, Silver Liakat–Medal 27.12.1915.*
Würth von Würthenau, Robert Emil	Captain	Prussian Army	1915/1918	As Turkish major, Military Mission and CO of Turkish Depot Regiment. Later with the German Asia Corps in Palestine. *Born 3.8.1879 in Staufen im Breisgau, died in Frankfurt 4.6.1943.*
Zachariae	Major	Prussian Army	1915/1918	As Turkish lieutenant colonel, Military Mission and Director of a Turkish Rifle and Ammunition Factory in Istanbul.
Zacharias-Langhans, Dr. Gotthard	Lieutenant (Marine-Oberassistenzarzt)	Navy (Medical)	1915/1917	Naval Field Hospital Taşkışla and Bosphorus–Anatolian Hospital. *EK II June 1915, Hamburg Hanse Cross 31.1.1916.*
Zähringer, Albert	Second Lieutenant	Army	1914/1918	Special Command (SoKo), artillery officer.
Zarnke	Captain	Army	1916/1918	Editor of the soldiers' magazine 'Am Bosporus'.
Zeiss, Heinz Dr.	Captain (Stabsarzt)	Army (Medical)	1916/1918	Medical Officer with the Fifth Army.

Name	Rank	Branch	Time	Assignment/Function/Awards/Notes
Zernov	Captain	Army	1915/1915	Turkish Air Arm.
Zickel, Heinrich Dr.	Captain (Stabsarzt)	Army (Medical)	1915	MO to engineers unit on Gallipoli.
Ziegler und Klipphausen, Johannes von	Lieutenant Commander	Navy	1915/1918	Engineer on the *Goeben*.
Ziegler, Tankred	Paymaster	Navy	1915/1916	*Goeben*
Zillmann, Richard	Sub Lieutenant (Marine-Ingenieur)	Navy (Engineer)	1916/1917	*Goeben*
Zimmermann, Heinrich	Lieutenant Commander (Marine-Stabsingenieur)	Navy (Engineer)	1914/1916	Chief Engineer *Torgut Reis*. *April 1915 EK II*
Zinke gen. Sommer, Otto	Lieutenant	Navy	1915	Commander of a Turkish torpedo boat.
Zipper	Captain	Army	1915	OC engineers unit on Gallipoli. *Due to dysentery, repatriated in August 1915 to Germany.*
Zirzow, Otto	Commander	Navy	1914/1916	Navigation officer, *Goeben*. *EK I November 1915*
Zrizen	Commander	Navy	1915	Navigation officer, *Goeben*
Zschech, Dr.Bernhard	Lieutenant Commander (Marine-Stabsarzt)	Navy (Medical)	1914/1917	MO on *Goeben*, Turkish Navy Field Hospital Taşkışla.
Zwirner, Kurt	Lieutenant	Navy	1916/1918	OC Rifle Platoon *Breslau*. *Killed when the Breslau went down on 20 January 1918 off Imbros; but on commemoration plaque in Tarabya.*

Appendix 2

Chronological list of German officers and men who died or were killed between 1914-1916 whilst serving in Turkey with units of the Ottoman Army, Navy and Air Arm engaged in the Gallipoli, Dardanelles and Black Sea theatres of war. The list excludes those killed or missing on the Breslau when she went down in 1918 (see Appendix 3)

This list is an extract from the:

- List of graves in the German Military Cemetery in Tarabya [605]
- Reports of the Mediterranean Division
- Casualty list of the Naval Shore Detachment [606]
- Casualty list of the Breslau [607]
- Files from the German Military Political Archives

No exact casualty figures for the Engineers Company are available; it is only known that three sappers were killed and two died.

Date	Name	Rank	Unit	Remarks
Unknown	3 German Sappers	Unknown	Guards Engineer Replacement Battalion	Buried Cham Burnu.
Unknown	1 German Sapper	Unknown	Guards Engineer Replacement Battalion	Unknown
Unknown	Reiter	Driver	Unknown	Killed on the Dardanelles, transferred to Tarabya.
Unknown	Stahl, Paul	Leading Seaman	Unknown	Killed or died on the Dardanelles, transferred to Tarabya.
Unknown	Wittkop, Wilhelm	Leading Seaman	Unknown	Killed or died on the Dardanelles, transferred to Tarabya.
28.08.1914	Szernik, Karl	Able Seaman	*Breslau*	Accidental death in transit.
14.11.1914	11 German seamen	Unknown	*Goeben*	Killed in a naval battle in the Black Sea.
21.11.1914	Zehner, Karl	Leading Seaman	*Goeben*	Buried Tarabya.
22.11.1914	Berneth, Fritz	Zimmermanns-Maat	*Nilüfer*	Killed when *Nilüfer* sank, buried Tarabya.
22.11.1914	Schwießelmann, Hans	Ordnance Lieutenant	Special Command (SoKo) as Torpedo & Mine Specialist	Unknown

Date	Name	Rank	Unit	Remarks
26.12.1914	Bode, Hermann	Leading Seaman	*Goeben*	Buried Tarabya.
26.12.1914	Osterkamp, Friedrich	Leading Seaman	*Goeben*	Buried Tarabya.
19.02.1915	Woermann, Hans	Sub Lieutenant (Navy)	CO of Fort Orhanié	Killed on the Dardanelles, transferred to Tarabya.
08.03.1915	Hilgendorff, Fritz	Lieutenant Commander	MMD, took part in operations against Suez Canal	Suicide in an hotel in Istanbul, buried in Tarabya.
18.03.1915	Brilla, August	Ober-Maat	Gunner at Fort Hamidié	Killed during the Allied fleet attack on the Dardanelles, transferred to Tarabya.
18.03.1915	Sommerfeld, Paul	Leading Seaman (Gunner)	Gunner at Fort Hamidié	
18.03.1915	Schildhauer, Erich	Able Seaman (Gunner)	Gunner at Fort Hamidié	
20.03.1915	Radau, Wilhelm	Artillerie-Maat	Gunner at Fort Hamidié	
03.05.1915	Prüntges, Gerhard	Leading Seaman	Naval Shore Detachment	Killed at Kereves Dere, buried at Gallipoli.
03.05.1915	Dathe, Werner	Leading Seaman	Naval Shore Detachment	Killed at Kereves Dere, buried at Gallipoli.
04.05.1915	Drechsler, Reinhold	Able Seaman (Gunner)	Naval Shore Detachment	Killed at Kereves Dere, buried at Gallipoli.
06.05.1915	Kutnick, Hinrich	Leading Seaman	Naval Shore Detachment	Killed on Gallipoli, transferred to Tarabya.
28.05.1915	Schelling, Karl	Lieutenant Commander	Unknown	Buried Tarabya.
04.06.1915	Haase, Johann	Able Seaman	Naval Shore Detachment	Killed at Sigindere.
04.06.1915	Gorzelski, Eduard	Leading Seaman	Naval Shore Detachment	Killed at Sigindere.
04.06.1915	Flesner, Gerhard	Able Seaman	Naval Shore Detachment	Killed at Sigindere.
04.06.1915	Hoheisel, Paul	Leading Seaman d. Res.	Naval Shore Detachment	Killed at Sigindere.
09.06.1915	Lass, Robert August Ludwig	Petty Officer (Ordnance)	Gunner	Killed at Kumkale.
09.06.1915	Schirrmacher, Paul Leo Gustav	Able Seaman	Gunner	Killed at Kumkale.
11.06.1915	Klitzke, Richart	Telegraphist		Killed during the naval battle between *Breslau* and a Russian destroyer in the Black Sea, buried Tarabya.
11.06.1915	Krauß, Friedrich	Leading Seaman		
11.06.1915	Maceirzhynski, Theodor	Leading Seaman	*Breslau*	
11.06.1915	Seitz, Engelbert	Able Seaman		
11.06.1915	Woide, Paul	Leading Seaman		
28.06.1915	Leipzig, Erich von	Colonel	Military Attaché German Embassy	Suspected suicide in Uzunköprü, buried at Tarabya.
28.06.1915	Brocken, gen. Brückers, Peter	Leading Seaman	Naval Shore Detachment	Killed at Sigindere.
01.07.1915	Hentschel, Fritz	Able Seaman	Torpedo Flotilla, assigned *Olga*	Died, buried Tarabya.
01.07.1915	Kleesattel, Adam	Able Seaman (Gunner)	Gunner	Killed on Gallipoli.

Date	Name	Rank	Unit/Ship	Notes
13.07.1915	Kalkowski, Otto	Able Seaman		Killed on Gallipoli.
18.07.1915	Bohnhof, Gustav	Leading Stoker	*Breslau*	Killed after striking a mine, all buried in Tarabya.
18.07.1915	Garbrecht, Richard	Leading Stoker		
18.07.1915	Hartmann, Emil	Stoker		
18.07.1915	Hein, Albert	Stoker		
18.07.1915	Strenge, Walter	Machinist Mate		
18.07.1915	Igel, Fritz	Stoker		
18.07.1915	Kroll, Franz	Machinist		
18.07.1915	Pechmann, Paul	Leading Stoker		
18.07.1915	Heller, Hans, Georg	Lieutenant	5th Army	Buried Tarabya.
20.07.1915	Eckert	Bosun's Mate		Killed on Gallipoli.
01.08.1915	Döring, Edmund	Senior Machinist Mate	*Goeben*	Buried Tarabya.
05.08.1915	Kurtz	Senior Gunners Mate	Gunner	Died of wounds.
05.08.1915	Krenzlin, Rudolf	Sapper	Engineers Unit Istanbul	Buried Tarabya.
08.08.1915	Denk	Petty Officer		Unknown
08.08.1915	Hildebrandt, Oskar	Sub Lieutenant (Navy Reserve)	Platoon Commander, Naval Shore Detachment of *Breslau*	Killed during the battle on Hill 971, buried at Deniz Dere.
08.08.1915	Dank, Matthias	Able Seaman	Naval Shore Detachment	Killed on Gallipoli, buried at Ismail Tepe.
08.08.1915	Klaus, Fritz	Able Seaman	Naval Shore Detachment	Killed on Gallipoli, buried at Kurt Dere.
10.08.1915	Buchmüller, Ernst	Leading Seaman	Naval Shore Detachment	Killed on Gallipoli, buried at Ismail Tepe.
15.08.1915	Huck, Otto	Leading Seaman	Gunner	Died of wounds, interred in Tarabya.
16.08.1915	Hispe, Martin	Able Seaman	Gunner	Killed on Gallipoli.
16.08.1915	Plitsch, Ernst	Able Seaman	Gunner	Killed on Gallipoli.
16.08.1915	Lorsking, Wilhelm	Gunner's Mate	Gunner	Killed on Gallipoli.
20.08.1915	Bierwagen	Sapper	Guards Engineer Replacement Battalion	Wounded and died on the same day in the field hospital at Aga Dere.
21.08.1915	Mühlenbach, Peter	Able Seaman	Gunner	Killed on Gallipoli.
September 1915	Kanter, Friedrich	Leading Seaman	Gunner	Killed on Gallipoli.
03.09.1915	Pehl	Gunner's Mate		Died of his wounds.
06.09.1915	Hammerschmidt, Georg	Leading Stoker	Torpedo Flotilla Istanbul	Died of typhus. Buried Tarabya.
07.09.1915	Peters, Wilhelm	Leading Seaman	Naval Shore Detachment	Killed on Gallipoli, escaped in June from British captivity, buried at Kilia Tepe.
16.09.1915	Kelb, Wilhelm	Sapper	Sapper Unit Istanbul	Buried Tarabya.
30.09.1915	Winter, Heinrich	Leading Gunner's mate	Unknown	Died of dysentery, transferred to Tarabya.
17.10.1915	Templin, Karl	Leading Stoker	Harbour division, Special Command (SoKo)	Killed during sea battle on the gun boat *Taschkeprü*, Buried Tarabya.

Date	Name	Rank	Unit	Remarks
17.10.1915	Rathert, Christian	Able Seaman	Naval Shore Detachment	Died of typhus on Gallipoli, buried at Kilia Tepe.
06.11.1915	Kraft, Werner	Sub Lieutenant	*Goeben*, Naval Shore Detachment Gallipoli	Died of typhus. Buried Tarabya.
07.11.1915	Danker, Hermann	Petty Officer	Special Command (SoKo)	Died of typhus. Buried Tarabya.
08.11.1915	Kaufhold, Hinrich	Able Seaman		Killed at Gallipoli.
11.11.1915	König, Friedrich Karl	Pilot	Turkish Air Arm at St. Stefano	Buried Tarabya.
16.11.1915	Trein, Hermann	Corporal	Artillery Dardanelles	Buried Tarabya.
21.11.1915	Schophoff, Wilhelm	Sergeant	Artillery	Buried Tarabya.
28.11.1915	Wachowiak, Peter Valentin	Leading Stoker	Steamer *General*	Buried Tarabya.
03.12.1915	Raydt	Lieutenant (Navy)	Destroyer *Yarhisar*	
03.12.1915	Mallus	Torpedo Machinist	Destroyer *Yarhisar*	
03.12.1915	Annes	Torpedo Machinist Mate	Destroyer *Yarhisar*	
03.12.1915	Gräfe	Torpedo Able Seaman	Destroyer *Yarhisar*	Missing after the destroyer *Yarhisar* was torpedoed on 3.12.1915 by the Allied submarine, HMS *E 11*.
03.12.1915	Voss	Torpedo Leading Seaman	Destroyer *Yarhisar*	
03.12.1915	Diessel	Torpedo Leading Seaman	Destroyer *Yarhisar*	
03.12.1915	Czemper	Torpedo Able Seaman	Destroyer *Yarhisar*	
03.12.1915	Wichert	Leading Telegraphist	Destroyer *Yarhisar*	
03.12.1915	Ruebe	Telegraphist	Destroyer *Yarhisar*	
07.12.1915	Rudat, Johannes	Leading Telegraphist	Special Command (SoKo)	Died during a battle between the *Intibah* with a submarine, Buried Tarabya.
07.12.1915	Schmidt, Franz	Leading Seaman	Minelayer *Intibah*	
08.12.1915	Müller, Georg Ernst	Leading Telegraphist	Assigned to *General*	Killed on 8.12.15 in the Marmara Sea, first buried in Bandirma, then Tarabya.
10.12.1915	Klähn, Walter	Stoker	Minesweeping Div. Bosphorus	Killed during a battle with a destroyer, Buried Tarabya.
10.12.1915	Schmidt, Franz	Leading Seaman	Unknown	Unknown
10.12.1915	Klaehn	Stoker	Unknown	Unknown
12.12.1915	Hecht, Wilfried	Able Seaman	Naval Shore Detachment	Killed on Gallipoli, buried on Kilia Tepe.
29.12.1915	Reinecke, Emil	Leading Seaman	Naval Shore Detachment	Killed on Gallipoli, buried on Kilia Tepe.
30.12.1915	Fack, Hans	Able Seaman	Unknown	Died of wounds, interred in Tarabya.

07.01.1916	Arendt, Franz	Lieutenant Commander (Stabsarzt)	Hospital ship *Reschid Pasa*	Buried Tarabya.
21.01.1916	Wienker, Heinrich	Machinist Mate	*Goeben*	Buried Tarabya.
26.03.1916	Dahms, Richard	Leading Stoker	*Breslau*	Accidentally killed by an explosion.
13.04.1916	Nippelt, Fritz	Sergeant Armourer	Military Mission	Buried Tarabya.
07.05.1916	Bettaque, Rudolf	Officer Candidate (Offizier-Stellvertreter)	Minesweeping Command	Killed on the Dardanelles, transferred to Tarabya.
29.05.1916	Köhler, Heinrich	Able Seaman	*Goeben*	Buried Tarabya.
29.05.1916	Preussner, Louis	Sergeant (Unteroffizier) (served as Turkish Second Lieutenant)	Flying Training School at St. Stefano	Crashed on 16.5.1916, died in the German Hospital, buried Tarabya.
02.07.1916	Galling, August	Able Seaman		Buried Tarabya.
12.07.1916	Runcke, Paul	Able Seaman	Steamer *General*	Buried Tarabya.
25.07.1916	Burgschat, Franz	Leading Stoker	*U 38*	Buried Tarabya.
02.09.1916	Winter, Georg	Able Seaman	*Goeben*	Buried Tarabya.
13.09.1916	Hünermörder, Paul	Able Seaman	Turkish Torpedo Boat Flotilla	Buried Tarabya.
17.09.1916	Hartig, Egon	Stoker	*Goeben*	Died of illness, buried Tarabya.
28.09.1916	Scheuble, Ernst	Leading Machinist Mate	Harbour Bosphorus	Buried Tarabya.
11.10.1916	Töpfer, August	Lieutenant (Ober-Ingenieur)	Armaments Office	Buried Tarabya.
18.11.1916	Wendt, Rudolf	Stoker	Assigned to *General*	Buried Tarabya.
20.11.1916	Scholz, Karl	Telegraphist	*Breslau*	Accidentally killed in transit.
07.12.1916	Gruber, Georg	Able Seaman	*U 46*	
07.12.1916	Hampel, Paulus	Leading Machinist Mate	*U 46*	Killed when the *U 46* sank off the mouth of the Bosphorus in the Black Sea after striking a mine. Buried Tarabya. The wreck of *U 46* is now on display in the Naval Museum in Istanbul.
07.12.1916	Heiling, Peter	Sub Lieutenant	*U 46*	
07.12.1916	Hoffmann, Albert	Leading Machinist Mate	*U 46*	
07.12.1916	Karkowski, Wilhelm	Engineer Candidate Officer	*U 46*	
07.12.1916	Lücken, Eduard	Machinist Mate	*U 46*	
07.12.1916	Meyer, Peter	Able Seaman	*U 46*	
07.12.1916	Neiling, Peter	Sub Lieutenant	*U 46*	
07.12.1916	Witt, Otto	Petty Officer	*U 46*	
21.12.1916	Gugat, Johann	Leading Seaman	Assigned to *General*	Buried Tarabya.
22.12.1916	Brockmann, Heinrich	Able Seaman	Assigned to *General*	Buried Tarabya.

Appendix 3

Crew list of those killed when the *Breslau* sank on 20 January 1918

List of the crew of the German light cruiser *Breslau*, who were killed when she went down after being struck by mines off Imbros on 20 January 1918. Of the 336 killed, only fifty-six, of whom twenty-two are unknown, were rescued from the sea or washed ashore on Lemnos or Imbros and buried there. There are no other known German graves on these islands.[607]

Hippel, Georg von	Captain/Kapitän z. S., Commandant	Homeyer, Otto	Lieutenant Commander / Kapitänleutnant
Sell, Friedrich Freiherr von	Lieutenant Commander / Kapitänleutnant	Deetjen, Hermann	Lieutenant / Oberleutnant z. S.
Zwirner, Kurt	Lieutenant / Oberleutnant z. S	Müller, Dr. Viktor	Lieutenant Commander Marine-Stabsarzt
Eschenbrenner, Dr. Hugo	Sub Lieutenant Marine-Assistenzarzt	Bothe, Hermann	Chief Petty Officer / Oberbootsmann-Maat
Kehlenbrink, August	Chief Petty Officer / Oberbootsmann-Maat	Sturm, Wilhelm	Chief Petty Officer / Oberbootsmann-Maat
Zahn, Otto Franz (Buried on Lemnos)	Chief Petty Officer / Oberbootsmann-Maat	Stetten, Hermann von	CPO Artificer Ober-Stückmeister-Maat
Tscheschner, Otto	CPO Artificer Ober-Stückmeister-Maat	Antes, Wilhelm	Petty Officer / Bootsmaat
Adomeit, Emil	Petty Officer / Bootsmaat	Becker, Guido	Petty Officer / Bootsmaat
Bischoff, Willy	Petty Officer / Bootsmaat	Grüning, Erich	Petty Officer / Bootsmaat
Gustin, Albert	Petty Officer / Bootsmaat	Heller, Karl	Petty Officer / Bootsmaat
Meine, Heinrich	Petty Officer / Bootsmaat	Schäl, Theodor	Petty Officer / Bootsmaat
Schmidt, Georg	Petty Officer / Bootsmaat	Schröder, Wilhelm	Petty Officer / Bootsmaat
Schütt, Paul	Petty Officer / Bootsmaat	Augner, Daniel	Leading Seaman/ Ober-Matrose
Bose, Waldemar Otto (Buried on Lemnos)	Leading Seaman/Ober-Matrose	Brandt, Karl	Leading Seaman/ Ober-Matrose
Braun, Richard	Leading Seaman/Ober-Matrose	Bröcker, Otto	Leading Seaman/ Ober-Matrose
Brückner, Max	Leading Seaman/Ober-Matrose	Bülow, Robert von	Leading Seaman/ Ober-Matrose
Feuerriegel, Wilhelm	Leading Seaman/Ober-Matrose	Friedrichs, Georg	Leading Seaman/ Ober-Matrose
Früh, Emil	Leading Seaman/Ober-Matrose	Gotthardt, Hubert	Leading Seaman/ Ober-Matrose
Hans, Robert	Leading Seaman/Ober-Matrose	Härtel, Georg (Buried on Lemnos)	Leading Seaman/ Ober-Matrose
Hartmann, Hermann	Leading Seaman/Ober-Matrose	Hauser, Alex	Leading Seaman/ Ober-Matrose

Haz, Karl	Leading Seaman/Ober-Matrose	Heß, Felix	Leading Seaman/Ober-Matrose
Jünemann, Wendelin	Leading Seaman/Ober-Matrose	Karsten, Robert	Leading Seaman/Ober-Matrose
Klingsiek, Wilhelm (Buried on Lemnos)	Leading Seaman/Ober-Matrose	Klühs, Otto Ernst (Buried on Lemnos)	Leading Seaman/Ober-Matrose
Lewinski, Leo	Leading Seaman/Ober-Matrose	Mangrapp, Gustav	Leading Seaman/Ober-Matrose
Mattäi, Ernst	Leading Seaman/Ober-Matrose	Müggenburg, Heinrich	Leading Seaman/Ober-Matrose
Nissen, Lorenz	Leading Seaman/Ober-Matrose	Nowack, Kurt	Leading Seaman/Ober-Matrose
Panjas, Johann	Leading Seaman/Ober-Matrose	Pauls, Willy	Leading Seaman/Ober-Matrose
Philipsen, Max	Leading Seaman/Ober-Matrose	Pippig, Bruno	Leading Seaman/Ober-Matrose
Pust, Franz	Leading Seaman/Ober-Matrose	Reich, Wilhelm	Leading Seaman/Ober-Matrose
Sack, Alfred	Leading Seaman/Ober-Matrose	Schiefer, Gustav	Leading Seaman/Ober-Matrose
Schipper, Kurt	Leading Seaman/Ober-Matrose	Sindt, Ernst	Leading Seaman/Ober-Matrose
Stahl, Paul (Buried Lemnos)	Leading Seaman/Ober-Matrose	Struck, Eduard	Leading Seaman/Ober-Matrose
Szusries, August	Leading Seaman/Ober-Matrose	Uhlig, Alfred	Leading Seaman/Ober-Matrose
Wenderoth, Franz	Leading Seaman/Ober-Matrose	Wernicke, Willi Paul (Buried Lemnos)	Leading Seaman/Ober-Matrose
Witt, Otto	Leading Seaman/Ober-Matrose	Witte, Johannes	Leading Seaman/Ober-Matrose
Wittkop, Wilhelm (Buried on Lemnos)	Leading Seaman/Ober-Matrose	Wolter, Albert	Leading Seaman/Ober-Matrose
Aufermann, Georg (Buried on Lemnos)	Able Seaman / Matrose	Ambrosius, Paul	Able Seaman / Matrose
Brandenburg, Otto	Able Seaman / Matrose	Brandt, Wilhelm	Able Seaman / Matrose
Beutel, Wilhelm (Buried on Lemnos)	Able Seaman / Matrose	Bieneck, Karl	Able Seaman / Matrose
Blümel, Wilhelm	Able Seaman / Matrose	Böckmann, Louis	Able Seaman / Matrose
Brellert, Paul	Able Seaman / Matrose	Christoff, Gustav	Able Seaman / Matrose
Doden, Mense	Able Seaman / Matrose	Enchelmaier, August (Buried on Lemnos)	Able Seaman / Matrose
Fock, Jakob	Able Seaman / Matrose	Herold, Hugo	Able Seaman / Matrose
Holzapfel, Wilhelm (Buried on Lemnos)	Able Seaman / Matrose	Karl, Erich	Able Seaman / Matrose
Kiedrowski, Franz von	Able Seaman / Matrose	Krieger, August	Able Seaman / Matrose
Kühn, Kurt	Able Seaman / Matrose	Leitner, Kajetan	Able Seaman / Matrose
Mess, Wilhelm (Buried on Lemnos)	Able Seaman / Matrose	Netzel, John	Able Seaman / Matrose

Otto, Cornelius	Able Seaman / Matrose	Otto, Richard	Able Seaman / Matrose
Pietsch	Able Seaman / Matrose	Prödel, Karl	Able Seaman / Matrose
Runto, Gustav	Able Seaman / Matrose	Schaller, Bruno	Able Seaman / Matrose
Schröter, Wilhelm	Able Seaman / Matrose	Seidel, Richard	Able Seaman / Matrose
Selewski, Ernst	Able Seaman / Matrose	Smolorz, Johann	Able Seaman / Matrose
Sniatecki, Sigismund	Able Seaman / Matrose	Springorum, Otto	Able Seaman / Matrose
Böhme, Erwin	Feuerwerker	Schramm, Friedrich	CPO Ordnance Ober-Feuerwerker-Maat
Krüger, Bernhard	CPO Ordnance Ober-Feuerwerker-Maat	Zernike, Wilhelm	CPO Ordnance Ober-Feuerwerker-Maat
Mohr, Wilhelm	Artilleriemechaniker-Maat	Schulze, Wilhelm	Artilleriemechaniker-Maat
Falk, Peter	Artilleriemechaniker-Ober-Gast	Krause, Ernst	Artilleriemechaniker-Ober-Gast
Korn, Ernst	Artilleriemechaniker-Gast	Laux, Ernst	Artilleriemechaniker-Gast
Weidemann, Wilhelm	Steuermann	Thom, Oskar	Obersteuermann–Maat
Richter, Max	Obersignal-Maat	Bergmann, Otto	Signal-Maat
Buchholz, Richard	Signal-Maat	Etzold, Emil	Leading Signaller Obersignal-Gast
Küstermann, Anton	Leading Signaller Obersignal-Gast	Laetsch, Kurt Johann (Buried on Lemnos)	Leading Signaller Obersignal-Gast
Loocks, Walter	Leading Signaller Obersignal-Gast	Staden, Peter	Leading Signaller Obersignal-Gast
Blümel, Richard (Buried on Lemnos)	Signaller Signal-Gast	Geßner, Walter	Signaller Signal-Gast
Güthlein, Georg	Signaller Signal-Gast	Kindereit, Karl	Signaller Signal-Gast
Speicher, Alfons	Signaller Signalgast	Adolph, Max	Telegraphist FT-Maat
Steffen, Hans	Telegrapher FT-Gast	Stagebaum, Leopold (Buried on Lemnos)	Telegrapher FT-Gast
Schüler, Karl	Telegrapher FT-Gast	Zilian, Rudolf	Telegrapher FT-Gast
Sienknecht, Johann	Oberwacht-Maat	Grabe, Hans	Marine-Stabsingenieur
Friede, Karl	Marine-Ingenieur-Aspirant	Kledehn, Fritz Georg (Buried on Lemnos)	Marine-Ingenieur-Aspirant
Becker, Wilhelm	Leading Machinist	Arnold, Hans	Machinist
Bartelt, Emil	Machinist	Borgmann, Walter	Maschinist
Bormann, Ernst	Machinist	Grüwell, Friedrich	Machinist
Machande, Paul	Machinist	Rebehn, Karl	Machinist
Axen, Heinrich	Marine-Ingenieur-Appl.	Scholz, Martin	Marine-Ingenieur-Appl.
Hartmann, Wilhelm	Chief Engineering PO	Jäppelt, Hans Arthur (Buried on Lemnos)	Chief Engineering PO
Künzel, Max	Chief Engineering PO	Vierkant, Max	Chief Engineering PO
Wortmann, Adolf	Chief Engineering PO	Bäßler, Alfred	Engineering PO
Bukowsky, Franz (Buried on Lemnos)	Engineering PO	Danschke, Richard	Engineering PO
Dreyer, August	Engineering PO	Dürrbaum, Gustav	Engineering PO
Dzink, Johann	Engineering PO	Ernst, Johannes	Engineering PO
Gäde, Christian	Engineering PO	Grau, August	Engineering PO

Grenda, Hermann	Engineering PO	Grimm, Alwin	Engineering PO
Herrmann, Wilhelm	Engineering PO	Heuck, Firedrich	Engineering PO
Hielscher, Fritz	Engineering PO	Hinrichten, Otto	Engineering PO
Jarren, Otto	Engineering PO	Kaschke, Franz	Engineering PO
Köster, Paul	Engineering PO	Lüderitz, Kurt	Engineering PO
Markfelder, Johann	Engineering PO	Moreitz, Walter	Engineering PO
Neukrich, Richard	Engineering PO	Pappert, Heinrich	Engineering PO
Radtke, Otto	Engineering PO	Rosenthal, Paul	Engineering PO
Schäfer, Erich	Engineering PO	Scheffer, Fritz	Engineering PO
Schönbrodt, Hermann	Engineering PO	Schönfeldt, Hans	Engineering PO
Schwider, Wilhelm	Engineering PO	Sprunk, Franz	Engineering PO
Unger, Rudolf Bruno (Buried on Lemnos)	Engineering PO	Weiße, Friedrich	Engineering PO
Atulla, Karl	Leading Stoker/Ober-Heizer	Behrendt, Helmut	Leading Stoker/ Ober-Heizer
Berndt, Felix	Leading Stoker/Ober-Heizer	Breitenfeld, Josef	Leading Stoker/ Ober-Heizer
Dittrich, Fritz	Leading Stoker/Ober-Heizer	Dix, Bruno	Leading Stoker/ Ober-Heizer
Falk, Paul	Leading Stoker/Ober-Heizer	Fiebig, Friedrich	Leading Stoker/ Ober-Heizer
Filius, Gabriel	Leading Stoker/Ober-Heizer	Fischer, Florian	Leading Stoker/ Ober-Heizer
Freier, Johann	Leading Stoker/Ober-Heizer	Grytz, Richard	Leading Stoker/ Ober-Heizer
Haase, Alwin	Leading Stoker/Ober-Heizer	Haselow, Rudolf	Leading Stoker/ Ober-Heizer
Hasselmann, Hans	Leading Stoker/Ober-Heizer	Heinh, Erich	Leading Stoker/ Ober-Heizer
Henkel, Paul	Leading Stoker/Ober-Heizer	Herbold, August	Leading Stoker/ Ober-Heizer
Jesautzki, Franz	Leading Stoker/Ober-Heizer	Kilguhs, Johann	Leading Stoker/ Ober-Heizer
Klatte, Karl	Leading Stoker/Ober-Heizer	Klohs, Otto	Leading Stoker/ Ober-Heizer
Klünder, Hugo	Leading Stoker/Ober-Heizer	Knickrehm, Heinrich	Leading Stoker/ Ober-Heizer
Koch, Richard	Leading Stoker/Ober-Heizer	Langel, Josef	Leading Stoker/ Ober-Heizer
Langhof, Rudolf	Leading Stoker/Ober-Heizer	Langlotz, Rudolf	Leading Stoker/ Ober-Heizer
Lück, Max	Leading Stoker/Ober-Heizer	Mainczhl, Franz	Leading Stoker/ Ober-Heizer
Marek, Albert	Leading Stoker/Ober-Heizer	Martens, Willi	Leading Stoker/ Ober-Heizer
Neidhard, Franz	Leading Stoker/Ober-Heizer	Patelschik, Franz	Leading Stoker/ Ober-Heizer
Piezt, Ignaz	Leading Stoker/Ober-Heizer	Rothkegel, August	Leading Stoker/ Ober-Heizer

Schlicht, Georg	Leading Stoker/Ober-Heizer	Schliewe, Franz	Leading Stoker/Ober-Heizer
Schmidt, Johannes	Leading Stoker/Ober-Heizer	Schramm, Franz	Leading Stoker/Ober-Heizer
Schulz, Rudolf	Leading Stoker/Ober-Heizer	Schuttler, Friedrich	Leading Stoker/Ober-Heizer
Schwan, Walter	Leading Stoker/Ober-Heizer	Sewerin, Walter (Buried on Lemnos)	Leading Stoker/Ober-Heizer
Sosnowski, Wilhelm	Leading Stoker/Ober-Heizer	Strube, Karl	Leading Stoker/Ober-Heizer
Suhrbier, Willi	Leading Stoker/Ober-Heizer	Teermann, Hermann	Leading Stoker/Ober-Heizer
Tesch, Otto	Leading Stoker/Ober-Heizer	Tetzloff, Wilhelm	Leading Stoker/Ober-Heizer
Trapp, Hermann	Leading Stoker/Ober-Heizer	Urban, Eduard Julius (Buried on Lemnos)	Leading Stoker/Ober-Heizer
Vierke, Willi	Leading Stoker/Ober-Heizer	Weißpflog, Kurt	Leading Stoker/Ober-Heizer
Winkler, Arthur	Leading Stoker/Ober-Heizer	Zander, Paul	Leading Stoker/Ober-Heizer
Zaretzke, Alfred	Leading Stoker/Ober-Heizer	Zech, Franz	Leading Stoker/Ober-Heizer
Zimmermann, Jakob	Leading Stoker/Ober-Heizer	Altmeyer, Jakob	Stoker / Heizer
Babrucke, Otto	Stoker / Heizer	Bauer, Karl	Stoker / Heizer
Beckmann, Johann	Stoker / Heizer	Biber, Michael	Stoker / Heizer
Bleser, Hans (Buried on Lemnos)	Stoker / Heizer	Brachnitz, Walter	Stoker / Heizer
Bräk, Bruno Paul (Buried on Lemnos)	Stoker / Heizer	Bürgelt, Kurt	Stoker / Heizer
Eberhardt, Fritz	Stoker / Heizer	Ehrhardt, Heinrich	Stoker / Heizer
Ermert, Karl	Stoker / Heizer	Erning, Gustav	Stoker / Heizer
Feidler, Friedrich	Stoker / Heizer	Fischer, Johann	Stoker / Heizer
Frank, Arthur	Stoker / Heizer	Freier, Friedrich	Stoker / Heizer
Golgowski, Walter	Stoker / Heizer	Hartwig, Erich	Stoker / Heizer
Hawener, Wilhelm	Stoker / Heizer	Heer, Konrad	Stoker / Heizer
Hirsch, Otto	Stoker / Heizer	Höser, Karl	Stoker / Heizer
Hoika, Anton	Stoker / Heizer	Kayser, Karl	Stoker / Heizer
Klages, Gustav	Stoker / Heizer	Klose, Anton (Buried on Lemnos)	Stoker / Heizer
Koch, Willi	Stoker / Heizer	Koppers, Johann	Stoker / Heizer
Masche, August	Stoker / Heizer	Müller, Oskar	Stoker / Heizer
Näth, Friedrich	Stoker / Heizer	Nauter, Josef	Stoker / Heizer
Niehoff, Rudolf Karl (Buried on Lemnos)	Stoker / Heizer	Pakulla, Josef	Stoker / Heizer
Pfaff, Friedrich	Stoker / Heizer	Pfahlert, Ernst	Stoker / Heizer
Piachnow, Fritz	Stoker / Heizer	Pleines, Hugo	Stoker / Heizer
Pömmerl, Franz	Stoker / Heizer	Probst, Johann	Stoker / Heizer
Prochert, Heinrich	Stoker / Heizer	Reinhardt, Arthur	Stoker / Heizer
Robakowski, Paul	Stoker / Heizer	Rößler, Georg Erich (Buried on Lemnos)	Stoker / Heizer

Schablitzki, Max	Stoker / Heizer	Scheuemann, Gustav	Stoker / Heizer
Schulze, Reinhold	Stoker / Heizer	Gebralla, Florian	Stoker / Heizer
Seifert, Karl	Stoker / Heizer	Siegert, August	Stoker / Heizer
Smolka, Ignatz	Stoker / Heizer	Wackerow, Ernst	Stoker / Heizer
Wehnke, Karl	Stoker / Heizer	Weiß, Anton	Stoker / Heizer
Werner, Artur	Stoker / Heizer	Widera, Karl	Stoker / Heizer
Winkler, Albin	Stoker / Heizer	Witte, Heinrich (Buried on Lemnos)	Stoker / Heizer
Wolff, Hans	Stoker / Heizer	Zander, Hugo	Stoker / Heizer
Gaffreh, Otto	Torpedo–Machinist	Behrens, Willi	Torpedo–Machinisten–Maat
Fiebig, Oskar	Torpedo–Ober–Heizer	Hempel, Fritz	Torpedo–Ober–Heizer
Guchalla, Florian	Torpedo–Ober–Heizer	Witt, Paul	Torpedo–Ober–Heizer
Maßholder, Franz	Torpedo–Heizer	Preilowski, Franz	Torpedo–Heizer
Ulrich, Karl	Torpedo–Heizer	Voigt, Hermann	Torpedo–Heizer
Trutnau, Wilhelm	Torpedo–Ober–Matrose	Müller, Oskar	Torpedo–Matrose
Ostermann, Henry	Torpedo–Matrose	Wiemeyer, Gerhard	Torpedo–Matrose
Böttcher, Walter	San.-Maat	Sondberg, Rudolf	Paymaster Zahlmeister–Appl.
Staats, Christian (Buried on Lemnos)	Ships' Writer Schreiber	Schneider, Paul	Ober–Matrose–VerwMt.
Gebauer, Reinhold	Ober–Bottelier	Wesemann, Paul	Hob.-Maat
Meyer, Heinrich	Leading Shipwright Ober–Zimmermanns–Gast	Gebhardt, Karl Ernst (Buried on Lemnos)	Shipwright Zimmermanns–Gast
Reichert, Erdfried (bestattet auf Imbros)	Shipwright Zimmermanns	Schlage, Friedrich	Shipwright Zimmermanns
Schulz, Paul	Painter Maler-Gast	Perske, Max Julius	Leading Cobbler Ober–Schuhmacher-Gast
Borgmann, Walter (Buried on Lemnos)	unknown	Felder, Hugo Alfred (Buried on Lemnos)	unknown

Notes by chapter

Note: Unless where otherwise stated, the originals for all references quoted are only in German
AA/PA   = Auswärtiges Amt/ Politisches Amt (German Foreign Office/ Political Office)
BA/MA = Bundesarchiv/Militärarchiv (Federal German Archives/German Military Archives)

Foreword

1. In Turkish accounts the fighting on Gallipoli is referred to as the 'Canakkale War'. As far as possible, in most cases names of people and places use the usual British terminology. Where a source for quotations has a previous English translation (e.g. *Five Years in Turkey* by Liman von Sanders) the appropriate original translation has been used wherever found.
2. Denizler Kitabevi, a bookshop in lstanbul in Istklal Cadessi, www.denizlerkitabevi.com
3. Website: www.thegallipolihouses.com

Chapter 1: German-Turkish military relationships through the ages until 1913

4. Wallach, Anatomie einer Militärhilfe, p. 15
5. Haupt, Deutsche unter dem Halbmond, p. 208
6. Even though German references used the name 'Constantinople' throughout until after the First World War, for various reasons this work uses 'Istanbul' exclusively; however, quotations may sometimes remain unchanged.
7. Wallach, Anatomie einer Militärhilfe, p. 24
8. Haupt, Deutsche unter dem Halbmond, p. 210
9. Tarabya is a suburb in northern Istanbul. The former summer residence of the German Ambassador is still there, set in eighteen hectares of parkland.
10. Friedrich Engels (1820-1895) also used to write military analyses and was therefore dubbed 'the General' by his friends.
11. The Crimean War, also known as the Orient War, took place in 1853-1856 between Russia on the one hand and the Ottoman Empire, France, Great Britain and Sardinia on the other.
12. Marx, Russlands Drang nach Westen, p. 24
13. Adamow, Die Europäischen Mächte und die Türkei während des Weltkrieges, p. 6
14. Adamow, Die Europäischen Mächte und die Türkei während des Weltkrieges, p. 6
15. Adamow, Die Europäischen Mächte und die Türkei während des Weltkrieges, p. 7
16. Mühlmann, Die deutschen Bahnunternehmungen, p. 123
17. Cust, Geschichte des Osmanischen Reiches, p. 304
18. Marx, Russlands Drang nach Westen, p. 96
19. The expression 'sick man of the Bosphorus' originated with Czar Nicholas I.
20. Rathmann, Stoßrichtung Nahost 1914 - 1918, p.15

21. Holborn, Deutschland und die Türkei 1878-1890, p. 11ff
22. On his arrival in Istanbul, von Sanders was also not met by representatives of the German Embassy for this reason. Liman von Sanders, Fünf Jahre Türkei, p. 12 (German only)
23. Wallach, Anatomie einer Militärhilfe, p. 29
24. Römer, Die deutsche und englische Militärhilfe für das Osmanische Reich, p. 27
25. Radke, Generalfeldmarschall Colmar Freiherr v. der Goltz Pascha, p. 55
26. Wallach, Anatomie einer Militärhilfe, p. 77
27. Wallach, Anatomie einer Militärhilfe, p. 32
28. Scherer, Adler und Halbmond, p. 475
29. Scherer, Adler und Halbmond, p. 475
30. Wallach, Anatomie einer Militärhilfe, p. 105
31. Römer, Die deutsche und englische Militärhilfe für das Osmanische Reich, p. 39
32. Römer, Die deutsche und englische Militärhilfe für das Osmanische Reich, p. 33
33. Römer, Die deutsche und englische Militärhilfe für das Osmanische Reich, p. 40
34. Adamow, Die Europäischen Mächte und die Türkei während des Weltkrieges, p. 14
35. Adamow, Die Europäischen Mächte und die Türkei während des Weltkrieges, p. 15 ff
36. Hallgarten, Imperialismus vor 1914, p. 165
37. Römer, Die deutsche und englische Militärhilfe für das Osmanische Reich, p. 54
38. Römer, Die deutsche und englische Militärhilfe für das Osmanische Reich, p. 55
39. Römer, Die deutsche und englische Militärhilfe für das Osmanische Reid1, p. 59
40. Römer, Die deutsche und englische Militärhilfe für das Osmanische Reich, p. 68
41. Römer, Die deutsche und englische Militärhilfe für das Osmanische Reich, p. 68
42. Römer, Die deutsche und englische Militärhilfe für das Osmanische Reich, p. 70
43. Mango, Atatürk, p. 113
44. Wallach, Anatomie einer Militärhilfe, p. 121
45. Morgenthau, Chapter I (Henry Morgenthau was the United Sates Ambassador in Istanbul from 1913-1916.)
46. Wallach, Anatomie einer Militärhilfe, p. 111 ff
47. Humann to Jäckh, from Yale University, no. HM 250, RCPN MS 467
48. Humann to Jäckh, from Yale University, no. HM 250, RCPN MS 467
49. BA/MA, N 156/10 Admiral Wilhelm Souchon: personal correspondence with his wife Violet.
50. Adamow, Die Europäischen Mächte und die Türkei während des Weltkrieges, p. 17

Chapter 2: Paving the way for the "Liman" Military Mission 1913

51. On 23 January 1913, Enver Paşa instigated a putsch against the government and the ruling Grand Vizier Kamil Paşa and then appointed Mahmud Şefket Paşa as Grand Vizier.
52. Cemal Paşa, Memoirs, p. 67 ff.
53. Comparable position to a Chief of Cabinet.
54. Fischer, Krieg der Illusionen, p. 485 ff
55. Morgenthau, Chapter XI (in English)
56. Wangenheim to Bethmann Hollweg, 26 April1913, GP 38, Nr.15439, p. 200 ff
57. Der Weltkrieg 1914 - 1918, Vol. 9, p. 167
58. Schulte, Vor Kriegsausbruch 1914, p. 32 ff
59. Mühlmann, Deutschland und die Türkei 1913-1914, p. 5 ff
60. Wallach, Anatomie einer Militärmission, p.125

61. Römer, Die deutsche und englische Militärhilfe für das Osmanische Reich, p. 77
62. Wallach, Anatomie einer Militärmission, p. 137
63. Wallach, Anatomie einer Militärmission, p. 137
64. BA/MA, W 10 / 51475, Personal notes of Mühlmann
65. Wallach, Anatomie einer Militärmission, p. 137
66. Liman von Sanders, Brief an das Reichsarchiv, 11 August 1924
67. Liman von Sanders, Fünf Jahre Türkei, p. 11
68. Mühlmann, Deutschland und die Türkei 1913-1914, p. 4
69. Fischer, Krieg der Illusionen, p. 486 ff. Fischer quotes from Russian sources, which apparently show that the Kaiser tasked the Military Mission with the 'Germanification' of Turkey and to build a 'new, strong army' for him (the Kaiser).
70. Liman von Sanders, Fünf Jahre Türkei, p. 12
71. Mühlmann, Deutschland und die Türkei 1913-1914, p. 3
72. Mühlmann documented the 'Contract concerning the creation of a German Military Mission to assist the reorganisation of the Imperial Ottoman Army', Deutschland und die Türkei 1913-1914, p. 88 ff
73. Mühlmann, Der Kampf um die Dardanellen 1915, p. 15
74. Fischer, Krieg der Illusionen
75. Liman von Sanders, Fünf Jahre Türkei, p. 12
76. Mehmet Raşa was the Ottoman Sultan from 1909-1918.
77. Morgenthau, Chapter II (in English)
78. Jacques Benoist, Mustafa Kemal, p. 115
79. Liman von Sanders, Fünf Jahre Türkei, p. 16 ff
80. AA/PA, Turkey 142, R 13319, Military report 5 dated 24 March 1914
81. Hindenburg, Aus meinem Leben, p.135
82. Morgenthau, Chapter II (in English)
83. Mango, Atatürk, p. 142
84. Liman von Sanders, Fünf Jahre Türkei, p.14
85. PA/AA, Lucius to AA, 11 Nov 1913, GP 38, No.15447, p.195
86. Hallgarten, Imperialismus vor 1914, p. 431
87. Adamow, Die Europäischen Mächte und die Türkei während des Weltkrieges, p. 73
88. Adamow, Die Europäischen Mächte und die Türkei während des Weltkrieges, p. 74
89. Trumpener, German Military Aid to Turkey, p. 13 (in English)
90. Kerner, The Mission of Liman von Sanders, p. 549 and p. 552 (in English)
91. Wallach, Anatomie einer Militärmission, p.141
92. AA/PA, GP 38, No. 15493, Wangenheim to Jagow, 17 Oct 1913
93. Adamow, Die Europäischen Mächte und die Türkei während des Weltkrieges, p. 77 ff, Memorandum to the Czar dated 23.12.1913
94. Adamow, Die Europäischen Mächte und die Türkei während des Weltkrieges, p. 83 ff
95. Wangenheim to AA, 23 Dec. 1913, CP 38, No. 15499, p. 273
96. Liman von Sanders, Fünf Jahre Türkei, p. 16
97. Liman von Sanders, Fünf Jahre Türkei, p. 16
98. Adamow, Die Europäischen Mächte und die Türkei während des Weltkrieges, p. 95
99. Adamow, Die Europäischen Mächte und die Türkei während des Weltkrieges, p. 102
100. Römer, Die deutsche und englische Militärhilfe für das Osmanische Reich, p. 80
101. Römer, Die deutsche und englische Militärhilfe für das Osmanische Reich, p. 81
102. Römer, Die deutsche und englische Militärhilfe für das Osmanische Reich, p. 93
103. AA/PA, Turkey 142. R 13319, Military Report 5 dated 24 March 1914

Chapter 3: The Military Mission (MM) and the Mediterranean Division (MMD) until Turkey's entry into the war

104. AA/PA Türkei 142, R 13319, von Mutius to AA 2 February 1914

105. Adamow, Die Europäischen Mächte und die Türkei während des Weltkrieges, p. 94

106. Miller, Superior Force: The conspiracy behind the escape of the Goeben and Breslau, Chapter 1

106a. Charles Lister, writing to the Hon Irene Lawley; Letters and Recollections with a Memoir by his Father, Lord Ribblesdale. Charles Scribner's Sons, New York, 1917. Charles Lister was a diplomat at the British Embassy in Istanbul until diplomatic relations with Turkey were broken off. He later joined the Royal Naval Division (Hood Battalion) as a sub lieutenant and served in Gallipoli.

107. Cemal Paşa, Erinnerungen, p. 114

108. AA/PA, Turkey 142, R 13319, Military report 5 dated 24 March 1914

109. Morgenthau, Chapter III (in English)

110. AA/PA, Türkei 142, R 13320, Telegram von Wangenheim dated 23 July 1914

111. Reissner, Die Europäischen Mächte und die Türkei während des Weltkrieges, 5.106

112. Cemal Paşa, Erinnerungen, p. 114

113. Mühlmann, Die deutsche Militär-Mission in der Türkei, p. 851

114. Mühlmann, Die deutsche Militär-Mission in der Türkei, p. 851

115. Mühlmann, Die deutsche Militär-Mission in der Türkei, p. 852

116. Liman von Sanders, Fünf Jahre Türkei, p. 34

117. Cemal Paşa, Erinnerungen, p. 115

118. Lorey, Der Krieg in den türkischen Gewässern, p. 3

119. BA/MA, RM 40/755, War Diary (WAR DIARY) of the Navy Mediterranean Division (MMD), p. 2

120. Mäkelä, Souchon, der Goebenadmiral, p. 85

121. House in the original ornamental decor and to the left is the salon, in which the German-Turkish alliance agreement was signed.

122. Cemal Paşa, Erinnerungen, p. 124

123. AA/PA, Türkei 142, R 13320, Telegrams of von Wangenheim and von Tirpitz dated 2 August 1914

124. Lorey, Der Krieg in den türkischen Gewässern, p. 5

125. Wchrle, Aus meinem türkischen Tagebuch, p. 1

126. BA/MA, 40/755 War Diary (WAR DIARY) of the Navy Mediterranean Division (MMD), p.7

127. Humann to Jäckh, from Yale University, No. HM 250, RCPN MS 467

128. Lorey, Der Krieg in den türkischen Gewässern, p. 27

129. This theory is examined in detail in G. Miller's 'Superior Force - The Conspiracy behind the Escape of the Goeben and Breslau', but is rejected. Miller primarily sees the escape of the MMD in the chain of unfortunate wrong decisions and only secondarily as caused by a conspiratorial intervention, which he suspected - if at all - was by the Greeks.

130. Lorey, Der Krieg in den türkischen Gewässern, p. 27

131. BA/MA, 40/755 War Diary (WAR DIARY) of the Navy Mediterranean Division (MMD), p.13

132. BA/MA, 40/755 War Diary (WAR DIARY) of the Navy Mediterranean Division (MMD), p.15

133. BA/MA, 40/755 War Diary (WAR DIARY) of the Navy Mediterranean Division (MMD), p.16

134. BA/MA, 40/755 War Diary (WAR DIARY) of the Navy Mediterranean Division (MMD), p.18

135. BA/MA, 40/755 War Diary (WAR DIARY) of the Navy Mediterranean Division (MMD), p.18

136. Kannengiesser, Gallipoli, p. 21

137. Cemal Paşa, Erinnerungen, p. 126

138. AA/PA, Türkei 142, R 13320, Telegram von Wangenheim dated 14 August 1914

139. Morgenthau, Chapter V (in English)

140. BA/MA, 40/755 War Diary (WAR DIARY) of the Navy Mediterranean Division (MMD) p. 20

141. Yavuz Celalettin, Die türkisch-deutschen Marinebeziehungen

142. AA/PA, Türkei 142, R 13320, Telegram von Wangenheim dated 14 August 1914

143. Morgenthau, Chapter V (in English)

144. Langensiepen et al, Halbmond und Kaiseradler, p.19

145. Yavuz Celalettin, Die türkisch-deutschen Marinebeziehungen

146. BA/MA, N 155, Lieutenant Commander Rudolph Firle: Diaries

147. Yavuz Celalettin, Die türkisch-deutschen Marinebeziehungen

148. Langensiepen et al, Halbmond und Kaiseradler, p. 15

149. Langensiepen et al, Halbmond und Kaiseradler, p. 17

150. Langensiepen et al, Halbmond und Kaiseradler, p. 14

150a. Charles Lister, Letter to the Hon. Irene Lawley p. 116 August 20, 1914. Letters and Recollections with a Memoir by his Father, Lord Ribblesdale. Charles Scribner's Sons, New York, 1917.

151. Langensiepen et al, Halbmond und Kaiseradler, p. 101

152. Langensiepen et al, Halbmond und Kaiseradler, p. 102

153. BA/MA, RM 5 /2355

154. Humann to Jäckh September 191 5, from Yale University, No. HM 250, RGPN MS 467

155. Lorey, Der Krieg in türkischen Gewässern, p. 44

156. BA/MA, N 155 / 21 Lieutenant Commander Rudolph Firle: Diaries

157. Römer, Die deutsche und englische Militärhilfe für das Osmanische Reich, p. 335

158. Yavuz Celalettin, Die türkisch-deutschen Marinebeziehungen

159. BA/MA, RM 40 /755, War Diary (WAR DIARY) of the Navy Mediterranean Division (MMD)

160. BA/MA, N 155/21, Lieutenant Commander Rudolph Firle: Diaries

161. Yavuz Celalettin, Die türkisch-deutschen Marinebeziehungen

162. Lorey, Der Krieg in türkischen Gewässern, p. 44

163. BA/MA, RM 40 / 755, War Diary (WAR DIARY) of the Navy Mediterranean Division (MMD)

164. Langensiepen et al, Halbmond und Kaiseradler, p. 20

165. Yavuz Celalettin, Die türkisch-deutschen Marinebeziehungen

166. Langensiepen et al, Halbmond und Kaiseradler, p.19

167. AA/PA, Türkei 142, R 13321, Telegram von Wangenheim dated 21 September 1914

168. Yavuz Celalettin, Die türkisch-deutschen Marinebeziehungen

169. Report by Humann 11.10.1914, from Yale University, No. HM 250, RGPN MS 467

170. Letter Humann to Jäckh dated 13.10.1914, from Yale University, No. HM 250, RGPN MS 467

171. From the notes by Humann, from Yale University, No. HM 250, RGPN MS467

172. From the notes by Humann, from Yale University, No. HM 250, RGPN MS 467

173. BA/MA, RM 40/755, War Diary (WAR DIARY) of the Navy Mediterranean Division (MMD)

174. Note by Humann dated 22.10. to Wangenheim, from Yale University, No. HM 250, RGPN M5 467

175. BA/MA, RM 40 / 755, War Diary (WAR DIARY) of the Navy Mediterranean Division (MMD)

176. Note by Humann dated 24.\00.12 hrs at night, from Yale University, No. HM 250, RGPN MS 467

177. From the notes by Humann, from Yale University, No. HM 250, RGPN M5467

178. BA/MA, RM 40 / 755, War Diary (WAR DIARY) of the Navy Mediterranean Division (MMD)

179. BA/MA, RM 40 / 755, War Diary (WAR DIARY) of the Navy Mediterranean Division (MMD)

180. BA/MA RM 40 / 755, War Diary (WAR DIARY) of the Navy Mediterranean Division (MMD)

181. Mühlmann, Das deutsch-türkische Waffenbündnis im Weltkriege, p. 23

182. Lorey, Der Krieg in den türkischen Gewässern, p.47

183. Yavuz Celalettin, Die türkisch-deutschen Marinebeziehungen p. 31

184. Langensiepen et al, Halbmond und Kaiseradler, p. 25

185. Langensiepen et al, Halbmond und Kaiseradler, p. 26
186. BA/MA, N 156/10, Admiral Wilhelm Souchon: Private correspondence with wife Violet 187. BA/MA, 1Uvt40/755, War Diary (WAR DIARY) of the Navy Mediterranean Division (MMD)
188. Langensicpen et al, Halbmond und Kaiseradler, p. 27
189. Liman von Sanders, Fünf Jahre Türkei, p. 45
190. BA/MA, RM 40/755, War Diary (WAR DIARY) of the Navy Mediterranean Division (MMD)
191. Morgenthau, Chapter XI (in English)
192. In the ancient seraglio of Topkapi, the Sultan, standing before the Prophet's mantle and in the presence of the Grand Vizier, Sheikh ül Islam, and a delegation of some Ministers from the great assembly, made the following address:

'I regard this patriotic proclamation to my nation as the most brilliant proof of the perseverance and firmness it will demonstrate in the defence of the Fatherland during this war we are fighting to defend our rights against three Great Powers.

We trust in the divine protection and assistance of the Prophet: I am convinced that we will be victorious. My children, so that the soil of the motherland will not be overrun by the enemies, so that the Muslim nation exposed for some time from all sides will be rescued, it is necessary that you show strength and endurance.

I hope for the mercy of God to hear our prayers spoken in this holy place.'
193. BA/MA, N 156/ 10, Admiral Wilhelm Souchon: Private correspondence with wife Violet

Chapter 4: Everyday life and work in the Military Mission (MM), the Mediterranean Division (MMD) and the Special Command (SoKo) in Istanbul

194. Kannengiesser, Gallipoli, p. 129
195. Kannengiesser, Gallipoli, p. 123
196. Wallach, Anatomie einer Militärmission, p. 150
197. Wallach, Anatomie einer Militärmission, p. 150
198. Wallach, Anatomie einer Militärmission, p. 151
199. Wallach, Anatomie einer Militärmission, p. 151
200. ΛΛ/PA, Türkei 142, R 13320, Telegram von Wangenheim dated 21 July 1914
201. BA/MA, RM 5 / 2361
202. Wallach, Anatomie einer Militärmission, p. 198
203. Wallach, Anatomie einer Militärmission, p. 199
204. BA/MA, RM 5/2358, Telegram SoKo
205. Wallach, Anatomie einer Militärhilfe, p. 199
206. BA/MA. RM 5 I 2358, Telegram SoKo
207. Wallach, Anatomie einer Militärhilfe, p. 200
208. Kannengiesser, Gallipoli, p. 138
209. Wallach, Anatomie einer Militärhilfe, p. 201
210. For example, the expedition to Persia under Wasmuth and Captain von Niedermeyer.
211. BA/MA, RM40/129
212. Kannengiesser, Gallipoli, p.136
213. Kannengiesser, Gallipoli, p.137
214. BA/MA, RM 40/129
215. BA/MA, RM 40/l29

216. AA/PA, Turkey 142, R 13334, Military Mission from 10.10.1915
217. BA/MA, RM 5/2358
218. AA/PA, Türkei 142, R 13334, 6.10.1915
219. Langensiepen et al, Halbmond und Kaiseradler, p. 58
220. Langensiepen et al, Halbmond und Kaiseradler, p. 58
221. Langensiepen et al, Halbmond und Kaiseradler, p. 61
222. Liman von Sanders, Fünf Jahre Türkei, p. 192
223. Morgenthau, Chapter IV (in English)
224. Morgenthau, Chapter VIII (in English)
225. BA/MA, RM 5/2360
226. BA/MA, RM 5/2404, Report by Admiral von Usedom, 20 July 1915
227. BA/MA, RM 5/2405, Report by Admiral von Usedom, 20 November 1916
228. BA/MA, RM 5/2358
229. BA/MA, RM 5/2358
230. BA/MA, RM 5/2358
231. Langensiepen et al, Halbmond und Kaiseradler, p. 130
232. Kopp, Das Teufelsschiff und seine kleine Schwester – Erlebnisse des *Goeben* Funkers Georg Kopp
233. BA/MA, RM 5/2359
234. Kannengiesser, Gallipoli, p. 166
235. BA/MA, RM 5/2357
236. BA/MA, RM 40/138 Tagesbefehle des Oberkommandos der Meeresengen, p. 194
237. BA/MA, RM 5/2385 ‚Türkische Overtüre‘ aus Abendausgabe Nr. 131 der Vossischen Zeitung ('Turkish Overture', from the evening edition no 131 of the Vossischen Zeitung)
238. BA/MA, RM 5/2385
239. BA/MA, RM 5/2358
240. BA/MA, RM 5/2355
241. Original picture is from the Australian War Memorial.
242. Wolfgang Schrader, born and educated in Istanbul, was locally conscripted as an able seaman, was at Gallipoli and worked as the Turkish translator for Lieutenant Adolf Hommel, Liaison Officer for the MMD and Turkish Fifth Army. This and other pictures are courtesy of the Schrader family. Coincidentally, Schrader's grandson, Jochen, is a personal friend and close neighbour in Heidelberg of the translator.
243. BA/MA, RM 5/2358
244. BA/MA, RM 5/2355
245. BA/MA, N 156/11, Admiral Wilhelm Souchon: Private correspondence with his wife Violet
246. BA/MA, N 156/11, Admiral Wilhelm Souchon: Private correspondence with his wife Violet
247. BA/MA, RM 5/2359
248. BA/MA, RM 5/2359
249. Langensiepen et al, Halbmond und Kaiseradler, p. 157
250. BA/MA, RM 5/2360
251. The Imtiaz Medal was created by Sultan Hamid II in 1883 to reward loyalty, courage, and virtue. This honour was also given to both nationals and foreigners in war and peace. According to Army Order 16 of 1915, the possessors of the Imtiaz Medal simultaneously received the War Medal. In the course of the war, battle clasps, either in silver or gold, were awarded, which could be attached to the medal ribbon. (Recipients included: von der Goltz, Felmy, Grumbckow, Kieslingstein, Range, Ristow, Rohrscheidt, von Sanders, Schleiff and von Usedom.)
252. The Liakat Medal, also created by Sultan Abdul II, was introduced on 22 April 1891 for nationals and foreigners and for both men and women. It was a lower order to the Imtiaz Medal. For merit in war, the

medal was awarded with a sabre clasp from 1915. Holders of the medal were entitled to wear the War Medal after it had been introduced. The Liakat Medal was awarded in either silver or gold. (Recipients included: Ackermann, Buddecke, Croneiss, Endres, Felmy, Grumbckow, Heintze, Klein, von Strempel, von Usedom and Valentiner.)

253. The Osmania Order of the Ottoman Empire was introduced on 4 January 1862 by Sultan Abdul Aziz. In 1867 the Order was expanded to four and in 1893 to five Classes. The First Class could also be awarded with diamonds for special merit. For valour in war, from 1915 the Order could also be awarded to military personnel 'with sabres', i.e. the sabres were added to the Osmania Order First Class with diamonds. (Recipients included: von der Goltz, von Falkenhayn, Grumbckow, Heuck, Ristow, Schlee, von Strempel, and Weidtmann.)

Interestingly enough, before the First World War this order was also awarded to British officers for service in Egypt and Sudan.

254. The Medjidie Order of the Ottoman Empire was founded on 29 August 1852 by Sultan Abdul Mecid I for all kinds of merit. Originally the Order was only awarded to military personnel in peacetime, but from 1915 onwards it was also awarded 'with sabres' for military valour in war. This Order was first awarded to nationals in 1852. Like the Osmania Order, it was also divided into five Classes and was often awarded to German officers who served in Turkey during the war. (Recipients included: Endres, von der Goltz, Grumbckow, Heuck, Kieslingstein, Kettner, Klein, Kümpel, Ristow, Schlee and Weidtmann.)

255. BA/MA, N 156/11, Admiral Wilhelm Souchon: Private correspondence with his wife Violet
256. BA/MA, RM 5/2359
257. BA/MA, RM 5/2361
258. BA/MA, N 156/11, Admiral Wilhelm Souchon: Private correspondence with his wife Violet
259. BA/MA, RM 5/2359
260. BA/MA, RM5/2361
261. Langensiepen et al, Halbmond und Kaiseradler, p. 62

Chapter 5: Fortification of the Dardanelles

262. Moltke, Letters, p. 100
263. Mühlmann, Schlachten des Weltkrieges, Bd. 16 Der Kampf um die Dardanellen, p. 50
264. Langensiepen, Halbmond und Kaiseradler, p. 103
265. Sanders, Fünf Jahre Türkei, p. 65
265. AA/PA, Türkei 142, R 13319, Military report 5 dated 24 March 1914
266. BA/MA, RM 40 / 755, War Diary (WAR DIARY) of the Navy Mediterranean Division (MMD)
267. Mühlmann, Das deutsch-türkische Waffenbündnis im Kriege, p. 21
268. BA/MA, RM 5 / 2404, Report by von Usedom 5 June 1915
269. BA/MA, RM 5 / 2355
270. Wehrle, Aus meinem türkischen Tagebuch, p. 34
271. Wehrle, Aus meinem türkischen Tagebuch, p. 34
272. BA/MA, RM 5 / 2404
274. Morgenthau, Chapter XVIII (in English)
275. Morgenthau, Chapter XVII (in English)
275. Schoen, Die Hölle von Gallipoli, p. 18
276. Lorey, Der Krieg in den türkischen Gewässern, p. 86
277. Mühlmann, Schlachten des Weltkrieges, Bd. 16 Der Kampf um die Dardanellen, p. 52

278. Langensiepen, Halbmond und Kaiseradler, p. 105

279. Souchon in War Diary (WAR DIARY) of the Navy Mediterranean Division (MMD), 27 August 1914

280. BA/MA, RM 5 / 2404, Report by von Usedom, 5. Juni 1915

281. BA/MA, RM 5 / 2404, Report by von Usedom, 31. Oktober 1915

282. BA/MA, RM 5 / 2404, Report by Captain Pieper

283. Lorey, Der Krieg in den türkischen Gewässern, p. 387 ff

284. BA/MA, RM 5 / 2356

285. BA/MA, RM 5 / 2358

Chapter 6: The Battle for the Dardanelles

286. Mühlmann, Das Deutsch-Türkische Waffenbündnis im Weltkriege, p. 39

287. Wallach, Anatomie einer Militärhilfe, p. 182

288. Wallach, Anatomie einer Militärhilfe, p. 172

289. Wallach, Anatomie einer Militärhilfe, p. 183

290. Schmiterlöw, Aus dem Leben des Generalfeldmarschalls Freiherr von der Goltz Pascha, p. 188

291. Mühlmann, Das Deutsch-Türkische Waffenbündnis im Weltkriege, p. 41

292. Wehrle, Aus meinem türkischen Tagebuch, p. 35

293. Wehrle, Aus meinem türkischen Tagebuch, p. 36

294. Mühlmann, Das Deutsch-Türkische Waffenbündnis im Weltkriege, p. 43

295. Mühlmann, Schlachten des Weltkrieges, Bd. 16 Der Kampf um die Dardanellen, p. 61 ff

296. Pomiankowski, Der Zusammenbruch des Ortomanischen Reidles, p. 114

297. Von Usedom, Report über die Kämpfe an den Dardanellen, p. 1 ff

298. Kannengiesser, Gallipoli, p. 62

299. Mühlmann, Schlachten des Weltkrieges, Bd. 16, Der Kampf um die Dardanellen, p. 63

300. Mühlmann, Das Deutsch-Türkische Waffenbündnis im Weltkriege, p. 45

301. Mühlmann, Das Deutsch-Türkische Waffenbündnis im Weltkriege, p. 46

302. Lorey, Der Krieg in türkischen Gewässern, p. 87

303. Langensiepen u. a., Halbmond und Kaiseradler, p. 105

304. Offizierstellvertreter (Warrant Officer) Rudolf Bettaque was killed on 7 May 1916 at Gallipoli during mine clearance and was buried in Gallipoli. Today his tombstone is in the military cemetery in Tarabya.

305. Langensiepen u. a., Halbmond und Kaiseradler, p. 106

306. Pomiankowski, Der Zusammenbruch des Osmanischen Reiches, p. 120

307. Yilmazer, The Air War Çanakkale

308. Mühlmann, Der Kampf um die Dardanellen, p. 71

309. BA/MA, N 156 / 12, Admiral Wilhelm Souchon: Private correspondence with wife Violet, Vol. 3, The number of German casualties in this report does not match with the records of Admiral von Usedom, who reported twenty-two dead or wounded German soldiers.

310. Von Usedom, Report über die Kämpfe an den Dardanellen,. 7 ff

311. Mühlmann, Der Kampf um die Dardanellen, p. 74

312. Langensiepen u. a., Halbmond und Kaiseradler, p. 131

313. Reichsarchiv, Der Weltkrieg 1914 -1918, Bd. 7, p. 336

314. Reichsarchiv, Der Weltkrieg 1914-1918, Bd. 7, p. 337

315. Reichsarchiv, Der Weltkrieg 1914 - 1918, Bd. 7, p. 338

Chapter 7: Preparing to Repulse the Allied Landing

316. Mühlmann, Der Kampf um die Dardanellen, p. 89,
317. Reichsarchiv, Der Weltkrieg 1914–1918, Bd. 9, p. 175
318. Liman von Sanders, Fünf Jahre Türkei, p. 73
319. Lorey, Der Krieg in türkischen Gewässern, p. 88
320. Liman von Sanders, Fünf Jahre Türkei, p. 76; here original translation of *Five Years in Turkey* by Colonel Carl Reichmann, U.S. Army (Retired) 1927 p. 56–57
321. Schmiterlöw, Aus dem Leben des Generalfeldmarschalls Freiherr von der Goltz-Pascha, p. 190
322. Schmiterlöw, Aus dem Leben des Generalfeldmarschalls Freiherr von der Goltz-Pascha, p. 190
323. BA/MA, N 156/12, Admiral Wilhelm Souchon: Privatkorrespondenz mit Ehefrau Violet
324. Wallach, Anatomie einer Militärhilfe, p. 178
325. BA/MA 40 I 73, Landverteidigung von Gallipoli, p. 12
326. Liman von Sanders, Fünf Jahre Türkei, p. 80; here original translation of *Five Years in Turkey* by Colonel Carl Reichmann, U.S. Army (Retired) 1927 p. 59–60
327. Mühlmann, Der Kampf um die Dardanellen, p. 84
328. Liman von Sanders, Fünf Jahre Türkei, p. 82; here original translation of *Five Years in Turkey* by Colonel Carl Reichmann, U.S. Army (Retired) 1927 p. 61
329. Liman von Sanders, Fünf Jahre Türkei, p. 82
330. Liman von Sanders, Fünf Jahre Türkei, p. 83 / here original translation of *Five Years in Turkey* by Colonel Carl Reichmann, U.S. Army (Retired) 1927 p. 62
331. Kannengiesser, Gallipoli, p. 80
332. Kannengiesser, Gallipoli, p. 81
333. Mango, Atatürk, p. 145
334. Pomiankowski, p. 129
335. ANPA, R 48065, Deutscher Botschafter an Auswärtiges Amt 23 September 1925
336. Görgülü, The Intentions of the Germans in Gallipoli, p. 1

Chapter 8: The Allied Landings on 25 April 1915

337. The portrayal of the fighting up to the withdrawal of the Allied troops, unless otherwise indicated, stems from: The battle for the Dardanelles (German Imperial Archives), Gallipoli (Kannengiesser) and Gallipoli (Robert Rhodes James).
338. 'Achi Baba' was the English name for Elchi Tepe
339. James, Gallipoli, p. 81 ff
340. BA/MA, W 10 I 51475, Notes by Mühlmann
341. Liman von Sanders, Fünf Jahre Türkei, p. 84; here original translation of *Five Years in Turkey* by Colonel Carl Reichmann, U.S. Army (Retired) 1927 p. 63
342. BA/MA, W 10151475, Notes by Mühlmann
343. James, Gallipoli, p. 101 ff
344. Westlake, British Regiments at Gallipoli, p. 88
345. 'Six VCs before breakfast.' VC = Victoria Cross, the highest decoration for bravery in wartime in the British Empire.
345a. Erickson, Gallipoli the Ottoman Campaign, Pen & Sword Books Ltd, 2010, p.73. Sergeant Yahya survived and was decorated.
346. Danışmann, Gallipoli 1915, p. 6

347. Broadbent, Gallipoli, p. 43
348. Broadbent, Gallipoli, p. 54
349. Broadbent, Gallipoli, p. 57
350. So named by the Turks as on 27 April it was the command post of Mustafa Kemal.
351. Broadbent, Gallipoli, p. 89
352. James, Gallipoli, p. 112
353. Lorey, Der Krieg in den türkischen Gewässern, p. 119
354. BA/MA RM 40 I 755, War Diary of the MMD, p. 144
355. James, Gallipoli, p. 166
356. James, Gallipoli, p. 168
357. James, Gallipoli, p. 168
358. Mango, Atatürk, p. 147

Chapter 9: The Fighting from 26 to 28 April 1915

359. Robert Rhodes James, Gallipoli, p. 135
360. BA/MA, W 10 I 51475, Notes by Mühlmann
361. BAIMA, W 10 I 51475, Notes by Mühlmann
362. Liman von Sanders, Fünf Jahre Türkei, p. 89 / here original translation of *Five Years in Turkey* by Colonel Carl Reichmann, U.S. Army (Retired) 1927 p. 67
363. BA/MA, W 10 /51475, Notes by Mühhnann
364. BA/MA, W 10 /51475, Notes by Mi.ihlmann
365. Kannengiesser, Gallipoli, p. 102;here original translation of *The Campaign in Gallipoli* by Major C.J.P. Ball, D.S.O., M.C. p.121
366. Kannengiesser, The Campaign in Gallipoli, p. 124
367. Kannengiesser, The Campaign in Gallipoli, p. 126
368. Robert Rhodes James, Gallipoli, p. 184

Chapter 10: The Three Battles for Krithia

369. Robert Rhodes James, Gallipoli, p. 171
370. Kannengiesser, Gallipoli, p. 128
371. Robert Rhodes James, Gallipoli, p. 171
372. Robert Rhodes James, Gallipoli, p.171
373. Robert Rhodes James, Gallipoli, p. 171
374. BA/MA, W 10 I 51475, Notes by Mühlmann
375. BA/MA, W 10 I 51475, Notes by Mühlmann
376. Robert Rhodes James, Gallipoli, p. 144
377. Robert Rhodes James, Gallipoli, p. 144
378. BA/MA, W 10 I 51475, Notes by Mühlmann
379. BA/MA, W 10 I 51475, Notes by Mühlmann
380. BA/MA, W 10151475, Notes by Mühlmann
381. Chambers, Gully Ravine, p. 28
382. BA/MA, W 10 1 51475, Notes by Mühlmann
383. Kannengiesser, Gallipoli, p.131

384. BAIMA RM 40 I 755, War Diary of the MMD, p. 146
385. BA/MA RM 401755, War Diary of the MMD, p. 158
386. Prigge, Der Kampf um die Dardanellen, p. 68 ff
387. BA/MA, W 10 151475, Notes by Mühlmann
388. Kannengiesser, Gallipoli, p. 134
389. BA/MA RM 40 /755, War Diary of the MMD p. 158
390. BA/MA RM 40 1755, War Diary of the MMD, p. 159
391. BA/MA, W 10 I 51475, Notes by Mühlmann
392. Kannengiesser, Gallipoli, p. 137
393. BA/MA, W 10 I 51475, Notes by Mühlmann
394. BA/MA RM40/76, p. 2
395. Prigge, Dardanellen-Kriegstagebuch, p. 71
396. BA/MA, W 10 I 51475, Notes by Mühlmann
397. Kannengiesser, Gallipoli, p. 137
398. Kannengiesser, Gallipoli, p. 138
399. BAIMA, W 10 / 51475, Notes by Mühlmann
400. BA/MA, W 10 /51475, Notes by Mühlmann
401. Robert Rhodes James, Gallipoli, p. 148
402. Kannengiesser, Gallipoli, p.139
403. Lorey, Der Krieg in den türkischen Gewässern, p. 124
404. BM/MA RM 40 I 76, p. 6
405. BM/MA RM 40 I 76, p. 6
406. Mühlmann, Notes by
407. Robert Rhodes James, Gallipoli, p. 157
408. BA/MA, RM 40 /755, p. 162
409. Liman von Sanders, Fünf Jahre Türkei, p. 100; here original translation of *Five Years in Turkey* by Colonel Carl Reichmann, U.S. Army (Retired) 1927 p. 76
410. In this quote, either the date of the second half of September or the name Colonel von Leipzig is incorrect, as Colonel von Leipzig died on 28 June 1915.
411. Sefik Okday, Der letzte Großwesir und seine preußischen Söhne, p. 62
412. Kannengiesser, Gallipoli, p. 142
413. Kannengiesser, Gallipoli, p. 145
414. BA/MA,RM 40/755, p. 164
415. Lorey, Der Krieg in den türkischen Gewässern, p. 125
416. Kannengiesser, Gallipoli, p. 168
417. AA/PA, Türkei 139, A 16680, Liman an Kriegsministerium vom 22.05.1915
418. BA/MA RM 40/755, p. 172
419. Kannengiesser, Gallipoli, p. 173
420. Wiesener, Adler, Doppelaar und Halbmond, p. 208
421. Kannengiesser, Gallipoli, p. 179, Leading Seaman Peters was killed on 7 September 1915 at Gallipoli.
422. Kannengiesser, Gallipoli, p. 179
423. Kannengiesser, Gallipoli, p. 178
424. AAIPA, Türkei 142, R 13331, Telegramm Nr. 1453, Von Leipzig an Auswärtiges Amt vom 23. Juni 1915
425. AA/PA, Türkei 142, R 13331, Telegramm Nr. 1463, Von Wangenheim an Auswärtiges Amt vom 25 June 1915
426. BA/MA, RM 40/129
427. BA/MA, RM 5 / 2404, Report Usedom 20.07. 1915
428. Robert Rhodes James, Gallipoli, p. 2

Chapter 11: Positional Warfare and the August Landing in Suvla Bay

428a. Adolf Horaczek, Als Deutscher Soldat 1914/1918 von der Westfront an die Osmanische Front p. 33

429. AA/PA, Türkei 142, R 13333, Erfahrungen aus dem Einsatz des Pionierkommandos vom 28.8.1915

430. AA/PA, Türkei 142, R 13332, Liman von Sanders, 18.8.1915

431. Liman von Sanders, Fünf Jahre Türkei, p. 103 431 Liman von Sanders, Fünf Jahre Türkei, p. 103; here original translation of *Five Years in Turkey* by Colonel Carl Reichmann, U.S. Army (Retired) 1927 p. 78

432. AA/PA, Türkei 142, R 13334, Telegramm 2254, Militärmission an Auswärtiges Amt vom 4. Oktober 1915

433. Kannengiesser, Gallipoli, p. 141 & 146

434. Kannengiesser, Gallipoli, p. 172

435. Kannengiesser, Gallipoli, p. 149 & 151

436. Lorey, Der Krieg in türkischen Gewässern, p. 127

437. BA/MA, RM 40 I 440 Gefechtsberichte der Landungsabteilung

438. AA/PA, Türkei 142, R 13333, Militärmission vom 26. September 1915

439. Liman von Sanders, Fünf Jahre Türkei, p.104; here original translation of *Five Years in Turkey* by Colonel Carl Reichmann, U.S. Army (Retired) 1927 p.79

440. Liman von Sanders, Fünf Jahre Türkei, p.106; here original translation of *Five Years in Turkey* by Colonel Carl Reichmann, U.S. Army (Retired) 1927 p.80–81

441. AAIPA, Türkei 142, R 13331, Telegramm Fürst Hohenlohe an General von Falkenhayn vom 25. Juli 1915

442. Liman von Sanders, Fünf Jahre Türkei, p.106; here original translation of *Five Years in Turkey* by Colonel Carl Reichmann, U. S. Army (Retired) 1927 p.81

443. Liman von Sanders, Fünf Jahre Türkei, p.107

444. Liman von Sanders, Fünf Jahre Türkei, p.107; here original translation of *Five Years in Turkey* by Colonel Carl Reichmann, U.S. Army (Retired) 1927 p.81

445. AA/PA, Türkei 142, R 13332, Telegramm 248, Gesandter Pless an Auswärtiges Amt vorn 1. August 1915

446. AAIPA, Türkei 142, R 13332, Telegramm 251, Gesandter Pless an Auswärtiges Amt vom 1. August 1915 im Anschluß an Telegramm 248

447. Liman von Sanders, Fünf Jahre Türkei, p.108; here original translation of *Five Years in Turkey* by Colonel Carl Reichmann, U.S. Army (Retired) 1927 p.82

448. Schmiterlöw, Aus dem Leben des Generalfeldmarschalls Freiherr von der Goltz-Pascha, p. 191

449. Robert Rhodes James, Gallipoli, p. 245

450. Robert Rhodes James, Gallipoli, p. 255

451. Liman von Sanders, Fünf Jahre Türkei, p. 109; here original translation of *Five Years in Turkey* by Colonel Carl Reichmann, U.S. Army (Retired) 1927 p.83

452. Kannengiesser, Gallipoli, p. 205-208

453. Kannengiesser, Gallipoli, p. 210

454. BA/MA RM 40 I 440, Casualty list German Naval Shore Detachment

455. Patton, The Defense of Gallipoli, p. 54

456. Liman von Sanders, Fünf Jahre Türkei, p.110; here original translation of *Five Years in Turkey* by Colonel Carl Reichmann, U.S. Army (Retired) 1927 p.84

457. Liman von Sanders, Fünf Jahre Türkei, p.111; here original translation of *Five Years in Turkey* by Colonel Carl Reichmann, U.S. Army (Retired) 1927 p.85

458. BA/MA RM 5 / 2356

459. Liman von Sanders, Fünf Jahre Türkei, p. 112; here original translation of *Five Years in Turkey* by Colonel Carl Reichmann, U.S. Army (Retired) 1927 p.

460. Guse, Die Türkei, p. 164

461. BA/MA, W 10/51475, Brief Willmer an von Sanders
462. BA/MA W 10/51475, Brief Sanders an Mühlmann
463. Das Ehrenbuch der Deutschen Schweren Artillerie, p. 276
464. Das Ehrenbuch der Deutschen Schweren Artillerie, p. 277
465. Das Ehrenbuch der Deutschen Schweren Artillerie, p. 278
466. Corbett, Naval Operations, Vol. III, p. 104
467. Liman von Sanders, Fünf Jahre Türkei, p. 114; here original translation of *Five Years in Turkey* by Colonel Carl Reichmann, U. S. Army (Retired) 1927 p.87
468. Kannengiesser, Gallipoli, p. 225
469. BA/MA, N 156/11, Admiral Wilhelm Souchon: Privatkorrespondenz mit Ehefrau Violet
470. BA/MA RM 40/440, Gefechtsberichte Landungsabteilung (After-action Reports German Naval Shore Detachment)
471. The British 10th (Irish), 11th (Northern), 13th (Western) [New Army, K1] Divisions and the 53rd (Welsh) and 54th (East Anglian) Territorial Divisions.
472. BA/MA RM S/2357
473. BA/MA RM 40 I 440, Gefechtsberichte Landungsabteilung (After-action Reports German Naval Shore Detachment)
474. Mango, Atatürk, p. 153
475. Metger/Goltz, Von Konstantinopel nach Ankara, p.143
476. Mango, Atatürk, p. 154
477. Mango, Atatürk, p. 155
478. BA/MA, RM 40 /440, Gefechtsberichte Landungsabteilung (After-action Reports German Naval Shore Detachment)
479. BA/MA, RM 40/440, Gefechtsberichte Landungsabteilung (After-action Reports German Naval Shore Detachment)
480. BA/MA, RM 40/440, Gefechtsberichte Landungsabteilung (After-action Reports German Naval Shore Detachment)
481. BA/MA, RM 5/2358
482. After Nish had been taken on 5 November 1915, the railway link to Turkey via Sofia was secured. Rail and maritime traffic were now open and thus fulfilled the purpose for which the German Supreme Army Command had participated in the campaign against Serbia. 'Aus IX. Band Die Operationen des Jahres 1915' aus der Reihe 'Der Weltkrieg 1914-1918', p. 254

Chapter 12: German support in the formation of the Turkish Air Arm and air operations at Gallipoli

483. AA/PA, Turkey 142, R 13322, Telegramme von Wangenheim dated 28 November 1914
484. BA/MA, L 05 1/1, Diary of Major (Ret'd) Erich Serno
485. St. Stefano is now the suburb of Yeşilköy; where the old airfield was situated is today the Turkish Air Force Academy as well as the Atatürk International Airport.
486. Werner, Boelcke, p. 175
487. Kannengiesser, Gallipoli, p. 144
488. Yilmazer, The Air War Çanakkale
489. Preussner was again stationed in early 1916 at San Stefano, where he was in charge of flying training. On 16.5.1916 he crashed on the airfield after a flying student, apparently in panic, blocked the joystick. Preussner died of his injuries on 29.05.1915 and was buried with full military honours in Tarabya.

490. BA/MA, RM 5 / 2387, Report about the Seaplane Detachment

491. BA/MA, RM 5 / 2387

492. BA/MA, RM 5 / 2387, Report by von Usedom, 10 September 1915

493. BA/MA, RM 5 / 2404, Report by von Usedom, 31 October 1915

494. BA/MA, RM 5 / 2387, Report about the night flight of aircraft tail number 237

495. BA/MA, RM 5 / 2387

496. BA/MA, RM 5 / 2405, Report by von Usedom, 30 May 1916

497. BA/MA, RM 5 / 2405, Report by von Usedom, 16 April 1917

498. This picture from the collection owned by Bülent Yilmazer shows several interesting details and clearly demonstrates the close cooperation between the Germans and the Turks. After production in Germany, because the aircraft were ferried immediately to the front, they still carried the German emblems. These were painted over in Turkey with the Turkish square, black national emblem. But as the paint composition was different, sometimes from a certain angle you could see both national emblems. The pilot is checking the wing fixture, whilst the observer gets final instructions from another German officer; a Turkish mechanic is working on the right wing and an Imam is giving his blessing for the sortie.

499. Buddecke, El Schahin, p. 74 ff

500. Buddecke, El Schahin, p. 74 ff.

501. Werner, Boelcke, p.174

502. Werner, Boelcke, p.174

503. Werner, Boelcke, p.174

503a. Emil Meinecke – Fighter Ace on the Dardanelles. Memoirs of Oberleutnant Emil Meinecke, Translated and Edited by Brian P. Flanagan, published in Cross and Cockade US Vol 12 No 3. p. 240

504. Werner, Boelcke, p.178

504a. Emil Meinecke – Fighter Ace on the Dardanelles. Memoirs of Oberleutnant Emil Meinecke, Translated and Edited by Brian P. Flanagan, published in Cross and Cockade US Vol 12 No 3. p. 241. After the war Meinecke discovered why he would not shake hands; it was because that Bysshe had just returned from leave, during which he had become engaged. Any married bliss would now have to wait until he was released as a PoW two years later.

504b. Emil Meinecke – Fighter Ace on the Dardanelles. Memoirs of Oberleutnant Emil Meinecke, Translated and Edited by Brian P. Flanagan, published in Cross and Cockade US Vol 12 No 3. p. 244

505. BA/MA, RM 40 / 129

506. Eberhardt, Unsere Luftstreitkräfte 1914-18, p. 210

507. Eberhardt, Unsere Luftstreitkräfte 1914-18, p. 210

508. Eberhardt, Unsere Luftstreitkräfte 1914-18, p. 212

509. BA/MA, RM 40 / 129

Chapter 13: German Engagement in Naval Operations at Gallipoli

510. BA/MA RM 40 I 755, p.165

511. BA/MA RM 40/755, p. 169

512. BA/MA RM 401755, p.168

513. BA/MA RM 40 I 454, p. 45

514. BA/MAN 155 I 24, p. 27

515. BA/MA, N 155 I 24, p. 27

516. BA/MA, N 155 I 24, p. 28

517. BA/MA, N 155 / 26, p. 56

518. Baumbach, Ruhmestage der deutschen Kriegsmarine, p. 103

519. BA/MA, N 155 / 24, p. 29

520. BA/MA, N 155 / 24, p. 30

521. BA/MA, N 155 / 24, p. 30

522. Lorey, Der Krieg in türkischen Gewässern, p. 14-1

523. BA/MA, N 155 / 24, p. 30

524. BA/MA, \1 155 / 24, p. 30

525. BA/MA, N 155 / 2, p. 80

526. Lorey, Der Krieg in türkischen Gewässern, p. 145

527. Lorey, Der Krieg in türkischen Gewässern, p. 146

528. Lorey, Der Krieg in türkischen Gewässern, p. 151

529. Hersing, U 21 rettet die Dardanellen, p.51 ff

530. Kannengiesser, Gallipoli, p. 168/9

531. Lorey, Der Krieg in türkischen Gewässern, p. 154

532. Hersing, U 21 rettet die Dardanellen, p. 59

533. Mackenzie, Compton. *Gallipoli Memories*, Cassell & Co Ltd., 1929, p. 75 (Mackenzie was at the time a lieutenant in the Royal Marines and attached to GHQ MEF.)

534. Liman von Sanders, Fünf Jahre Türkei, p. 102; here original translation of *Five Years in Turkey* by Colonel Carl Reichmann, U.S. Army (Retired) 1927

535. Liman von Sanders, Fünf Jahre Türkei, p. 9; here original translation of *Five Years in Turkey* by Colonel Carl Reichmann, U.S. Army (Retired) 1927

535a. Pless was the seat of the Prince of Pless, located in the then Silesia. Kaiser Wilhelm II also held conferences there. [Translator's note: The Prince of Pless was married to Daisy, the sister of Lieutenant Colonel George Cornwallis-West, Scots Guards, who was the first CO of the Anson Battalion, Royal Naval Division. He left the Battalion before it sailed to Gallipoli.]

536. Liman von Sanders, Fünf Jahre Türkei, p.191; here original translation of *Five Years in Turkey* by Colonel Carl Reichmann, U.S. Army (Retired) 1927 p. 150

537. The book by Hersing, entitled: 'U 21 rettet die Dardanellen'.

Chapter 14: The Allied Withdrawal from Gallipoli

538. BA/MA, RM 5 / 2404, Report von Usedom, 31. Oktober 1915

539. Kannengiesser, Gallipoli, p. 245

540. Kannengiesser, Gallipoli, p. 248/9

541. Kannengiesser, Gallipoli, p. 250

542. BA/MA, RM 40 / 207.5.74

543. Kannengiesser, Gallipoli, p. 253/4

544. BA/MA, RM 40 / 440, Gefechtsberichte Landungsabteilung (After-action Reports German Naval Shore Detachment)

545. Kannengiesser, Gallipoli, p. 257/8

546. BA/MA, RM 40 / 440, Gefechtsberichte Landungsabteilung (After-action Reports German Naval Shore Detachment)

547. Schweder, lm Türkischen Hauptquartier, 5. 158

548. BA/MA, RM 40 / 440, Gefechtsberichte Landungsabteilung (After-action Reports German Naval Shore Detachment)

549. Pomiankowski, Der Zusammenbruch des Ottomanischen Reiches
550. BA/MA, RM 5 / 2359
551. BA/MA, RM 5 / 2405, Report von Usedom, 30. Mai 1916
552. BA/MA, RM 5 / 2404, Report von Usedom
553. BA/MA, RM 5/2360, Brief Humann an Kapitän z. S. Ackermann
554. 'teptil hava' (climate changer) describes a man who was diagnosed as 'needing a change of climate' by military doctors and then sent home for months. Kannengiesser noted: 'Naturally these 'teptil hava' from their homes later attempted to obtain extensions of leave by lawful or unlawful methods. They never reported back at the right time, often not at all, to their regiments. So the 'teptil hava' slid unnoticed into the class of deserters.' p. 193
555. Mühlmann, Der Kampf um die Dardanellen, p. 164

Chapter 15: The Time after the Battles of Gallipoli

556. BA/MA 40/426, WAR DIARY German Naval Shore Detachment, p. 43
557. BA/MA 40/426, WAR DIARY German Naval Shore Detachment, p. 250
558. However, fourteen German officers and 134 men, including fourteen Turkish crew members were rescued; *vide* Lorey, German Naval Shore Detachment on Gallipoli, p. 126
559. Langensiepen u. a., Halbmond und Kaiseradler, p. 207
560. This statement was, along with some other traditional lore, told to the author by Mr. Richard Maier, former employee of the German Consulate General and later administrator of the estate in Tarabya.
561. AA/PA, Türkei 141, R 13334, Telegram No. 2391 Ambassador to the Foreign Office of 18 October 1915

Chapter 16: The German Military Cemetery in Tarabya

563. AA/PA, R 48065, Deutsche Botschaft über Deutsche Kriegsgräber in der Türkei vom 12. March 1925
564. There were once warm healing springs in this area, which caused it to acquire the Greek name *Therapia* (healing), which was later mutated into Tarabya. Following a big earthquake in 1894, which almost completely destroyed the whole town, these springs were buried and remain dried up to this day.
565. Metger/Goltz, Von Konstantinopel nach Ankara, p 287
566. Mäcklä, Souchon, der Goebenadmiral, p 48
567. Kannengiesser, Gallipoli, p 62
568. Von Usedom, Report über die Kämpfe an den Dardanellen, p 8
569. Schweder, Im Türkischen Hauptquartier, p 202 ff
570. BA/MA, RM 40 / 440, Unterlagen Landungsabteilung
571. Gebhard Bieg, Ein Grabstein für Deutsche Gefallene der Schlacht von Gallipoli im Depot der Troja-Grabung
572. Schweder, Im Türkischen Hauptquartier, pp 115 und 160. The monument no longer exists, as it apparently had to make way for a Turkish radar station.
573. BA/MA, RM 40/440, Unterlagen Landungsabteilung
574. Bean, Gallipoli Mission, p 45
575. AA/PA, Türkei 142, R 13333, Telegramm 2153, Botschafter an Auswärtiges Amt vom 23 September 1915
576. AA/PA, R 48065, Der Deutsche Militär Bevollmächtigte vom 6 April 1918
577. BA/MA, RM 40 *I* 729, p 18
578. Fischbacher, Tarabya, p 12

579. Von Wangenheim died from a heart attack on 25 October 1915 in Istanbul.
580. Fischbacher, Tarabya, p 12
581. When compared with many other artists of his generation in the First World War, Georg Kolbe was very privileged. He did not have to go to the front and even as a soldier could continue his work. He remained from 1917 to 1918 in Istanbul in order to create other works of art.
582. Metger/Goltz, Von Konstantinopel nach Ankara, p 301
583. Thaus/ Dönitz, Kreuzerfahrten der Goeben und Breslau, p 272
584. Späterer Mitbegründer des Volksbundes Deutscher Kriegsgräberfürsorge
585. Auswärtiges Amt, Akte R 48065
586. AA/PA, R 48064, Schreiben Stresemann an Auswärtiges Amt vom 12 October 1922
587. AA/PA, R 48064, Deutscher Vertreter bei der Königlich Schwedischen Gesandtschaft in Konstantinopel an das Auswärtige Amt vom 17 August 1921
588. German Ambassador in Istanbul from 1924-1932, later in Ankara.
589. After the Kaiser did not like it, apparently the sculpture was not erected in place but stored in Tarabya.
590. Nadolny, Mein Beitrag, p 93
591. AA/PA, R 48065, Report Botschafter an Auswärtiges Amt vom 12 March 1925
592. List of the fallen from the files of the cemetery administration dated 31 March 1937
593. AA/PA, R 48065, Report Botschafter an Auswärtiges Amt vom 23 September 1925
594. AA/PA, R 48065, Report Botschafter an Auswärtiges Amt vom 23 September 1925, Anlage
595. AA/PA, R 48066, Report Deutsche Botschaft an Auswärtiges Amt vom 15 April 1932
596. AA/PA, H 48066, Report Deutsche Botschaft an Auswärtiges Amt vom 28 June 1935
597. AA/PA, R 48066, Report Deutsche Botschaft an Auswärtiges Amt vom 1 July !936
598. Jäschke, Die Türkei in den Jahren 1935-1941
599. Schweder, Im Türkischen Hauptquartier, p 243
600. Liman von Sanders, Fünf Jahre Türkei, p 169
601. Schmiterlöw, General-Feld Marschall von der Goltz-Pascha, p 210
602. Langensiepen u. a., Halbmond und Kaiseradler, p 155
603. Morgenthau, Kapitel XXVII

Epilogue

604. Schweder, Im Türkischen Hauptquartier, p 240 ff

Appendix 2

605. List of the buried from the files of the cemetery administration from 1927, 1987 and 2007
606. BNMA, RM 40 / 440, Notes by der Landungsabteilung
607. Hüner, Unter zwei Flaggen, p 258 ff

Bibliography

Name	Title	Year	Publisher
Adamow, E. (Redaktion)	Die europäischen Mächte und die Türkei während des Weltkrieges. Konstantinopel und die Meerengen. Nach den Geheimdokumenten des ehem. Ministeriums für Auswärtige Angelegenheiten	1932	Dresden, Band 1-4
Alp, Tekin	Türkismus und Pantürkismus	1916	Deutsche Orient Bücherei-Band:2, Herausgeber: Ernst Jäckh, Verlag Gustav Kiepenheuer, Weimar
Anonym	Gallipoli. Der Kampf um den Orient	1916	Berlin, Scherl-Verlag
Anonym	Die Tragödie Deutschlands	1923	Stuttgart, Verlag Ernst Heinrich Moritz
Bachmann, Martin	Tarabya – Geschichte und Entwicklung der historischen Sommerresidenz des deutschen Botschafters am Bosporus	2004	Deutsches Archäologisches Institut
Baer, C.H.	Der Völkerkrieg – Eine Chronik der Ereignisse seit dem 1. Juli 1914. 17. Bd. Feb. 1916 bis Aug. 1917	1918	Verlag Julius Hoffmann, Stuttgart
Baumbach, Norbert	Ruhmestage der deutschen Kriegsmarine	1933	Verlagsbuchhandlung Broschek & Co, Hamburg
Bean, Charles	Gallipoli Mission	1990	Crows Nest
Becker, Helmut	Äskulap zwischen Reichsadler und Halbmond.	1990	Herzogenrath, Verlag Murken-Altrogge
Benoist-Mechin, Jacques	Die Türkei 1908-1938 – Das Ende des Osmanischen Reiches.	1989	Vaduz. Zug, Swan-Verlag
Benoist-Mechin, Jacques	Mustafa Kemal. Begründer der neuen Türkei	1955	Düsseldorf/Köln, Diedrichs
Bergmann, Werner	Im Namen Seiner Majestät des Sultans	2002	Aufsatz aus: Orden und Ehrenzeichen, Nr, 19, 4. Jg.
Bieg, Dr. Gebhard	Ein Grabstein für Deutsche Gefallene der Schlacht von Gallipoli im Depot der Troia-Grabung		Tübingen
Bleek-Schlombach, E.	Allah il Allah. Mit den Siegesfahnen an den Dardanellen und auf Gallipoli	1916	Leipzig

Bolz, Alexander	Gallipoli 1915: Der Kampf um die Dardanellen im Ersten Weltkrieg	1995	Lüneburg Albecht-Verlag, 1995
Brandenburg, Erich	Von Bismarck zum Weltkriege. Die deutsche Politik in den Jahrzehnten vor dem Kriege.	1925	Berlin
Brauns, Dr. Nikolaus	Die Deutsch-Türkischen Beziehungen vor dem Ersten Weltkrieg 1914		
Broadbent, Harvey	Gallipoli – the fatal shore	2005	Helicon Press, Sydney
Buddecke, Hans Joachim	El Schahin (Der Jagdfalke). Aus meinem Fliegerleben	1918	Berlin
Busch, Fritz Otto	Der Deutsche Seekrieg. Band 1: Unsere Marine im Weltkrieg	1934	Berlin, Brunnen-Verlag
Celalettin, Yavus	Die türkisch-deutschen Marinebeziehungen zu Beginn des Ersten Weltkrieges	1997	Marineforum, 1997/3+4
Chessum, D.J.	An Essay on Admiral Souchon – the man who changed the world	2002	
Corbett, Sir Julian Stafford	British Naval History, Vol III		
Cornevin, R.	Geschichte der deutschen Kolonisation	1974	Hermann Hübener Verlag
Craig, Gordon A.	Die preussisch-deutsche Armee 1640-1945	1960	Düsseldorf, Droste-Verlag
Danişman, Hasan	The Gallipoli Campaign of 1915. Lone Pine Dairy of Lt. Mehmed Fasih	1997	Istanbul, Denizler Kitapevi
Danişman, Hasan	Gallipoli 1915, Day one Plus...	2007	Istanbul, Denizler Kitapevi
Dede, Klaus	Prophet wider Willen. Die erstaunliche Karriere des türkischen und deutschen Generalfeldmarschalls Freiherr von der Goltz	1991	Die Zeit, Nr. 6-1. Februar 1991
Demirhan, Pertev	Generalfeldmarschall Freiherr von der Goltz: Das Lebensbild eines großen Soldaten	1960	Göttinger Verlagsanstalt
Dewitz, Prehn von	Der Kampf um Konstantinopel	1915	Kiepenheuer, Weimar
Dietrich, Anne	Deutschsein in Istanbul	1998	Leske & Budrich
Djemal Pascha	Hatirat (Tagebuch)	1920	Istanbul
Djemal Pascha, Ahmed	Erinnerungen eines türkischen Staatsmannes	1922	München
Drexler, Josef	Mit Jildirim ins Heilige Land – Erinnerungen und Glossen zum Palästina-Feldzug 1917/1918	1919	Selbstverlag des Verfassers
Eberhardt, Walter von	Unsere Luftstreitkräfte 1914 – 1918	1930	Berlin, Vaterländischer Verlag
Endres, Franz Carl	Die Türkei. Bilder und Skizzen von Land und Volk	1917	München, Beck

Name	Title	Year	Publisher
Epkenhans, Michael (Hrsg.)	Das ereignisreiche Leben eines „Wilhelminers" (Albert Hopman)	2004	R. Oldenbourg Verlag, München
Erickson, Edward.J.	Ordered to Die. A History of the Ottoman Army in the First World War	2001	Westport
Eşref, Ruşen	Mustafa Kemal über die Dardanellenkämpfe im Weltkriege	1933	Leykam-Verlag, Graz
Etschmann, Dr. Wolfgang	‚Wüstensturm' im Jahr 1917. Die Schlacht um Gaza-Bersheba vor 75 Jahren.	1992	Aufsatz: Truppendienst, 4/92
Euringer, Richard	Vortrupp PASCHA - die erste Expedition deutscher Flieger in die Wüste bis zum Suezkanal	1937	Deutsche Buchgemeinschaft, Berlin
Feldmann, von	Das „Oberkommando der Meerengen" in den Dardanellen 1914 bis 1918	1939	Marine-Rundschau
Fetzer, Dr. C.A.	Aus dem Thessalischen Feldzug der Türkei	1898	Stuttgart und Leipzig, Deutsche Verlags-Anstalt
Fischbacher, Georg	Tarabya	1982	Zeitschrift des Volksbundes Deutsche Kriegsgräberfürsorge
Fischer, Fritz	Griff nach der Weltmacht. Die Kriegszielpolitik des kaiserlichen Deutschlands 1914-1918	1977	Düsseldorf, Droste
Fischer, Fritz	Krieg der Illusionen. Die deutsche Politik von 1911 bis 1914	1969	Düsseldorf, Droste
Frey, Waldemar	Kut-El-Amara. Kriegsfahrten und Erinnerungsbilder aus dem Orient	1932	Brunnen-Verlag, Berlin
Friedrich Scherer	Adler und Halbmond. Bismarck und der Orient 1878-1890	2001	Paderborn, Schöningh 2001 Otto-von-Bismarck-Stiftung, Wissenschaftliche Reihe; Bd. 2
Fuhrmann, Malte	Den Orient deutsch machen, Imperiale Diskurse des Kaiserreiches über das Osmanische Reich	2002	Berlin
Gaerte, Dr. Felix	Das Kaiserliche Palais in Istanbul	1989	Universität Istanbul
Gleich, Gerold von	Vom Balkan nach Bagdad. Militär-politische Erinnerungen an den Orient	1921	Berlin
Goltz, Colmar Frhr. v.d.	Der Thessalische Krieg und die türkische Armee	1898	Berlin, Mittler & Sohn
Goltz, Colmar Frhr. v.d.	Denkwürdigkeiten	1929	Berlin, Mittler & Sohn

Goltz, Colmar Frhr. v.d.	Karte der Umgegend von Constantinopel. Beschreibung		Berlin, Schall & Grund
Goltz, Colmar Frhr. v.d.	Anatolische Ausflüge	1896	Berlin, Schall & Grund
Goltz, Colmar Frhr. v.d.	Bilder aus der türkischen Armee	1897	Militärwochenblatt, 82. Jg, Nr. 38, Berlin
Görgülü, Ismet	German Claims on Canakkale Victory	1995	Atatürk Research Center, Issue 25/1995
Görgülü, Ismet	The Intentions of the Germans in Gallipoli		
Gründer, Heinz	Die Kaiserfahrt Wilhelms II. ins Heilige Land 1898. Aspekte deutscher Palästinapolitik im Zeitalter des Imperialismus, in: Dollinger, Heinz / Gründer, Horst / Hanschmidt, Alwin (Hg.)	1982	Münster, Festschrift für Heinz Gollwitzer zum 65.Geburtstag am 30. Januar
Guhr, Hans	Als türkischer Divisionskommandeur in Kleinasien und Palästina	1937	Berlin, Mars-Verlag
Guse, Felix	Die Kaukasusfront im Weltkriege – bis zum Frieden von Brest	1940	Leipzig, Koehler & Amelang
Gutsche, Willibald	"Pilgerfahrt" zu den heiligen Stätten. Die Orientreise Kaiser Wilhelms II. 1898, in: Gutsche, Willibald / Kaulisch, Baldur (Hg.): Bilder aus der Kaiserzeit 1897 bis 1917	1985	Köln
Hallgarten, George W. F.	Imperialismus vor 1914. Die soziologischen Grundlagen der Außenpolitik europäischer Großmächte vor dem Ersten Weltkrieg	1963	München, C. H. Beck
Haupt, Werner	Deutsche unter dem Halbmond. Die Geschichte der deutschen Militärberater in der Türkei	1967	Deutsches Soldatenjahrbuch 1967, München
Hedin, Sven	Bagdad-Babylon-Ninive	1918	Brockhaus Verlag Leipzig
Heimann, Karl	Briefstempel der Deutschen Militärmission in der Türkei	1998	Soest, Poststempelgilde
Heinrich	Deutsche Kraftfahr-Truppen Sonderkommando 500 in der Türkei	1916	
Heinsius, Paul	Admiral Wilhelm Souchon	1964	Deutsches Soldatenjahrbuch 1964
Helfferich, Karl	Die deutsche Türkenpolitik	1921	Berlin
Helfferich, Karl	Der Weltkrieg	1925	Karlsruhe
Hersing, Otto	U 21 rettet die Dardanellen	1932	Leipzig, Verlag Hase & Koehler
Herzfeld, Hans	Die Liman-Krise und die Politik der Großmächte in der Jahreswende 1913/14	1933	Berliner Monatshefte 11

Name	Title	Year	Publisher
Heymann, Carl (Verleger)	Der Kriegsverlauf. Zwölf Monate in amtlichen Nachrichten, Noten und Urkunden. August 1914 – Juli 1915	1915	Berlin
Hildebrandt, Karl-Heinz	Das Osmanische Reich: Deutschlands ‚Vietnam' im Ersten Weltkrieg	1995	Aufsatz: ‚Alte Kameraden', 43, 7/8 Aug.
Hildebrandt, Karl-Heinz	Das Deutsche Asienkorps und die Militärmission Liman von Sanders	1993	Aufsatz: Kampftruppen 3/93
Hindenburg, v.	Aus meinem Leben	1934	Leipzig, Hirzel Verlag
Hirschfelder, Heinrich	Das Kaiserreich 1871-1918	1987	Buchnersverlag, Bamberg
Holborn, Hajo	Deutschland und die Türkei 1878-1890	1926	Berlin
Holzhausen, Rudolf H.J.	Die deutsch-türkischen Operationen gegen den Suez-Kanal und im Sinai-Gebiet während des Ersten Weltkrieges	1957	Wehrwissenschaftliche Rundschau (1957), S. 157-167.
Hopkirk, Peter	Östlich von Konstantinopel	1996	Europaverlag
Horaczek, Adolf	Als Deutscher Soldat 1914/1918 von der Westfront an die Osmanische Front	2014	Rolf H Arnold, Publisher; epubli GmbH, Berlin
Hüner, Hans	Unter zwei Flaggen		Verlag „Breslau–Midilli", Potsdam
Jäckh, Ernst	Der aufsteigende Halbmond.	1911	Fortschritt Verlag, Berlin
Jäckh, Ernst	Die deutsch-türkische Waffenbrüderschaft	1915	Deutsche Flugschriften (24. Heft) Berlin, Stuttgart
Jäschke, Gotthard	Die Türkei in den Jahren 1935 – 1941	1943	Leipzig
James, Robert Rhodes	Gallipoli	1999	London, Pimlico
Kampen, Wilhelm van	Studien zur deutschen Türkeipolitik in der Zeit Wilhelm II.	1968	Dissertation der Philosophischen Fakultät der Christians-Albrechts-Universität zu Kiel
Kannengiesser, Hans	Gallipoli. Bedeutung und Verlauf der Kämpfe 1915	1927	Berlin, Schlieffen Verlag
Kannengiesser, Hans	Original translation of 'The Campaign in Gallipoli' by Major CJP Ball, DSO, MC	1927	Hutchinson and Co (Publishers) Ltd
Keilbach, Rainer	Professor Dr. med. Dr. phil. h.c. Ernst Rodenwald	2004	Aufsatz aus: Orden und Ehrenzeichen, Nr. 30, 6. Jg
Kerner, Robert J.	The Mission of Liman von Sanders	1928	Slavonic Review 6 (1927/28)
Kessel, Eberhard	Moltkes erster Feldzug	1939	Berlin, Mittler
Kiesling, Hans von	Mit Feldmarschall von der Goltz Pascha in Mesopotanien und Persien	1922	Leipzig
Kiesling, Hans von	Soldat in drei Weltteilen	1935	Leipzig
Klinghardt, Karl (Hg.):	Denkwürdigkeiten des Marschalls Izzet Pascha	1927	Koehler Verlag, Leipzig

Kober, August Heinrich	Europäische Fürstenhöfe damals – Zwischen Donau und Bosporus	1938	Frankfurt, Societäts-Druckerei
Kopp, Georg	Das Teufelsschiff und seine kleine Schwester - die Abenteuer der Kreuzer Goeben und Breslau	1930	Koehler Verlag, Leipzig
Kraus, Th u. Dönitz, Karl	Die Kreuzerfahrten der Goeben und Breslau	1933	Deutscher Verlag, Berlin
Kressenstein, Friedrich Frhr. Kress von	Mit den Türken zum Suezkanal	1938	Berlin, Vorhut-Verlag
Kuscubasi, Esref	Turkish Battle at Khaybar	1997	Istanbul
Laar, Clemens	Kampf um die Dardanellen	1936	Gütersloh, Bertelsmann-Verlag
Laar, Clemens	Kampf in der Wüste	1936	Gütersloh, Bertelsmann-Verlag
Langensiepen, Nottelmann, Kriesmann	Halbmond und Kaiseradler	2000	Hamburg
Lawrence, T.E.	Die sieben Säulen der Weisheit, dt. Übersetzung	1988	Leipzig, List
Lettow-Vorbeck	Die Weltkriegsspionage	1931	München, Moser
Lindow, Ernst	Freiherr Marschall von Bieberstein als Botschafter in Konstantinopel 1897-1912	1934	Danzig
Lorey, Hermann	Die deutsche Landungsabteilung auf Gallipoli	1928	Marine-Rundschau 1928
Lorey, Hermann	Der Krieg in den türkischen Gewässern. Zweiter Band: Der Kampf um die Meerengen	1938	Berlin
Lorey, Hermann	Der Krieg in den türkischen Gewässern. Erster Band: Die Mittelmeer-Division	1928	Berlin
Ludwig, Emil	Die Fahrten der Goeben und der Breslau	1916	Fischer-Verlag, Berlin
Ludwig, Erich	Moltkes Briefe aus der Türkei	1923	Berlin, Hafen-Verlag
Mackenzie, Compton	Gallipoli Memories	1929	Cassell & Co Ltd
Marx, Karl / Engels, Friedrich	Russlands Drang nach Westen. Der Krimkrieg und die europäische Geheimdiplomatie im 19.Jahrhundert	1991	Zürich
Majoros, Ferene	Das Osmanische Reich 1300-1922	2002	Bechtermünz Verlag
Mäkelä, Matti	Souchon der Goebenadmiral greift in die Weltgeschichte ein	1936	Braunschweig
Malade, Theo	Von Amiens bis Aleppo. Aus dem Tagebuch eines Feldarztes.	1930	Lehmanns Verlag, München
Mango, Andrew	Atatürk	1999	The Overlook Press, New York
Meinecke, Emil	Emil Meinecke – Fighter Ace on the Dardanelles. Memoirs of Oberleutnant Emil Meinecke, Translated and Edited by Brian P. Flanagan		Cross and Cockade US Vol 12 No 3

Name	Title	Year	Publisher
Metger,Jörg u. Goltz Gabriel	Von Konstantinopel bis Ankara	2006	Ankara, Selbstverlag
Militärgeschichtliches Forschungsamt	Deutsche Militärgeschichte. Band 3, Abschnitt V: Von der Entlassung Bismarcks bis zum Ende des Ersten Weltkrieges.	1983	München, Bernhard & Graefe
Moltke, Helmut von	Unter dem Halbmond: Erlebnisse in der alten Türkei 1835 - 1839 / Helmuth v. Moltke. Hrsg. von Helmut Arndt	1984	Tübingen, Erdmann
Moltke, Helmut von	Briefe über Zustände und Begebenheiten in der Türkei aus den Jahren 1835-1839	1911	Berlin
Moltke, Helmut von	Der russisch-türkische Feldzug von 1828 und 1829 (Nachdruck)	1877	Berlin, Reimer
Mönch, Viktoria	Dr. Friedrich Huttner – ein bayrischer Militärapotheker im türkischen Dienst	1982	Wehrmedizinische Monatsschriften
Moorehead, Alan	Gallipoli	1956	New York, Harper & Brother
Morgenthau, Henry	Ambassadors Morgenthau's Story	1921	Doubleday, Page & Company, New York
Mücke, Hellmuth von	Ayesha	1916	August Scherl Verlag, Berlin
Mücke, Hellmuth von	Die sagenhafte Fahrt des Emdenlandungskorps	1915	August Scherl Verlag, Berlin
Mühlmann, Dr. Carl	Oberste Heeresleitung und Balkan im Weltkrieg 1914/1918	1942	Berlin, Limpert Verlag
Mühlmann, Dr. Carl	Der Kampf um die Dardanellen 1915	1927	Berlin, Verlag Gerhard Stalling. 1. Aufl.
Mühlmann, Dr. Carl	Die deutsche Militär-Mission in der Türkei	1938	Wissen und Wehr 12/1938
Mühlmann, Dr. Carl	Das deutsch-türkische Waffenbündnis im Weltkriege	1940	Leipzig, Koehler & Amelang
Mühlmann, Dr. Carl	Deutschland und die Türkei 1913-1914. Die Berufung der deutschen Militärmission nach der Türkei 1913, das deutsch-türkische Bündnis 1914 und der Eintritt der Türkei in den Weltkrieg	1929	Berlin
Mühlmann, Dr. Carl	Die deutschen Bahnunternehmungen in der asiatischen Türkei 1888-1914	1926	Weltwirtschaftliches Archiv 24
Nadolny, Rudolf	Mein Beitrag	1935	Wiesbaden, Limes Verlag
Neulen, Hans Werner	Adler und Halbmond. Das deutsch-türkische Bündnis 1914-1918	1994	Frankfurt

Neulen, Hans Werner	Feldgrau in Jerusalem. Das Levantekorps des kaiserlichen Deutschland	1991	München, Universitas
Niedermayer Oskar von	Unter der Glutsonne Irans -Kriegserlebnisse der deutschen Expedition nach Persien und Afghanistan	1925	Dachau, Einhorn-Verlag
Niedermayer Oskar von	In der Hölle Irans Iran		München Verlag Josef Kösel & Friedrich Pustet
Niedermayer, Oskar Ritter von	Der Vordere Orient. Eine wehrpolitisch-strategische Analyse	1940	Militärwissenschaftliche Rundschau (1940)
Nowarra, Heinz J.	Eisernes Kreuz und Balkenkreuz	1968	Verlag Dieter Hoffmann, Mainz
O`Connor, Neal W.	Aviation Awards of Imperial Germany in World War I and the men who earned them	1990	Princeton, New Jersey
Okay, Kurt	Enver Pascha. Der große Freund Deutschlands	1935	Berlin
Okday, Sefik	Der letzte Großwesir und seine preußischen Söhne	1991	Göttingen
Özer, Sener	Die Geschichte der deutsch-türkischen Beziehungen von den Anfängen bis zur Gegenwart unter besonderer Berücksichtigung der Militärpolitischen Aspekte	1990	Hamburg, FüAkBw, Jahresarbeit LGAN 88
Patton, G.S. Jr.	The Defense of Gallipoli. A General Staff Study	1936	Hawai, Fort Shafter
Pomiankowski, Joseph	Der Zusammenbruch des Ottomanischen Reiches	1969	Graz, Akademische Druckanstalt
Prigge, E.R.	Der Kampf um die Dardanellen	1916	Deutsche Orient Bücherei Band: 13, Herausgeber: Ernst Jäckh, Verlag Gustav Kiepenheuer, Weimar
Purves, Alec A.	The Medals Decorations & Orders of the Great War 1914 - 1918	1989	J. B. Hayward & Son, Polstead, Suffolk
Radke, Heinz	Generallfeldmarschall Colmar Freiherr v. der Goltz Pascha	1991	Deutsches Soldatenjahrbuch 1991
Rathmann, Lothar	Die imperialistische Nahostpolitik des kaiserlichen Deutschland	1962	Berlin (Ost)
Rathmann, Lothar	Stoßrichtung Nahost 1914-1918. Zur Expansionspolitik des deutschen Imperialismus im 1.Weltkrieg	1963	Berlin (Ost)
Rehbein, Arthur	Ehrenbuch der grünen Farbe	1926	Schulz u. Pasche, Berlin
Reichsarchiv Bd. 16	Der Kampf um die Dardanellen	1916	Oldenburg, Stalling Verlag
Reventlow, Graf Ernst von	Deutschlands auswärtige Politik 1888 - 1914	1916	Berlin, Mittler

Name	Title	Year	Publisher
Rodenwaldt, Ernst	Seuchenkämpfe – Bericht des Hygienikers der V.- kaiserlich-ottomanischen Armee	1921	Heidelberg, Carl Winter's Universitätsbuchhandlung
Rodenwaldt, Ernst	Ein Tropenarzt erzählt sein Leben	1957	Stuttgart, Enke-Verlag
Römer, Matthias	Die deutsche und englische Militärhilfe für das Osmanische Reich 1908-1914	2007	Peter Lang, Europäischer Verlag der Wissenschaften, Frankfurt am Main
Sanders, Liman von	Fünf Jahre Türkei / von Liman von Sanders Auflage 2., durchges. Aufl.	1920	Berlin, Scherl
Sanders, Liman von	Original translation of "Five Years in Turkey" by Colonel Carl Reichmann, U. S. Army (Retired)	1927	London Bailliere, Tindall & Cox
Schäfer, Carl Anton	Deutsch-türkische Freundschaft	1914	Stuttgart/Berlin, Deutsche Verlags-Anstalt
Schellendorf, Bronsart von	Ankara und Enver-Pascha	1936	Orientrundschau (früher Mitteilungen des Bundes für Asienkämpfer), XVIII. Jg. Nr. 2, Berlin
Scherer, Friedrich	Adler und Halbmond. Bismarck und der Orient 1878-1890	2001	Paderborn
Schmid, Alois	Schmid Alois. München-Bagdad	1916	München
Schmiterlöw, Bernhard von	Aus dem Leben des Generalfeldmarschall Freiherr v.d. Goltz-Pascha	1926	Berlin, Verlag R.S. Koehler
Schoen, Walter von	Die Hölle von Gallipoli	1937	Berlin, Deutscher Verlag
Schulte, Bernd	Vor Kriegsausbruch 1914. Deutschland, die Türkei und der Balkan	1980	Düsseldorf
Schweder, Paul	Im Türkischen Hauptquartier	1916	Leipzig, Hesse & Becker
Sefik, Okday	Der letzte Großwesir und seine preußischen Söhne	1991	Muster-Schmidt Verlag, Göttingen
Serman, Emil	Mit den Türken an der Front	1915	August Scherl Verlag, Berlin
Simon-Eberhard, Max	Mit dem Asienkorps zur Palästinafront	1927	Berlin
Snelling, Stephen	VCs of the First World War: Gallipoli	1999	London
Souchon, Wilhelm	Das Logbuch des Admirals, Erinnerungen von Exzellenz Souchon Pascha	1933	Weser Zeitung, Nr:512-516
Steuber, Werner	Arzt und Soldat in drei Erdteilen	1940	Berlin, Vorhut
Steuber, Werner	„Jildirim": Deutsche Streiter auf heiligem Boden / nach eigenen Tagebuchaufzeichnungen und unter Benutzung amtl. Quellen des Reichsarchivs	1926	Oldenburg, Stalling

Stürmer, Harry	Zwei Kriegsjahre in Konstantinopel. Skizzen deutsch-jungtürkischer Moral und Politik	1917	Lausanne
Teske, Hermann	Von der Goltz: Ein Kämpfer für den militärischen Fortschritt	1957	Göttingen, Musterschmidt-Verlag
Travers, Tim	The Ottoman Crisis of May 1915 at Gallipoli	2001	War in History
Tröbst, Hans	Soldatenblut. Vom Baltikum zu Kemal Pascha	1925	Leipzig, Verlag R.S. Koehler
Trota, Wilhelm von	Unter dem Halbmond im Weltkriege	1916	Berlin
Trumpener, Ulrich	Germany and the Ottoman Empire 1914-1918	1968	Princeton
Trumpener, Ulrich	German Military Aid to Turkey in 1914. An Historical Re-Evaluation	1960	The Journal of Modern History 32 (1960), S.145.
Trumpener, Ulrich	Liman von Sanders and the German-Ottoman Aliance	1966	Journal of Contemporary History 1
Ullrich, Volker	Entscheidung im Osten oder Sicherung der Dardanellen: das Ringen um den Serbienfeldzug 1915	1982	MGM
Unger, Michael	Die Bayerischen Militärbeziehungen zur Türkei vor und im Ersten Weltkrieg	2003	Frankfurt
Usedom, Guido von	Zusammenfassender Bericht über die Kämpfe an den Dardanellen vom 19. Februar bis 20. April 1915	1915	SoKo der deutschen Marine in der Türkei, Chanak, Mai 1915
Valentiner, Max	U 38 – Wikingerfahrten eines deutschen U-Bootes	1937	Berlin, Ullstein-Verlag
Van der Vat, D	The Ship which changed the world – the escape of the Goeben to the Dardanelles in 1914	1986	Adler&Adler, Bethesda
Wagner, Reinhold	Moltke und Mühlbach zusammen unter dem Halbmonde 1937-1839	1893	Berlin, Verlag von A. Bath
Wallach, Jeduha L.	Anatomie einer Militärhilfe – Die preußisch-deutschen Militärmissionen in der Türkei 1835-1919	1976	Düsseldorf, Droste Verlag
Wath, W.	Breslau - Midilli. Ein Jahr unter türkischer Flagge. Selbsterlebtes an Bord des Kreuzers nach Tagebuchblättern.	1917	Druck u. Vlg. August Scherl, Berlin
Wehrle	Aus meinem türkischen Tagebuch.	1926	München, Die schwere Artillerie Nr. 3/4

Name	Title	Year	Publisher
Weist, Wolfgang, Dr.	Des Kaisers Reise in den Orient 1998		
Werner, Prof. Dr. Johannes	Boelcke – der Mensch, der Flieger, der Führer der deutschen Jagdfliegerei		Leipzig, Koehler & Amelang
Wiegand, Theodor	Halbmond im letzten Viertel,	1985	Verlag Philip von Zabern, Mainz
Wiesner, Ernst	Adler, Doppelaar und Halbmond. Der Verbündeten Siegeszug durch Balkan und Orient in kriegerischer, wirtschaftlicher Bedeutung.	1915	Hamburg, Hansa-Verlag
Yilmazer, Bülent	The Air War Çanakkale	2005	Milsoft
Zabel, Rudolf	Im Kampfe um Konstantinopel und die wirtschaftliche Lage der Türkei während des Weltkrieges	1916	Leipzig, Thomas-Verlag
Zentner, Christian	Der erste Welt Krieg, Daten, Fakten, Kommentare	2000	Moewig-Verlag
Archive Documents / Archivunterlagen			
T.C. Genelkurmay Baskanlığı	Birinci Dünya Harbi'nde Türk Harbi V. Cilt Çanakkale Cephesi Haekatı (Haziran 1914 – 9 Ocak 1916)	2002	Ankara
	Aus den Aufzeichnungen und Briefen aus dem Besitz von Ernst Jäckh, Nr. HM 250, RGPN MS 467	2001	Yale University Library, P.O. Box 208240, New Haven, USA

Files from Federal Archives or Military Archives / Akten Bundesarchiv / Militärarchiv (BA/MA)	
BA/MA, W 10 / 51475	Brief Willmer an von Sanders
BA/MA, W 10 / 51475	Brief Sanders an Mühlmann
BA/MA, W 10 / 51475	Eigene Aufzeichnungen Mühlmann
BA/MA, RM 5 / 2404	Bericht Usedom 18.12.1914
BA/MA, RM 5 / 2404	Bericht Usedom 05.06.1915
BA/MA, RM 5 / 2404	Bericht Usedom 20.07.1915
BA/MA, RM 5 / 2404	Bericht Usedom
BA/MA, RM 5 / 2404	Bericht von Usedom, 31. Oktober 1915
BA/MA, RM 5 / 2404	Bericht Pieper 25. 01.1916
BA/MA, RM 5 / 2405	Bericht von Usedom, 30. Mai 1916
BA/MA, RM 5 / 2405	Bericht von Usedom, 20. November 1916
BA/MA, RM 5 / 2405	Bericht von Usedom, 16. April 1917
BA/MA, RM 5 / 2355 – 2361	Schriftverkehr/Fernschreiben Sonderkommando
BA/MA RM 40 / 4	Akten der Mittelmeerdivision: Politische Nachrichten und allgemeine Nachrichten und Admiral Stab, September 1914 – September 1917
BA/MA RM 40 / 54	Akten der Mittelmeerdivision: Die Mittelmeerdivision August 1914 – April 1915

BA/MA RM 40 / 55	Akten der Mittelmeerdivision: Zusammenstellung des Sonderkommandos, August 1914 – September 1915
BA/MA RM 40 / 62	Akten der Mittelmeerdivision: Bericht über die ersten Maßnahmen in den Dardanellen, 1914
BA/MA RM 40 / 129	Persönliche Unterlagen
BA/MA RM 40 / 138	Akten der Mittelmeerdivision: Tagesbefehle des Oberkommandos der Meerengen, Bd. 1 (August 1914 – Juni 1917)
BA/MA RM 40 / 440	Akten der Mittelmeerdivision: Unterlagen Landungsabteilung
BA/MA RM 40 / 454	Akten der Mittelmeerdivision: Operationsbefehle, September 1914 – Juli 1915
BA/MA RM 40 / 755	Kriegstagebuch des Kommandos der Mittelmeerdivision vom 22. Oktober bis 30. November 1914
BA/MA, N 155 / 21	Korvettenkapitän Rudolph Firle: Tagebücher
BA/MA, N 156 / 10	Admiral Wilhelm Souchon: Privatkorrespondenz mit Ehefrau Violet, Bd. 2 (17. Mai – 26. August 1914)
BA/MA, N 156 / 11	Admiral Wilhelm Souchon: Privatkorrespondenz mit Ehefrau Violet, Bd. 3 (30. August – 9. Dezember 1914)

Files from Foreign Office or Political Archives / Akten Auswärtiges Amt / Politisches Archiv (AA/PA)

Lucius an AA	11. Nov. 1913, GP 38, Nr.15447
Wangenheim an Jagow	17. Dez. 1913, GP 38, Nr.15493
Wangenheim an AA	23. Dez. 1913, GP 38, Nr. 15499

Index